JERUSALEM

Syracuse Studies on Peace and Conflict Resolution
Robert A. Rubinstein, *Series Editor*

Jerusalem

CONFLICT & COOPERATION
IN A CONTESTED CITY

Edited by Madelaine Adelman
& Miriam Fendius Elman

SYRACUSE UNIVERSITY PRESS

ISBN: 978-0-8156-3339-6 (cloth)   978-0-8156-5252-6 (e-book)

Library of Congress Cataloging-in-Publication Data

Jerusalem : conflict and cooperation in a contested city / edited by Madelaine Adelman and Miriam Fendius Elman.
     pages cm — (Syracuse studies on peace and conflict resolution)
   Includes bibliographical references and index.
   ISBN 978-0-8156-3339-6 (cloth : alk. paper) — ISBN 978-0-8156-5252-6 (ebook)
1. Jerusalem—Ethnic relations—Congresses.   2. Jerusalem—History—Congresses.
3. City planning—Jerusalem—Congresses.   4. Jerusalem—Social conditions—21st century—Congresses.   5. Jerusalem—In art—Congresses.   6. Arab-Israeli conflict—Influence—Congresses.   I. Adelman, Madelaine, editor of compilation.   II. Elman, Miriam Fendius, editor of compilation.   III. Adelman, Madelaine, author. Sex and the city: The politics of Gay Pride in Jerusalem.
   DS109.9.J4573 2014
   956.94'42054—dc23   2014008022

For our parents

Madelaine Adelman

Miriam Fendius Elman

Contents

Photographs and Table

Photographs

Table

Preface

TRAINED IN DIFFERENT methodologies for the production of knowledge and typically housed in different physical locations on the university campus, anthropologists and political scientists rarely have the inclination or the opportunity to engage in collaborative work. In completing this book, we have had the good fortune to work at two institutions, Arizona State University and Syracuse University, that value cross-disciplinarity and provide incentives for social scientists and humanists to build bridges across the (sometimes artificial) boundaries that divide them.

At Arizona State University (ASU), we are grateful to the Jewish Studies Program, the Department of Religious Studies, the Sandra Day O'Connor College of Law, the Center for the Study of Religion and Conflict (CSRC), the Department of Political Science and the School of Global Studies (now the School of Politics and Global Studies), the School of Justice and Social Inquiry (now part of the School of Social Transformation), and the Department of Languages and Literatures, for generously funding the conference "Jerusalem Across the Disciplines," which took place on the Tempe ASU campus on February 19–21, 2007, and provided us with the opportunity to discuss and improve draft chapters of this book. Our special thanks goes to then interim director of the Jewish Studies Program, Joel Gereboff, for supporting the idea for this book from the start and encouraging us to pursue it. We also thank Alan Artibise, then executive dean of the College of Liberal Arts and Sciences and Deborah Losse, then divisional dean of humanities, for so warmly welcoming our many visiting scholars and lending their support to this interdisciplinary endeavor. Lastly, we thank then administrative assistant of the Jewish Studies Program, Dawn Beeson; graduate students Scott Cooper and Ramazan Kilinc; and undergraduate students Graham Berry, Jeremy Browning, Philip Kuhlman, and Matthew Williams who willingly gave much of their time over the Fall 2006 and Spring 2007 semesters to make the conference the success that it was.

At Syracuse University, we thank the Maxwell School's Moynihan Institute for Global Affairs for supporting our efforts to turn the conference proceedings into a book and for offering to us its many seminar spaces, which became an ideal intellectual home for our continued conversations. We have benefitted greatly from the constructive suggestions for revision that have been offered by many colleagues, themselves experts on the city of Jerusalem, and especially Yitzhak Reiter and Daphne Tsimhoni. We also thank Yael Zerubavel who served as discussant for an earlier draft of the book's introductory chapter, presented at the annual conference of the Association of Jewish Studies in Washington, DC, December 21–23, 2008. In both Arizona and the greater Syracuse area we have given numerous talks on the book project, receiving helpful feedback from both academics and the general public. We thank the Maxwell School, Hendricks Chapel at Syracuse University, the Intergroup Relations Center at Arizona State University, Colgate University, Lemoyne College, Temple Concord of Syracuse, NY, and Congregation Beth Shalom-Chevra Shas of Dewitt, NY, for inviting us to speak, for the warm reception we received, and for the insightful comments from audience participants.

At Syracuse University Press, we have had the pleasure to work with an outstanding publishing team. We thank the press's former executive editor, Mary Selden Evans, who was excited about the book from the start and encouraged us to submit a final manuscript. Jennika Baines expertly shepherded the book's initial manuscript through the first stages of review. Erica Sheftic assisted us with quickly addressing our many questions. We also extend our gratitude to Suzanne Guiod, who, in taking over the project midstream, provided invaluable assistance and guidance. Two sequential reviews helped to make this book a much better product. We thank the press's anonymous reviewers for their valuable constructive criticism. Lastly, we have had the enormous good luck to have worked with an incredible series editor, Robert Rubinstein, who helped us every step of the way and in more ways than we could every possibly repay.

We began this book in 2007 as Israelis and Jews worldwide celebrated the fortieth year of Jerusalem's reunification. It seems only fitting that the book would go into production in 2012, as Israelis rejoiced during another Jerusalem Day, marking the unification of the two halves of the city following the 1967 war. In the intervening years, as we and our chapter collaborators wrote and revised the book, the gulf between the festive happiness of the Jews and the increasing alienation and despair of the city's Palestinian residents has only widened. Along with this central contestation between Jewish and Palestinian Jerusalemites, conflicts between other constituents of Jerusalem—secular and religious, Ashekanzic and Sephardic, Christian and Muslim, male and female, rich and poor, city and suburb—have also increased. Often on the front pages of the news, the city has become an international problem, of concern and interest to billions of people, many of whom have never set foot in either East or West Jerusalem, or its many holy places. Engaging in each of these many conflicts, this book also offers reminders of the cooperative outcomes that have sometimes been realized, both in the past and currently. Our hope is that the city's many conflicts will give way to more cooperative solutions in the future.

MADELAINE ADELMAN, *Tempe, Arizona*
MIRIAM FENDIUS ELMAN, *Syracuse, New York*

JERUSALEM

Introduction

Knowing Jerusalem through Disciplinary
Conflict and Cooperation

MIRIAM FENDIUS ELMAN AND MADELAINE ADELMAN

ON MAY 19, 2011, US President Barack Obama delivered his second major speech on American diplomacy in the Middle East and North Africa.[1] In his remarks the president congratulated the peoples of the region for challenging authoritarian rule and pledged continued US support for the "Arab Spring." Given the momentous events unfolding in the region, much of the speech was devoted to an assessment of the causes and consequences of the political upheavals in the Arab world, and to the role that the United States would play in facilitating the region's democratization. Yet the President also devoted attention to the Israeli-Palestinian conflict. By including the conflict in his remarks (albeit at the very end), President Obama underscored both the United States' national interest in the conflict's resolution, and the link between a renewed peace process and the success of the region's democratization efforts.

---

1. President Obama delivered his first speech to the region in Cairo in June 2009. The speech was well received both because it advocated for a new US approach to the Muslim world, and because of President Obama's demand for an Israeli settlement freeze and his explicit recognition of the "intolerable" situation of the Palestinian refugees. By contrast, because the President set no precondition on Israel that it cease settlement activity prior to the resumption of negotiations, and because the speech downplayed the refugee problem, his May 2011 speech has been widely interpreted as unbalanced in favor of Israel.

Not surprisingly, the president's speech quickly generated criticism, especially with regard to his proposed plan for moving Israeli-Palestinian negotiations forward. Much of this criticism zeroed in on President Obama's insistence that Israel must return to the "1967 lines with mutually agreed swaps." Yet many observers also questioned President Obama's strategy to defer the conflicts over the future status of Jerusalem and the plight of the Palestinian refugees to a later phase of negotiations. Interestingly, both Palestinian and right-of-center Israeli commentators—two constituencies that are rarely in agreement—took issue with President Obama's endorsement of a gradualist approach.

To be sure, in advocating for postponing various important issues for a later time, President Obama was hoping that, by agreeing to some provisions of a final deal first, Israelis and Palestinians would, over time, build up mutual trust and confidence in each other and would thus be able to resolve the more contentious issues down the road. Indeed, such a strategy—based on the principle of "sliding into peace"—had been the hallmark of the Oslo peace process since its inception in 1993 (Nusseibeh 2008). Roundly criticizing this deferment strategy, however, Palestinian observers and their supporters noted that by excluding the "Jerusalem problem," President Obama's plan provided little incentive for Palestinians to return to the negotiating table. Specifically, by requiring that the borders of the new Palestinian state be agreed upon prior to negotiations over the city, President Obama was in fact supporting Israel's position on the status of Jerusalem's holy sites and the neighborhoods of East Jerusalem. That is, President Obama was endorsing a unified Jerusalem as Israel's capital, with both western and eastern parts of the city under Israel's continued sovereignty. In the words of one commentator, "Leaving Jerusalem out of the negotiating process is in effect an uncritical acceptance of Israel's insistence that the city as a whole belongs exclusively to Israel. . . . It must be understood, I believe as an unscrupulous American acceptance of Israel's position on Jerusalem, which is not only a betrayal of legitimate Palestinian expectations of situating their capital in East Jerusalem but also a move that will be received with bitter resentment throughout the Arab world" (Falk 2011; see also Zunes 2011).

For their part, commentary from right-wing Israeli circles also reflected a similar concern with President Obama's approach. In particular, the argument here was that shifting the issue of Jerusalem to a later stage of negotiations would leave Israeli negotiators with few bargaining chips, while tackling all the core issues at once would facilitate trade-offs.[2] Furthermore, Israeli commentators noted that entering into peace talks without Jerusalem on the table could be interpreted as an acknowledgement that the Jewish neighborhoods in East Jerusalem, not to mention the Western Wall and the Jewish Quarter of Jerusalem's Old City (none of which Israel controlled prior to the June 1967 war), were settlements and occupied Palestinian land.

It is not surprising that President Obama's suggestion that Israelis and Palestinians reach agreement on border and security issues before dealing with the status of Jerusalem was met with staunch criticism. Many observers of the Israeli-Palestinian conflict have long argued that such a two-stage process is what ultimately derailed the Oslo peace process in the 1990s. As Gilead Sher (2008, 304) notes, sidestepping "an issue loaded with potential deal-breakers" in order to make progress on other less highly charged issues was a "logical ploy," but it proved counterproductive both because progress made on the easier issues did not ensure that the other core issues could be resolved, and because the phased process invariably empowered spoilers who would focus attention on all the unaddressed issues instead of highlighting the concessions and accommodations that were gradually being made. It was also predictable that Jerusalem in general—one of the most contested cities in the world—would become a key focus of both the Israeli and Palestinian critique of President Obama's speech. After all, both Israelis and Palestinians claim the city as their national heritage on the basis of their religious and historical attachments

---

2. Sari Nusseibeh (2008, 200–201) notes that trade-offs might have been what Yasser Arafat had in mind when he refused to concede Palestinian sovereignty over East Jerusalem and the Haram al-Sharif at the 2000 Camp David II summit. By standing firm on the primacy of the Jerusalem issue, Arafat may have hoped that his Palestinian constituents would be more willing to compromise on the issue of a Palestinian right of return.

to it. The conflict over Jerusalem is thus a microcosm of the larger conflict between Jews/Israelis and Muslim/Christian/Arab Palestinians.

As a city holy to Jews, Muslims, and Christians, Jerusalem has been the site of contestation—often violent—between its rival religious bodies (Reiter 2013). But contention in Jerusalem would continue even if the political sphere was dominated by a single faith. As F. E. Peters (2008, 17–18) recently pointed out, "were the Christians and Muslims voluntarily to withdraw from Jerusalem and [were] all other political claims presently . . . surrendered to the Israelis, the city would be a no less contentious place. Secular and religious Israelis, reform and [O]rthodox Israelis, the Ministry of Religious Affairs and the Department of Antiquities all have enough Jewish holy place issues between them to keep them angry for generations." Conflict in the city predates the start of the Israeli-Palestinian conflict in the mid-nineteenth century and the inhabitants of the city have a long experience with inter- and intra-communal conflicts. Over the centuries various Christian denominations, for example, have contested—frequently through the use of force—the Church of the Holy Sepulcher, even as they disregarded the Temple Mount/Haram al-Sharif, leaving this sacred space to a contestation between Jewish and Muslim believers (Hassner 2009). The ultra-Orthodox Jewish community has often sparred with the city's secular and non-Orthodox Jewish residents. An example of this contention occurred in the summer of 2008 with the celebratory opening of the new Chords Bridge at the entrance to the city. The event set off a heated argument about the influence of ultra-Orthodox city residents after municipal officials insisted that a women's dance troupe scheduled to perform wear more modest costumes out of respect for religious Jerusalemites in the audience. Continuing conflicts between Jewish denominations over the right of women to pray at the Western Wall has also dominated the news in recent years (Rudoren 2012; Kershner 2013a, 2013b; Sattath 2013). Most recently, mass demonstrations in downtown Jerusalem, which have brought thousands into the streets to protest a shortage of affordable housing and declining social welfare benefits, underscore economic disparities in the city and an ever widening gap between wealthy Jerusalemites and the city's poor.

Yet Jerusalem is not only a place of contention and violence. In fact, many cooperative arrangements between the city's inhabitants have emerged over the millennia. Most notably, the early years of Islamic rule over the city was a period in which Jewish and Muslim residents developed an amicable relationship. Early Muslims perceived the religious importance of Jerusalem primarily on the basis of its biblical/Jewish heritage. Indeed, they acknowledged that the members of the Jewish faith also had a legitimate attachment to the Holy City and did not seek to impose an exclusively Islamic representation of Jerusalem's holiness (Mourad 2008). In contemporary times, while Muslim scholars and politicians have increasingly sought to promote Jerusalem as an exclusively Islamic sacred space, holy sites in the city have not all been characterized by Jewish/Israeli-Arab/Palestinian conflict. In northern Jerusalem, for example, the Tomb of the Prophet Samuel/Nabi Samwil—which has a mosque built atop a synagogue—has been a shared holy site for centuries, with none of the violent confrontations that have occurred at the Temple Mount/Haram al-Sharif, the Tomb of Joseph in Schechem/Nablus, or the Cave of the Patriarchs in Hebron (Reiter 2009).

This book explores the diversity of conflict and cooperation in modern Jerusalem.[3] It is different from existing work in that it is neither a chronology of the history of the city nor of the extended conflict over it. Several key studies trace Jerusalem's pre-modern and modern history (Armstrong 1997; Levine 1999; Chapman 2004; Gold 2007; Gilbert 2008). Our aim is not to duplicate this work but rather to consider how different disciplinary theories and methods contribute to the study of conflictual and cooperative outcomes in the city from the nineteenth century to pres-

---

3. The modern history of Jerusalem can be separated into four periods: the final years of the Ottoman Empire's rule over the city until the First World War; the British Mandate period from 1917 through 1948; the period from 1948 until 1967, during which the city was divided with Israel in control of the city's western half and the Hashemite Kingdom of Jordan in control of the eastern part; and the contemporary period, which began immediately following the 1967 war when Israel effectively annexed East Jerusalem (Mayer and Mourad 2008, 9).

ent times. The essays in this volume touch on a variety of issues that relate to Jerusalem and its impact on the Israeli-Palestinian conflict from when the conflict between competing Zionist and Palestinian nationalisms first emerged. Several contributions to the book center on political decision-making; others focus less on the national and more on the local and social. While Jerusalem's centrality to the Israeli-Palestinian conflict is explored, in the pages that follow we seek to uncover this centrality through the lens of multiple disciplines, and not only the political.

Moreover, the Israeli-Palestinian conflict is only one facet of our coverage. Several chapters also cover issue areas that are unevenly explored in recent studies of the city. These include Jerusalem's diverse communities, including secular and Orthodox Jewry and Christian Palestinians; religious and political tourism and the "heritage managers" of Jerusalem; the Israeli and Palestinian gay community and its experiences in Jerusalem; and visual and textual perspectives on Jerusalem, especially in architecture and poetry. To be sure, we recognize the need to focus on Jerusalem in the context of the Israeli-Palestinian ethno-nationalist conflict. Integral to the study of contemporary Jerusalem are the Palestinian right-to-sovereignty and claims to illegally appropriated lands, and Israel's acute insecurity and how this gives rise to its exclusivist territorial claims in Jerusalem and elsewhere. Yet, in the chapters that follow, we also note that Jerusalem should be seen as a physical and demographic reality that must function for all its communities, and within which its diverse communities can have a stake. It is at once a multicultural city, but one that is unlike other multi-ethnic cities such as London, Toronto, Paris, or New York.

In order to best flesh out the range of conflicts and cooperative relationships that have emerged in Jerusalem, this book offers insight derived from different disciplinary methods, theories, perspectives, and representational techniques. It considers the similarities and differences across the disciplines in their respective "readings" of Jerusalem, and the diverse cultural, legal, social, political, religious, textual, and physical issues that are implicated in its study. The volume brings together scholars from across the humanities and social sciences to explicitly engage a key analytical question that has been left implicit in most treatments of the city: How does disciplinary training influence the study of Jerusalem?

While the study of Jerusalem has long been recognized to be a field of inquiry requiring multiple approaches, scholars of Jerusalem have not been particularly self-conscious about how their disciplines have guided the questions they ask about the city, the methods they use to investigate it, and the answers they provide. In contrast to the existing scholarship on the city, this book's contributors, many of whom have written extensively on the topic of Jerusalem, share substantive disciplinary insights about the city while at the same time considering the real (and sometimes false) boundaries between the disciplines. Several of the chapters that follow assess how a single discipline—such as political science (Elman), history (Saposnik), religious studies (Zank), literary criticism (Ginsburg), or anthropology (Bowman and Woodward)—helps (and sometimes hinders) in the explanation of key events and developments in the city. Others offer insight into how a collaboration across disciplines, for example between sociology and religious studies (Friedland and Hecht), or geography and political science (Klein), yields new knowledge. Still others illustrate how our understanding of Jerusalem's diverse intra- and inter-communal conflicts and cooperative arrangements are informed via cross-disciplinary fields of study, such as justice studies (Adelman) and tourism studies (Timothy and Emmett). In recent years, scholarship in both the social sciences and the humanities has taken a "cross-disciplinary turn." Numerous new pedagogical works (along with funding opportunities) endorse the superiority of interdisciplinary knowledge and call for more intentional collaboration across disciplines. In this book we are agnostic as to whether discipline-specific, interdisciplinary, or cross-disciplinary approaches render better understandings of Jerusalem. Our goal is not to advocate for one or another mode of knowledge production, but to reflect on how our own disciplinary backgrounds have shaped our study of Jerusalem.

Jerusalem in the Context of Conflict and Cooperation

Much of the recent literature on Jerusalem has been focused on the city in the context of the Israeli-Palestinian conflict and is generated by historians or political scientists. This is not surprising because Jerusalem has been at the center of this conflict from its start. And in recent years, Jerusalem has experienced more terrorist violence than any other Israeli city.

During the Second Intifada from 2000 to 2006, West Jerusalem became the preferred target for Palestinian terrorists; several Hamas cells established bases in the eastern part of the city. However, up through the second half of the nineteenth century, Jewish-Arab relations in Jerusalem were fairly cordial, with considerable commercial interaction. Arab merchants and landowners profited from the increased income that Jewish immigrants brought by renting properties and increased commerce and trade. Jews were tolerated by the Muslim population and were granted some measure of religious freedom. Helping to foster this coexistence was a lack of nationalism, since Jews came to the city primarily in order to fulfill religious obligations. As Zionism became more influential within the city's Jewish immigrant community, however, relations between Jews and Arabs became increasingly polarized (Khalidi 1992; Talhami 2000).

At the turn of the century, Jewish immigration to Palestine increased. In 1850, Jews comprised 40 percent of a population of 15,000. By 1880, Jews formed a majority in the city—17,000, or 55 percent out of 31,000. In the late nineteenth century, the rising Jewish population in the city led to the building of new Jewish suburbs outside of the Old City's walls. By 1946, 60 percent of Jerusalem's population was Jewish as compared with only 31 percent of Palestine's population overall. Several prominent Arab Jerusalemite notables were influential in fashioning the Palestinian response to Zionism. It was the mayor of Jerusalem, Zia al-Khalidi, who wrote to his friend, Zadoc Khan, the chief rabbi of France, recognizing the historical and religious rights of Jews to Palestine while also warning that a mass resettlement of Jews would lead to violent conflict with local Arabs (Nusseibeh 2007, 23). The mufti of Jerusalem, Hajj Amin al-Husaini, notorious for his anti-Semitic views and for his collaboration with the Nazi regime during the Second World War (he spent the war years in Berlin, mobilizing Bosnian Muslims for the SS), restricted Jewish prayer at the Western Wall and was instrumental in inciting rioting against the Jewish inhabitants of Jerusalem (Armstrong 1997, 376–77, 380–82). One of the first large-scale outbreaks of violence between Jews and Arabs during the British Mandatory period occurred in Jerusalem. During the "Wailing Wall incident" of August 1929, a peaceful demonstration of Zionist groups in the

Old City triggered Arab rioting that resulted in the deaths of 133 Jews and 116 Arabs (Friedland and Hecht 1998, 140–41; Nicholson 2012).

Jerusalem was the scene of violent clashes between Jewish forces and the British authorities, which culminated in the terrorist bombing of the British government offices at the city's King David Hotel in July 1946. After Arab Palestinians rejected the November 1947 United Nations parti- tion resolution, they attacked Jewish towns and villages, including several Jewish neighborhoods in Jerusalem. When the armistice between Jordan and Israel was signed two years later, Arab residents of West Jerusalem left this part of the city, while Jews evacuated the Jordanian-controlled Old City. Although today the dispute between Israelis and Palestinians over Jerusalem centers primarily on East Jerusalem and the Temple Mount/ Haram al-Sharif, also at issue are the rights of the approximately 30,000 Palestinian refugees who left West Jerusalem in 1948 and who have been unable to return to these areas of the city (Khalidi 1992, 136; Ju'beh 2001).

During the civil war that erupted between the Jews and Arabs in the wake of the British withdrawal from Mandatory Palestine, the most noto- rious acts of terrorism occurred in and around Jerusalem, including the April 9, 1948, Irgun and Lehi attack on Deir Yassin, an Arab village at the western entrance to Jerusalem, during which over 100 Palestinian civil- ians were murdered, and the reprisal Palestinian massacre of ninety Jew- ish nurses and doctors traveling to Jerusalem's Hadassah Mount Scopus Hospital. Some of the fiercest fighting during the 1948 war took place in Jerusalem. It was the siege of the city that has formed the basis for the Israeli nationalist narrative that the war was fought by the weak against the mighty (Shlaim 2001; Morris 2008).

Research on Jerusalem tends to follow the chronological trajectory of the conflict. Recent scholarship on the 1967 war has suggested that prior to Jordan's attack on Jewish areas in western Jerusalem, the Israeli gov- ernment had no irredentist designs on Jordanian-controlled East Jerusa- lem or on the Old City. In fact, even after the Jordanian shelling of West Jerusalem began, many in the Israeli government and military continued to voice opposition to capturing this part of the city (Brecher 1978, 23–25; Goddard 2010, 149). At the time, Defense Minister Moshe Dayan, noting that capturing the Temple Mount/Haram al-Sharif site could complicate Israel's relations with the Christian world, famously noted, "I don't need that Vatican; leave it alone." Similarly, Prime Minister Levi Eshkol advised caution, noting, "We have to weigh the diplomatic ramifications of conquering the Old City. Even if we take the West Bank and the Old City, we will eventually be forced to leave them." On several occasions during the war, Jordan's King Hussein was given the opportunity to stand down. In return, Israel would withdraw its forces and retain Jerusalem's status quo (Oren 2005; Naor 2005; Golani 1999).

Researchers suggest that little deliberation was taken in the decision to extend Israeli law to East Jerusalem and the Arab areas surrounding it on June 18, 1967, or on Knesset legislation at the end of the month that declared Jerusalem to be "one city, indivisible, the Capital of the State of Israel." By the end of June 1967, over sixty square kilometers of East Jerusalem, including nearly thirty surrounding villages in the West Bank, were effectively annexed to West Jerusalem as the city's municipal lines were redrawn. The city expanded to three times its size, absorbing nearly 70,000 Palestinians within its new municipal boundaries (Golan 2011). The fact that these policies generated hardly any debate is curious given that they represented a marked divergence from earlier Zionist policies regarding the city. Earlier Zionist positions on the city were notable for their flexibility and were pragmatic responses to the political circumstances of the times (Mayer 2008). For Zionists in the first few decades of the twentieth century, Jerusalem evoked an image of a religious, past-oriented city at odds with the new Hebrew culture and *sabra* mentality. Indeed, Israel's founders identified far more with Tel Aviv, Haifa, and other Israeli coastal towns. To be sure, even early Zionists saw the city as central to the Jewish faith, and would have preferred a state that included Jerusalem's holy sites. Yet, in 1937, when the partition of Palestine was first debated in international forums, the Zionist Executive hoped only to retain the western suburbs of Jerusalem and the Mount Scopus enclave for the new capital of the Jewish state. In 1947, David Ben-Gurion and other Zionist leaders were willing to forfeit control over Jerusalem so as not to risk the loss of international support for partition (Brecher 1978, 14–15; Goddard 2010, 135). Nevertheless, in June of 1967, "Israelis quickly made up their minds that the 'liberation' of Jerusalem was 'irreversible'" (Chapman 2004, 145).[4]

Since 1967, Israel has sought to transform the demographic and physical facts of the city in a way that confirms the national Zionist project. As Simone Ricca (2005, 52) notes, "The military conquest of Jerusalem necessitated the city's physical transformation . . . in order to adapt a typical Middle Eastern, medieval and mainly Arab city to the symbolism and requirement of a modern Jewish state." Eleven Jewish neighborhoods were built in East Jerusalem on land annexed by Israel. These became suburban residential communities connected to the western parts of the city by a system of roadways. During the 1980s, seven of the ten fastest growing settlements were located in the metropolitan area of Jerusalem. Today, the majority of the roughly half million Israeli settlers live just beyond the Green Line in suburban housing developments located within, and adjacent to, metropolitan Jerusalem and Tel Aviv (Allegra 2011).

In order to build these new neighborhoods, not only was Arab Palestinian land confiscated for public usage, but the growth of Arab communities was restricted by withholding building permits; designating numerous areas surrounding Arab neighborhoods as "green" and thus closed to housing development; revoking Jerusalem residency status to Palestinians who moved beyond the city limits even for short periods of time; setting high charges for building licenses in Arab communities of East Jerusalem; and denying Arab residents of the city government subsidies for home purchases, which are available to Jewish residents. Within the Old City, the Jewish Quarter was also expanded by expropriating Arab property and redrawing its boundaries. Jeff Halper (2011, 74), director of the Israeli Committee against House Demolitions (ICAHD), claims that since Palestinian residents of Jerusalem cannot easily acquire permits to build on the land that they own in East Jerusalem, some 25,000 housing units are currently lacking for the Palestinian sector.

---

4. For an important challenge to this representation of the city, see The Museum on the Seam, located on Jerusalem's Highway 1, between East and West Jerusalem (http://www .coexistence.art.museum).

Demographically, in order to strengthen the state's claim to exclusive control of the city, Israel's policies in Jerusalem have sought to increase the Jewish population. The city's municipal boundaries were redrawn (in 1967, and recently via the line of the separation wall) to avoid heavily populated Arab areas; to maximize the availability of land for new, and the expansion of older, Jewish neighborhoods; and to foster industrial and high-tech industry that would bring more Jewish Israelis to the city. Yet, the commitment of successive Israeli governments to "greater Jerusalem" and the image of East Jerusalem as an integral part of the state also meant a willingness to treat East Jerusalemite Palestinians as different from Palestinians living in the West Bank or Gaza. Jerusalem's Arab population became permanent Israeli residents ("blue card" holders) with: the right to vote in municipal elections; freedom of movement, speech, and association; and the ability to collect a variety of welfare benefits granted to all Israeli citizens, including health insurance, pensions, unemployment compensation, child allowances, and free public schooling.

In short, for over forty-five years Israel has been creating a geographical and political reality in Jerusalem that makes it difficult to contemplate a re-division of the city (Azoulay 2008). Menachem Klein (2008, 56) notes that "Jerusalem is the pinnacle of what has been Israel's national project since 1967: settling Jews in the territories it won control of in the war of that year. In no other populated Palestinian territory has Israel reached the same level of achievement—annexation and the creation of near demographic parity with the original population." For East Jerusalemite Palestinians this has created a dual legal status. According to international law, East Jerusalem is occupied territory that will eventually be handed over to a sovereign Palestine. According to the official Israeli position, though, East Jerusalem is an integral part of the state of Israel. Palestinians in Jerusalem thus "share a sense of transience. . . . They are not preoccupied with institution building because they are waiting for the Israelis to withdraw; they do not engage in collective efforts to build infrastructure as they await the advent of Palestinian sovereignty" (Yair and Alayan 2009, 245).

Jerusalem has long been at the center of political contests over land. Long-held Muslim waqf (religious authority) claims that Israel is trying to undermine the foundations of the Temple Mount/Haram al-Sharif in order to destroy the al-Aqsa Mosque and the Dome of the Rock and create space for the rebuilding of the third Jewish Temple are fueled by the activities of a small group of Jewish ultra-Orthodox Jerusalemites working under the auspices of fringe organizations, such as the Temple Institute in the Jewish Quarter of the Old City (Sales 2013). Prior to 1948, such claims were fabricated by Palestinian political leaders in order to generate anti-Zionist uprisings. Yet, in September 1996, then Israeli prime minister Benjamin Netanyahu's decision to open a subterranean tunnel running along the foundation of the Western Wall, ostensibly to redirect tourist traffic to the Via Dolorosa in the Old City's Muslim Quarter, was perceived as another attempt at religious sabotage. The violent rioting sparked by the opening of the Western Wall tunnel resulted in the first clashes between Palestinian Authority security forces and the Israel Defense Forces (IDF) since the signing of the Oslo Accords. Increasing collusion between Jewish religious messianists and premillennialist Christian groups, and in recent months, the targeting of several mosques and Arab property in East Jerusalem as part of a vigilante backlash to Israel's dismantlement of Jewish homes built on private Palestinian land (i.e., the "Price Tag" campaign), has contributed to the Palestinian insistence that Israel must relinquish sovereign control of the area. At the same time, the desecration of synagogues and other Jewish sacred sites in areas controlled by the Palestinian Authority, and violent attacks on Jewish worshippers at these places, has convinced many Israelis that Jerusalem's holy sites should remain under Israeli control. Significantly, a 2007 poll showed that only 6 percent of Palestinians think that it is very important to allow Jews to visit their holy sites in Jerusalem, and 35 percent would not grant Jews any access at all.

Since 1967, when Israel took control of what had been Jordanian East Jerusalem, Israel's leadership has sought on numerous occasions to reaffirm the state's exclusive sovereignty over its "eternally unified capital." In 1980, Israel's Knesset passed a law that affirmed the city's status as the "complete and united" capital of Israel, and a 2010 law requires approval by popular referendum or a two-thirds Knesset majority for any withdrawal from East Jerusalem. In the 1990s, during the years of the Oslo peace process, prime ministers Yitzhak Rabin, Shimon Peres, and

Benjamin Netanyahu, despite their differences on other issues, agreed that Jerusalem was not negotiable. Accordingly, the self-governing Palestinian Authority created by the Oslo agreements had no jurisdiction in Jerusalem. Yet, the Oslo peace process—which began auspiciously with the signing of the Declaration of Principles in September 1993 and a handshake between former enemies on the White House lawn—and three Nobel Peace prizes did challenge a number of taboos on the city. These included the Israeli claim that Jerusalem would remain an undivided city under its exclusive sovereignty (Lustick 2008). The fact that Israel's political leaders did not view Jerusalem as part of the deal makes this new shift in Israeli public opinion all the more significant.

As the Oslo peace process unraveled, more work was done highlighting the reasons for its demise and the role that Jerusalem played (Rabinovich 1999; Ross 2004; Ben-Ami 2006; Maoz and Nusseibeh 2000; Agha and Malley 2001; Hassner 2003). In the aftermath of the failed Camp David 2000 and Taba 2001 final status negotiations, and the start of the Second Intifada, additional monographs and articles have been published on the Israeli-Palestinian "battle for Jerusalem"; the steps that need to be taken to resolve the conflict over the city's future (Klein 2003, 2007; AbuZayyad 2001; Baskin 2001a; Morris 2002; Gorenberg 2000; Segal et al. 2000; Khalidi 2001); and external or internal socio-political obstacles along the way (Abu El-Haj 2001; Sorkin 2005).

Much recent scholarship on the failed Camp David negotiations in July 2000 suggests that Jerusalem was the central stumbling block. Political scientist Menachem Klein argues that (after much wrangling) an agreement had largely been reached over final borders, refugees, and settlements, and that these issues did not derail the process. Instead, the intransigence and insensitivity of both negotiating teams over Jerusalem's holy sites are key to understanding the failure of the final status negotiations. Disagreement over whether Israel or the new Palestinian state would have sovereignty over the Temple Mount/Haram al-Sharif derailed the negotiations. The ultimate failure of the Camp David negotiations are linked to Arafat's refusal to recognize Jewish historic and religious claims to the Temple Mount and to then Israeli prime minister Ehud Barak's insistence that the Palestinian delegation agree to the construction of an area for Jewish prayer there (Hammami and Tamari 2000; Baskin 2001a; Ben-Ami 2006, 246–60; Sher 2008).

Many commentators on the Israeli-Palestinian conflict consider Jerusalem to be at the heart of the conflict, and therefore the key to its resolution. Indeed, the recent Palestinian uprising was named the "al-Aqsa intifada" due to the central role that Muslim holy sites have played in the latest phase of the Israeli-Palestinian conflict. Dozens of reports suggest ways for sharing the city, including the Old City and its holy sites (Romann and Weingrod 1991; Lustick 1993–94; Friedland and Hecht 1996b; Kaminker 1997; Albin 1997; Benvenisti 1996; Emmett 1996; Shalakany 2002; Cheshin, Hutman, and Melamed 1999; Wasserstein 2001; Klein 2001). As Ruth Lapidot (1994) notes, "A solution to the conflicts about Jerusalem is a sine qua non for the achievement of a viable and durable peace in the area." The publication of these reflections on the conflict has coincided with a burgeoning literature on the city generated by Israeli and Palestinian think tanks; documentaries and films on the city; and a proliferation of web-based information and internet sites devoted to tracking political and religious developments in the city in real time, including the development and impact of the wall separating Jerusalem from parts of the West Bank (see the appendix to this volume for suggested Internet resources). Recent initiatives have also sought to reimagine the future of the city of Jerusalem, such as Michael Sorkin's 1999 gathering to heal Jerusalem through architectural interventions as documented in his edited volume, *The Next Jerusalem* (2002), and the Massachusetts Institute of Technology's ongoing Jerusalem 2050 project. Israel's fortieth anniversary of the 1967 war, and the sixtieth year of independent statehood, celebratory events that for Palestinians marked an ongoing occupation and their own elusive quest for a national homeland, have also led to renewed attention to the war and its consequences, including Israel's settlement project and the annexation of East Jerusalem (Klein 2005; Segev 2007; AbuZayyad 2007; Gorenberg 2006; Zertal and Eldar, 2007).

Researchers also have sought to place the present conflict over Jerusalem in historical perspective, and have revisited Jewish, Muslim, and Christian spiritual and physical legacies on the city (Khalidi 1992; Eade and Sallnow 1991; O'Mahoney 1995; Asali 1997; Armstrong 1998; Breger and Idinopulos 1998; Levine 1999, 2008; Gilbert 1996; Dumper 2002; Cline 2004). Chapman (2004, 69) notes that "[a]lthough the Temple was mere rubble for 600 years and the site was then completely taken over by another religion (Islam), Jerusalem continued to generate a powerful spiritual energy for the Jewish people." From this perspective, any kind of division of the city recalls the Jewish experience of persecution and exile (Albin 1997, 123). As Rabbi Daniel Feldman (2008, 57) recently puts it, "The Jewish people's connection to Jerusalem transcends words, as well as time and space. Within the Jewish soul there is a longing for Jerusalem that defies rational explanation." The term Zionism itself refers to Mount Zion, which overlooks the Temple Mount/Haram al-Sharif site, and incorporates the concept of Jerusalem (Reiter 2008, 6).

Jerusalem is not only linked to Zionism and it is not merely the capital of a modern sovereign Jewish state. Many Jews worldwide view the city as an integral part of the identity of the entire Jewish people: the "eternal capital" for 3,000 years. The Jewish holiness of the Temple Mount derives from the biblical narrative, primarily the Book of Samuel and the Book of Kings, and the rabbinic texts, including the Mishna and the Talmud. Daily, Sabbath, and festival prayers and liturgy include descriptions of the Temple rituals, and the destruction of the Temple is commemorated in celebratory and mourning occasions throughout the Jewish life cycle (Reiter 2013, 120–21). Jerusalem, the destroyed Temple, and a yearning to return to Jerusalem in order to rebuild the Temple and restore the divine presence to the Holy City thus figure prominently in the Jewish faith (Levine 2008). Indeed, viewed as central to generations of Jews and to Judaism itself, some Israeli politicians have argued that their government should not negotiate over Jerusalem without consulting the Jews of the Diaspora (see, for example, Sharansky 2008).

Similar claims are increasingly being voiced by Palestinian negotiators, too, who argue that Jerusalem belongs to all Muslims. The city is holy for Muslims because of its biblical significance, the Prophet Muhammad's association with the city, the fact that Jerusalem was the first direction of prayer for Muslims (qibla), the major Islamic shrines of the Dome of the Rock and the al-Aqsa mosques, and 1,300 years of continuous

Muslim rule of the city (Reiter 2008, 2013).[5] Muhammad's night journey, during which he was (either literally or in a vision) transported from Mecca to Jerusalem, meeting there with Abraham, Moses, and Jesus prior to ascending to heaven, reflects both the continuity between Islam and Judaism and Christianity, and the significance that Muslims attach to the city. According to Muslim tradition, the magic steed—Buraq—that Muhammad rides during the night journey was tethered to the al-Aqsa Mosque's entrance. As Reiter (2008) explains, in the past this place was identified at the south of the Haram al-Sharif compound. Following the events of 1929, however, it became identified with the Western Wall. Thus, currently the Western Wall (for Jews, the Wailing Wall) is known as al-Buraq Wall to Muslims.

As the third most sacred site to Islam, Muslims believe that the Haram al-Sharif cannot be ceded to non-Muslim authority. That is, it is in trust to the Muslim waqf and cannot be willingly transferred to another's sovereignty. Jerusalem's sanctity for Islam figures centrally in the Palestinian intifada literature, despite the fact that most Palestinian and Israeli Palestinian novelists and poets are secular. Glorious periods of Islam's past are recounted in the literature, especially Saladin's re-conquest of the city from the Crusaders. Here, the parallel to the intifada is clear: Muslims must recapture Jerusalem from the foreign occupier (Elad-Bouskila 1999, 127–38). However, as Reiter (2008) suggests, contemporary Muslim thinking holds that all of Palestine is waqf, and not only Jerusalem.

According to researchers, Jerusalem became holy for Christians because it is where Jesus Christ lived, was crucified, and resurrected. The Church of the Holy Sepulcher has been the locus of Christian pilgrimage since it was built in 335 CE. Yet, Jerusalem became central to Christianity only after the fourth century, when Constantine sought to create a

5. According to Jewish faith, the Dome of the Rock and al-Aqsa mosques were built over the ruins of the ancient Jewish Temple; the Western Wall is part of the outer wall of what was the Second Temple compound. In this chapter we thus use the double terminology of Temple Mount/Haram al-Sharif when referencing this area of the Old City.

Christian empire with Jerusalem as its holy city. Prior to this, Christianity devalued the physical site of the Temple. Rather, Jesus would replace the Temple, and Christians would be able to worship in any physical place. As Chapman (2004, 48) notes, "the city of Jerusalem [had] very little significance for the disciples of Jesus." Although it is the "heavenly Jerusalem" that symbolizes the city of God for Christians, Christian pilgrims from all over the world experience God in the earthly city of Jerusalem, which is viewed to be the site of salvation in the messianic age. For Christian dispensationalists, the city figures prominently in beliefs about the end of the world and the second coming of Christ. Christian dispensationalism, often referred to as Christian Zionism, predates the Jewish Zionist movement by at least half a century. Indeed, its modern form began to develop in the beginning of the nineteenth century, long before Herzl wrote his seminal text, *The Jewish State*. For dispensationalists, Jerusalem is viewed as physical, literal space. The central theological premise is that the city must come under the control of the Jewish people prior to Christ's resurrection. According to many dispensationalists, Zionism and the founding of Israel, and especially the 1967 war, are signs from God of the fulfillment of biblical prophesy. It follows from this view that Christians must support Israel, and in particular Jewish claims to exclusive control over the city.[6] In August 1969, an Australian tourist who set fire to the al-Aqsa Mosque was influenced by this Christian messianism, and evangelical Christian Zionists continue to fund Jewish groups that seek to purchase property in East Jerusalem and the Old City's Muslim Quarter.

Nonetheless, it would be a mistake to assume that such religious attachments are unchanging and static. In fact, religious attachments to the city, especially among Jews/Israelis and Muslims/Palestinians, have shifted in reaction to changing political situations (Armstrong 1998;

6. For more on Christian Zionism and its growing popularity among millions of Christians in the United States and worldwide, see Chapman (2004, 108–27), Lukens-Bull and Fafard (2007), and Shindler (2000). For more on the rift between Christian Zionists and Christian Palestinians, see Dumper (2002).

Golani 1999; Karmi 2001; Kimmerling 2001; Naor 2005; Mourad 2008). For Muslim Palestinians, for example, the political importance of the Haram al-Sharif increased because of Zionist immigration (before 1948) and, since 1967, because the Old City is under Israeli control (Nicholson 2012). If not in the past, for Palestinian leaders and the Palestinian public today, sovereignty over the Haram al-Sharif and the Old City (even including the Western Wall) is "fundamental to Palestinian needs: the end, not the starting point of discussion" (Bell et al. 2005, 5). Unlike its relationship to Judaism, Jerusalem was never a political center for Islam. However, contemporary scholars of Islam have sought to connect the two sacred mosques in Mecca with those in Jerusalem in order to highlight Jerusalem's high status. They have also emphasized the view that the Canaanites and Jebusites who preceded the ancient Hebrews in the city were Arab tribes with whom the Palestinians can associate themselves (Reiter 2008, 28, 72; 2013, 124). In fact, since 1967, Palestinians (and Arabs and Muslims worldwide) have been engaged in intense efforts to both elevate Jerusalem's status in Islamic and Arab history and mythology and to denigrate Jewish links to the city. Recently, for example, Palestinian officials—including the Palestinian Authority—have denied any Jewish historical connection to the Western Wall. This campaign has been so successful that should Palestinian negotiators agree to grant Israel control over parts of the Temple Mount/Haram al-Sharif compound in future negotiations, it is unlikely that the Muslim world would support it. As Yitzhak Reiter (2008, 4) argues, "The Islamization of Jerusalem in response to the extension of Israeli sovereignty over Jerusalem demonstrates that religion in general and religious meaning in particular cannot be overlooked in political analysis and must be factored into political solutions."

Jewish Israeli positions on the city have been equally fluid and dynamic. For the last 1,300 years, the Temple Mount/Haram al-Sharif has not been an active site of Jewish worship. Since 1967, Israel's sovereignty there has been merely symbolic with day-to-day religious practice under the supervision of the Muslim waqf. Long-standing religious edicts prohibiting Jews from entering the site have made the Western Wall the holiest accessible space.[7] Some religious interpretations suggest an increased sanctity of Jerusalem in the modern era due to restored Jewish control of the city; others question whether Jerusalem's holiness extends beyond the borders of the Old City, which constituted ancient Jerusalem, to encompass contemporary Jerusalem (Feldman 2008, 58–59). Interestingly, between 1949 and 1967 the Israeli government did not spend much time or effort in attempting to gain access to the Jewish holy sites in Jordanian controlled East Jerusalem. While Israeli military and political leaders did try to capture the Mount Scopus area, there was little interest in the holy places of the Old City or in the Mount of Olives. As Motti Golani (1999, 585) notes, "The Israeli government did not seem overly perturbed that its citizens were denied access to the holy places." Israelis in general, and Jerusalemites in particular, grew accustomed to the division of the city. For both the Israeli public and Israel's leadership, attention was focused on the western part of the city, which became the locus of the Israel's political, economic, educational, cultural, and even religious institution building (Mayer 2008).

The fact that attachments to the eastern part of Jerusalem have been historically constructed helps to explain recent contestations over the city's future. Recent polls show that a majority of Israelis oppose any peace deal that would involve handing over the Temple Mount/Haram al-Sharif site. According to a 2005 poll, only 9 percent of Jewish Israelis were willing to allow sovereignty over the Temple Mount/Haram al-Sharif to pass completely to a new Palestinian state; 51 percent insisted on exclusive Israeli control of the site, with only 36 percent willing to share it (Shragai 2005). Similarly, in 2009, "more than two thirds of the Jews in Israel oppose[d] relinquishing sovereignty over the Temple Mount, the holiest place to the Jews" (Inbari 2009, 272). Yet 40 percent of Israeli Jews also believe that Israel should relinquish control of the city's Arab neighborhoods in return

---

7. For more on the origins of these positions, their endorsement by Israel's religious establishment, and recent attempts by rabbinic authorities affiliated with Israel's settler movement to turn the Temple Mount/Haram al-Sharif into an active Jewish holy site, see Inbari (2007, 2009).

for a final status agreement.[8] Both former prime minister Ehud Olmert and Israel's current prime minister Benjamin Netanyahu have sparred over the issue of Jerusalem, with the former open to negotiation over the city's status and the latter insisting that "dividing Jerusalem would be a moral and historical mistake."[9]

The point of departure for this volume is that the continuing debate over Jerusalem's future cannot be divorced from the realities of urban life in the eastern and western parts of the city. In the first decades following the 1967 war, the Arabs of East Jerusalem enjoyed the material benefits and personal rights that the extension of Israeli law brought. In its first few decades, the occupation of East Jerusalem was therefore easier and milder than that of the West Bank or Gaza (Klein 2007, 82; Benziman 2008). In fact, East Jerusalem thrived economically for some decades (Rekhess 2008, 269). This initially lucrative position of East Jerusalemite Palestinians vis-à-vis Palestinians in the West Bank and Gaza, however, has not been sustained. Israeli Jewish neighborhoods of East and West Jerusalem have flourished. Communities such as Pisgat Ze'ev, Neveh Ya'acov, Gilo, East Talpiot, and Har Homa were planned and constructed with the support of the government and included new schools, commercial districts, parks, and synagogues. Meanwhile the Arab neighborhoods have languished. Communities such as Beit Hanina and Shuafat have been unable to get a municipal plan approved that would legalize the building of new homes (Cheshin, Hutman, and Melamed 1999, 52–55). Including its Palestinian population, Jerusalem is now the poorest city of Israel. It continues to lack the high tech and financial sectors that have flourished in Tel Aviv and other urban centers in Israel. Arab East Jerusalem remains underdeveloped and underserviced as successive Israeli

8. Poll results from March 19 to 27, 2008, Ma'gar Mochot polling agency. Reported in *Begin-Sadat Center for Strategic Studies Bulletin* (Begin-Sadat Center for Strategic Studies 2008, 3).

9. Netanyahu presented his views on the future of Jerusalem at an April 2008 conference sponsored by the Begin-Sadat Center for Strategic Studies at Bar-Ilan University. These were reiterated in speeches to a joint session of the United States Congress and to AIPAC in May 2011.

governments have given the lion's share of municipal resources over to the western part of the city.

Indeed, Jerusalem never became the multi-cultural city that its long-time mayor, Teddy Kollek, hoped it would become (MacLeish 1968). Due to the persistent neglect of East Jerusalem's municipal services, schools, roads, and other essential infrastructure was, and remains, far inferior to that enjoyed by Jewish residents in the western (and eastern) parts of the city. The intifadas, growing unemployment, the militarization of life in the city, and the lack of law enforcement, has placed parts of East Jerusalem, including a-Tur, Silwan, and Ras al-Amud, on the path to becoming slum neighborhoods with a variety of social ills including drugs, crime, and a rise of religious extremism (Klein 2008, 69). Moreover, while Israel decided to unite Jerusalem, it has failed to apply the law equally to East Jerusalem. For example, the Israeli justice system rejects collective punishment in West Jerusalem and other Israeli cities, while it condones such policies in the eastern half of Jerusalem where the Arab families of terrorists are routinely harassed and where the homes of the families of militants have been frequently destroyed (Benziman 2008). In sum, Israel has failed to unify a city that remains an urban space inhabited by two distinct peoples who have unequal rights and responsibilities to the state, and have little interaction or connection to each other. This division of the city, along with the neglect of basic social services in the Arab eastern part, has led to a growing resentment among Arab Jerusalemites. That Palestinians from East Jerusalem have perpetrated the recent terrorist attacks in the city is indicative of this growing political and religious radicalization.[10]

Students of Jerusalem have long argued that politics and religion are interrelated. The religious is never purely an issue of belief, but is always framed as a political problem; the political is never totally secular, but

---

10. During 2008, for example, there was a significant rise in the number of East Jerusalem residents involved in terrorist activities. During the first half of 2008, seventy-one Palestinians residing in East Jerusalem were arrested for suspected terrorist involvement, compared with thirty-seven in all of 2007. See the Meir Amit Intelligence and Terrorism Information Center (ITIC), Israeli Intelligence Heritage and Commemoration Center, report on "Jerusalem as a Focus for Terrorism" (2008, 4).

quickly morphs into an affront to religious sensibilities—thus, for example, the fusion of nationalism with messianism fueled the post-1967 building frenzy in and around Jerusalem's newly acquired lands. Established in 1974, Israel's settlement movement, the *Gush Emunim* (Bloc of the Faithful), aimed to settle the occupied territories, including East Jerusalem and its Arab neighborhoods, in order to repopulate the biblical land of Israel. The conquest of East Jerusalem and the Old City in June 1967—outcomes that had more to do with chance and the exigencies of battle—were immediately viewed as miracles and the beginning of a divine redemption. For many, withdrawing from the conquered territories in return for peace with neighboring countries was seen as sacrilege and a rejection of divine command. As Motti Inbari (2007, 2009) has recently noted, the political possibility that control over the Temple Mount/Haram al-Sharif compound could be transferred to the Palestinians during the course of the Oslo peace process resulted in shifts to long-standing religious rulings regarding the site. Rabbinic authorities affiliated with the settler movement, the Council of Yesha Rabbis, issued a series of rulings that both permitted and encouraged Jews to enter the Temple Mount, thus challenging the mainstream religious view that entry onto it is forbidden. It is not a coincidence that these challenges occurred in the mid-1990s: "since the emergence of the Oslo accords and discussion of the division of sovereignty in the 'Holy Basin' (the Western Wall and the Temple Mount) there has been an increasingly strong counter-reaction demanding that Jews enter the site and create facts on the ground" (Inbari 2007, 44). Since 2003, when the area was re-opened to Jewish visitors after a three-year closure during the Second Intifada, dozens and often hundreds of religious Jews have visited the Temple Mount/Haram al-Sharif each month.

An elusive Israeli-Palestinian peace has left the city deeply divided along ethnic lines. As Menachem Klein (2005, 53) argues, Jerusalem is a frontier city: "Thick ethnic-national, political, community, religious, historical, and cultural walls separate the Jewish from the Arab side of the city." For years, the city has also been off-limits to the majority of Palestinians living adjacent to it in the West Bank, although, since the end of the Second Intifada Israel has increasingly permitted hundreds of thousands of Palestinians to enter Jerusalem without a permit during Ramadan

(International Crisis Group 2012b, 14). Various road blocks, curfews, and closures instituted since the early 1990s have cut off Palestinians living in the West Bank from the holy places of the Old City and from political and cultural institutions in East Jerusalem. Mobile road blocks and police checkpoints have created a "soft" border between West and East Jerusalem. Today there are very few sites in which Jewish and Arab residents of the city interact with each other. Yet, it is the separation wall encircling Jerusalem, which Israel began constructing in 2002 as part of its counter-terrorism strategy, that represents the most dramatic change affecting the residents of Jerusalem since 1967. The wall creates a "hard" separation of metropolitan Arab East Jerusalem from the West Bank, thereby separating approximately 250,000 Palestinians—10 percent of the total West Bank population—from their social, political, economic, and cultural hinterland. The separation wall excludes many communities that were once part of Jerusalem from the city, and greatly expands the city's municipal boundaries. Numerous recent studies have examined the far-reaching ramifications of the separation wall on the daily lives of Palestinian Jerusalemites, on the urban infrastructure of East Jerusalem, and on the Jewish settler communities (see, for example, Wharton 2007; Vitullo 2005; Isaac and Khalilieh 2011). Some of these barriers have been put into place for security considerations and have reduced the threat of terrorism for Israelis living within the 1949 borders, including west Jerusalemites. Yet, recent scholarship on the vast "system of walls" that Israel has designed concurs that it is primarily meant to both protect Jewish settlers and to create "facts on the ground" that limit the territorial concessions that Israel will ultimately have to make in any final settlement.[11]

Economics is as central as politics to Jerusalem's contemporary reality. New Jewish communities have been constructed with the financial support of the government; Arab neighborhoods have languished. The result is that after four decades of Israeli rule of "undivided" Jerusalem,

---

11. For useful overviews of the separation wall in Jerusalem and its consequences for Palestinians and the peace process, see Klein (2005; 2007, 81–99), Seidemann (2005), Khamaisi and Nasrallah (2006).

there are neighborhoods in East Jerusalem that still lack adequate sanitation services. Large numbers of both religious and secular Israeli Jewish Jerusalemites are poor, and becoming poorer. But the situation is worse for Jerusalem's Arab population. In 2000, an estimated 57.7 percent of East Jerusalem's Palestinian residents lived beneath the poverty line. By 2007, the municipality recorded 62 percent of East Jerusalemite families living under the poverty line (M. Klein 2005, 68; 2008, 61). Today, 60 percent of non-Jews, compared to 23 percent of Jews in the Jerusalem municipality, fall below the poverty line (International Crisis Group 2012a, 3; Halper 2011). Foreign demand for housing property in West Jerusalem has contributed to high prices and a lack of middle-class housing options. Many of the city's current building projects are luxury second-homes for Jews who live outside of Israel, and prices per square meter typically range from $7,000-$10,000, well outside of the affordability range of most city residents. The recent construction of the separation wall around Jerusalem has also contributed to a housing shortage and high rents and housing prices in East Jerusalem and the Old City, as thousands of Palestinians who once lived outside of the city are moving back within municipal boundaries so as not to lose their Israeli-issued identity cards and the social services they bring (Bell et al. 2005, 9).

Yet, as we demonstrate in the essays for this volume, schisms in the city do not only reflect Palestinian-Israeli fault lines. Deep divisions between religious and secular, and between Ashkenazi and Sephardic Jews, also characterize the city (Fenster 2005; Friedland and Hecht 1996b). Whereas all cities must face the challenges of governing with respect to both individual and group rights, Jerusalem represents an extreme example of the difficulties of managing cities where residents have contradictory needs and identities. Group rights to maintain differences increasingly clash with residents' individual rights. For example, secular women's rights to the city's public spaces are frequently pitted against the rights of religious minorities, as in the case of the segregated Mea Shearim neighborhood, a "modesty gated area" servicing the ultra-Orthodox community (Fenster 2005). Unlike other Israeli cities—B'nei Brak, Beitar Ilit, and Emmanuel—where the majority Jewish population is ultra-Orthodox, Jerusalem is unique in that a large religious population exists alongside a secular majority as well as secular political, economic, and cultural institutions of the state. As Roger Friedland and Richard Hecht (1996b, 113) note, conflicts between religious and secular Jews in Jerusalem is exacerbated by the tendency of the ultra-Orthodox to seek monopoly control over the city spaces that they enter. Since Judaism is not a private confession but a system of laws regulating both private and public life, behavior in the outside community is important. Public violations of the Sabbath and codes of modesty and kashrut cannot be tolerated not only because observant Jews have an obligation to ensure that fellow Jews keep the laws of the Torah, but also because such violations profane the community. These controversies are likely to increase in the years ahead. While nearly 70 percent of the city's population are Jews, within the Jewish population it is the religious sector that is growing. In the 1990s, for example, 72 percent of Jerusalem's Jewish elementary school children attended state religious schools compared to only 26 percent in Tel Aviv (Vinitzky-Seroussi 1998, 187). Orthodox Jews also comprise the majority of voters in municipal elections. Since 1990, thousands of young, secular and well-educated professionals have departed for other Israeli locales: "The people who seem likely to remain are the ultra-religious, the Yeshiva students, and the poor. There is less and less to sustain Jerusalem as a vibrant Western city" (Shavit 2002, 57).

Currently, notwithstanding the inclusive rhetoric of the city's new mayor, Jerusalem is governed by a coalition of right-of-center Israeli nationalists and ultra-Orthodox religious groups who discriminate against secular Jews and the Palestinian population (the latter have little influence in municipal affairs since most Arab Palestinian Jerusalemites have long boycotted municipal elections). In this competition over the identity of the city, secular Jews and Palestinians struggle against Jewish and Islamic groups who claim the right to determine the city's character. As middle class Israelis continue to migrate away from Jerusalem—driven out by high housing costs, limited employment opportunities, and violence—the growth of Jerusalem's religious population and the predominance of the ultra-Orthodox on the city council raises the concern that the city's religious community will dictate its future (Winer 2013). Indeed, Jerusalem is increasingly seen as representing a religious and right-wing nationalist Israeli identity. Tel Aviv, by contrast, appeals to a more secular and left-of-center segment of Israel's population. The recent disagreement between Jerusalem mayor Nir Barkat and Jerusalem coalition government member Rachel Azaria, who is against gender segregation in the ultra-Orthodox neighborhood of Mea Shearim, highlights these ongoing rifts. In October 2011, Mayor Barkat dismissed Azaria citing loyalty to city council policy and procedural issues related to Azaria's opposition to the municipality (Hasson 2011).

On top of these divisions, a variety of issues associated with community planning—planning that equitably organizes urban space including housing, water planning, sewage and waste removal, industry and trade, education, transportation, and environmental concerns—are also central to the city's future. While the future of Jerusalem is certainly a political question that involves clashing claims regarding sovereignty and identity, like any other city its urban planners, engineers, educators, and technocrats must come up with ways of handling the myriad problems associated with service provision and property rights in modern urban space. Seen from this perspective, the study of Jerusalem is viewed less as a "political space of competing ideological units" and more as, for example, a "technical space in need of garbage-collection maintenance." For technocrats, after all, whether Israelis or Palestinians have sovereignty over the Temple Mount/Haram al-Sharif is unimportant. What they would like figured out is more mundane, such as whether it is better for the city's residents that the municipal service collecting the garbage left by the thousands of pilgrims visiting the holy compound be a public or private company (Shalakany 2002, 441–42).

This book builds on previous scholarship on Jerusalem by focusing on different types of cooperative and conflictual relationships that have occurred in the city's modern past and in recent years, and those that might emerge in the future. Chapters 1, 2, and 3 examine a diverse set of conflicts and cooperative outcomes that are marked by the intersection of Jerusalem's politics and its religious symbolism. In chapter 1, Miriam Fendius Elman considers the extent to which religious myths surrounding Jerusalem contributed to the demise of the Oslo peace process and the start of the Second Intifada. In chapter 2, Richard Hecht and Roger Friedland discuss how power is integral to the sacred, as illustrated by religious movements in Israel and Palestine using sacred sites to promote their definitions of political space. In chapter 3, Michael Zank explores how, by offering multiple and contradictory views on Jerusalem as a real and ideal city, scripture is an expression of discontent with the actual earthly city of Jerusalem. Zank explains how spiritual orientations toward the holy city have always interacted with more mundane and secular concerns, such as political survival and governance.

The next set of chapters discusses the contestation over different visions or representations of Jerusalem among early Zionists. In chapter 4, Shai Ginsburg probes the merits and pitfalls of the genre of political poetry in general, and the work of Uri Tsvi Greenberg in particular. In some of his earlier work, Greenberg emphasizes individual pain and suffering and his alienation from the collective, portraying Jerusalem as a utopian vision that provides personal deliverance. In his later work, however, Greenberg sets Jerusalem within the "discourse of national command and mission." In these poems, Jerusalem becomes a marker of a new Jewish experience, where Jewish tradition is reinvigorated by the energy of the Zionist project in Palestine. Yet Ginsburg argues that Greenberg's poetry is quite different from other Labor poetry of the time in which Jerusalem plays a minor role. By emphasizing the ruin of Jerusalem in his poetry, Greenberg offered an alternative reading of Zionism and a harsh criticism of the political and cultural hegemony of the Labor movement. In chapter 5, Arieh Saposnik explains that there were actually two "Jerusalems" in the early Zionist imagination—one evinced ambivalence toward a city viewed as intolerant and unclean; the other viewed Jerusalem as a sanctified city. Saposnik shows how Zionism ultimately reconciled these tensions by transforming the city from a "center of reviled exile" into the "very heart of the land of redemption." Jerusalem thus became the centerpiece for a new national sacrality in which the secular—Hebrew culture and political power—became sacred.

Chapters 6, 7, and 8 move beyond elites and public policy to consider conflictual and cooperative outcomes within particular, specific communities and neighborhoods. The focus of these chapters is on ordinary, non-elite residents of the city and their everyday lives, and is marked by an analysis that involves close interaction and identification with the subjects of study. In chapter 6, Menachem Klein reviews the history of the small village of Nu'man (Khirbet Mazmuria), located on the southeastern border of the Jerusalem municipal line. In addition, he discusses the various types of walls and borders that have existed in Jerusalem since 1947, and how these have shaped power relationships in the city and group identities. Klein suggests that more attention should be paid to Israeli-Palestinian interactions (not necessarily always conflictual) that take place next to these boundaries and in contexts where they are porous. In chapter 7, Glenn Bowman discusses his own experiences doing fieldwork in Jerusalem's Old City, which inevitably involved developing a close relationship with his subjects. In critiquing anthropology's study of Jerusalem, he argues that the field is bifurcated between an anthropology of the city's historical past and a political anthropology that has too quickly moved away from a close observation of social and cultural configurations to providing expert solutions to the Jerusalem "problem." In chapter 8, Madelaine Adelman traces tensions between the growth of public support in Israel for its gay community and newly forged religious-nationalist cooperative ties in Jerusalem that have worked against this community. In examining a very local controversy surrounding the venue of the 2006 WorldPride parade, the "parade in which nobody marched," she shows who was against the event, how they organized to oppose it, and the ways in which national conflicts informed the handling of a gay pride event in the city.

A final set of chapters moves beyond national and local conflict and cooperation to consider its international dimensions. In chapter 9, Mark Woodward shows how Jerusalem impacts Muslim religious rituals even in places outside of the Middle East, and the lives of Muslims who have never actually visited the city. Woodward reveals the symbolic replication of Jerusalem in the Javanese city of Kudus (a Javanese transliteration of the Arabic *Quds*), a shrine city in Indonesia with a population of 135,000, an important pilgrimage site, and a center of Islamic learning since the sixteenth century. Woodward discusses the founding of the city and its principle mosque, and the extent to which legends concerning direct contacts with Jerusalem contributed to the religious legitimacy of Javanese territories and communities. In chapter 10, Dallen Timothy and Chad

Emmett discuss how competing religious attachments to Jerusalem and differential power relationships contribute to conflicts surrounding Jerusalem's heritage sites and to seemingly innocuous activities in the city such as tourism. The authors explain why Jerusalem's tourist spaces have become increasingly segregated and how this has exacerbated Israeli-Palestinian—as well as Christian/Jewish/Muslim—conflicts in the city.

Jerusalem across the Disciplines

Extant work on Jerusalem typically does not self-consciously probe disciplinary advantages and limitations. Beyond the general claim that religion and politics both matter, there is little discussion of how diverse fields contribute to the study of the city, or how studying the city might illuminate strengths and weaknesses of the disciplines themselves. While a number of seminal studies on Jerusalem were written prior to the 1990s (e.g., Elon 1989; Ben-Arieh 1984; Benvenisti 1976), as noted above there has been a significant increase in publications on the city during the last decade. During this period, over a dozen books and scores of journal articles have been published on the topic of Jerusalem.[12] Some of these academic works focus on the city's religious significance and the ways in which attachments to the city's sacred sites have been the source of multiple conflicts (Chapman 2004; Inbari 2007; Goddard 2010). Others focus on the politics of Jerusalem

---

12. In this book we focus primarily on English language sources. In the context of Jerusalem studies, this proves less of a hindrance than might otherwise be the case. Since Israeli, Palestinian, and other scholars in the Middle East and Europe want to "get their message out," they typically prefer to publish their work in English. Many monographs on the city initially published in Hebrew and Arabic are frequently translated into English for publication by either US or UK presses. Moreover, many of the journals that publish work on the city are printed in the English language: *Israel Studies, Journal of Palestine Studies, Jerusalem Quarterly File*, and the *Palestine-Israel Journal of Politics, Economics and Culture*. Data and analyses on the city available from think tanks and on the World Wide Web are also easily accessible in English (for example, see this book's Appendix for suggested Internet sources). Our decision to focus on English language sources should thus not be viewed as a slight to locally produced knowledge in the Middle East region. Noteworthy recent books on Jerusalem published in Hebrew include Shragai (1995), Amirav (2002, 2007), and Berkovits (2006). In Arabic, see Muwassi (1996) and Nassar (2005).

and its impact on the larger Arab-Israeli and Israeli-Palestinian conflicts (Dumper 2002; Klein 2007; Gold 2007) or on how legal principles—such as sovereignty and territoriality—impact the city's status and the likelihood for conflict resolution (Shalakany 2002).

Researchers in the humanities and social sciences have each advanced recent scholarship on Jerusalem. The overwhelming majority can be found in political science and focus on decision-making, state-level politics, and the significance of Jerusalem in various efforts to resolve the Israeli-Palestinian conflict. Literary scholars have examined the representation of the city in Israeli Jewish and Palestinian literature and art (Omer-Sherman 2006; Parmenter 1994; Rogers 1999; Elad-Bouskila 1999; Harb 2004). Urban planners have reimagined the layout and architecture of the city (Segal, Tartakover, and Weizman 2003; Sorkin 2002; Weizman 2007). Scholars from disciplines such as anthropology and art history have begun to rethink the place of archeology in Jerusalem (Abu El-Haj 2006, 2001, 1998; Wharton 2006) and there has been an increasing interest in the politics of space and place as it relates to the city's past and present. Historians have considered the ways in which Jerusalem has been "documented" over time, for example, in the way that nineteenth century European photographers presented the city as an authentic biblical site of holy ruins relevant to Europe, rather than as a living place inhabited by local residents (Nassar 2005, 2006). Education researchers have examined how Jewish high school students in Jerusalem interpret key events in Jewish history (Porat 2004) and the reality of day-to-day schooling in East Jerusalem, where the curriculum is determined by the Palestinian Authority, while hiring, salaries, and infrastructure funding is under Israel's jurisdiction (Yair and Alayan 2009). Medical research has revealed the psychological phenomenon known as the Jerusalem Syndrome (Amirav 2007; Van der Haven 2008). Scholars also have begun to compare Jerusalem to other highly contested cities (Samman 2007). Still other scholarly works reflect on how Jerusalem represents a microcosm of larger social and cultural influences (Fenster 2005; Gavriely-Nuri 2007) and on how symbolic and physical urban space influences Jerusalem's political and sociological dynamics (Misselwitz and Rieniets 2006). Ethnographies of Jerusalem are surprisingly limited typically to discrete studies of "sub-cultural" groups, and members of marginalized communities (Dominguez 1989).

Two publications stand out for us as prototypical models of scholars seeking to utilize disciplinary insights in order to better understand conflict and cooperation in Jerusalem. Bernard Wasserstein (2001) offers a concise history of Jerusalem and its antagonists since the Ottoman period. He shows how disputes over control of the city and the status of its holy sites have been a microcosm of larger global and regional conflicts. Wasserstein's study conveys how religion and politics have intersected in Jerusalem's history (for example, in his rich description of how Mufti Hajj Amin al-Husayni exploited the sanctity of Jerusalem for Muslims so as to solidify his control of Palestine and wrest it away from competing Palestinian families). In particular, the book explains why the Jewish and Palestinian nationalist movements ultimately clashed, yet shows that this outcome was not necessarily inevitable.

Of the many monographs written on Jerusalem, Meron Benvenisti's *City of Stone* (1996) is one of the most interdisciplinary. Although Benvenisti does not explicitly refer to competing disciplinary theories or methods of analysis, his book deftly interweaves multiple dimensions of Jerusalem's past and present: urban and municipal planning, political parties, demographics, religious beliefs, nationalisms, and historical memories. He manages to account for the raw emotions of Jerusalem's communities, providing one of the best explanations for Israel's controversial actions in Jerusalem in June 1967. Benvenisti also gives voice to Jerusalem's competing communities: secular and religious Jews, East Jerusalemite Muslim Palestinians and Palestinian Israelis, Christian Zionists and Christian Palestinians. Blending the genres of historical analysis, biography, and contemporary political commentary, *City of Stone* is a tour de force. In depicting the complexity of intra- and inter-communal conflicts in Jerusalem, it remains of the best books written on the city in recent years.

Inspired by this scholarship, we seek to uncover new issue areas linked to conflict—and at times cooperative endeavors—within Jerusalem's diverse communities and neighborhoods, and its governance and development. In the pages that follow we discuss Jerusalem's elites and its politicians (Elman). But we also consider the everyday formation and practice of identity, religion, and social movements among the city's non-elite. The essays in this book touch on secular-religious conflicts in Jerusalem's Jewish community (Adelman), the significance of Jerusalem for communities outside of the city (Timothy and Emmett, and Woodward), the role that Jerusalem played for Europeans in the 1800s and early Zionists thereafter (Saposnik and Ginsburg), and pedagogical approaches to the city (Zank). To explore these issues, the contributors to the volume bring to bear the insights of different disciplines.

Multiple Jerusalems

In the following chapters, scholars from a diverse set of fields openly discuss the rules and assumptions embedded in their respective disciplines along with the merits and pitfalls of their own disciplinary engagement with Jerusalem. In so doing, we offer various models of cross-disciplinary engagement, ranging from reflexive discussions of disciplinary insights and boundaries, to interdisciplinary conversations, to new trans-disciplinary paradigms. Taken as a whole, the book offers scholars of Jerusalem in particular, and those interested in fostering cross-disciplinary engagement in other fields of inquiry in general, with a set of flexible blueprints from which to begin to create new forms of knowledge.

This book brings together multiple perspectives on and "readings" of the Israeli-Palestinian conflict, and especially how it has evolved in Jerusalem.[13] Indeed, the city carries multiple meanings according to its successive and simultaneous residents and rulers. During its history, Jerusalem has experienced "twenty ruinous sieges, two intervals of total destruction, eighteen reconstructions, and at least eleven transitions from one religion to another" (Chapman 2004, 8). It follows that reconciliation of enduring rivalries between the nation and sub-state actors often involves an acknowledgement of counter-narratives and, typically, of past wrongdoings (Silverstein and Makdisi 2006, 9–18). Nowhere is this more evident

---

13. For useful overviews of the Israeli-Arab conflict in general, and the Israeli-Palestinian conflict in particular, see Dowty (2008), Fraser (2004), Wasserstein (2003), Nusseibeh (2007), Khalidi (2006), Morris (1999), and Golani and Manna (2011).

than with regard to the Israeli-Palestinian conflict. The recent revisiting of Zionist culpability in creating the refugee crisis of 1948, and acknowledgement of the Palestinian tragedy, for example, has had a significant impact on Israel's positions regarding the peace process. Israeli politicians well-versed in the "new history" of Israel's early years have remarked that these alternative readings of the state's origins influenced their negotiating positions with the Palestinians (Ben-Josef Hirsch 2007, and see Bar-On 2006).

Nevertheless, rather than making productive use of these tensions, most scholarly work on the Israeli-Palestinian conflict in general, and the dynamics of the conflict in Jerusalem in particular, is partisan, some of it overtly so. For example, while Dore Gold's (2007) book describes well the role that the violent conquest of Jerusalem plays in Sunni and Shiite apocalyptic movements, and how these ideas have begun to infiltrate the Palestinian community, it dodges any discussion of how the belief systems and practices of Christian Zionists or messianic Jews have affected religious tolerance and freedom in the city (Shindler 2000; Lukens-Bull and Fafard 2007; Armstrong 1998; Dumper 2002). Unfortunately, much of the existing work on the city reads as either firmly pro-Palestine/anti-Israel or pro-Israel/anti-Palestine. It is rare to find a study that acknowledges the aspirations and motivations of each side, or that recognizes the mistakes and egregious excesses of both.[14]

By contrast, contributors to our volume recognize the voices of Jerusalem's multiple constituencies, including Jews (secular and Orthodox) and Palestinian Arabs (Muslim and Christian).[15] This volume's point of departure is Jerusalem in the mid-nineteenth century, when the "problem of Jerusalem" first emerged and demanded political and religious solutions. Several of the contributions show how, in the conflict over Jerusalem's holy sites, the distinction between politics and religion has been

14. For notable exceptions see Ben-Ami (2006) and Reiter (2008).

15. Christians today are a minority of the Palestinian population and only 20 percent of the Arab population of the Old City of Jerusalem is Christian. Since 1993, Palestinian Muslim-Christian conflicts have increased significantly in Jerusalem. For more on recent attacks on Christian holy sites and discriminatory practices taken against Palestine's Christian communities, see Tsimhoni (2005).

blurred (Friedland and Hecht, and Saposnik). The Arabs and Jews of Palestine have each married nationalistic designs to religious symbols, and religious sites have often been turned into nationalist symbols (Benvenisti 1996; Reiter 2008).

A number of contributors to this book demonstrate how Israel has been, through its architecture, museums, literature, educational programs and celebrations, overstating the Jewish connections to Jerusalem while denying Muslim and Arab legacies (Timothy and Emmett). Such an erasure of local inhabitants of the city occurs in the famous Israeli song, "Jerusalem of Gold," considered by many to be Israel's unofficial national anthem. In one line of the song, a reference to the "empty market square" conveys Israel's "blindness" to Arab residents of the Old City who lived there before the 1967 war (Gavriely-Nuri 2007, 105). The city of Jerusalem continues to constitute a contested site for cultural production, sometimes producing bizarre outcomes among its divergent citizenry. Consider, for example, Israel's recent plan to build a Museum of Tolerance on the site of an ancient Palestinian cemetery in Jerusalem, Ma'man Allah, or Jerusalem mayor Nir Barkat's attempt to turn Silwan, a village southeast of the walled Old City where some 7,500 Palestinians live, mostly in homes built without legal permits, into an archeological park—the City of David and the Garden of King Solomon. By emphasizing the shared heritage of the three Abrahamic faiths, mayor Barkat hopes to create a new tourist attraction for Christian, Muslim, and Jewish tourists, even if a residential neighborhood is undermined in the process (Bronner 2009; Bronner and Kershner 2009; Oppenheimer 2011). Israeli architecture and text serve to erase competing nationalist claims to the city, since they emphasize the lack of any nation in Jerusalem other than the Davidic Kingdom of Israel and the post-1948 Israeli state. As Benvenisti (1996, 8) aptly puts it, Jerusalem's history is a "vast quarry from whose stones a magnificent edifice dedicated to the cult of Israeli Jerusalem has been constructed" (see also Azoulay 2008).

This book should be read as a work of scholarship rather than partisan polemic. The book includes contributions by authors who, in their other work, have been highly critical of Israeli positions and actions, and the chapters also reflect a critical perspective of Israeli policy. However, the book also eschews a stance that denies Israelis and Palestinians in general, or Israeli and Palestinian Jerusalemites in particular, the right to live in peace and with dignity and security, which is sadly the tenor of some recent work on the city. Beyond that, our authors vary to some degree regarding the legitimacy of the Israeli state and Zionism, pathways to a Palestinian state, and the future of Jerusalem in the context of a binational state or the two-state paradigm.[16]

Despite these different positions on Jerusalem's past and future, the view which unites many students of the Israeli-Palestinian conflict (along with Palestinians, and increasingly Israelis themselves) is that Israel's post-1967 settlement project has been an error of colossal proportions. Indeed, since the early 1990s a new consensus has emerged that views continued Israeli control of the majority of the West Bank as both a security and economic liability. Poll data and electoral returns demonstrate that most Israelis are determined to maintain the exclusively Jewish nature of Israel, and they now see that withdrawal from the major population centers of the West Bank and dismantling most of the Jewish Israeli settlements there is the only way of achieving this goal (Waxman 2008). Former Israeli foreign minister and Oxford-trained historian Shlomo Ben-Ami (2006, 331) reflects on this new public opinion when he observes that "demography and territory, the two pillars of the Zionist enterprise, cannot be reconciled unless Israel abandons her territorial ambitions and departs from the unrealistic, and morally corrupting, dream of possessing the biblical lands of Eretz-Israel."[17] Public support for the disengagement from Gaza and Olmert's policy of "convergence," the unilateral removal of isolated

16. We purposely use the term Israeli, recognizing that Israel's continued existence as a *Jewish* democratic state is also contested. For more on this debate, see especially Kimmerling (2001), Dowty (1999), and Smooha (2004). For discussions of the binational versus two-state solution to the Israeli-Palestinian conflict, see, for example, Inbar (2009), Benvenisti (2007), and Morris (2009).

17. While many of the chapters that follow reference Israel's settlement project in general, our focus here is on how these policies have impacted those who live in Jerusalem and its environs. For overviews of the history of Israel's settlement and occupation policies since 1967, the settlement movement, and the expansion and development of Jewish settlement in the West Bank and Gaza, see, for example, Zertal and Eldar (2007), Haklai (2006), Gorenberg (2006), Sprinzak (1991), and Newman (1985).

settlements even in the absence of a negotiated agreement, and the building of the separation wall is consistent with this new outlook.

Yet, while there is growing acceptance of the need to withdraw from territory occupied in the June 1967 war, most Israelis—and many Jews worldwide—do not include Jerusalem in this equation. As Benjamin Netanyahu recently noted in his remarks to the American Israel Public Affairs Committee (AIPAC) on March 22, 2011—"Jerusalem is not a settlement, it is our capital." A majority of Israelis agree with him. As noted in a recent report by the International Crisis Group (2012a, 4), "What Palestinians and most of the world call settlements are, for Israelis of all stripes, established towns and neighborhoods, firmly rooted in the Israeli consciousness as Jewish and so deeply woven into the fabric of Jerusalem and Israel writ large that their ultimate disposition is taken for granted."

Not only is there a deep Jewish spiritual connection to the city, but a number of Jerusalem's contested spaces are places where Jews lived for hundreds of years—prior to being expelled by foreign rulers. Sheikh Jarrah is a case in point. This Palestinian neighborhood north of the Old City is also the site of the compound of Shimon HaTzadik (Simon the Just), the great high priest from the Second Temple era who is believed to be buried there. A small Jewish community settled near the tomb in the late 1800s, but was forced to leave the area in 1948 when Jordan took control of the eastern portions of the city. In the 1950s, some thirty Palestinian families moved into the neighborhood with the permission of the United Nations Relief and Works Agency (UNRWA) and the Jordanian authorities, paying nominal rent on their homes. Following the 1967 war, however, Israel demanded that these residents pay their rent—at market rate—to a special Israeli authority set up to collect the fees. In the meanwhile, a Knesset committee sought to register the properties with the Israel Lands Authority based on nineteenth century documents attesting to the fact that they were owned by Jews. Most of the Palestinian families refused to pay any rent to Israeli authorities, a position that has become the basis of the legal claim against the families today. The Israeli courts have ordered evictions from the disputed residences and Jewish Israeli settlers have various plans to build in the neighborhood (Reiter and Lehrs 2010). The neighborhood continues to be a site of Arab-Jewish violence, most recently during the annual Flag Day parade honoring the forty-fourth anniversary of the 1967 war in June 2011 (Lidman 2011).

While cooperative solutions will need to be found for Jerusalem's shared heritage, Israel's continued policy of encircling West (predominantly Jewish) Jerusalem with Jewish neighborhoods in the eastern half of the city, and of settling Jews and building Jewish religious establishments in the heart of Arab neighborhoods in East Jerusalem, has caused animosity and perpetuated injustices (Goodman 2011, 185–200; Ofran 2012). As Marco Allegra (2011, 12) recently notes, "Israel's policy in Jerusalem . . . has created a deeply contested and polarized city, and coexistence between Jews and Palestinians has been progressively deteriorating." In recent years, Israel has approved plans for the expansion of many neighborhoods located within the city limits set by Israel after the 1967 war. For example, thousands of new housing units were approved in 2010 and 2011 for the communities of Gilo, Har Homa, Ramat Shlomo, and Ramot (International Crisis Group 2012a, 2012b). In 2012, in reaction to the General Assembly resolution that upgraded Palestine to a non-member observer state, Israel announced plans to build further residential units in East Jerusalem. While the resumption of peace talks in the summer of 2012 and recent negotiations over Iran's nuclear program have led Israel to halt some of this construction (notably in the controversial E1 area that abuts the Jewish settlement of Ma'ale Adumim), other new housing plans are moving forward (Sternman 2013; Rudoren 2013b, 2013c; Peace Now 2013). For example, in addition to Sheikh Jarrah noted above, Jewish settler purchases of buildings in the Arab neighborhoods of Abu Dis, Ras al-Amud, Jabel Mukaber, and Silwan continue to inflame tensions with over 2,000 Israeli Jewish settlers now living in the midst of these Palestinian communities in and around Jerusalem's Old City (Klein 2010, 58–69; Klein 2011; Rudoren 2013a).

Since 1967, the "lack of reference" for Palestinian residents of Jerusalem—including the many former West Bank Palestinians who are now caught in the seam between the 1949 municipal boundary and the recently constructed separation wall—is intolerable because they are neither allowed to be fully Israeli nor fully Palestinian (see, for example, Khalidi 1992; Abu Shamseyeh 1999; Talhami 2000; Wharton 2007; Vitullo 2005; Klein 2005; Klein 2007, 81–99; Seidemann 2005; Khamaisi and Nasrallah

2006). Sarah Kaminker (1997, 14) concludes that the "critical element of democratic city planning—the relatively equitable distribution of community resources—has been crushed to make way for the 'new' Jerusalem." Since 1967, the Israeli state and municipal government's urban policy of ensuring the preponderance and dominance of Jerusalem's Jewish community has rendered the notion of a unified multicultural city a fiction that is founded on discrimination and the use of force (Anderson 2005; Safier 2001). It is questionable whether this policy can be sustained in the long term; demographics suggest otherwise. In 1967 the population of Jerusalem was 74 percent Jewish and 26 percent Arab. Today, due to the high Palestinian growth rate coupled with secular Jewish Israeli flight from the city, the city is 64 percent Jewish and 36 percent Arab (Benari 2012).[18]

Disciplinary and Cross-Disciplinary Engagements of Jerusalem

In recent years, moving between or beyond what some call "mono-disciplinarity" has become an increasingly popular way of thinking about and organizing knowledge. As a result, a wide range of cross-disciplinary scholarship has emerged as valuable models for solving some of the world's most complex problems (Klein 1990, 1996; Fiore 2008; Feller 2007; Sa 2008). Proponents argue that discipline-bound "lone scholars", and the rigid university structures that support "silo" research, impede scientific progress. Instead, advocates of interdisciplinarity argue that cross-disciplinary engagements aid researchers who want to pursue answers

18. In 2011, Jerusalem's population was 804,000, making the capital Israel's largest municipality, with its residents comprising nearly 10 percent of the country's total population. According to figures released by Israel's Central Bureau of Statistics (CBS), 499,400 Jews resided in the city by the end of 2011. There were 281,000 Muslims, 14,700 Christians, and a further 9,000 residents with no stated religious affiliation (Fiske 2013; Benari 2012). In total, from 1967 through 2011, the city's population grew by 200 percent, with the Jewish population increasing by 157 percent and the Arab population increasing by 327 percent. In 2010, 474,000 residents (both Jews and Arabs) lived in areas added to the municipality in 1967; these residents represent 60 percent of Jerusalem's total population. In these areas of the city, the data show that there were 192,000 Jewish and non-Arab residents (accounting for 41 percent of the population in these East Jerusalem neighborhoods) and 280,000 Arabs, constituting 59 percent of the population living in these areas (Benari 2012; see also Choshen et al. 2013, 7–9).

to real-world problems that otherwise would go unsolved if left to the domain of one discipline or another. Widespread interest in cross-disciplinary research can be traced in part to the range of meanings and practices associated with the concept. Here, Julie Klein's (1990, 55–73) "lexicon" of interdisciplinarity, which distinguishes between disciplinary (stand-alone), multidisciplinary (additive), interdisciplinary (integrative) and transdisciplinary (generative) research remains especially useful.

Disciplinary or mono-disciplinary research, which could be conducted by one or more researcher from the same area of inquiry, relies on the theories, epistemological frameworks, and methods agreed upon within that area of inquiry. These agreed-upon components produce a set of questions that are possible to ask, a toolkit that researchers draw from in order to answer those questions, and criteria with which they judge the results. Disciplines constitute a way of approaching and understanding the world. Scholars immersed in a discipline can easily take on, without much reflection, this worldview—to the point where it may become difficult to either articulate the many assumptions that make up their discipline or to appreciate the value of another discipline. That is not to say that scholars are hermetically sealed within isolated towers of knowledge. The boundaries between disciplines—or the bridges that traverse disciplines—are messier than any typology can allow for.

Multidisciplinary research, typically conducted by a set of researchers from distinct disciplines, is considered additive: adding the insights of two or more disciplines to answer a research question. Said another way, multidisciplinary research is akin to "parallel play" with researchers focusing alongside each other on the same question, but approaching it in disciplinarily unique ways that, when shared, reveal something new that otherwise would have been hidden had the team members worked in isolation. Faculty commonly refer to "interdisciplinary" research when in fact they are describing a form of "multidisciplinary" research where a team of discipline-based scholars collaborate strategically, and on a contingent basis, on a shared research topic or question.

Interdisciplinary research, which could be conducted by one or more researchers, is considered integrative: borrowing and/or mixing the theories, epistemological frameworks or methods from two or more disciplines. Interdisciplinary research can be further differentiated between "cognate interdisciplinarity," for example, research within the natural sciences, social sciences or the humanities, and "radical interdisciplinarity": research that *crosses* the domains of the natural sciences, social sciences, and the humanities (Petts, Owens, and Bulkeley 2008, 596–97). Scholars trained within a particular discipline (e.g., political science, psychology, philosophy) can work toward interdisciplinarity, a process that requires considerable time, coordination, communication, and cooperation. Scholars who have been trained in what might be termed "encouraged interdisciplinarity," for instance, a graduate degree in anthropology with a certificate in women's studies, or "intentional interdisciplinarity," a graduate degree in social science, have a head start in the pursuit of such interdisciplinary research.

Lastly, transdisciplinarity is a generative approach to knowledge, typically deployed to solve complex problems that have eluded promising solutions. The term draws on the notion of interdisciplinarity in that it refers to a synthesis of theories and methods that breakdown the constituent components of any one or more disciplines to generate something new. Yet, the term also refers to the intentional production of socially-useful knowledge in which researchers seek to fill the gap between "knowledge production in academia" and "knowledge requests for solving societal problems" (Hadorn et al. 2008, 4; Rhoten 2003). Furthermore, transdisciplinarity relies on the experience and vision of relevant (typically non-academic) actors. Thus, in transdisciplinary research, "problems are formulated from the very beginning within a dialogue among a large number of different actors and their perspectives," and the resulting knowledge is "socially robust" in the sense that the research produced is communicable and useful for society (Nowotny 2004). In this way, transdisciplinary scholarship combines interdisciplinary approaches to knowledge production with the philosophy and practice of community-embedded and stakeholder-focused policy relevant research.

The contributors to this book seek to advance knowledge about the city of Jerusalem—one of the most contested urban spaces in the world—by explicitly asking how what we do in our disciplines problematizes our study of Jerusalem. Our point of departure is an acknowledgment that each discipline has different expectations about what Jerusalem tells us. Given the complexity of the subject, no single method, theory, or approach can claim to provide a full account of the city, but each discipline makes unique contributions to its study, contributions enhanced by the mindfulness of the contributions made by others. The book highlights how various disciplines approach the same subject (Jerusalem) and the same issues—conflict and cooperation within neighborhoods and communities, and contestation over governance, citizenship, development, and movement—in order to show where the gaps between the disciplines lie. It thus seeks to offer fresh insight into the study of Jerusalem, while also providing an instructive set of models for both disciplinary and cross-disciplinary engagement.

Some authors show how their understanding of the city has been shaped by their home discipline: Elman, Bowman, Ginsburg, and Zank in particular assess disciplinary strengths and weaknesses on a given contested issue or problem. Here, the goal is not to morph or integrate knowledge into something that transcends a specific discipline, but to probe the value and limits of each disciplinary approach, whether along theoretical, methodological, or empirical lines. In some respects, this type of cross-disciplinary engagement is the easiest to undertake, and it is thus not surprising that so many of this book's contributors (and many others!) work within this mode when claiming to do "interdisciplinary" work. After all, this model does not require high levels of proficiency or expertise in another discipline. Rather, it requires a self-conscious probing of one's own disciplinary training and guild rules, with an eye to assessing their benefits and drawbacks. It also requires a large dose of humility—that is, the recognition that one's own field does not have all the answers and that other disciplines have something valuable to contribute. In a sense, this is interdisciplinarity as Rashomon.

A different approach to cross-disciplinary engagement is suggested by a second group of chapters authored by Saposnik, Klein, Hecht and Friedland, and Timothy and Emmett. Unlike our first set of authors, who each approach their study of Jerusalem from the perspective of a particular discipline, albeit cognizant of its limitations, the authors in our second set seek to move beyond specific disciplinary boundaries, and self-consciously attempt to locate and pinpoint fruitful linkages to alternative modes of inquiry. Such cross-disciplinary engagement goes further toward a synthesis of two (or more) disciplinary approaches—these chapters are thus good examples of what we mean by interdisciplinary research. In fact, in at least one of these cases (Hecht and Friedland), the authors have worked together for so long that their work has developed from a multi-disciplinary to interdisciplinary approach.

Still other chapters in this volume study Jerusalem by working within fields of study that transcend single disciplines. The essays by Woodward and Adelman are the most ambitious in their attempt to bridge the boundaries of disciplinary "bunkers." They each adopt a transdisciplinary or post-disciplinary approach. These two chapters offer an analysis of Jerusalem that is not easily located in any particular discipline, nor is it easy to unpack the ways in which these authors "mix and match" disciplinary approaches (as is possible with our second set of chapters).

To be clear: we are not arguing that cross-disciplinary engagement is somehow "better" than disciplinary research. As the chapters that follow demonstrate, Jerusalem can be usefully examined through the lenses of specific disciplines just as it can via disciplinary boundary-crossings. Our goal is twofold: to inspire scholars to be more explicit in identifying how their disciplines shape their understanding of Jerusalem, and to underscore the difficulty inherent to studying Jerusalem from a single disciplinary perspective. Jerusalem is a city of contrasts. Cafes and night clubs sit alongside synagogues; state-of-the-art medical research takes place along with cutting edge and contested archeological digs; Judaica stores, convents, and mosques share space only a few blocks away from high rise apartments and pricey hotels; neighborhoods marked by poverty and gentrification share the city landscape (*Eretz* 2008; Gonen 2002). The city—a physical disputed space that is very real for the people who live there—is also an imagined space for billions of other people worldwide. It resides in the collective hopes, memories, and dreams of those who define it as sacred. We hope that in the pages that follow we do justice to the multiple dimensions of the city and its diverse communities, and in so doing we illuminate the possible ways that Jerusalem and other contested modern urban spaces might be studied across the disciplines.

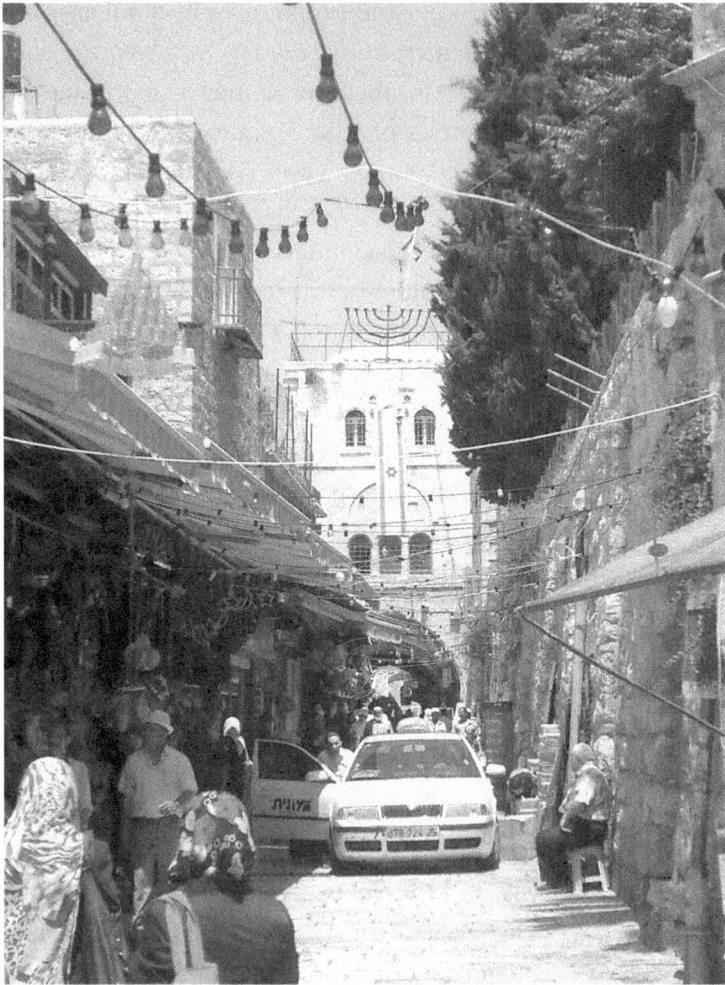

1. A Jewish home in the Christian Quarter of the Old City, Jerusalem. July 2012. Courtesy of Mathew Rommel.

2. The Tomb of the Prophet Samuel in north Jerusalem. March 2008. Courtesy of Miriam Fendius Elman.

3. The Western Wall Plaza in Jerusalem's Old City. July 2012. Courtesy of Miriam Fendius Elman.

4. The recently renovated Hurva Synagogue in Jerusalem's Old City. July 2012. Courtesy of Miriam Fendius Elman.

5. A Jewish residence in the Sheikh Jarrah neighborhood, East Jerusalem. July 2012. Courtesy of Miriam Fendius Elman.

1

Jerusalem and the Demise of the Oslo Peace Process

The Contributions (and Limitations) of a Political Science Approach

MIRIAM FENDIUS ELMAN

We shall extra-territorialize Jerusalem, so that it will belong to nobody and yet everybody; and with it the Holy Places which will become the joint possession of all Believers—a great condominium of culture and morality.

—Theodor Herzl (1896)

We hereby inform the people of Israel and the entire world that under heavenly command we have just returned home in the elevations of holiness and our holy city. We shall never move out of here.

—Rabbi Zvi Yehuda Kook (1967)

Even if we conquer the Old City and the West Bank, in the end we will have to leave them.
—Levi Eshkol (1967)

On the question of Jerusalem, we said that this government, just like all its predecessors, believes there are no differences of opinion in this House over the eternalness of Jerusalem as Israel's capital. United and unified Jerusalem is not negotiable and will be the capital of the Israeli people under Israel's sovereignty and the subject of every Jew's yearnings and dreams forever and ever.

—Yitzhak Rabin (1993)

Our policy on Jerusalem is the same policy followed by all Israeli governments for 42 years, and it has not changed. As far as we are concerned, building in Jerusalem is the same as building in Tel Aviv.

—Benjamin Netanyahu (2010)

47

HOW MUCH DID conflict over Jerusalem contribute to the demise of the Oslo peace process? Despite a burgeoning literature in political science on the collapse of the Israeli-Palestinian peace efforts that began with such promise in the early 1990s, Jerusalem has not figured very prominently in the majority of this work. The political science literature brings to bear a host of factors that led to the outbreak of Second Intifada. These include continued Israeli settlement activity in the West Bank and Gaza; Palestinian suicide terror campaigns; delays in Israeli redeployment; the increasing militarization of Fatah; and Israel's counter-terrorism responses, particularly under then Israeli prime minister Benjamin Netanyahu. While political scientists do consider contestation over Jerusalem—especially during the final status negotiations at Camp David in 2000—as critical to understanding the ultimate failure of the Oslo peace process, for the most part political scientists have tended to see Jerusalem as a microcosm of larger trends and patterns, rather than as reflecting a set of concerns unique to the city.

For example, continued settlement activity in East Jerusalem is considered part of the larger problem of the Israeli "occupation-oriented mindset." Moreover, key events that took place in Jerusalem throughout the 1990s are glossed over and are not considered central to Oslo's failure. Specifically neglected in the literature are the 1996 violent clashes between Palestinian Authority forces and the Israel Defense Forces (IDF) over excavations at the Noble Sanctuary (Haram al-Sharif)/Temple Mount (Har HaBayit); Ariel Sharon's ill-conceived visit to the Temple Mount/ Haram al-Sharif in September 2000; and Netanyahu's poorly timed decision to commence Jewish housing construction in southern Jerusalem at Har Homa (Jabal Abu Ghneim).

In this essay, I suggest that this cursory treatment of Jerusalem in the political science literature is largely due to methodological preferences and professional "guild rules." Perhaps owing to the fact that contemporary political science still tends to favor comparative research over area and regional studies in general, and single case studies in particular, political scientists who study international relations have typically viewed the breakdown of the Oslo peace process as a case study for generalizable causal statements that can be applied to other conflicts outside of the

Israeli-Palestinian example. To be sure, many political scientists are skeptical of attempts to construct a representative sample of events and they recognize that generalizations tend to be conditional rather than universal (Lebow 2000–2001). Methods that focus on within-case analysis—including approaches more consistent with the historian's craft, such as narrative, process tracing, path dependence, and counterfactual analysis—are also growing in popularity. Nonetheless, political science continues to give pride of place to cross-national and cross-temporal empirical validation of theoretical propositions. Even political scientists deeply engaged in the details of a single case have an overriding interest in using such specific historical or contemporary contexts to help substantiate or disconfirm broad theoretic premises about the way states and sub-state actors interact (Elman and Elman 2008, 364). As Jack Levy (2001, 82) notes, political scientists are "consumed by the question of how to generalize beyond their data to the larger universe from which their data were selected" (see also Gerring 2004).

All this is not to say that the political science literature on Oslo's demise is unhelpful or incorrect. On the contrary, by focusing on Israeli and Palestinian decision-makers as rational, strategic calculators this literature offers a useful corrective to approaches that emphasize "ancient ethnic hatreds." It provides considerable analytic leverage in understanding both the road to Oslo, as well as its eventual failure. My purpose in this essay is thus not to propose the rejection of the political science literature, but rather to show how a focus on Jerusalem complements the explanations offered. In turn, while I suggest that political science has certain limitations, I also consider how it offers valuable insight to the study of the city.

The Discipline of Political Science and the Study of Jerusalem

Political scientists have a long tradition of favoring explanations of social behavior that are grounded in rational choice and strategic interaction.[1]

---

1. On the dominant role of rational choice explanation in the international relations subfield of political science, see, for example, Katzenstein, Keohane, and Krasner (1999). For a critique, see Walt (1999).

For example, while political psychology and constructivist approaches (devoted to the study of cognitive and motivational biases, and identity and ideology respectively), are important areas of political science research on international relations (IR), much of the subfield is given over to explanation that emphasizes the cost–benefit calculations of rational decisionmakers in the face of external or domestic constraints and opportunities. Explanation of social behavior tends to be interest-based—aspects of culture, including religion, are often given short shrift. As one prominent political scientist has recently noted, social scientists in general do not pay much attention to religion, finding it "uninteresting if not embarrassing" (Jervis 2002, 37). Despite the resurgence of religion, the IR discipline's epistemological foundation rests on secularist assumptions (Hurd 2007). Moreover, most modern IR theories emphasize rational calculation as opposed to emotion and emotional relationships (Crawford 2000). It is thus not surprising that political scientists studying the Oslo peace process in the 1990s have steered clear of Jerusalem. A dedicated investigation into the role that Jerusalem played in the demise of the Oslo peace process invariably requires attention to the religious and emotive responses that the city generates—something that political science "guild rules" tend to eschew.[2]

Perhaps even more important than the emphasis on rational choice are methodological leanings that value the identification and explanation of recurring patterns of behavior. Political scientists tend to formulate and test general theoretical propositions, and causation is typically established in the context of a comparison across cases (Ray 1995, 131–57). In political science it is customary to show how specific events are instances of general trends and patterns. Explanation is centered on comparing a specific event to a representative sample or relevant population of similar cases and demonstrating that the event at hand fits into a general pattern

---

2. There are some indications that this is changing. The American Political Science Association recently launched a new section on religion and politics, and Cambridge University Press also publishes a new journal on the topic. For recent work on the relationship between religion and international relations, see, for example, Fox (2001), Philpott (2002), Fox and Sandler (2004), Haynes (2005), Hurd (2004), Hallward (2008), Warner and Walker (2011), and Desch and Philpott (2013).

(ibid., 134–38). Thus, the Cold War, the United States invasion of Iraq, or the breakdown of Oslo are only interesting (to political scientists) insofar as they are examples of, respectively, enduring rivalries in bipolar international systems, great power military interventions in the periphery, and negotiation failure. As political science methodologist John Gerring (2004, 344–45) notes: "[A] case study refers to a set of units broader than the one immediately under study. . . . Case studies are not immaculately conceived; additional units always loom in the background. . . . Studies of a war are studies of war, studies of a farming community are studies of farming communities everywhere, studies of individuals are studies of humanity, and so forth."

Given this disciplinary preference for theories that cross space and time, it is not surprising that the idiosyncratic issues and concerns of a particular Israeli/Palestinian city, which are unlikely to transfer or replicate well for other inter-group conflicts or contested urban spaces, do not receive the lion's share of attention.[3]

Historians and other scholars in the humanities, of course, reject this view that causation requires the observation of a large number of cases. For historians, the social world is complex and characterized by path dependence, contingency and catalysts, feedback loops, and equifinality, or many different paths to the same outcome (see, for example, Ingram 1997, 2001; Gaddis 1997, 2001; and Schroeder 1997, 2001). Consequently, historians tend to see the single event as far more representative than the political scientist's cluster of cases, and it is researched more thoroughly and set in a broader context. Historians see as unhelpful the political scientist's attempt to detach events from their "temporal moorings," treating them as discrete and comparable, or to use fragments of history to illuminate theory (Ingram 1997, 2001). A growing number of political scientists are sympathetic to these criticisms. Indeed, qualitative methodologies have experienced a renaissance in recent years and the new literature on qualitative methods is now extensive and includes a number of new

3. For more on the methodological preferences of scholars who study international relations, see Elman and Elman (2008, 2001, and 1997), and Elman (2005).

texts (Brady and Collier 2004; George and Bennett 2005; Goertz 2006; and Gerring 2007). These methods have also become more deeply embedded in graduate student training programs and more institutionalized in the profession (Bennett and Elman 2007; Collier and Elman 2008). Yet, while political scientists do note the difficulties associated with theory building and testing, most political scientists do not accept the historian's skepticism of generalizable theory. Today, IR theorists are more likely to eschew monocausal, parsimonious analysis in favor of examining nonlinearity and the interaction effects of multiple chains of causation. But they are still unwilling to give up the attempt to delineate a universe of events, and to construct a representative sample of them (see, for example, Van Evera 1997; Thompson 2003).

The Political Science Literature on Oslo's Demise

In his essay "The Second Intifada: Background and Causes of the Israeli-Palestinian Conflict," Jeremy Pressman (2003) suggests that laying the blame for the outbreak of the Second Intifada on Ariel Sharon's visit to the Temple Mount/Haram al-Sharif on September 28, 2000, "overplay[s] the role of individual leaders and overlook[s] a wider array of elite decisions and deeper political and social conditions." Pressman links the Second Intifada to Israel's continued occupation of the West Bank and Gaza: "Palestinians expected their lives to improve in terms of freedom of movement and socioeconomic standing; when both worsened, significant resentment built up in Palestinian society." Pressman is certainly correct to point to dashed Palestinian expectations. By 2000, 60 percent of Palestinians were living under the jurisdiction of the newly formed Palestinian Authority (PA), and the IDF had redeployed from all major Palestinian population centers (six Palestinian cities and 450 villages and hamlets were evacuated by the IDF as part of the Oslo II agreement). Yet, the third redeployment stipulated by the Oslo Accords had not taken place and the transitional phase of the agreements had missed numerous deadlines. The Camp David permanent status talks of July 2000 took place when the PA was only in full control of roughly 18 percent of the occupied territories and in joint control of only another 24 percent. The army had pulled back from major Palestinian population centers, but Israeli settlements remained and in fact had expanded. Nor was the territory under Palestinian control contiguous: a strong IDF presence remained in between Palestinian controlled villages and cities (Rabbani 2001; Klein 2003, 151).

In Pressman's view, while Israel's continued occupation provides the context for understanding the demise of the peace process, the proximate cause is the militarization of Israeli-Palestinian interactions. According to Pressman, this is typical of a security dilemma in which each side sees itself as reactive and defensive and the other as acting offensively. Thus, central to Pressman's account is an attempt to ground the Israeli-Palestinian conflict in the 1990s in a generalizable statement about "spirals of insecurity." As Pressman notes, the violent confrontations that ensued following the opening of the tunnel running underground along the Western Wall in 1996 prompted Israel to embark upon a new policy in which the IDF would hit back hard against any future Palestinian rioting. Known as "Operation Field of Thorns," this military plan envisioned a harsh response to any renewed violence. On its part, factionalism within Fatah led to the emergence of a young guard for which armed conflict was the major currency of political power. Significantly, this young guard rejected negotiation as the route to ending the occupation. Its members believed that only a Palestinian counter-offensive would force Israel to make necessary diplomatic concessions. Given Palestinian beliefs in the efficacy of using force, and Israel's preparations to use force if needed, Pressman argues that the policies of each side reinforced negative views of the adversary. It is thus not surprising that the protests of September 2000 resulted in a rapid escalation of the Israeli-Palestinian conflict.

Pressman's discussion of the demise of the Israeli-Palestinian peace process in the 1990s is compelling, but where does Jerusalem fit into this account? In Pressman's view, Ariel Sharon's visit to the Temple Mount was merely a "spark that set the second intifada into motion." That is, it was simply a trigger (rather than a cause) for the major confrontation that followed. I believe that Pressman underestimates the impact that Sharon's actions had on the peace process, particularly since they came so soon after the breakdown of negotiations at Camp David. In fact, the failed Camp David negotiations are crucial for understanding why Sharon's Jerusalem visit had such an explosive impact. The failure to resolve the problem of Palestinian refugees and disputes over final boundaries certainly contributed to the failure to reach an agreement.[4] Eventually, however, compromises were reached on these issues and it was Jerusalem that became the "make or break" of the entire negotiations (Sher 2006, 99, see also 125–29; Chapman 2004, 177–78). Sharon's decision to visit the Temple Mount was so volatile precisely because Jerusalem was central to the negotiation failure at Camp David.

Indeed, Israel's demand at Camp David to have some form of sovereignty on the Haram al-Sharif/Temple Mount was clearly a deal-breaker. Although then Israeli prime minister Ehud Barak supported the creation of two capitals for two states in Jerusalem, the proposal entailed Israel's annexation of the three main Jewish settlement blocks in East Jerusalem, thus effectively splitting the West Bank in two. In fact, the Israeli position was inconsistent with the US proposal for shared sovereignty of the Old City, which afforded Palestinians sovereignty over the Christian and Muslim holy sites and Israel sovereignty over the Jewish and Armenian quarters. From the Israeli perspective, Muslim and Christian holy sites and the Arab neighborhoods inside the Old City as well as those immediately outside of it (Sheikh Jarrah, Wadi al Joz, Ras al-Amud, Abu Tor, and Silwan) would only receive an expanded form of Palestinian political autonomy; Israel would still retain overall sovereignty in these areas (Klein 2003, 71). Dennis Ross (2007) has argued that President Clinton's "ideas" or "parameters" proposed at Camp David "would have been guided by the principle that what is currently Jewish will be Israeli and what is currently Arab will be Palestinian, meaning that Jewish Jerusalem—East and West—would be united, while Arab East Jerusalem would become the capital of the Palestinian state." But it is clear that Prime Minister Barak and his negotiating team did not concur (see Sher 2006, 67, 70–71, 74–79, 105).

---

4. At Camp David in 2000, Israel proposed including in its final borders the settlements where most Jewish Israelis in the West Bank reside. While over 80 percent of Israeli settlers would have thus been incorporated into the state, some 100,000 Palestinians would have also found themselves living within Israeli territory. Presumably these Palestinians would have required relocation, adding to the refugee problem.

President Clinton proposed to vertically divide the Haram al-Sharif/ Temple Mount in such a way that Palestinians would control the surface while Israel would control the areas underground. In principle, Israel was prepared to accept this compromise proposal. In the event, however, Yasser Arafat would reject anything less than full sovereignty in all Palestinian areas of East Jerusalem, geographic contiguity of the future Palestinian state, and full Palestinian sovereignty over the Haram al-Sharif. Here, Arafat relied on an official Palestinian Authority fatwa issued by Sheikh Ikrima Sabri, the chief mufti of Jerusalem and the Palestinian Territories, which ruled that the land of Palestine is holy Islamic waqf land and that it was forbidden (*haram*) for Palestinians to accept compensation for it (Reiter 2007, 178; 2013, 127). According to Shlomo Ben-Ami (2006, 248–50, 256–58), Arafat focused far too much attention on the "Islamic value of Jerusalem" and made the city into a "personal obsession," thereby preventing agreement at Camp David, and later at Taba (see also Sher 2006, 37–38, 52, 82–85, 137). The Palestinian delegation's denial of a Jewish historical and religious connection to the Temple Mount also contributed to the failure of the negotiations (Klein 2003, 76, 81; Reiter 2008, 1).

In the aftermath of the failed summit, Ariel Sharon's police-escorted visit to the Temple Mount/Haram al-Sharif underscored Israel's commitment to retaining sovereignty of the site.[5] By granting and offering protection for Sharon's visit, the Israeli government linked the failure of Camp David—and the Oslo period as a whole—to an event in Jerusalem that galvanized the Palestinian street. Thus, the appearance of Sharon, a symbol of Israeli aggression, on Islam's holiest site in Palestine contributed to the outbreak of the intifada. It was not merely a trigger.

Indeed, Pressman's downplaying of Sharon's government-approved visit to the Temple Mount/Haram al-Sharif neglects how the al-Aqsa Mosque became the preferred site to launch political protest. In August

5. Sharon did not have a religious incentive to visit the site. Rather, it is likely that he made the trip in order to wrest political power away from his Likud party rival, Benjamin Netanyahu. He may have calculated that his image among right-wing Israeli voters would be strengthened as the visit would serve to underscore that, under his leadership, the Likud party would not negotiate over the Temple Mount.

1996, as the Oslo process began to unravel, Arafat had called for a general strike and a demonstration at the Temple Mount/Haram al-Sharif—the first protest against Israeli policies that had been organized since the Oslo accords were signed (Bruck 1996, 85). Nor is it trivial that the second Palestinian uprising was referred to as the al-Aqsa Intifada, or that the venue for the initial protests was once again Jerusalem's Muslim holy site.

Although many among the Palestinian leadership sought to prevent Sharon's visit (Klein 2003, 98), there are some indications that his "photo-op walk" had actually been agreed upon in advance. Jibril Rajoub, then a key leader in the Palestinian Authority's security forces, noted that if Sharon did not enter the Haram mosques "there will not be any problem." But Hamas had already circulated statements to its members calling on them to confront Sharon and prevent the attempt to "demolish the Aqsa Mosque and build the so-called Jewish temple in its place." After Sharon's hour-long visit, which occurred without much incident, both Marwan Barghouti and Yasser Arafat provocatively called on the entire Arab and Islamic world to "move immediately to stop these aggressions and Israeli practices against holy Jerusalem." The imam at the Haram al-Sharif told the approximately 20,000 worshipers gathered on the day following Sharon's visit that the Jews were plotting to take down the mosque and replace it with a synagogue. It was at this point that worshipers ran to the cliff overlooking the Jewish Wailing Wall and began throwing stones and other debris on the worshipers below. By day's end fourteen police and over two hundred Palestinian demonstrators were injured; six Palestinians were dead (Gutmann 2005, 33–37). These events on the Temple Mount/Haram al-Sharif were broadcast over the Palestinian Authority's radio station and the description of the confrontations implied that Palestinians were fighting to defend the mosques against an enemy intent on killing innocent Muslim worshippers (Klein 2003, 98–99). Weeks of rioting ensued with the loss of upwards of 600 lives and more than 5,000 injured.

Like Pressman, in analyzing the outbreak of the Second Intifada, political scientist Mia Bloom (2004) emphasizes the importance of the Israeli occupation. For Bloom, Palestinians' dashed expectations of greater freedoms under the Oslo process contributed to a growing support for terrorism, which multiple Palestinian groups used to their advantage.

In Bloom's account Palestinian organizations began employing terrorism as a way to compete for "market share" among Palestinian voters. As they became more and more outraged by the perceived sham of Oslo, Palestinians increasingly began to support the use of violence. Palestinian organizations accordingly shifted their strategies to engage in terrorism as a way of mobilizing support. In turn, the excessive use of force and collective punishment on Israel's part to combat terrorism—check points, border closures, economic sanctions, home demolitions, targeted assassinations—further de-legitimized the peace process and the Palestinian Authority, and contributed to a general feeling of hopelessness. The important point here is that Bloom intends for her explanation of the breakdown of the peace process to be generalized to other cases of revolt against occupation, and to contribute to a larger debate on uprisings and the use of terrorism as a rational choice for challenging occupations by democratic states (see, for example, Pape 2003).

Bloom's argument is provocative, and it is certainly the case that in Palestine's democratizing state in the 1990s the use of force was used as a means of mobilizing the vote, with more and more groups jumping on the "suicide-bombing bandwagon" to garner a positive image among the Palestinian populace. But Bloom's central argument that the Israeli occupation begot Palestinian violence begs the question of why terrorism emerged as the method of choice in the early 1990s, when Israel was turning over Jericho and redeploying elsewhere, and at a time when Prime Minister Yitzhak Rabin refused to let terrorist acts hinder progress toward peace. The wave of Hamas suicide attacks in February and March 1996 occurred *after* the transfer of Palestinian cities in January 1996, during a period when Palestinians had every reason to believe that further territorial concessions would be forthcoming. As Yuval Elizur (2003, 115–16) notes, "The Rabin and Peres governments . . . held an attitude toward Arab terrorism quite different from that of their successors. Both prime ministers refused to let violence deter progress toward peace and stuck to the slogan 'We must fight terrorism as if there are no hopes for peace and we must strive for peace as if there is no terror. . . . ' When Sharon became prime minister, succeeding Ehud Barak in early 2001, he advocated a policy very different from Labor's: no negotiations without a total cessation of violence first."

Thus, contrary to Bloom's claims, terrorism was used in the early 1990s not because the Israeli occupation was deepening (it was actually contracting!), but because certain Palestinian groups were bound to emerge as political losers if the Oslo process succeeded. That is, suicide bombing was a way for rival organizations to slow the tide of improved relations between the nationalist, secular Palestinian Authority and Israel. The bombings enabled these groups to play a spoiler role and increased precisely at those moments when the peace process was moving forward. The Israeli public and leadership expected the Palestinian Authority to curb terrorism, and they assumed that Arafat had the capacity to control it, especially after his electoral victory in 1996. Thus, terrorism worked to convince Israel that it did not have a partner for peace.

As the violence continued, Israel's trust in the peaceful intentions of Arafat and the Palestinian Authority plummeted. What Hamas hoped was that the violence would provoke a harsh Israeli response, thus undermining Arafat, Fatah, and the Oslo process and improving its own domestic political position. That Israel fell into this trap is one of tragedies of the Oslo years.

Typical of political science explanations, Bloom's analysis of the collapse of the peace process rests on broad trends and patterns in the dyadic Israeli-Palestinian conflict; the rational (albeit counter-productive) choices that each actor made; and the inevitable unintended consequences and unexpected outcomes that resulted from their policies. Noteworthy for our discussion here is the fact that many of the suicide bombings that took place in the 1990s occurred in Jerusalem (a point Bloom ignores). Also problematic is her treatment of Palestinian public opinion. Bloom does not differentiate the views of West Bank Palestinians from the views of Palestinians living in Gaza or East Jerusalem. To be sure, although Jerusalem was not part of the area that fell under Palestinian Authority jurisdiction, it was in Jerusalem that the Palestinian nationalist movement gained strength. Due to their special status, East Jerusalemite Palestinians could move about more freely and were less subject to censorship than Palestinians in the West Bank and Gaza. As a result, East Jerusalem quickly became the political and cultural locus of Arab Palestine. Even so, East Jerusalemite Palestinians did not participate in the terror campaigns of the 1990s, and "stood firmly against terrorist attacks, more so than Palestinians nationwide" (Klein 2001, 212). Indeed, what has radicalized Jerusalem's Palestinians has been Israel's counter-terrorism response, in particular the building of the separation barrier (Kreimer 2005).

Lastly, consider Ron Pundak (2001) and Jerome Slater's (2001) treatments of Oslo's demise. Unlike Pressman and Bloom, neither Pundak nor Slater explicitly attempt to ground Israeli-Palestinian relations in the 1990s within generalizable theories of international relations. Both are more interested in demonstrating how the deterioration of the peace process was the result of Oslo's failure to resolve key features of the conflict, namely the Palestinian right of return and Israeli settlement policy. Like Pressman, Pundak also suggests that Ariel Sharon's visit to the Temple Mount/Haram al-Sharif was "the match that ignited the powder keg which had threatened to explode for years." Here, too, Sharon's visit is seen as merely a trigger, and not important in and of itself.

To be sure, Pundak and Slater each devote attention to the Camp David talks, and both consider the proposed solutions to resolving the conflict over Jerusalem that were raised and rejected. Each also emphasizes Barak's flawed negotiating style at the summit, which was apparent during the talks over the city's future. Both Slater and Pundak criticize Barak's demand to change the status quo on the Temple Mount/Haram al-Sharif by proposing to build a Jewish synagogue on the upper part of the Mount. Pundak suggests that Barak's negotiating team was insufficiently prepared to discuss final status issues regarding Jerusalem and would have done better by leaving Jerusalem to the end of the talks. Instead, the summit discussions involved an "exaggerated focus on Jerusalem." Indeed, by demanding Jewish prayer on the Temple Mount/Haram al-Sharif, Barak played into the long-standing Muslim fears regarding Israel's true intentions for the al-Aqsa Mosque area (Gorenberg 2000; Klein 2003, 162–63). Barak's demand was especially idiosyncratic given Israel's long-standing policy in Jerusalem of separating religious status from political sovereignty, as demonstrated by Jordan's control of Jerusalem's Muslim holy sites since 1967, and the PA's day-to-day administration of them since 1993.

Yet, in each essay the "problem of Jerusalem" is buried within a larger discussion of the historical origins of the conflict and the individual failures of particular statesmen (especially Netanyahu, Barak, and Arafat). For Pundak the central reason for Oslo's collapse was Israel's policies between 1993 and 1999, including the continuation of settlement activity; increased checkpoints and IDF activity in the occupied territories; isolated Palestinian enclaves cut off from each other and surrounded by Israeli communities; and border closures that drastically limited employment opportunities for Palestinians in Israel. Pundak does take the Palestinian leadership to task for failing to realize how terrorism would alter Israeli public opinion, continuing anti-Israel incitement and media propaganda, insisting on the right of every Palestinian refugee to return to within the Green Line, and "expressing doubts about the importance and holiness of the Temple Mount for the Jewish people." But his main focus is on Israeli policies in the occupied territories. These policies led the Palestinian leadership to reach the conclusion that "Israel did not in fact want to end the occupation and grant the Palestinian people their legitimate rights."

For Slater, the central reason for Oslo's demise is that Israel did not go far enough in the permanent-status negotiations at Camp David. Like Pundak, Slater's position is that Israel bears the greater share of the responsibility for the collapse of peace process in the 1990s. The Israeli negotiators failed to see that from the Palestinian perspective, they had already made the most important territorial concession—accepting a Palestinian state on only 22 percent of Mandatory Palestine. Arafat's condition for accepting agreement was thus 100 percent of the occupied territories (with certain exchanges to accommodate forty-plus years of Israeli settlement). Slater argues that Arafat could not sign on to the Israeli offer, which provided far fewer concessions than is typically claimed. While both authors make cogent arguments, it is not clear in either of these analyses how much Jerusalem mattered to Oslo's collapse. That is, if agreement could have been reached on Jerusalem, would the peace process have derailed, nevertheless?

Jerusalem as Catalyst: Rethinking Oslo's Failure

As discussed in the previous section, the political science literature on Oslo's collapse tends to emphasize underlying causes and treats the

Israeli-Palestinian peace process as a case study for broader theorizing on international relations. While the literature makes an important contribution, it ignores the presence of catalysts that were independent of the numerous and deep-seated underlying causes identified. As suggested by Richard Ned Lebow (2000–2001, 2003), political scientists have a tendency to take catalysts for granted. As long as underlying conditions are present, some incident or event will eventually spark conflict. Catalysts, however, are not merely triggers. Often, in the absence of a catalyst, conflict may not occur because certain dynamics are not set into motion. As Lebow (2000–2001, 592) explains, an analysis of catalysts requires accepting that international outcomes are often the result of accidental conjunctures—"the concatenation of particular leaders with particular contexts, and of particular events with other events is always a matter of chance, never of necessity."

The role of Jerusalem in Oslo's demise provides a useful example of how catalysts work. Indeed, Jerusalem is central to an understanding of the increasingly militarized Israeli-Palestinian interactions during the 1990s. For example, it was Netanyahu's authorized opening (at then-mayor of Jerusalem Ehud Olmert's urging) of the Hasmonean Tunnel running close to the Temple Mount in September 1996 that led to the first clashes between Palestinian Authority forces and the IDF, in which fifteen Israelis and over seventy Palestinians were killed. The September 1996 clashes were the most violent that the occupied territories had experienced since 1967 (Rabbani 2001, 69). But these events were also significant because in earlier years joint Israeli and Palestinian security forces had successfully worked together to ensure the peace. In the period immediately after the signing of the Declaration of Principles, Arafat suppressed Hamas, arresting over 2,000 operatives and imprisoning dozens of Hamas leaders. Thus, if terrorism is the key to understanding the growing Israeli disillusionment with the Oslo Accords, then Jerusalem is the key to understanding the ultimate failure of the peace process. That is, had the Palestinian Authority and Israel been able to continue joint policing operations to pacify terror cells, then the security provisions that Israel ultimately undertook as part of its counter-terrorism effort—measures that were largely seen as collective punishment by the Palestinians—need not have been implemented. The peace process would have moved forward. In short, the clash at the Temple Mount/Haram al-Sharif in 1996 was not a "one-off" event. It is unlikely that another provocation would have had the same impact. Indeed, the 1996 events in Jerusalem were catalysts to everything that came after. They are integral to an understanding of how terrorism and Israeli-Palestinian militarization contributed to Oslo's demise.

In this regard, conflict over Har Homa is also worth noting. Olmert's insistence that Netanyahu authorize building the long-planned Jewish neighborhood of Har Homa was controversial because it blocked the contiguity of the Palestinian East Jerusalem neighborhood of Sur Baher with Bethlehem and the village of Beit Sahur. As Sarah Kaminker (1997, 6) has observed, Har Homa, while within Jerusalem's municipal boundaries in the southwest of the city, is "a geographical area in the center of a region that is entirely Palestinian. The region is populated only by Christians and Muslims, who live in the style traditional to Arab towns and villages." From the Palestinian viewpoint, the fact that Israel was moving forward with Har Homa not only meant another Jewish community in East Jerusalem, but it signaled Israel's continued attempts to prevent Palestinian contiguous control of land that would become part of a Palestinian state, and potentially its new capital. That Israel was attempting to create a strip of Jewish living communities that would connect East Talpiot to Gilo was particularly infuriating to the Palestinians because it was happening during the Oslo process, at a time when the two sides should have been working to create a viable two-state solution. As in the case of the 1996 tunnel excavations, the events at Har Homa were important insofar as they contributed to the Palestinian sense that Oslo had changed nothing. As Idith Zertal and Akiva Eldar (2007, 167) point out, "Har Homa became a symbol of the Palestinian struggle."

Considering the significance of Netanyahu's actions in 1996 requires that we raise the counterfactual: Would the peace process have progressed had Yitzhak Rabin not been assassinated?[6] As I suggest below, with regard to Jerusalem, Rabin was as hawkish as his Likud rivals. Nevertheless, it is

6. For more on counterfactual analysis, see, for example, George and Bennett (2005, 230–31) and Lebow (2007).

unlikely that Rabin would have sabotaged the Oslo process as persistently as Netanyahu did by continuing to establish new Jewish Israeli housing settlements, confiscating land for new settlements, or expanding existing ones. In addition, given his views prior to his death, I believe that Rabin would have continued to see breeches of the Oslo Accords as the actions of a Palestinian minority, and would not have held the peace process hostage to Arafat's curbing of all anti-Israel terrorism (for a similar argument, see Rosenblum 1998).

The Contributions of a Political Science Approach to Jerusalem Studies

Political Parties

Political science has a rich tradition of examining the effects of institutions on political party behavior, and the influence of parties on domestic and foreign policies. With regard to Israel, there is a considerable body of literature that considers how its parliamentary system—by privileging small political parties—influences Israel's war decisions, its policies toward the occupied territories, and its stance in peace negotiations (see, for example, Elman 2000; Spruyt 2005; Elman, Haklai, and Spruyt 2013).

Party politics offers an important framework for understanding Jerusalem. In Israel's formative years, the city was dominated by revisionist parties and their paramilitary organizations: the Irgun Zvai Leumi (Etzel) and Lehi, known by the British as the Stern Gang. These parties were in direct competition with the mainstream Labor-dominated Zionist leadership, and Jerusalem soon became linked to the inter-party conflicts of the day. Menachem Begin, as leader of the Irgun, tried to turn Jerusalem into a separate bastion of his revisionist party, despite the fact that war with the Arabs loomed large and military unification was all the more necessary. Jerusalem is thus central to the Altalena episode, in which Ben Gurion sent the Hagana to prevent the Irgun from unloading weapons off a ship bound for Tel Aviv. The weapons would have assisted the Irgun in its attempt to consolidate its position in Jerusalem.

In contemporary Israeli politics, Jerusalem has continued to be a locus for party competition. Policies for Jerusalem under Likud-led and

Labor-led governments have noticeably diverged. When Israel captured the Old City in the 1967 war it was Labor-affiliated Israeli defense minister Moshe Dayan who ordered the removal of the Israeli flag from the Temple Mount/Haram al-Sharif and initiated what became the status quo on the site: the prohibition of Jews from praying on the upper part of the Mount so as to avoid religious conflict with Palestinians and the larger Muslim world. In June 1967, Prime Minister Levi Eshkol stated that the administration of the site's mosques would remain in the hands of Muslim clerics. During the Oslo years, however, this long-standing injunction was diluted as both Netanyahu and Barak's policies toward Jerusalem were influenced by attempts to placate the religious right, whose political parties were important government coalition members.

As mayor of Jerusalem for nearly three decades, Teddy Kollek (who mostly ran as an independent) faced different sets of constraints when the Likud party came to power in 1977. Kollek's ("mosaic") policy for Jerusalem was based on "self-segregation." It envisioned a Jerusalem with co-existing ethnic and religious communities. Significantly, Kollek rejected attempts by Jewish religious groups to build homes within East Jerusalem's Arab neighborhoods. The dramatic increase in Jewish home purchases in the Muslim and Christian quarters of the Old City and in other predominantly Arab neighborhoods of East Jerusalem occurred only during the Olmert/Netanyahu period. Olmert encouraged Jewish settlement in the Muslim quarter of the Old City, and in Silwan, Ras al-Amud, and Wadi Joz. Right-of-center Israeli politicians (including Begin, Olmert, and Netanyahu) also supported the groups seeking to secure Jewish prayer on the Temple Mount, such as Ateret Kohanim and the Temple Mount Faithful. These were policies that Kollek had never advocated, and that Labor-affiliated prime ministers had never endorsed.

Indeed, Kollek strived to keep East Jerusalem closer in character to West Jerusalem, which was governed by democracy, and less akin to the West Bank, which was administered by military rule. During the First Intifada, Kollek actively protested collective punishment measures against Arab communities in East Jerusalem, including house demolitions and the cutting off of city services. He insisted on traveling in East Jerusalem without a security detail, and wanted residents to move about freely throughout the city. As Cheshin, Hutman, and Melamed (1999) note, "The right wing Likud Party's 1977 election victory had a profound effect on Israeli policy in East Jerusalem," not least because the Likud was closer ideologically to the settler movement. Jewish housing in Arab neighborhoods thus increased in the 1980s, something that Kollek adamantly opposed. At the same time, when in the late 1980s Kollek tried to get approval for 12,000 Arab housing units in the north of the city, the Likud-controlled government ministries refused to authorize approval (Friedland and Hecht 1996b, 199). Kollek tried in vain to prevent Jews from moving into the Muslim quarter of the Old City and other Arab neighborhoods within the municipal boundaries. Despite these efforts, however, Kollek was not successful. Then housing minister Ariel Sharon moved into a renovated apartment there in December 1987; Jewish settlers moved into Silwan in October 1991, also with the assistance of the Housing Ministry (Dumper 2002, 62). Indeed, the mainly right-of-center governing coalitions from 1979 to 1991 refused to entertain any possibility of change in Jerusalem's status, and continued to create "facts on the ground" by confiscating land, constructing new Jewish neighborhoods, and restricting Arab housing permits within the municipal boundaries. A commission (the Klugman committee) found that millions of dollars in state funds had been spent during the Likud years to move Jewish families into Arab neighborhoods of Jerusalem (Dumper 2002, 66).[7]

When the Likud's Ehud Olmert became mayor, Israel's Jerusalem policy reflected attempts to create new facts of the ground that would improve Israel's position vis-à-vis Jerusalem in final-status negotiations (Mayer 2008, 239). Much attention has been placed on the Netanyahu/Olmert policy of withdrawing the residency permits of Palestinians who had moved outside of the city's municipal boundaries. Yet, Olmert also

---

7. Some scholars of Jerusalem have a less sanguine view of Kollek. For example, Cheshin, Hutman, and Melamed (1999, 16) argue that the mayor's priority was to increase a Jewish presence in all parts of the city and that he did for its Arab residents only what was required to keep them from rebelling. Kollek is, after all, famous for having remarked in an October 1999 interview that "[f]or Jewish Jerusalem I did something during the last 25 years. . . . For East Jerusalem? Nothing!"

sought to increase Israel's control over East Jerusalem by funneling more city funds to Arab neighborhoods. As Olmert noted, "[t]he key to the unity of Jerusalem lies in real equality between Arabs and Jews." Olmert argued that Israel's failure to provide comparable infrastructure and services for Jerusalem's Palestinians was benefiting the Palestinian Authority, which was quickly moving in to fill the void despite the Oslo agreement's ban on its activity in the city. Until Olmert became mayor, for over four decades East Jerusalem had been largely left under-developed and under-serviced compared to West Jerusalem and other Israeli cities. It had been so under both left-wing and right-wing municipalities and national governments. Ironically, Olmert's policy that re-emphasized Israel's "one Jerusalem" also meant more services to Arab East Jerusalem. In fact, twenty times more money was allocated annually to basic infrastructure in Arab neighborhoods than during the previous Kollek/Rabin/Peres years combined.

Despite the real differences in Labor versus Likud policies for Jerusalem, however, we should also not over-exaggerate them. It was under successive Labor-led governments that Israel settled East Jerusalem. After all, between 1968 and 1970 the first Jewish neighborhoods in East Jerusalem were built, in French Hill and Ramot Eshkol, and then in Ramot, Gilo, and East Talpiot. Labor-led governments also authorized the construction of Ma'ale Adumim, despite protest from Kollek. From the early days of the Oslo process, Rabin stood firm on a united Jerusalem, which he insisted in speech after speech would remain "eternally" under Israeli sovereignty (Hulme 2006, 112–16; Ross 2004, 91). Prior to Rabin's assassination, "Jewish settlement in an ever-expanding Jerusalem continued" (Slater 2001, 177). Olmert's position toward Orient House was consistent with the general approach of Israel's right-wing toward Jerusalem: no Palestinian representation or the trappings of a state in the city. While left-wing Knesset members visited the building in the 1990s and tried to keep it open, it was the Rabin government that set up road blocks outside of it.

Under the Labor-led government of Ehud Barak, Jewish settlement expansion in East Jerusalem, and elsewhere on the West Bank, increased at the greatest rate since 1992. In 1999, Barak visited Ma'ale Adumim telling its residents that the community was part of "greater Jerusalem" and would not be relinquished to Palestinian control. As Bill Hutman and Amir

Cheshin note, Barak repeated the mantra of every Israeli prime minister before him: "Jerusalem will remain forever the undivided capital of Israel."

Nationalism

The origins and consequences of nationalism is a cottage industry in the political science subfields of comparative politics and international relations. In recent years, for example, there has been a proliferation of studies on how nationalism is invoked to justify violence and war and how political leaders play the "nationalist card" in order to discredit competitors in newly democratizing states (see, for example, Van Evera 1994; Snyder 2000; Gagnon 1994–95).

Nationalism provides an important perspective for the study of Jerusalem because it was not inevitable that the city would figure so centrally in the Zionist nationalist project. To be sure, Jerusalem has always been central to Jewish consciousness, even as its political importance has vacillated. Experts on Jerusalem discuss at length the fact that for the greater part of the pre-modern period, Jewish settlement in Jerusalem was sparse. Nevertheless, the city has always resonated in Jewish thought (including in Jewish halacha, aggada, tefilla, and kabbala). Today, Israelis (and Jews outside of Israel) speak readily of how Jerusalem is the symbol of nationalist pride. The sacred Western Wall, after all, is also the site of Israeli military induction ceremonies. Yet, Israel's early Zionists did not embrace Jerusalem, viewing it instead as a backwater city populated by anti-Zionist *haredim*.[8] As Bernard Wasserstein (2001, 4; see also 48–49) puts it, "The early Zionist settlers in Palestine from the 1880s onwards, and particularly the social Zionists, who arrived in large numbers after 1904, looked down on Jerusalem and all it stood for in their eyes by way of obscurantism, religiosity and squalor."

The leadership of the Jewish community in Palestine (the *Yishuv*) initially accepted the United Nation's General Assembly resolution that would establish a *corpus separatum* in Jerusalem. Far from insisting on

---

8. For an extended discussion of the Jewish Orthodox anti-Zionist position and its advocates in Jerusalem, see Friedland and Hecht (1996b) and Friedman (2002).

Jewish exclusive political rights, the Yishuv was willing to accept an international regime for the Old City (Goddard 2010, 128–31). When the state of Israel was declared on May 14, 1948, no mention was made of Jerusalem; a Jewish Agency representative at the United Nations later indicated that Tel Aviv would be the seat of government (Wasserstein 2001, 151). In fact, Jerusalem was marginalized for much of the Yishuv period and only took on significance in the aftermath of the 1948 war. Menachem Klein (2002, 139) notes that even at the start of the 1948 war, Israel did not invest the same amount of effort to gain control of the Old City as it did to conquer West Jerusalem: "[Israel] assumed that a conquest of the eastern part of Jerusalem, with its Christian and Islamic Holy Places, would eventually lead to the ousting of Israel from the western city as well."

The fact that West Jerusalem was under siege and that some of the fiercest battles of the 1948 war were fought over Jerusalem goes far in explaining the emergence of the city in Israeli national consciousness. As Avi Shlaim (2001, 89–90) argues, it was during the first round of international fighting with the regular Arab armies, including the Jordanian Arab Legion, from May 15, 1948 through June 11, 1948, that the "collective Israeli memory of the 1948 war was formed." During this period, the "fate of the newly born Jewish state seemed to hang in the balance" and the Jewish community suffered heavy losses (see also Ben-Ami 2006, 56). An estimated 10,000 shells were fired in Jerusalem in the first three weeks of the international war. Fierce fighting between Jewish and Jordanian forces inflicted severe damages and civilian casualties and by May 28 the Jewish quarter of the Old City surrendered. Nevertheless, Ben-Gurion rejected an IDF request to launch a counteroffensive for Jerusalem. As Wasserstein (2001, 163) notes, Ben-Gurion feared "international complications if Israel were to move into the old city."

Jerusalem's significance for Israeli nationalism received another boost in subsequent years. It is worth considering how Israel would have acted in the immediate aftermath of the 1967 war had Jordan respected a Jewish right of access to the Western Wall, and had the Western Wall, Jewish synagogues in the Old City, and thousands of Jewish gravestones on the Mount of Olives not been destroyed and desecrated in the intervening years of Jordanian rule in East Jerusalem. Friedland and Hecht (1996b, 33) note that the Jordanians had built a latrine right up against the Western Wall, and Marshall Breger and Thomas Idinopulos (1998, 13) point out that "[s]o severe were Jordanian restrictions against Jews gaining access to the Old City that visitors wishing to cross over from west Jerusalem (at the Mandelbaum Gate) had to produce a baptismal certificate." In June 1967 Israeli policies were decidedly chauvinistic. Consider the quick demolishing of the entire residential Maghrebi quarter abutting the Western Wall, de facto annexation of Jordanian Jerusalem, and the extension of the city's municipal boundaries. Yet, it is impossible to make sense of these actions without an account of Jerusalem from 1948 to 1967, and the denial of Jewish religious rights during this time. As Meron Benvenisti (1996, 81) eloquently writes: "It is easy to imagine the force of the Jews' angry feelings and the lust for revenge that accumulated over the years, and the period (1947–67) of being denied access to the Wall only increased their longing to return to this remnant of the Temple. That torrent of feelings was loosed on the eighth of June, 1967, when the first Israeli soldiers reached the paved area in front of the Wall."

Even with the increased standing of Jerusalem in Israel's national consciousness in the aftermath of the 1948 war, however, it is not the case that Israel had designs on East Jerusalem, or considered wresting it away from Jordan. Before 1967 there were very few Israeli politicians voicing an interest in East Jerusalem. When the 1967 war broke out, Israeli leaders promised Jordan that the IDF would not attack if its army stood down. In the event, Jordan attacked West Jerusalem and the IDF went on the offensive, expelling the Jordanian army from the eastern part of the city. Arguably Israel might have attempted to trick King Hussein into attacking as a pretext for a land grab, but Jordan did not have to take the bait. Indeed, had Jordan refrained from shelling West Jerusalem, it is unlikely that Israel would have used force to reclaim East Jerusalem. After all, by 1967 Israelis had grown accustomed to an internationally divided Jerusalem and had accepted partition of the city. It is unlikely that this state of affairs would have changed had Jordan not joined the war. However, Israelis have long justified the state's position on East Jerusalem by claiming that a vacuum of sovereignty existed in the area *until* Israel occupied it by a legal act of self-defense in the 1967 war.

In addition to providing insight into Israeli nationalism, an understanding of Jerusalem and its relevance for the development of Palestinian nationalism also provides an important corrective to claims of an historic Palestinian *political* attachment to the city. To be sure, the Palestinian nationalist movement had its roots in Jerusalem. The prominent Muslim families of Jerusalem—the Khalidis, Husaynis, and Dajanis—were among the first to voice concerns in the Ottoman parliament over Jewish immigration. Yet, what experts on the city demonstrate is that Arabs long considered the Islamic sites of the Old City of Jerusalem religiously, rather than politically, important. Chad Emmett (1996, 236) notes that when Palestine was conquered by the Muslim Arabs, a provincial capital was established at Ramla. Because Muslim leaders recognized the religious significance of Jerusalem, a sanctified city, they rejected viewing it as a political center. Jerusalem became more important to Palestinians from the 1920s on, with the rise of Jewish Palestinian and Arab Palestinian nationalist claims. Yet, Jerusalem was not mentioned in the Palestinian National Charter in 1964 or in 1968. Indeed, East Jerusalemite Palestinians identified with the Hashemite Kingdom; Jordan in turn sought to curb nascent Palestinian nationalism in its part of the city. Increased emphasis on the city emerged as other Arab states began to link East Jerusalem with the future capital of a sovereign Palestinian state. But it was not until 1988 that a major Palestinian document mentioned Jerusalem as the future capital of the State of Palestine.

Democracy

It goes without saying that the origins, development, and consequences of democracy and competing regime types is at the heart of the study of political science. With regard to Israel, political scientists who focus on international relations have considered the extent to which Israel's policies conform to, or contradict, the notion that "democracies do not fight each other" (see, for example, Elman 1997). This has necessitated a consideration of whether Israel is a democracy, a topic that has generated a significant debate in Israel Studies and the subfield of comparative politics more generally.

Sammy Smooha (2002, 2004) has argued persuasively that Israel should be considered an ethnic democracy. As such, Israel denies its minorities complete membership and full equality even as it empowers them with the right of protest and to "wage a struggle for improving status." Israel is not a liberal democracy because of the institutional dominance of the Jewish majority. Unlike liberal democracies, which rest on a civic nationalism, Israel is the Jewish homeland, not a state of and for its citizens. It thus fails to forge its citizens into a unified civic nation, and instead privileges the ethnic majority in policy and practice (Peleg and Waxman 2007).

Viewing Israel as a Jewish and democratic state provides considerable leverage for understanding Israel's policies with regard to Jerusalem. It is clear that since 1967 Israel has sought to establish Jewish control over both West and East Jerusalem, and to create conditions that would encourage Jerusalem's Arab residents to relocate to the West Bank. Underscoring the contradictory practices of an ethnic democracy, consider the following policies: constructing and subsidizing Jewish neighborhoods in East Jerusalem; respecting freedom of religion (i.e., the 1967 Law for the Protection of the Holy Places; the autonomy of the Supreme Muslim Council; and the shari'a courts); expropriating privately owned Arab land for public use; creating "green" zoning laws (*shetach nof patuach*) to prevent Palestinians from building on Palestinian-owned lands; granting Arab residents of Jerusalem municipal voting rights and residence status; increasing efforts to convince Arab residents to go to the polls; not imposing the Israeli curriculum in East Jerusalem schools; and neglecting Arab East Jerusalem neighborhoods, which were left bereft of city services.

Experts on Jerusalem have written extensively on how Jerusalem's municipal planning has sought to limit the growth of the Arab population in East Jerusalem even as it has worked to ensure an expanded Jewish presence in the area. The policy was based on the premise that if Jewish growth was restricted to West Jerusalem and Arab growth to the eastern part of the city, then this would provide the pretext for the city's re-division between Israel and a future Palestinian state. This policy of maintaining a demographic advantage over the Arab population of East Jerusalem population has succeeded. By 2000, approximately 165,000 Jews resided in the Jewish neighborhoods of East Jerusalem, accounting for 38 percent of the city's total Jewish population and 48 percent of the overall population in East Jerusalem. By 2011, there were 192,000 Jewish residents in East Jerusalem (Benari 2012). As Amir Cheshin, Bill Hutman, and Avi Melamed (1999) put it, "Israel's plan to bring Jews to East Jerusalem, and keep the Arab population down or out, seems to have worked." Nevertheless, Jerusalem experts agree that Israel's policy has failed to truly unify the city. This failure to integrate Jerusalem is best conveyed by the fact that the vast majority of Israelis have never visited the Arab neighborhoods of the city (except for the Old City), while Jerusalem's Palestinians do not spend time in West Jerusalem, except for those who work in the Jewish part of the city.

The Limitations of a Political Science Approach to Jerusalem Studies

Most of the literature on Jerusalem treats the "Jerusalem problem" as a political problem involving competing nationalisms and politically motivated violence. What becomes clear from considering the city's history, however, is that events there often tend to take on a life of their own, unconnected to the political events of the day. This is particularly the case in the Old City, where long held beliefs about Jewish aspirations to destroy the Muslim mosques have led to violent clashes irrespective of the current state of Israeli-Palestinian affairs or developments in the peace process. That communal violence in Jerusalem cannot be readily predicted by (or read off of) the larger Israeli-Palestinian conflict underscores the limitations of a political science approach to the study of the city.

Consider, for example, the October 1990 clashes on the Temple Mount, which resulted in the deaths of seventeen Muslim worshippers. The Temple Mount Faithful had received a police permit to perform a Sukkot festival ritual at the Gihon Spring below the Temple Mount. A rumor spread among the Muslim population that the group was planning to lay the cornerstone of the new Jewish temple on the Mount. Hundreds of Muslims converged on the site just as thousands of Jews gathered at the Western Wall below for the traditional priestly benediction. A riot erupted, with Muslim worshippers raining stones down on the packed plaza below, and the police opening fire. Sparked by long held Muslim beliefs regarding Jewish aspirations for the Temple Mount, this incident—the most violent incident in the Old City since 1967—was not directly connected to, or the result of, the broader Israeli-Palestinian conflict.

The 1990 clashes mirror earlier instances in which religious expression served to fuel political violence, but were not simply a reflection of political contestation. For example, in April 1920 an outbreak of communal violence in Jerusalem seemed unconnected to the politics of the day. Here too, the conflict was sparked by a religious celebratory event (in this case the festival of Nebi Musa, the prophet Moses). Though not driven by politics, the 1920 riots had far-reaching political consequences. They marked the first outbreak of Arab-Jewish violence in Jerusalem under British rule, and they led to the appointment of Hajj Amin-al-Husayni as grand mufti of Jerusalem, a post granted in return for the promise to prevent any outbreaks of violence during future religious events. Yet, as leader of the Arab Palestinian nationalist movement, the mufti continually spoke of the threat to the Haram al-Sharif arising from Jewish plans to rebuild the Temple.

All this does not mean that religion cannot be a force for peace. For example, the fact that the Israeli rabbinate continues to forbid entry to the Temple Mount has helped to dampen conflict by facilitating Muslim clerical control of the holy sites and reinforcing the position of both the Israeli police and secular courts that prevented Jewish prayer on the Temple Mount (at least until the 1980s). Religious perspectives may also facilitate conflict resolution over the city's future status. Jordan's King Hussein put forward one of the more interesting proposals during the Oslo period, suggesting a council of representatives from the Christian, Jewish, and Muslim communities that would administer the Old City, whose sovereignty would be "left to God." This position is important because, in de-linking politics from Jerusalem's sanctity, creative possibilities for conflict resolution become available. After all, the Temple Mount/Haram al-Sharif is sacred to Jews and Muslims not merely because of Israeli sovereignty or Palestinian de facto day-to-day control of the site. Since religion determines sanctity, Israel and Palestine can each be guardians of Jerusalem's holy sites without either side having to impose or concede sovereignty (see Klein 2007, 116–17).

In sum, as Silvio Ferrari (2002, 226) points out, while the political stage is dominated by two actors, the Israelis and the Palestinians, from the religious point of view, political control over the city and the debate over boundaries and territory are not the primary issues and the cast of characters is different: the main actors are not Israelis and Palestinians but Jews, Christians, and Muslims. The upshot is that many of the explosive clashes in the city are not easily linked to the politics of the moment. They are better viewed instead as emotive/religious (and largely spontaneous) responses driven by myths, symbols, and beliefs. Palestinians and Muslims worldwide have long believed that Zionism's true objective is to destroy the mosques on the Haram al-Sharif and rebuild the Jewish Temple there (Goldhagen 2013, 336–39). They see the schemes and plots of marginal Jewish extremists as representing Israel's true intentions (Benvenisti 1996, 73–75). Because of these beliefs, and the capacity for political leaders to use them for nationalist purposes, Jerusalem's holy sites continue to be flashpoints for violence. While progress on other issues of the conflict may be reached, they can be easily negated by a seemingly insignificant event in the Old City.

Conclusion

In the end, the Oslo peace process collapsed because it allowed both sides to ignore their most important points of contention. The 1993 Declaration of Principles did not require the Israelis to stop settlement in the West Bank, Gaza, or East Jerusalem, and did not provide a means for committing the Palestinians to disarm and reject violence. Yuval Elizur (2003, 109) argues that "Oslo was premised on the principle of 'sliding into peace.' Its negotiators were convinced that the more both sides enjoyed the fruits of the initial agreement, the more flexible they would become regarding what were once thought the most divisive questions: namely, settlements, borders, Jerusalem, and control of the holy places" (see also Kittrie 2003).

Oslo failed because it was sold to the Israeli and Palestinian public as delivering far more than it could. Israelis expected Oslo to mean the end of violence; Palestinians thought it meant an end to occupation. In reality, the 1990s saw a reduction in both violence *and* occupation. Under Israeli prime ministers Rabin, Peres, Netanyahu, and Barak, Israel continued to redeploy from major Palestinian populations centers; a Palestinian Council was elected; and Palestinians gained administrative control over much of the Palestinian West Bank population. Israel also conceded that Jerusalem would be subject to negotiation on permanent status. To be sure, Israel's concessions occurred in fits and starts, and many deadlines lapsed. None-theless, it is a mistake to claim that the occupation was deepening dur-ing these years. For its part, the Palestinian Authority did at times reign in terrorism during the 1990s. This was imperfect, and Arafat often allowed violence to flare up as a way of improving the Palestinian negotiating posi-tion. Nevertheless, it would be wrong to claim that Arafat never worked to suppress terrorism. Between September 1995 and February 1996, for exam-ple, Hamas and the Palestinian Islamic Jihad were on the run. Later, in the first nine months of 2000, only one Israeli died from Palestinian terrorism (Margalit 2000). Without the fanfare of high-level diplomacy, including the widely televised handshake between Rabin and Arafat on the White House lawn and the Nobel peace prizes, these steps toward peace might have been seen by both Israelis and Palestinians for what they really were—fragile and tentative moves forward. Instead, *because* of the Oslo agreements them-selves and the false hopes that they raised, throughout the 1990s both sides invariably saw the cup as half empty rather than half full.

How does Jerusalem factor into this explanation for Oslo's demise? Most students of the Israeli-Palestinian conflict suggest that had the "problem of Jerusalem" been dealt with early on in the Oslo process, it would have constituted an important confidence-building measure that could have ameliorated other setbacks to the peace process, led to com-promises on other issues, and forestalled divisive events like the 1996 tunnel excavations or Ariel Sharon's visit to the Temple Mount/Haram al-Sharif. The Oslo agreements said little about Jerusalem, other than that the newly formed Palestinian Interim Self-Government Authority would have no jurisdiction there. Yet Jerusalem was very much on the minds of Israelis and Palestinians. Indeed, because of the Oslo timetable, both sides rushed to establish facts on the ground in the city that each hoped would improve their respective bargaining positions in final status negotiations. Addressing the problem of Jerusalem in 1993 would have prevented this dynamic. The road not taken in 1993 would not have been an easy one; yet, it was not impossible given that final status issues (including Jerusalem) were raised and debated later, when the prospects for peace were not as great. In fact, Jerusalem had been put on the agenda first as early as 1967. The British ambassador to the United Nations had urged that Jerusalem be considered a "gateway to peace" and that it not be relegated to the last item on the agenda of Arab-Israeli negotiations (Wasserstein 2001, 232).

While Jerusalem was off the table during the Oslo years, the September 1993 Israeli-Palestinian Declaration of Principles (DOP) did reflect a new Israeli flexibility on the city. The DOP permitted East Jerusalemite Palestinians, for the first time, to vote in Palestinian national elections. Earlier this initiative had been rejected on the grounds that the city, including its eastern environs, was part of the State of Israel. By 1993, however, Israelis were willing to "leave the way open for interpretations" defining East Jerusalem as part of the West Bank (Benvenisti 1996, 47). Later, at the Camp David summit negotiations in the summer of 2000, Israel came even farther in its offer to the Palestinians, particularly with regard to Jerusalem. Israel had always claimed exclusive control of the city, united under Israeli sovereignty, with limited municipal power sharing and functional rights for Arab residents (for example Kollek's plan for a network of Jewish and Arab city boroughs). But at Camp David and the subsequent negotiations at Taba, Egypt in January 2001, Israeli negotiators considered dividing the city: Israel would annex the major Jewish settlements in East Jerusalem and the Jewish Quarter of the Old City; the new Palestinian state would gain full sovereignty over the Arab neighborhoods, including the Muslim and Christian quarters of the Old City. That is, the Oslo peace process reinforced the fact that "Israeli beliefs in the immutability of expanded Jerusalem are not hegemonic" (Lustick 1993–94, 48). For its part, at Taba the Palestinian Authority accepted Israel's annexation of the Jewish neighborhoods in East Jerusalem and the Etzion and Ariel blocks of settlements along the Green Line. In fact, by 2003, as reflected in the Geneva Agreement, both Israelis and Palestinians had come considerable distances to close the gap on their differences regarding the city's future status (Klein 2003, 125; 2007).

The rejection of the offers made in 2000 to 2001, and the eruption of a second violent Palestinian uprising, was a severe blow to Israel and appeared to confirm the claim that Palestinians would never settle for a two-state solution. Today, after years of suicide bombings, kidnappings, and rocket attacks, the Israeli position has hardened even further. Israelis are fearful that accommodation will be interpreted as a sign of weakness and that further withdrawals from the occupied territories will provide new bases of operations for Palestinian rejectionist groups. To be sure, most Israelis realize that the occupation, long justified on security grounds, has become a security liability. Most Israelis now want a state that will support Zionism and Israel's Jewish identity, and they now accept that relinquishing Jewish settlement in (most of) the West Bank is the only way to achieve this outcome (see Waxman 2008; Bar-Tal, Halperin, and Oren 2010). Nonetheless, Israelis are becoming increasingly convinced that Palestinians have unlimited demands, and it is not clear that the new Israeli consensus for withdrawal from the occupied territories extends anymore to Jerusalem.

In 1991, a majority of Israelis polled were more willing to support withdrawal from parts of the West Bank than from East Jerusalem, even if doing so would mean international recognition of the Jewish areas of Jerusalem as Israel's capital (Albin 1997, 138). By May 2000, nearly 30 percent of Israelis polled were willing to relinquish East Jerusalem in a final peace settlement (Breger 2002, 11) and a sizeable number of Israelis (45 to 54 percent) were willing to grant Palestinians control over the Muslim holy places on the Temple Mount/Haram-al Sharif and accept a Palestinian capital at Abu Dis (Segal et al. 2000). Even as late as 2008, negotiations between then Israeli prime minister Olmert and Palestinian president Mahmoud Abbas showed a "good deal of agreement." Both agreed to place the Holy Basin under international control and Abu Mazen agreed that thirteen post-1967 Jewish neighborhoods in East Jerusalem could revert back to Israel in a final deal (Golan 2011).

But these offers are now no longer on the table. With Hamas a major political organization in eastern Jerusalem, and a rise in terrorism in Jerusalem since the start of the Second Intifada (600 attacks occurred in the city between 2000 and 2004), concerns that withdrawing from this area would result in terror attacks originating from it have become more pervasive in the public discourse (see Shragai 2008). Fifty-six percent of

Israelis now believe that any part of Jerusalem given to the Palestinians would likely serve as a base for terrorist acts against Israel and 60 percent believe that a deal over the city would not end Palestinian claims against Israel or bring an end to Palestinian violence. Indeed, recent polls find that a large majority of the Jewish public (between 50 and 60 percent) now disagrees with the position that if there is a peace agreement that includes appropriate security arrangements, the Arab neighborhoods in East Jerusalem can be transferred to the Palestinians (Israel Democracy Institute, The Peace Index, December 2012, July 2013). And between 70 and 90 percent of Israelis polled now oppose a peace deal that would hand Jerusalem's Old City and the Temple Mount/Haram al-Sharif over to Palestinian sovereignty (Reiter 2008, 159; Bar-Tal, Halperin, and Oren 2010, 75). Sixty percent of Israelis are also not in favor of joint Israeli-Palestinian administration of Jerusalem's holy places (Israel Democracy Institute, The Peace Index, April 2008). And with Israel continuing to expand Jewish housing into the Old City and East Jerusalem (including, once again, new housing for the contested neighborhood of Har Homa), there appears to be less and less willingness to adhere to the "Clinton parameters" and the principles established at Camp David and Taba, i.e., relinquishing what is Jewish to Jews and what is Arab to Arabs.

Consider, too, Israel's building of the separation barrier in the Jerusalem area. The barrier has saved Israeli lives. It has rerouted the location of terror attacks and there has been a clear decline in the number of successful attacks and Israeli casualties. As Daniel Byman (2006, 105) notes, "After the fence was completed in the northern part of the West Bank in 2003, the number of Israelis killed by attackers originating from that area plummeted." According to some on the Israeli left, the barrier also advances the peace process insofar as it requires those Israelis on the "wrong side" of the wall to re-think the state's commitment to their communities (Kreimer 2005).[9] Yet, the separation barrier is not conducive to a resolution of the "Jerusalem problem." It prevents the emergence of a viable Palestinian

9. Excluding East Jerusalem, currently approximately 190,000 Israelis live in the 8 percent of the West Bank that is between the Green Line and the current route of the separation

capital in East Jerusalem by presenting yet another eastward expansion of Jerusalem's municipal boundaries (especially the E-1 plan for Ma'ale Adumim). It separates a number of Palestinian neighborhoods in northern Jerusalem from the rest of the city (Dahan 2013, 73–76) and also disenfranchises those Palestinians who live in the seam between the Green Line and the newly constructed barrier (east of the Green Line but west of the separation barrier). The separation barrier is thus counterproductive to any lasting solution to the conflict. Daniel Seidemann (2005) puts the problem well: "Physical barriers are a legitimate defensive measure in the war on terror. But the city's complexity also dictates that the barrier in Jerusalem can only be a limited tactical tool providing short term stability until such a time as a political process can resume. In the long run, the existence of the wall in Jerusalem and a nonviolent equilibrium between Israelis and Palestinians are mutually incompatible."

Palestinian negotiating positions have also hardened. In the early 1990s, Palestinian leader Yasser Arafat was willing to sign a peace agreement with Israel even if it meant postponing a resolution on Jerusalem. The negotiations advanced without Jerusalem (Bruck 1996; Benvenisti 1996, 47). No Palestinian leader will take such a position today, not even the moderate Mahmoud Abbas (Abu Mazen) who orchestrated the Oslo negotiations in secret, drafted the Beilin-Abu Mazen agreement in November 1995, and was Arafat's second in command. Indeed, the Palestinian leadership and public (and much of the Muslim world) have come to accept the claim that Jerusalem (and perhaps all of Palestine too) is holy Muslim waqf land and as such no part of it can be renounced, despite the fact that this notion is not rooted in Islamic legal texts or in historical practice (Reiter 2007, 2008; Gold 2007, 10–18).

Palestinian secular and religious leaders today publically reject Jewish historical and religious ties to the Temple Mount. By extension, many also reject Judaism's connection to the land of Israel and the legitimacy of the Jewish people's return to their homeland (Reiter 2008, 53–58). Indeed,

---

barrier. Some 50,000 Israeli settlers located on the east, or wrong side, of the barrier would have to move westward (see Makovsky 2006, vii, 14).

only 6 percent of Palestinians think that it is very important to allow Jews to visit their holy sites in Jerusalem. Nearly 35 percent would not grant Jews any access to Jerusalem's holy sites at all (Klein 2007, 123). By contrast, in the 1990s, Arafat and the Palestinian Authority were willing to entertain the idea that Israel would incorporate the large settlement blocks adjacent to the Green Line and they also conceded that as part of a final status agreement Israel would retain control over the Jewish Quarter of the Old City and sovereignty over at least the exposed part of the Western Wall (the Wailing Wall) and the Jewish neighborhoods in East Jerusalem (Albin 1997, 138; Breger 2002; Segal et al. 2000). Today these concessions have little support.

The Oslo process, culminating in the Camp David and Taba summits, shattered a number of taboos regarding Jerusalem. For Israelis it led to a new public discourse on the elusive goal of uniting the city and opened up the possibility of dividing and, ultimately, sharing it. The mantra that "Jerusalem cannot be divided" that had dominated public discourse for a generation could be "interpreted less strictly" (Sher 2006, 125) to allow for creative solutions. For Palestinians, it prompted a revision of the long-held demand for full Israeli withdrawal to the pre-1967 borders as they began to accept the special relationship that Jews (both religious and secular) had with Israel's capital. This new flexibility, however, was short lived. For Israelis, the city has once again become nonnegotiable. The preservation of Israeli sovereignty over Judaism's historical and religious heartland has once more placed Jerusalem off the table. For Palestinians, full sovereignty over the holy Haram al-Sharif compound has become a red line and they appear unwilling to give up their goal of its liberation.

Ironically, despite this apparent impasse over the city's future, the international community continues to view negotiations as the best route forward. Indeed, in a recent brief to the US Supreme Court, the Obama administration argued that the status of Jerusalem should be resolved by negotiations between Arabs and Israelis.[10] Unfortunately, today the

10. The case, Zivotofsky v. Clinton, 566 U.S. ___, 132 S. Ct. 1421 (2012), considered the extent to which the US Congress is entitled to play a role in recognizing the sovereignty of

prospect for a negotiated settlement to the "Jerusalem problem" appears bleaker than ever before. To be sure, Israelis and Palestinians have both come far in closing the distance that divides them. Once rejecting the very idea of a Palestinian people, much less a Palestinian state, the majority of Israelis now support the creation of a Palestine alongside Israel (Magal et al. 2012). Even right-wing Israeli politicians have come to accept the two-state solution and have conceded the 1967 lines with land swaps as the basis for a final status agreement (Golan 2009). For their part, Palestinians also support—in large majorities—a two-state solution to the conflict (Telhami and Kull 2013). Notwithstanding the views of some in the Palestinian diaspora and other rejectionist groups, most Palestinians accept the reality of Israel. Yet, for all this progress, there remains the intractable issue of Jerusalem. Here, in the final account, it is likely that conflict resolution will require third-party intervention in order to overcome mutual intransigence.

---

foreign countries. At issue was a 2002 statute that grants US citizens born in Jerusalem the right to designate Israel as their country of birth. Since the law was passed, US presidents have refused to follow it on the grounds that it trespasses the executive's constitutional authority to conduct foreign affairs. While the case was essentially one involving executive-congressional powers, it was also likely to have far-reaching impact on US policy with respect to Jerusalem (Liptak 2011; Levinson 2011). Reversing an earlier D.C. Circuit ruling, on March 26, 2012, the Supreme Court decided that Zivotofsky's claim that his passport should read "Israel" should be remanded to the lower courts for review. On July 23, 2013, the US Court of Appeals for the District of Columbia held that the statute was an unconstitutional intrusion on the president's exclusive power to recognize foreign nations.

2

Sacred Urbanism

Jerusalem's Sacrality, Urban Sociology,
and the History of Religions

ROGER FRIEDLAND AND RICHARD D. HECHT

FOR MORE THAN twenty years, we collaborated across our disciplinary
boundaries, as urban sociologist and as historian of religions, to understand and interpret the religion and politics of Jerusalem. Even though
both of us had been on the same campus for several years before going to
Jerusalem, we hardly knew one another and in our recollections of that
early period, we had only one very, very brief discussion about matters
unrelated to Jerusalem. We both came to Jerusalem in the early 1980s, each
with separate thoughts of writing a book on Jerusalem as a sacred city. We
met again by sheer chance on the Mount Scopus campus of the Hebrew
University. Roger was a Fulbright scholar working in the faculty of geography (much of his work to that date was on the geography of corporate
headquarters). Richard was serving a two-year administrative assign-
ment as the director of the University of California's Education Abroad
Program in Israel. We each concluded that we did not know enough about
the other's field to write the books we wanted to write—everything
about Jerusalem's religions, it seemed to us, was political, and everything
about Jerusalem's politics was religious. We needed one another's disciplinary knowledge to carry out our intended projects. Thus, over a Shab-
bat dinner (and Roger continues to recall the meal I cooked more than a
quarter century ago—carrot salad with caraway seeds and pea soup from
a *Telma* or *Osem* package) our collaboration began.

The collaboration changed us as individual scholars in fundamental and unexpected ways as we went about our work. Jerusalem became a platform for us to take up other issues that we thought important to our disciplines—religion and politics (at the time we began our research the topic of religion and politics was just beginning its gestation), religion and nationalism, religion and nation-state formation, and religion and violence. From our research and these issues we developed a series of undergraduate lecture courses and graduate seminars. The first time we offered our lecture course "Religion and Politics in the City: The Case of Jerusalem," twelve students enrolled. Eight of the students had been with us in Jerusalem and the four others were friends of theirs. The last time we offered the course in 2008, the enrollment had grown to 175 students. Our courses became venues where students from sociology and religious studies confronted the complexities of the city, and we worked through conceptual and theoretical problems that arose as we sought to bring our trainings and disciplines together in our collaboration. We moved from scholars who mutually and respectively mistrusted religion and social scientific explanations as reductionisms to a position that might be described as "neo-Durkheimian," or just "Durkheimian," where the city's communities—*haredim*, mainline Zionists, what we called the messianic suburbanites, Palestinian nationalists, Palestinian Islamists, and the tourists—became collective representations that provided conflictual meanings for daily life in the city and drove the contemporary city's politics.

Our title for this chapter is intended to recall Mike Davis's *Magical Urbanism: Latinos Reinvent the U.S. City* (2001). Davis makes a number of important points in that little book. The central argument is that while there is much abstract talk in urban planning and architectural schools about "reurbanization," Latino and Asian immigrants are "reurbanizing" American cities on an epic scale. In Davis's words, "All of Latin America is now a dynamo turning the lights back on in the dead spaces of North American cities." But equally important in this book is the subtext that Davis has elaborated in all of his books: urban space cannot be separated from culture, as many urban planners would suggest in their designs for public spaces, governmental buildings, power, water and sewage infrastructure, and road patterns. Planners may think that public spaces are a tabula rasa, functional, neutral space, and without meaning, awaiting their imprint, but all spaces are freighted with private and public meanings. Spaces already have meaning before the architect or the planner marks the first line on paper. Demographic change and legal or illegal immigration are not really the issue. The urban space of the city is changing, and with it, new meaning systems are at play in the American city. Davis notes that "Hispanic" and "Latino" are no longer synonymous with "Catholic." He writes (ibid. 13–14):

> Certainly syncretic New World Catholicism with a thousand and one Aztec and African gods masquerading as *santos*, remains, together with the mother tongue, the most important common heritage of Latino immigrant communities. And few cross-cultural trends are as impressive as the recent flocking of other Latin American Catholics and even Anglo New-Agers to the cult of Mexico's Virgin of Guadalupe (who also reincarnates the powers of the goddess Tonantzin) as she made her way *al otro lado*. (A digital laser replica of her image recently completed a triumphal procession of the Los Angeles archdiocese. "The 3-by-5 foot copy, blessed by the [P]ope, toured some 50 local parishes before a farewell appearing in front of 50,000 worshippers at the L.A. Coliseum.") Yet if murals of La Morena, radiant in her blue, star-studded shawl, sanctify the sides of *tiendas* from San Diego to Atlanta, the adjoining storefront will most likely be a Pentecostal church. In the city that the *pobladores* named "Nuestra Señora" (La Reina de Los Angeles), Spanish-language Protestant denominations (especially Pentecostals) are running neck-to-neck with the Pope. Latinos equally reinvigorate US Catholicism (supplying 71 percent of its growth since 1960) *and* energize its evangelical competitors. In this new dispensation, the traditional antinomy of Latino/Hispanic versus Protestant collapses, and, as Carlos Monsiváis wryly suggests, the immigrant may now pray to the Virgin of Guadalupe: "*Jefecita*. I am still faithful to you, who represents the Nation, even though I now may be Pentecostal, Jehovah's Witness, Adventist, Baptist or Mormon."

Davis underscores with this passage that all urban space is connected to culture and religion. But something else is concealed here that takes us to the case of Jerusalem. Urban planners cannot really control the meanings that are being attached to urban space. This becomes even more difficult when space is understood as an extension of the sacred. Indeed, the combination of the sacred and place set in motion historical processes and perhaps even trans-historical processes that overtake and then overwhelm planning.

Here we intend to share what we have learned about the urban sacrality of Jerusalem through our collaboration across our disciplines. We begin with a discussion of how sacred space has been theorized. Certainly, in the history of religions, we have few theoretical discussions about how sacred space operates in the social world. But, likewise, urban sociology has shown itself to be uninterested in the operations of the sacred in society or within the urban context beyond its ability to "rationalize" social behaviors. David Rapoport, our colleague at UCLA, who has done pioneering work on religion and violence, noted several years ago that political scientists rarely pay attention to the importance of space in their analyses of political conflict. He has sought to remedy that by considering the space of the nation-state, especially since 1945 (although his analysis reaches back to the 1880s), and making his central question: How might the massive redrawing of political boundaries be related to the steady expansion of the number of conflicts? (Rapoport 1996). We hope that the "anatomy" of sacred space that we provide here will contribute to a better understanding of the relationships between sacred space or site and politics.

Second, we take up two interesting cases where important dynamics of sacred space are suggested, which we describe as "building the sacred" and "rites of way." We illustrate the first, "building the sacred," through the Saudi efforts to support the renovation of Muslim sacred sites in Jerusalem in 1994, and the centralization of Jerusalem in Palestinian Muslim discourse and in the larger Muslim world. We discuss the second, "rites of way," by considering the clash between religious nationalist Jews and the Greek Orthodox community in the Christian quarter of the Old City in 1990.

Let us begin with the most basic observation and something that all of us know. Almost every scholarly and popular article, essay, and book on Jerusalem begins with a statement such as the following: "Jerusalem is a sacred or holy place, center, site to Judaism, Christianity and Islam, the three great monotheistic religions." If this description is not found in the first sentence it will be there very early in the discussion. But what exactly does this mean to call Jerusalem a sacred or holy place? Of course we know about the historical materiality of the city and its meanings for the three religions. But that does not answer our question. For almost a decade the Palestinian Academic Society for the Study of International Affairs (PASSIA) had sustained dialogues on Jerusalem with Israeli and Palestinian scholars and a range of political figures from the city of Jerusalem. In almost all of these dialogues the sacrality of Jerusalem is a significant descriptor. For example, Mahdi Abdul Hadi, the director of PASSIA, enumerates the "dimensions" that must be considered in any solution to the problem of Jerusalem. Among them, of course, is "the religious component" that Abdul Hadi (1998, 96–97) describes as follows:

> The religious claims of the three monotheistic religions to Jerusalem are each unique, with each religion having its own form of attachment to different places in the city. Jerusalem's holiness complicates any attempt to solve the Question of Jerusalem and is often used or manipulated to attain nonreligious goals. Yet, the meaning of religious attachment to the city was and remains a major concern. As well as its Jewish heritage, Jerusalem is a city with Arab, Islamic and Christian heritage. Its Islamic identity derives from the fact that it was the site of Prophet Mohammed's nocturnal journey, Isra' and Mi`raj, the original *qibla* for Moslems, and the site of Islam's third holiest shrine, [a]l-Aqsa Mosque. It is also the site of the Holy Sepulcher, other important churches, and the Mount of Olives. . . . Limiting the problem to the Holy Places is not appropriate; the right to live and to practice one's religion in the city must be guaranteed. This is what an open city must provide for. We have all learned from the experience of sharing religious sites, such as the Abraham Mosque in Hebron; exclusivity, however, is also not an answer. We need to understand the other's religion in order to be able to reach an agreement. Religion has to be seen in the context of the land, the people, and their rights.

This is a statement describing the holiness of Jerusalem and it has several interesting components. Abdul Hadi underscores that the holiness of the city complicates a resolution to the conflict over the city. He notes that there are religious attachments to the city and seems to believe that those attachments arise from the religious or mythological history of the city for Muslims, Christians, and Jews. Note that there is no mention of the Temple Mount or the Western Wall or the collective, historical memory of Jews that infuses the space of the city. Abdul Hadi also indicates that the religious problem cannot be limited to the Holy Places, but must include freedom of religious practice. Neither sharing of holy places nor exclusivity in those places is without problem, and he proposes that (1) there is need for mutual understanding among the religions if there is to be an agreement, and (2) religion must be seen in the context of land, people, and national or civil rights.

But there is something strange in this description. He writes that the city's holiness "is often used or manipulated to attain nonreligious goals." This statement reflects some understanding of the nature of religion or the sacred that perhaps privatizes or isolates it and takes it out of the political; there are religious goals and nonreligious goals. Yet, this statement is contradicted by the concluding proposals in which religion must be seen in the context of land, people, and rights—that is, where religion is political. We think this contradiction, and indeed Enlightenment understanding of religion, reflects the central problem that we had to address in our collaboration: What is the meaning of sacred place?

Theorizing Sacred Centers

The tradition of scholarship on the sacred represented by Mircea Eliade (1959) might be labeled "the transcendental tradition of the sacred." If you were to imagine the sites that are conjured up by this tradition, you would have to think of them as occupying determinate, but non-concrete locations, consisting of symbolic space on the one hand, and an autonomous phenomenological order on the other. Together these two orders produce an ontological break with ordinary social physics and the profane flow of lived experience. Scholars of the sacred either make the materiality of place—its physicality, its stones and steps, columns and transepts, its tracery—irrelevant, a media that has no significance in itself, or they reduce it to sacred signage—stone and masonry linguified, its materiality an expression of cultural forces located elsewhere. In the former, place is the container for the cosmological; in the second it is its materialization. In neither case does its material existence figure in its significance. In hindsight now we can understand why this "transcendental tradition of the sacred" made irrelevant the concrete, material, and immanent formations of space. The genealogy of this tradition reaches back to Rudolf Otto (1917) whose very definition of *das Heilige* negated any significant meaning to its manifestation in the empirical world. Perhaps if Arnold van Gennep's understanding of the "pivoting of the sacred" as outlined in his *Rites of Passage*—namely that the sacred is never found in an abstraction—had been made as central as Otto's, we would not be able to describe this as the "transcendental tradition of the sacred."

Studies of sacred centers must take the theoretical lessons of place seriously, in that place is a category that is both "out there" in the material world and "in here" in the culturally informed horizon of personal experience. Place, and sacred place in particular, cannot be reduced to one side or the other without doing violence to its constitution. As Nicholas Entrikin (1991) has pointed out, there is a "betweenness" to place.

Places are both organizations of material objects that afford particular cultural understandings *and* the cultural orders that shape their production and appropriation. Ironically, students of religion have much to learn from the new "strong program" in the sociology of science, which points to the constitutive role of technical objects, including scientific laboratories and their standardized instrumentation and architectonics, in the production of truth (Gieryn 1998; Shapin 1998). Architecture, in particular, points beyond the linguistic model in which the referent does not do any signifying work itself.

The productivity of place was also important to critical theorists like Walter Benjamin. Benjamin (1996) read the shopping arcades, the industrial exhibitions, and the industrial design of his day as pointing to the way in which material objects carry, in a contradictory distributed cognition, both the utopian desires and the commodified repressions of his age. The material world, as in his reading of the planetarium as a new individualized, ocularized relation to the awesome cosmos, affords particular structures of experience, of historical consciousness. Benjamin understood place as inseparable from the body and memory. Thus, place was a pivot of the Proustian *mémoire involontaire*, as Graeme Gilloch (1996, 179) has written—the sudden, spontaneous recollection in which the past and the present recognize one another. Indeed, one of the most important conclusions that we have reached in our collaboration for this volume is that we must take the constitutive role of the materiality of sacred places, and the cultural work they do, into account.

It is not only the *locus classicus*, Mircea Eliade, who mentalizes the materiality of sacred place. Paul Mus, the esteemed Buddhologist whose massive study of Barabadur remains a landmark achievement in this phenomenological tradition, does likewise. For him, the monument replicates the symbolism of Mount Meru, the center of the world, which is carried in every parasol of every Buddhist monk and which, as a mandala, becomes a diagram for the interior soul of the believer. Symbolism and phenomenology are one. Mus, for example, does not consider how this great monument is directly related to the great kingly empires of Java and Southeast Asia more generally.

The theoretical vaporization of sacred places has dual intellectual sources, both modern and classical. Scholars of the sacred have generally positioned sacred place as a cathected object in opposition to the modern, an expressive refuge from its time of becoming. Sacred place is not, then, an object subject to interested social practice. But the dematerialization of the sacred also draws on classical sources, which almost always locate being, the medium of sacred experience, in such a way that brackets its material instances. The spatial figures on neither side.

This approach has inimical consequences. The immaterial quality of sacred sites allows scholars to strip the sacred of its central properties—its power. The phenomenological tradition assumes that it is precisely the exteriority of the sacred, including the sacrality of place, to the material world that gives it such power, power able to hold the material world at bay, and indeed transform it utterly. Its irreducibility to the profane is what enables it to change the profane world.

Places whose meanings are located in numina, in symbol and belief, need not therefore be joined to power, in the ordinary sense of control over symbols, bodies and things in space and time, or in their very constitution. Nor are such sacred places questioned about who and how the sites are controlled, how they are constructed and reconstructed, and how and when different groups can access them. Authority to speak the word, to visit the place, to control its rites all involve questions of power, a power historians of religions have tended to bracket. The classical strategy of analysis is, in fact, a strategy to purify purity, to sacralize the sacred, to make power's constitutive role irrelevant, if not invisible, to the sacred, a sacred that is itself assumed to be a source of power. This certainly has something to do with the Enlightenment tradition in which religion was envisioned to be a private confession, a domain over which the state had no legitimate jurisdiction.

The Case of Nazareth

Just like economics, which refuses to grant the category of power any theoretical place in its intellectual architecture, yet cannot theorize the conditions under which the boundaries of the marketplace will be respected or transgressed, so historians of religions likewise push it beyond the pale. Yet power, and the adjudication of access, is absolutely essential to the organization and constitution of sacred sites. This is particularly the case where, as often happens, divergent communities or groups contest control and interpretation of sacred sites. The examples are legion, but let us briefly consider a case near, but outside Jerusalem—the plaza in front of Nazareth's Basilica of the Annunication. Much like Bethlehem, Nazareth has become decreasingly Christian in composition. Nazareth, a Palestinian city that ended up within the territorial limits of the state of Israel in 1948, has long had a Christian majority population. Even though the Palestinian Christians have migrated out of the region at a much greater rate than Palestinian Muslims, in part as a result of their higher levels of education, the Christians of Nazareth held a substantial majority as late as two decades ago, repeatedly electing the Communists (Hadash) to municipal office. Christian Palestinians, fearing an Islamization of Palestinian politics, were attracted to the political left for its commitment to secularity. Palestinian Muslims, as a result of their greater in-migration and their relatively higher birth rates, steadily increased their numbers in the city. In the 1998 municipal elections, the Muslims made their move and their party, United Nazareth, was able to take half the city council seats. The Christian Communist mayor was unable to form a governing coalition to rule the city.

Daphne Tsimhoni (2005) has provided the most detailed account of the conflicts, which stretch over three successive national governments, those of Benjamin Netanyahu, Ehud Barak, and Ariel Sharon, from 1997 to 2003. She locates the crisis in a number of factors—the breakdown of demographic equilibrium of the city and the loss of its Christian majority; expansion of poverty among the Muslim population; the growing social gaps between Christians and Muslims, which then provided the access point for the Islamic movement in Nazareth to challenge Christian dominance in the economy and in civic society in Nazareth. Here, we touch only upon a few of the events (Breger, Reiter, and Hammer 2010).

While Nazareth's militant Palestinian Muslims refused to participate in national Israeli elections, they found another way to confront the Jewish state—in the real estate of Christ. The Franciscan custos of the Holy Land, the Catholic guardians of sacred sites, had long planned to build an enormous church that would function as the Latin parish church for Nazareth, incorporating both the Crusader and Byzantine churches on the site, as well as the Grotto of the Annunciation. The proposal had received Israeli government approval as early as 1969. By the late 1990s, and in preparation for "Nazareth 2000," the city's celebration of the Christian Jubilee, building a plaza for an expected million pilgrims became urgent.

In 1997, led by the Islamic Movement, the Muslims declared the plaza a sacred endowment (or "waqf") and the burial site of Shihab al-Din, a nephew of Salah al-Din, the Muslim conqueror of the Holy Land in the twelfth century. The Muslims constructed a protest tent in the plaza, refused to move and demanded a mosque be built on the site to rival the Basilica of the Annunciation. The Nazareth District court found in 1998 in favor of the city and ordered the Muslims' tent removed. However, the municipality, fearing violence, was slow to act. The Muslims appealed the decision to the Israeli Supreme Court. Nazareth's mayor argued that the land had once belonged to the Jordanians; it was now state land, and thus Israel had the ultimate jurisdiction. On the Latin Easter of 1999, communal violence erupted in which Muslims stoned and firebombed Christian cars and businesses. The Netanyahu government did little to defuse the dangerous situation that was threatening to erupt into more extensive violence. In late 1999, the newly elected Barak government appointed a ministerial committee to find a compromise that in October 1999 offered the Muslims an opportunity to build a small mosque on the site, and they would be given, in exchange for the removal of the tent, state land elsewhere in the city for schools and mosques.

Salman abu Ahmed, the leader of the elected Muslim Movement's members in the city council immediately applauded the committee's decision and termed the Vatican's involvement through the Latin patriarch and the custos as "foreign interference in Nazareth's internal affairs" (Pinto, Algazy, and Gal 1999). Before the ministerial committee had reported its decision, the new sitting prime minister, Ehud Barak, had already been petitioned by the Latin patriarchate, the Greek patriarchate, the Armenian patriarchate, and the Franciscan custos. On September 11, 1999, they had written to him rejecting any Islamic claim: "the place currently proposed for the building of a mosque—besides being government-owned property—is not compatible with the larger vision of peace and harmony among all the faith communities of Nazareth and will remain an unfortunate source of friction and dispute in the future" (Gal and Eldar 1999).

By the late 1990s, the Vatican had a privileged diplomatic position from which to pursue and negotiate its interests as a result of the December 1993 Fundamental Agreement between the Holy See and the State of Israel, which established reciprocal diplomatic relations. In this agreement both Israel and the Vatican agreed to respect the "'Status Quo' in the Christian Holy Places." The Status Quo in the Holy Places is that labyrinthine compilation of decrees and agreements allocating time and space among the competing Christian communities in the major Christian holy places. While in the past, the "Latins"—as the Catholics are known in Jerusalem and the historic Holy Land—had used the influence of the colonial powers to alter their disadvantaged situation, or played the bargaining chip of promises to rebuild most of the holy places in exchange for a more equitable division of time and space within them, the Vatican's position now seemed to be that an unprecedented emphasis upon ecumenicism would gain them what power and money could not.

As the only world religion that has a sovereign personality in Israel, the Latin church was in a privileged position to defend its interests in Nazareth. And the basilica in Nazareth is not the Holy Sepulcher in Jerusalem. This is Israel's uncontested sovereign territory; this is a Catholic shrine, not one parceled out among several Orthodox Christianities. If the Vatican could not defend its interests in Nazareth, it certainly could not defend them in Jerusalem. Israel had agreed to spend $100 million in Nazareth to subsidize the costs of the million pilgrims expected for the 2,000-year anniversary of Christianity. Both Pope John Paul II and the State of Israel at that time were hoping for a papal visit to Israel. The Pope had long expressed to his closest advisors and friends his desire to visit the Holy Land, and especially Jerusalem, as his health declined. It was agreed that the Pope would visit Jerusalem in April 2000, but the Vatican, which had refused to release the Pope's itinerary for his Easter visit, threatened to cancel the visit in the event that the Muslims were allowed to build a mosque in Nazareth: "It is hoped that the Israeli government authorities," declared Joaquin Navarro-Valls, the Vatican spokesman, "considering the value that the city of Nazareth holds for all of Christianity, will know how to assure the respect of the Christian sanctuary and its free and peaceful access to pilgrims" (Pinto 1999).

The threat to cancel the papal visit to Israel did not yield immediate results. Shlomo Ben-Ami, then public security minister, who chaired the ministerial committee, commented that he believed the Pope's visit would continue as scheduled. Speaking at a meeting with Michel Sabbah, the Latin patriarch of Jerusalem, Ben-Ami noted, "I think that the visit of the Pope is of an importance far beyond a particular question, however important that question may be. And I am sure that the millenarian meaning of the visit is stronger than a particular case." Ben-Ami perhaps reasoned that the symbolism of this Pope marking the 2,000th anniversary of Christianity in Jerusalem would outweigh the controversy in Nazareth. But Sabbah interjected that the Roman Catholic Church "is not opposed to the building of synagogues, churches and mosques, but in proper places." Sabbah once again asked Ben-Ami to reconsider the recommendation of his committee (Pinto and Algazy 1999).

With no reconsideration in the offing, the Roman Catholic, Greek Orthodox, Armenian Orthodox patriarchs and the Roman Catholic custos announced that they would close their churches to protest the government's decision to build the mosque. In their letter to Israeli president Ezer Weizman they wrote that building a mosque so close to the Basilica of the Annunciation was a political and discriminatory act. The Christian hierarchy, rather than direct their ire at the Muslim Movement, attacked the government of Israel. How different, they noted, was the current intolerant and tense atmosphere to the nearly 500 years of peaceful co-existence between Christians and Muslims in the Holy Land under the Ottomans and the British. The letter added that the government's mistaken and unprecedented decision would undermine Jewish-Muslim relations not only in Jerusalem but throughout the country.

The Christian authorities did not close all their churches in the Holy Land. Those under the Palestinian Authority in the West Bank and Gaza would remain open. The spokesman for the Latin Patriarch said "the entity to be punished by this action is Israel. The Palestinians have proven that they are better at protecting minority rights" (Orme 1999; Algazy 1999a, 1999b). In the context of diplomatic relations between Israel and the Vatican, this was shocking language. The office of the Latin patriarch's use of the term "entity" recalled the Vatican's position of nonrecognition of Israel prior to its 1993 accord establishing reciprocal diplomatic relations. It also conjured the Palestinian Liberation Organization's (PLO) language of nonrecognition prior to the decision of the Palestinian National Congress in November 1988 agreeing to the partition of Palestine into two states. Prime Minister Barak and, after him, Prime Minister Sharon came under increasing pressure from the Vatican, and then president George W. Bush whose supporters also saw the situation in Nazareth as a contest between Christianity and Islam. Ultimately, Sharon would reverse the course of the governments before his and end the Nazareth affair by ordering government bulldozers to demolish the basement foundations of the Shihab al-Din Mosque that had been built in the plaza.

The case of Nazareth is instructive in that it alerts us to the full range of politics—juridical, diplomatic, national, and municipal—in the constitution of this sacred site, not only regarding what it means, but how it will be used. The disposition of this sacred site is contingent not only on Israeli-Palestinian political negotiations, but the balance of political forces within the Palestinian community between those who would ground their political identities in Islam and those who take a more nationalist or socialist point of view, and of course, the rights of diverse religious authorities vis-à-vis each other and the state. Here, if the militant Palestinian Muslims seek to nationalize the site, the Christians in large part are attempting to build a transnational Christian pilgrimage site. Thus, the struggle to control a sacred site must be understood in tandem with the struggles to control the interpretation of sacred texts, in the sense that control here is bound to the site's signification. In this case, by seizing the site, Palestinian Muslims are making a hermeneutical assertion that they, too, have an account of Jesus's mother, Mary.[1]

Building the Sacred: The Case of Jerusalem

In Israel and Palestine, politicized religious movements have consistently used sacred sites as a way to promote their definition of the territory, and hence both the nature of their claim to it and the primacy of that claim. In the case of Nazareth's Basilica of the Annunciation, the Islamic Movement asserted that this is waqf land (and it was unclear throughout the controversy whether waqf referred to something limited like the plaza) consonant with Hamas's claim that all of Palestine is waqf, and not a profane territory that can be ceded through treaties made under coercion to infidels. By taking the land, based on this claim that the sacred site is waqf land covenanted by Allah, Muslim activists perform that belief, a performance to which the sacrality of the site is critical. This parallels

---

1. In the Qur'an and its early exegeses, the Moses narrative of the Hebrew Bible and the Jesus narrative of the New Testament are conflated on the basis of Moses's sister Miriam (Arabic Maryam) and Mary (Arabic Maryam). Mary, the mother of Jesus, is the daughter of Imran's wife (i.e., Amran, the father of Moses). But more importantly the Qur'an argues the prophylactic prayer of Mary's mother protects her and Jesus from Satan's assault, intended to implant sin within her. Mary becomes the archetype of the chaste woman and because of her great virtue with regard to her chastity, God miraculously creates Jesus within her (see Newby 1989, 205–11).

the strategy of the Gush Emunim (Bloc of the Faithful) and the religious Zionist settlers, who, over the last three and half decades, have initiated their settlement drives by illegally occupying what they believe are sacred sites, tombs and ancient yeshivot in particular. The Jewish settlement movement began with an occupation of Hebron, the city where Abraham and his family are buried, and from which David began his drive for kingship. Hebron combines in one location both the space of the first covenant between God and the Jews in the tomb of Abraham, and political power as exemplified by David. The religious Zionist strategy likewise expresses the sanctity of the land and its status as a covenantal gift, not mere territory.

The question then becomes: what are the conditions under which different religious communities contest and indeed share sacred sites? Access to sacred places and even the site itself are ultimately dependent on state power. In our work on Jerusalem's sacred urban real estate, we have detailed the development of an enormously complex corpus of property rights, guaranteed and eventually codified by the state, whose content changed with who exercised sovereign control over Jerusalem and the geopolitical structure of influence in which different religious communities could differentially assert themselves.

The co-presence of divergent religions in a single site does not necessarily lead to conflict, nor depend on state orchestration.[2] Yet places that undergird belief, that choreograph movement, that sustain collective iden-

2. One of our students, Anna Bigelow, who now teaches in the Department of Philosophy and Religion at North Carolina State University, Raleigh, has been studying a sacred shrine, the tomb of a Muslim *pir*, Sheik Sadrudin Sadr-i Jahan, in the Punjab. This shrine has been long shared by Muslims, Hindus, and Sikhs—a sharing interrupted neither by the partition of 1948 nor the Sikh assassination of Indira Gandhi and the subsequent bloody communal riots that convulsed all of India. Even during the Hindu nationalist Ayodhya campaign, there was no significant violence there. Bigelow examines the process by which these different groups both construct a common symbolic world at the same time as they choreograph their co-presence at the site. The absence of conflict here is even more extraordinary given the political meanings that attach to this site. The site sits in the only Muslim-majority city in the Indian Punjab. The sheik whose tomb it is was given the land as a dowry when he married the daughter of the first Lodhi emperor of India in the fifteenth century.

tity, are enormous sources of political power. It is no wonder that states have sought to control them, and indeed often to base their legitimacy upon that control, or as has often happened, to build their own sacred centers over them. Neglecting the relation between power and the sacred site severely limits our ability to appreciate the enormous importance that sacred sites have had in the formation of nation-states themselves (or in those political units that preceded the nation-state). In fact, sacred centers, and the politicized pilgrimages that they afford, have been essential to the formation of modern collectivities.[3]

If we consider sacred centers only as ideas or symbols come to ground, as sites where a different order of experience is available, then we will neither be able to understand the enormous power of religion in the modern world, nor the ways in which power has always been integral to the constitution of the sacred. But there is more. If we cannot understand the role of power in the constitution of the sacred, then we

---

The sacred site and the princely state were ruled by descendents of the sheik until 1948. See Bigelow (2010).

3. A few examples provide cases in point. For example, consider the role of the Virgin of Guadalupe shrine in Mexico City, which proved critical as an alternative center of orientation and politicized pilgrimage to that of the Spanish colonial National Cathedral for Mexican revolutionaries (see Elizondo 1997; Brading 2001, 312–22). It was evident in the case of Palestinian pilgrimage to *Nebi Musa*, the Palestinian Muslim site in which Palestinians believe Moses is buried, that first created cross-local Palestinian identities at the beginning of the twentieth century (see Friedland and Hecht 1996a). It was clear in the case of Poland, where the pilgrimage to the Virgin of Jasnagorna was essential during the days of Soviet hegemony in providing a context for an anti-Soviet Polish nationalism to which, of course, the Vatican provided substantial financial and diplomatic support. In Spain, pilgrimage to Santiago de Compostella was essential to the formation of Catholic resistance against Muslims, to the formation of the modern nation-state of Spain, to the Spanish Civil War, and most recently even to the creation of the European Economic Community. In France, pilgrimage to the Sacré Coeur in Paris, built in the aftermath of the defeat of the Paris Commune and the Austrian invasion, was an important medium by which the French nation-state was both legitimated and defined (see Harvey 1985, 221–50). And in India, the Hindu nationalists have used politicized pilgrimage to Ayodhya, the birthplace of Ram, the foundational Hindu sovereign, as one of the most effective techniques to mobilize the population and to push their program to redefine the substance of Indian citizenship.

will also not be able to advance our understanding of the sacred as a necessary constituent of power. Scholars of religion who claim to study Jerusalem or Benaras should also have something to say about the role of mass pilgrimage, rite, and sacred place in the formation of the secular nation-state, as in the case of the March on Rome and its ritualized reenactments in Mussolini's Italy as analyzed by Simonetta Falasca-Zamponi (1997), or the importance of the magnificent cosmological gardens that Chandra Mukerji (1997) has shown to be critical in the formation of the territoriality of the absolutist French state. Joining the political content of sacrality and the sacred content of power is essential to making the study of religion and urban sociology central to the analysis of religio-political conflicts.

As we worked on Jerusalem and other sacred places, we began to formulate a series of fifteen "axioms" that we believe help us to understand the extensive powers of sacred places (see Friedland and Hecht 2006). These axioms attempt to formulate specific relationships between the three constituents of sacred place—place, memory, and power. "Place" refers to material, physical, or geographic sites and also immaterial or imagined sites. "Memory" refers to collective and individual memory as well as historical memory. "Power" refers both to the manifestations of the sacred as well as the cultural powers of place (e.g., political, economic, and aesthetic). The assumption that is made about sacred places is that their sacrality remains static. We believe that this static view, which can be used to characterize Madhi Abdul Hadi's description of Jerusalem or the entire phenomenological tradition that culminates in the work of Eliade, is the result of reading texts. The static textual reading of sacrality then becomes the *sacrality* of the site. When scholars and negotiators wrestle with Jerusalem's holiness, the holiness that is so difficult and often called an "intractable" problem may not represent how holiness or sacrality is being understood or experienced in the living texts of contemporary Jews, Christians, and Muslims.

These axioms then present a dynamic view of sacrality in which the meaning of that sacrality is always being interpreted, reinterpreted, challenged, assimilated, and synthesized by the contemporary communities. Also, and we think, it is equally important that the static view of sacrality conceals how social groups use sacrality to define themselves and their politics as we have described above. This also means that there may be radically different understandings of sacrality in a single community. We recall a time many years ago when we invited Salam Mariati, who was then chair of the Southern California Council on American-Islamic Relations (CAIR), to come to our class to speak on the topic of Jerusalem in Islam. He, of course, discussed the Isra' (Muhammad's night journey from Mecca to Jerusalem), but said nothing about the Mi'raj (the purification and ascension of the sleeping Muhammad from the Ka'bah into heaven, later integrated into the tale of the night journey) to our students. We asked him about the Mi'raj and he responded that that is a local tradition and is not grounded in the Qur'an and the authentic traditions about the Prophet, his wives, and his companions. Mariati is a Saudi and to make Jerusalem the place from which the Prophet climbed into the heavens would undercut the Saudi claim about Mecca and Medina. But, here we see a conflict between Palestinian Muslims and what they believe are the sources of Jerusalem's sanctity versus the Saudis.

For our purposes here we invite a consideration of three of the axioms we have discussed at length elsewhere. These axioms can be grouped together under the larger thematic title, "Building the Sacred":

> *Axiom 4.* Power and memory must be located at the very beginning. Power and memory are not late-comers. In order to institutionalize a cosmology, it must be put in place. This is what makes it accessible to non-reading and nonliterary oriented people. People don't read texts (as scholars do), but enact texts. They go to places and they enact rituals.
>
> *Axiom 9.* They [sacred spaces] can be mapped through the geographer and cartographer's skills, but they are the territory of imagination, enwrapped in the ribbons of memory, a territory asymmetrical with maps.
>
> *Axiom 14.* Central places, holy places, sacred places, and memory places are filled with history. But the superabundance of history allows one to escape the conditionings of history. The very limitations of space allow transcendence on the wings of memory.

These suggest that the sacrality of a site is constantly being built and refashioned by the people who use the site, by people who imagine the site, and by people who experience history in or at the site. The examples of this building of the sacred are countless.

Jerusalem is but one example. On January 2, 2007, Jerusalem's long-time mayor, Teddy Kollek, died. There is much to say about his twenty-eight years as the mayor of Jerusalem, but many articles written about his life and accomplishments stressed that he was the greatest "builder" of Jerusalem since David or Solomon or Herod or Suleiman. Building the sacrality of a site does not necessarily require building religious places, for in the case of Kollek he built many structures in the city. All of them contributed to building Jerusalem's sacrality in the second half of the twentieth century.

Kollek inherited a divided city. From 1948 to the Six-Day War of June 1967, the eastern parts of the city were ruled by the Jordanians. It was a very small city with a population on both sides—Jordanian Jerusalem and Israeli Jerusalem—of 267,000. While the major Israeli political institutions, the Knesset, and many ministerial offices had been built in the divided city after 1948, the city remained stagnant, a backwater of Israel. It was a city with few economic opportunities. While the city had been proclaimed the capital of the infant state, there was little there to support tourists for more than a single day's visit. There were few hotel rooms and the city's most historic and sumptuous hotel, the King David, could use only half of its rooms—and not those that looked out over the Old City's walls—due to Jordanian sniper fire. There were few restaurants and it was rumored that the sidewalks were rolled up at sunset. Jerusalem was the end. Literally, the city was at the end of a thin corridor that was sur-rounded on three sides and jutted into Jordanian territory. One American Jewish artist decided to uproot himself in 1965 from New York, where there were too many distractions and move to Jerusalem, where nothing was happening. "Then Teddy was elected," he told us, "then the Six-Day War happened, and everything began to change. Jerusalem became the center of the world."

Let's take another example. In April and June of 1994, the monthly newsletter of the Royal Embassy of Saudi Arabia in Washington, DC carried two announcements. The first of these announcements in April was given under the headline "King Fahd's Jerusalem Fund and Palestinian

Initiatives Praised," and went on to describe that the king, as custodian of the two holy mosques, had set up a fund for the repair and mainte-nance of the Islamic holy sites in Jerusalem. In addition, the king gave a donation of 200,000 Saudi riyals (or approximately $53,333) to the fami-lies of the Palestinians killed by "Jewish settlers" during and after the Hebron massacre carried out by Baruch Goldstein on February 25, 1994. The initiative and the donations were praised by Saudi newspapers. *Okaz*, a newspaper based in Jeddah, wrote that the unsolicited actions demon-strated Saudi Arabia's dedication to providing moral and material sup-port for Arabs and Muslims everywhere. *Al-Yom*, a newspaper based in Dammam, took note that the initiatives had been welcomed and praised not only by Palestinians, but also by Arabs and Muslims throughout the world. The newspaper said "King Fahd's donation to the families of the murdered worshippers at the Ibrahim Mosque in Jerusalem [sic] will help ease their burden as many have lost their breadwinners." It added that the fund set up for the repair and maintenance of the Islamic holy sites in Jerusalem would "restore several structures of great religious and his-toric significance to Arabs and Muslims and preserve them for future generations" (see Royal Embassy of Saudi Arabia newsletter, April 1994, 6). In June, Saudi Arabia's US embassy newsletter carried the headline, "Saudi Arabia Funds Restoration of Islamic Holy Sites in Jerusalem." The article described the Saudi intention to work closely with the United Nations Educational, Scientific and Cultural Organization (UNESCO) and to provide funds to restore al-Aqsa. The newsletter summarized the announcement in April and again stressed that this was part of Saudi Arabia's "long-standing policy of serving Arab and Islamic interests." The article also noted that renovations and expansions at Mecca and Medina had just been completed, and now it "is only natural for Saudi Arabia to do all it can to preserve Islam's third holiest shrine." Thirty years before, Saudi Arabia had funded preservation projects in Jerusalem. King Fahd had by April contributed more than $2.3 million, which included his April donation and $1.8 million in 1992 to do initial surveys for the renovations (Royal Embassy of Saudi Arabia newsletter, June 1994, 4).

The Saudi funding of renovations to al-Aqsa Mosque and the Dome of the Rock, and the Haram al-Sharif is an assertion of Saudi power over the Islamic holy places in Jerusalem. They came at a time when the Palestinian Authority was removing Jordanian religious authorities from the religious leadership of Jerusalem and the West Bank. King Hussein had seemingly renounced any Jordanian interests in the West Bank in July 1988. But the Jordanian infrastructure continued to operate until the signing of the Oslo Agreement in September 1993. The Jordanians continued to fund the religious authorities, mosques, and schools. Jerusalem remained a central preoccupation for the Hashemites. Shortly before the Gulf War of 1991, King Hussein funded a project that re-guilded the Dome of the Rock. The Hashemites were the guardians of the third holiest place for Islam, something that clearly contributed to the legitimacy of the regime. Thus, the Saudi fund to build or rebuild the sacrality of Jerusalem undercut both the Palestinians and the Jordanians.

Perhaps a more powerful example of this building of the sacred is how Jerusalem has been centralized among the Palestinians and in the larger Islamic world. Indeed, Islam has followed the same course that Jews and Israelis pursued in their building of the sacred. Yitzhak Reiter, who has studied the Islamic administration of Jerusalem for more than twenty years, has an extraordinary study on this topic (see Reiter 2008). Reiter describes one of the most puzzling moments in the Camp David II discussions when the Clinton proposal to divide sovereignty at the Temple Mount/Haram al-Sharif was rejected by Arafat when he claimed that the Jews had no real connection to the Temple Mount, and that al-Aqsa and all of Jerusalem belong to the entire Muslim nation. What did Arafat mean? Reiter shows that a solution that would divide Jerusalem in any way has become much more difficult and more problematic than ever before as the result of a number of historical and political dynamics. He concludes (2008, 160, emphasis in original) this important study by writing that:

> The upgrading of Jerusalem's sanctity in contemporary Muslim awareness, the denial of any Jewish connection to Jerusalem and of the legitimacy of a Jewish presence in the city and on the Temple Mount, the development of a new historical, religious, and political ethos that accentuates Jerusalem's importance to Arabs and Muslims, and the fact that the consent of important Muslim political leaders will have to be

obtained in order to reach an agreement regarding Jerusalem—all of these factors significantly restrict the Palestinians' flexibility in negotiations over the future of the city and its holy places. *Dividing sovereignty over the Temple Mount/al-Aqsa between Jews/Israelis and Muslims/Palestinians, whether on a geographical or a functional basis, does not appear to be a practicable option.*

In this environment all that is possible at the present time and into the foreseeable future is a cultural initiative that would aim to achieve some knowledge base to educate the respective Israeli and Palestinian publics of the legitimate "religious and cultural rights of the various parties involved" and a political possibility of achieving a "consensual arrangement involving the two parties which would suspend issues of sovereignty over the site, freezing the existing proprietorships of the holy places until a detailed agreement may be reached regarding the administration of the various sites within Jerusalem's historical and sacred space, which some international entity has the responsibility of maintaining order in those places" (ibid.).

Reiter develops what he calls a "dynamic sacrality" to the Muslim understanding of Jerusalem's sanctity, which he traces through the Umayyads, the Ayubbids, Hajj Amin al-Husseini, and then finally to the challenge posed by Israeli control over East Jerusalem. Political or sovereign control of a sacred space changes the meanings of the place. One might put that in this formulation: ritual rites and meanings are determined by political rights and meanings. As the Israelis built the sanctity of the city after the Six-Day War, Palestinians and Muslims built its Islamic sanctity as a strategy of resistance. The narrative that Reiter tells includes many details, and here we only have space to present a few of his interpretations.

He titles his second chapter "Elevation in Sanctity of al-Aqsa and al-Quds," and he shows meticulously how Palestinians have developed new myths regarding the al-Aqsa Mosque, using it as the focal point for the "resanctification" of the Haram al-Sharif. He notes how dramatically different this is from the position taken by the influential Hanbali jurist Ibn-Taymiyya in the thirteenth and fourteenth centuries who ruled that the sanctity of Jerusalem was canceled when the Prophet Muhammad changed the *qibla* from Jerusalem to Mecca. Reiter (2008, 18) writes that:

> Nearly all of the Muslim publications that I have seen on the subject of Jerusalem avoid mentioning Ibn-Taymiyya, despite the fact that this Muslim legal authority is an important source of inspiration for fundamentalist Islam and that Islamic movements make use of other texts of his. . . . Muhammad Shurab, a Saudi historian . . . whose book on the history of Jerusalem and al-Aqsa Mosque is sold in Jerusalem in stores near the Aqsa site . . . is one of the only authors who dares to cite Ibn-Taymiyya's opinion and to dispute his assertions. In his opinion, the Rock was not the first direction of prayer in Islam, but rather al-Aqsa Mosque, and he maintains that there is no proof that the Prophet ascended to heaven from the Rock or that the Jews prayed in its direction.

Among the new myths being produced are those that ascribe greater antiquity to al-Aqsa (e.g., that it was built by Adam or that Solomon renovated the compound), and he writes that "contemporary Muslim authors are turning a collection of ancient traditions into a myth, one intended to accord Jerusalem and the sacred Islamic site within it, special historical and Islamic primordial depth" (Reiter 2008, 26). Other efforts include extending the period of time in which Jerusalem served as the first *qibla* from seventeen months to more than four years in order to intensify Jerusalem's importance. The Isra' and Mi'raj, the Night Journey of the Qur'an's Sura 17 and the Prophet's ascension to heaven are understood to have taken place earlier than the Hijra (when Muhammad left Mecca), both of which are intended to equate Mecca and Jerusalem. Reiter finds many pictorial representations that draw this equation, although medieval representations show only the Ka'bah (a shrine in the Great Mosque in Mecca, from where Muhammad ascended to heaven, considered to be the most sacred by Muslims), and he concludes that both the Isra' and the Mi'raj were "dormant" concepts until the 1920s when Hajj Amin al-Husseini initiated his own campaigns, far less successful than the campaigns that have gone on since 1967. Indeed, the popularity of annual Isra' and Mi'raj day in the Palestinian and the larger Arab and Muslim world attests to the intensification of Jerusalem's sacral importance. Likewise, the obligation to visit al-Aqsa has become common discourse, along with ideas that Jerusalem is Islam's defensive stronghold, and that Jerusalem is the place where the dead will be resurrected and to which the Muslim messianic figure will come at the end of time. All these are additional markers of this intensification.[4]

Part of this new Islamic discourse is intended to deny the authenticity of the Jewish connection to Jerusalem. Reiter begins with Arafat's statement when he was visited in Ramallah by Arab leaders from Israel telling him that Solomon's Temple was in Yemen. This was not Arafat's total detachment from reality and Reiter shows how this statement belongs to a very sophisticated discourse that has emerged since 1967 in new Islamic writing that disputes Jewish assertions regarding Jerusalem. The new claims are that the Jewish historical presence in the city was only brief; the Temple never existed and if it did it was Solomon's private chapel or prayer room; and the Western Wall or *kotel* is a Muslim holy site and was only interpreted by Jews as their holy site in the 19th and 20th centuries for political purposes. If Solomon had a temple it was none other than the al-Aqsa, which was built in the primordial past by Adam. But then Reiter points out that there are many Islamic texts that recognize the Temple and the Jewish presence in Jerusalem. These are authentic ancient Islamic motifs that are contradicted by Muslim writers since 1967. For example, and there are many others, Reiter (2008, 46) quotes Kamil al-Asali, a Palestinian-Jordanian historian, on the Jewish connection to the Temple Mount, as saying that all the things that are identified with the Jews on the Temple Mount are "all folklore, lacking any basis. . . . David and Solomon and all of the figures and patriarchs from Abraham on were raised by Islam to the status of prophets, and thus it is not surprising that structures and sites are associated with them. . . . Modern archeology has not succeeded

---

4. This idea that Jerusalem is the defensive stronghold was elaborated in several Hamas leaflets during the First Intifada where the Palestinian community as a whole was deemed *murabitun*, which refers to the Muslims who settled on the frontiers during the Muslim conquests. Their defense of the borders of the *ummah* was considered a religious obligation (see Mishal and Aharoni 1994).

in proving that the site on which the Temple stood is located in this place, since no remnants of the Temple have survived." This discursive negation of the claims to the existence of the Temple has a broad reception in the Muslim world and has thoroughly been incorporated into Muslim public awareness. Yet, Reiter notes that the classic Islamic view does not deny Jewish traditions, history, and heritage in general, or those aspects of Jewish tradition that connected to Jerusalem in particular.

Rites of Way: The Case of St. John's Hospice

In his book *Jerusalem and Its Role in Islamic Solidarity*, Yitzhak Reiter notes that sovereignty changes the meaning of sacred; we, too, underscored that ritual rites and meanings are determined by political rights and meanings. This is essentially our third axiom: "Rites depend on Rights—the very construction and officiation of any sacred site, no matter how meager, has a component of authority. The idea of 'freedom of religion'—religion outside the control and domination by the state is a very new historical form." This can be seen in a number of cases in Jerusalem, perhaps most directly in how the Status Quo in the Holy Places functions.

Shortly after the Six-Day War the Knesset approved "The Law for the Protection of the Holy Places" (June 27, 1967), which stipulated that "the Holy Places will be protected from desecration or any other harm or anything that might affect the access of believers or their feelings for those places." The law most importantly gave the management of the holy places to the religious communities that maintained them. This reconfirmed the Status Quo in the Christian and Muslim holy places in Jerusalem, and the only place where this significantly changed was at the Western Wall. The British had failed to clarify the management of control of the Western Wall in the years following the 1929 violence and preferred to allow it to remain this way. With the Jordanians controlling the Old City and East Jerusalem, the management of the Western Wall was a moot question, although the Jordanians failed to meet the requirements of the 1948 armistice, which provided for free access to the Western Wall, the Jewish cemeteries and tombs on the Mount of Olives, and the Tomb of Rachel.

Meron Benvenisti (1976, 263–66; 1983, 42–43) points out that the communities in the Holy Places—both Muslim and Christian—fully expected the Israelis to change the status quo in their locations. Certainly this was the case for the Christians, who were experiencing lingering disputes over the control of ritual time and space at the Church of the Holy Sepulcher and the Church of the Nativity. However, the Knesset's "Law for the Protection of the Holy Places," regardless of whether it was fully implemented or not, was motivated by the values of a liberal democracy. Abba Eban, the Israeli foreign minister, took full advantage of the law to underscore that the unification of Jerusalem was thus "an advance toward the situation of peace, reverence, sanctity, and free access that is the main objective of the world community in relation to the historic and religious interests here involved." He termed the law "[t]he first law in modern history enacted for the protection of Holy Places from desecration." He also stressed Israel's willingness to hand over the holy places to independent management. The state had no interest beyond protecting them and providing access to them. Eban said, "Never in human memory has there been any disposition by any government in the region to exclude the Holy Places from its exclusive and unilateral control. This therefore is a statement of great significance, not only in the history of our region, but in the history of mankind" (Benvenisti 1976, 266). Of course, this statement failed to include the British, who had done virtually the same thing in their principle of "exclusive and unilateral control," which guided their attempts to neutralize the rivalries between Christian communities. The Catholic view that they were the "first among equals" would provide many difficulties in the years that followed.

There was a deep irony in the Law for the Protection of the Holy Places. The Knesset's liberal democratic values foreclosed the possibility of controlling the Temple Mount. Religious nationalists in the next decades came to understand this as a ceding of the religious and national center of the Jewish people to profane outsiders and there would be efforts, both legal and extra-legal to change the status quo on the Temple Mount.[5] Here, even though the Law for the Protection of Holy Places gave

5. For important summaries of the efforts to change the status quo on the Temple Mount, see Friedland and Hecht (1991), Reiter (2002), and Ramon (2002).

control to the Muslims, it did not disconnect politics from the meaning of the Holy Places.

We can also illustrate this third axiom through an event that took place in April 1990 when a group of approximately 150 Jewish settlers moved into the St. John's Hospice in the Christian Quarter of the Old City, relatively close to the Church of the Holy Sepulcher. Throughout the 1980s Jewish groups were first reclaiming and purchasing Jewish residences within the Old City, and then in several other locations outside the Old City in Silwan, Ir David, Sheikh Jarrah, and Keren Ha-Mufti. Each case was contested in the streets and in the courts. Menachem Klein (2001, 263–64) notes that

> from the beginning, these purchases by Jews have led to a series of legal battles between the purchasing organizations and the Palestinian owners, and in most cases the purchasers have won. . . . The evacuation of the Arab tenants has produced not only legal and political questions, but also moral dilemmas and human tragedies. The Jozlan family, with 28 members, had lived in Silwan for 32 years. The court ruled in favor of the Jewish purchaser, the Elad organization, and the family was required to evacuate the house so that the new owners could take possession. The fact that the Jozlan family possessed an official certificate from the Jewish National Fund testifying to their having saved Jews during the 1929 riots was no avail. Elad activists explained their attitude towards the Jozlans: "The most important thing in this place is its location and importance. . . . [T]o leave and not evacuate them is to miss the most important thing, which is that the City of David is ours."

Here, the settlers understood that they were reclaiming the City of David, the foundational beginning of the Jewish nation, and what they learned to do over more than two decades was to utilize the power of the Israeli state. In some cases the government supported their efforts of settlement, and in other cases they cleverly exploited rivalries within the national government, much like their predecessors in the Gush Emunim settlement movement had done in the West Bank and Gaza beginning in 1968 and continuing to the present.

The St. John's Hospice is a seventy-two room building that historically had housed Greek Orthodox pilgrims to the city. On April 11, 1990, members of the Yeshivat Ateret Cohanim—which was, at that time, already well-experienced in urban settlement—moved into the building. Since the early 1980s, the group almost exclusively focused its educational activities around preparing its students for the return of the sacrificial ritual of a third messianic temple and occupying residences in the Muslim and Christian quarters of the Old City. The settlers had rented the building from its Greek Orthodox owners through a Panamanian holding company. The move triggered a demonstration outside the hospice in which the Greek Orthodox patriarch was pushed and shoved. Ten Christian denominations closed their churches for one day in protest. This included the Church of the Holy Sepulcher, which closed its doors for the first time in 800 years (Murphy 1990, A4).

The incident with the Orthodox patriarch has been described as a public humiliation. Here is how Michael Dumper (1997, 194–95) describes the incident:

> The attempt by the Patriarch Diodorus to restore control over the building led to a physical confrontation during which the Patriarch himself was pushed to the floor by the settlers. The public humiliation of the Patriarch symbolizes the political changes that were taking place within church-state relations in East Jerusalem. Here was the leader of the most ancient Christian community in Jerusalem, who had cooperated with the Israeli state at the risk of his own standing among his community, acceded in the sale and leasing to Israel of precious land in the city, successfully obstructed for many years any concerted Christian opposition to the Israeli annexation of the city, and allowed himself to be paraded by municipal officials as the authentic Christian response to Israeli rule; here he was treated by some North American roughnecks as if he was of no consequence whatsoever, and without any intervention by the Israeli government to restore his dignity and status.

Dumper's account seems intemperate. On May 20, 1990, the patriarch gave an interview that challenged the reading that Dumper gives to the incident. A reporter for the Cypriot newspaper *Alethia* asked, "Your Beatitude, is it true that you had been humiliated and beaten up by a group of Israeli soldiers in the course of the reaction and the protest during the events?"

The Patriarch responded that "the truth" was that he was pushed by the "protesting worshippers." (Consulate General of Israel in Los Angeles 1990). Note that the perpetrators of the incident are no longer settlers, nor the Israeli police. Ultimately, the courts forced the students out of the building and voided the rental agreement.

The incident at St. John's Hospice quickly became an international incident. John Cardinal O'Connor, archbishop of New York City, in an article in *Catholic New York* noted that the incident was part of a larger anti-Christian policy in the state of Israel. Teddy Kollek immediately responded with an open letter to the Archbishop. Noting that he found the incident reprehensible, Kollek urged Christian leaders in Jerusalem not to overreact, despite the pressure being brought to bear by the PLO (Kollek 1990).

On May 15, 1990, Chaim Herzog, then president of Israel, wrote to the Metropolitan Paisios, the Greek Orthodox primate of North and South America, concerning an article the primate had written. Herzog pointed out that the Greek Orthodox Church in Jerusalem refused to sell the property to two Jerusalem Christian groups who offered $2 million. They wanted more money, and they received it from the Jewish settler group. St. John's Hospice is not a few meters from the Church of the Holy Sepulcher as the primate had written, and as any visitor to site could see. Herzog wrote that the church did not protest the sale of property in the area of the Holy Sepulcher to Muslim residents of the city. He lamented that the protest was initiated only when it was discovered that Jews were involved in the transactions. Herzog underscored that the Hospice is not holy space and, accordingly, can be treated like any other high-priced real estate transaction between a buyer and a seller or lessor and lessee. He also noted the many other instances in which the Greek Orthodox Church sold properties owned by it to either Jews or Muslims.

Here, President Herzog alludes to the role of the Greek church as one of the major landowners in Jerusalem and to its selling or long-term leasing of land, usually through Armenian intermediaries—as was the case in the St. John's Hospice incident. President Herzog was critical of the description of the St. John's Hospice as a holy place, and certainly that critique might be valid for the Greek Orthodox who knew that the site was merely an abandoned hospice. But, for the settlers, this indeed was sacred real estate and the Israeli state had provided the mechanism for a "rite" of settlement. The settlers had paid $4 million to sublet the property. It was learned later in April that the Housing Ministry, run by David Levy in Yitzhak Shamir's caretaker government, had provided $1.8 million and these funds had been approved by the Finance Ministry (Brinkley 1990).

An important study yet to be done concerns how the settlers, from the takeover of the Park Hotel in Hebron in 1968 through the illegal settlement "hilltop" outposts built during the Barak and Sharon governments, utilized rituals to control the spaces they occupied. Here, the work of Neil Jarman (1997) and Jarman and Dominic Bryan (1996) on the Protestant and Catholic parades in Northern Ireland (which have often been the trigger for communal violence) is important to our discussion. Jarman and Bryan argue that the parades are staged in what they call "interface zones," where Protestant and Catholic neighborhoods abut. In some cases the interface zones have been cleared of any housing units as the result of the violence; in other cases the neighborhoods in the interfaces are divided by walls and fences designed to separate the communities. Jarman and Bryan argue that the parades are intended to convert the space of the opposing communities into the territory of the marchers, even if this is only temporary. The spatial areas that the settlers have chosen are as clear as the interface zones of the Protestant and Catholic neighbors in the urban arenas of Northern Ireland. During the first decade of settlement, the interface zones were between the communities. For example, the Yeshivat Ataret Cohanim was originally located on the border between the Jewish Quarter and the Muslim Quarter. Later in the 1980s and early 1990s, the Ataret Cohanim struck deep into the Muslim Quarter or, in this case, the Christian one. Despite the distances from the boundary interfaces, the settlement became the ritual of controlling space, and as is suggested by the admission that Israel had contributed to the leasing of the property, the ritual of settlement, the "rite," was connected to the "right" of the state.

Conclusion

Let us return to our collaboration and one of the themes of this volume. The primary focus of our research on Jerusalem is not political policy.

There are some political scientists who are now taking the issue of sacred space very seriously in their attempt to formulate policy. For example, Ron Hassner (2003) argues that there are two characteristics of sacred space that need to be reconsidered in finding political solutions to disputed sacred sites. These are centrality and exclusivity. He considers the two prevailing policy approaches to disputes over sacred space—the Hobbesian approach, which rejects the symbolic dimension of these disputes and treats them as if they were standard territorial disputes, and the Huntingtonian view that these disputes are the products of religious forces that are beyond the influence of political actors. Hassner offers an alternative to these that takes the indivisibility of sacred space seriously "while considering the ways to problematize the social production and deconstruction of the sacred in pursuit of a solution for these disputes" (ibid.).

We are interested in understanding and interpreting the structure of sacred space. The concreteness of that space is at the center of our work. Concreteness means that sacred spaces have real histories and thus are fluid (not the static space that Mircea Eliade and many others within the phenomenological study of religion have described). Concreteness also means that sacred spaces have real politics (again not the apolitical spaces envisioned and described by the phenomenologists). Both of these, history and politics, suggest a number of important dynamics that we have described in this chapter. Sacred spaces are always being built and rebuilt; their sacredness is elaborated, changed, and expanded with meanings overlaying other older or contemporary meanings. The meanings of sacred spaces are much like the concentric rings of an onion. Sacred spaces are not separate from the powers of the state; they are deeply connected to the state in whatever form that takes. Stated differently, sacred spaces are deeply connected to sovereignty or the ability of the state to control its boundaries and control the meanings that are given to its important national sites.

The Israelis did something that was unique in terms of modern states. In the days and weeks immediately following the Six-Day War, the Jewish state did not attempt to erase the Muslim presence and authority on the Temple Mount/Noble Sanctuary. The Muslims perhaps expected that; certainly the Christians in the Church of the Holy Sepulcher jockeyed to exploit the change of sovereignty in the Old City. Each community hoped to claim more time and space for themselves in the central holy place of Catholic, Orthodox, and Middle Eastern Christianities. But the Israelis did nothing to upset the status quo in the holy places. Perhaps the one exception was the Abu Madyan waqf adjacent to the Western Wall. Indeed, the expectation of changes of ritual subsequent to changes of control and presence in the holy places confirms our third axiom that ritual rites depend on state rights and power. We believe that the Law for the Protection of the Holy Places was motivated by the values of a liberal democracy, an Israel very different than the Israel that recently celebrated the fortieth anniversary of the Six-Day War.

Of course, there will be those who will counter that Israel was motivated by a more practical concern to ensure the support of the international community for its rule of East Jerusalem and a united Jerusalem. But the Israeli state could not have anticipated how the sanctity of Jerusalem would be built in subsequent decades by Jews, Christians, and Muslims. By allowing Muslims to control the Temple Mount, the Jewish state set into motion forces that could not be managed. The Israelis had ceded authority over the central holy place of the Jews to the control of the Muslims. It would not take very long before this symbolic vacuum at the center of the national history of the Jewish people created a new generation of activists who would challenge the presence of the profaning "other" at the birthplace of the nation (see Friedland and Hecht 1991, 1996b; Shragai 1995; Reiter 2002; Ramon 2002). Some of these activists would read the space of the Temple Mount as a ritual site that was bound up in *halakchic* issues, which were once thought to be insurmountable until the "days of the messiah." Others read the space as national space—the place where David had founded the Kingdom of the Jews. In either case, the absence of Jewish control at the center was not just a scandal; the nation was incomplete. Hindu nationalists realized the very same contradiction with the Muslims occupying the birthplace of the Hindu nation at Ayodhya. In both cases, the absence of the exercise of the "rights of way" provoked not only a ritual contradiction, but also a national one.

3

Jerusalem in Religious Studies

The City and Scripture

MICHAEL ZANK

IN THIS CHAPTER, I reflect on Jerusalem as a holy city from the perspective of religious studies. It is obvious that Jerusalem and its holy places exert extraordinary attraction. The city means a lot to many people. Despite the many books that have been written about the city, including a few widely noted recent ones by Simon Goldhill (2008), Simon S. Montefiore (2011), and James Carroll (2011), not to mention the amazing Karen Armstrong (1997), retelling the city's history alone is not enough to understand Jerusalem's peculiar status. If our focus is on the religious qualities of the city, the history we're interested in is the history of the formation of Jerusalem as a religious symbol. Needless to say, the considerations here presented are merely gesturing toward a more sustained theoretical engagement.

There are several obstacles to the study of Jerusalem from a religious studies perspective. The first problem is the vastness of the topic. There are four thousand years of documented history to consider, each period requiring different specialized knowledge. When it comes to conceptualizing Jerusalem's religious qualities, one is drawn into a maze of different conceptions of the holy. And finally, the fact that Jerusalem is not simply a holy place but a concatenation of holy places in a living and contested city makes it difficult to say where religion ends and politics begin.

The modern conversation about religion has been shaped by two ideas: the Protestant focus on the inner life and the Enlightenment idea of a separation of church and state. But Jerusalem's character and status were shaped in an age when public sacrifices and rites of purification still mattered and politics and theology were commingled. Western educated people tend to see holiness as an inner or private quality rather than an aspect of public order. It therefore takes a certain effort to imagine what Jerusalem's holiness meant to pre-modern people and how our modern sensitivities have reconfigured Jerusalem as a symbol of the divine. Furthermore, many of the contemporary tensions over how to handle Jerusalem arise from the fact that a plurality of pre-modern ideas of holiness persist and compete with a plurality of modern ones, not to speak of ideologies of secularism and nationalism. No shared concept of holiness prevails in this city holy to Jews, Christians, and Muslims, making it a daunting task to describe and classify the city's symbolic qualities beyond merely cataloging them. To gain a point of departure for our investigation, something by which we may orient ourselves in the history of Jerusalem's holiness, I propose to focus on Scripture as the source of the city's symbolic meaning.[1]

To begin, I will review what Jerusalem classically or conventionally means to Jews, Christians, and Muslims in symbolic terms. I then briefly restate why it is Scripture in particular that has made Jerusalem what it is for us as Jews, Christians, and Muslims. The next question I consider is how Jerusalem's "extraordinary" holiness to Jews, Christians, and Muslims can be distinguished from the "ordinary" holiness it enjoyed before the rise of Scripture. Having distinguished two periods in the history of Jerusalem as a symbol, namely, before and since Scripture, I turn to the question of periodization as a device of historiography, propose a division of Jerusalem's history as a symbol of the sacred on the basis of Scripture as a turning point, and articulate some of the presuppositions of this new periodization. The last section shows how Scripture and the art of reading

---

1. In this chapter I use "Scripture" (singular, capitalized) to refer to a complex but unified phenomenon of authoritative canons of holy writ and their attendant interpretive traditions, a phenomenon similarly constitutive to several traditions, including Jews, Samaritans, Christians, Muslims, and Zoroastrians.

fostered by scriptural religions have shaped the ways in which pilgrims experience Jerusalem, namely, as a text to be studied and deciphered. I end with a few pedagogical considerations.

Jerusalem as a Symbol

A symbol is "something visible that by association or convention represents something else that is invisible."[2] Similarly, according to the *Shorter Oxford English Dictionary*, a symbol may be described as an "outward sign" that is correlated with an inner meaning.[3] The symbol is more generally defined as "a thing conventionally regarded as representing, typifying, or recalling something else by possessing analogous qualities or by association in fact or thought; *esp.* a material object representing an abstract concept or quality."[4] How does Jerusalem symbolize? The religious traditions under consideration teach us to consider the city a symbol, and I consider this symbolizing or interaction between a concrete and manifest thing and its invisible meanings, known by revelation only, as symbolic of how these traditions work. This symbolizing is emblematic of scriptural traditions more generally.[5]

The invisible or higher reality represented by the city of Jerusalem is the divine city or, rather, those attributes of the divine that can be represented, such as perfect governance, an insight the ancients intuited from the regularity of the motion of the heavenly bodies.[6] All ancient cities were configured to serve the divine powers that govern the forces of nature and

---

2. See *AudioEnglish.org* (2005, s.v. "symbolisation").

3. See *Shorter Oxford English Dictionary on Historical Principles* (2003, s.v. "symbol").

4. Ibid.

5. Compare to Wheatley (1969). Wheatley, professor of geography at the University of London, speaks of the city in general, whereas my study of Jerusalem attempts to determine *how* Jerusalem is configured as a symbol. I agree with Wheatley that the city as such has symbolic qualities and am delighted that urban geography is paying heed to this kind of hermeneutic approach.

6. On the significance of astronomy to the ancient conceptions of governance, see, e.g., Halpern (2003).

protect the citizenry in return for their devotion. Cities and gods stand in a mutually beneficial, though incontrovertibly hierarchical relation. Jerusalem's uniqueness rests not in its function as a temple city but in its transformation into the token of a new, more dialectic form of belief in divine presence, represented through markers of absence, memory and anticipation such as the remnants of the ancient temple (Western Wall), the empty tomb of Christ, or the rock of Prophet Muhammad's mystical ascent.

In Hebrew, the city can be referred to as *ir ha-qadosh*, "city of the holy," that is, the city of a deity that the scriptural traditions consider sacrosanct and beyond representation. Like other ancient civilizations, Jewish tradition forbade the mundane use of the name of God for fear of abusing it. When the temple was in existence, before 70 CE, the high priest would call on the name of the deity on the Day of Atonement. After the temple was destroyed, the presence of the divine indwelling or *shekhinah* was thought to linger near its ruins, hence the desire to be as near as possible to the place where God—or more precisely, his sacred name—used to be called upon. There is a paradox at the core of the rabbinic tradition, namely, that although divine redemption requires collective implementation of the Mosaic Torah, the fulfillment of many commandments requires the existence of a temple where alone many of the cultic obligations of the Torah can be enacted. Redemption and the coming of the messianic age therefore entail a rebuilding of the temple, but the temple needs to exist for the commandments to be fulfilled that might hasten redemption. As long as Jews held no political sway over the territory of the former temple, the goal of rebuilding remained within the spheres of prayer and mysticism. Nineteenth-century liberal Jews even completely disavowed the idea of a resumption of the sacrificial services and eliminated all references to a return to Zion and rebuilding of the temple from their prayers. All this changed with the modern Zionist movement and the establishment of the State of Israel in 1948. With the June 1967 conquest of what is now often referred to as the "sacred basin," the coming of redemption has become dangerously real and a powerful incentive for Jews, as well as Christians, to force the end.

For Christians,[7] the holiness of Jerusalem is located where Christ, the son of God and redeemer, walked, suffered, died, appeared after his resurrection, and was taken up into the heavens. Christian tradition has identified these places, sometimes on the basis of sound historical information and sometimes on the basis of mere tradition. The importance of these places has been to allow Christians to physically and emotionally relive the particular events in the life, death, and resurrection of Christ in their putative original locations. Of equal importance to the location of the suffering and death of Jesus is the place where Christ was born, which is enshrined in the Church of the Nativity in Bethlehem. Since the fourth century, when pious attention shifted for the first time to the events and places of the life of Jesus, of the saints, and of the prophets who had foretold the coming of the Savior, the Holy Land as a whole became the subject of learned attention and verification; Eusebius of Caesarea's *Onomasticon* (2005) identified the villages, cities, and landscapes of Palestine by their biblical names, and commemorative buildings, churches, basilicas, and monasteries were established to allow Christian pilgrims to experience the factuality of the history of Christ and the saints. The reality of the sacred places reaffirmed the authority of the sacred scriptures and of their plain meaning, which the Orthodox Church defended against Gnostics and Docetists. The locations of the events of the life, death, and resurrection of Christ were mapped onto Roman Aelia Capitolina (a city built by Emperor Hadrian on the site of Jerusalem, which was then in ruins) and the landscape of Aelia was mapped onto Scripture. City and Scripture mutually reinforced one another and provided a concrete scaffold for the edifice of Christian doctrine and its manifestation in a Greco-Latin-Byzantine *Hierapolis Hierousalem* (Greek for "holy city Jerusalem").

Islamic tradition states that the first direction of prayer (in Arabic, *qibla*) was the "city of the holy house" (*madinat bayt al-maqdis*). The Qur'an

7. When speaking of Christians, Jews, or Muslims in broadly abstract terms I mean ideal types that represent common notions that may be ignored or disavowed by particular individuals or contested by entire sub-groups. Generalizations of this kind are reductions inevitable in expositions, such as the present one, that paint in broad strokes.

refers to a "distant sanctuary" (*masjid al-aqsa*) where Prophet Muhammad was shown divine secrets and the Hadith affirms that the place of the prophet's "Night Journey" (the *Isra'*) and ascent (the *Mi'raj*) was none other than Jerusalem. Muslims understand Muhammad's mission as a restoration of the original religion of Abraham, as a completion of the chain of prophets, and as a reiteration of the original intention of Allah. Islam completes, augments, and corrects rather than displaces its monotheistic competitors. Jewish and Christian presence in *Al Quds* and in the "House of Islam" more broadly, is not perceived as an aberration but as the norm. The early Arab Muslim rulers accordingly readmitted the Jews to Jerusalem. The manner in which most Muslim rulers, following law and precedent, have handled the plurality of communities attached to the Holy City is emblematic of Muslim attitudes toward Christians and Jews more broadly, which is grounded in the Qur'an's view of the place of the Jewish and Christian scriptures in the history of revelation.

Jews, Christians, and Muslims are attached to the Holy City, but just as their respective histories and collective memories are internally complex and different from one another, so Jerusalem entered into their respective collective experience and imagination in different ways. Jerusalem and ancient Jewish history are intimately connected, as is evident from Jerusalem's role in the sacred literature of the Jews, including but not limited to the Tanakh, which is also part of the Christian canon of sacred scriptures. Although the Qur'an places no particular emphasis on Jerusalem, this fact alone does not indicate how or why Jerusalem figures in Islamic history and imagination. Even though Jerusalem and other names of the city appear in Tanakh hundreds of times, the Torah refers to the city explicitly only once, namely, in Genesis 14:18–20 ("And Melchizedek king of Salem brought forth bread and wine[,]" etc.), a passage that raises more questions than it answers. What becomes clear when looking at Jewish, Christian, and Muslim traditions on Jerusalem and its holiness is that in all three traditions the notion of why Jerusalem is special is mediated or conveyed by instruction based on scripture, tradition, and interpretation. Jerusalem's symbolic meaning arises from the scriptures of the Jews, from the exemplary position of Jewish history and experience, as enshrined in these scriptures, and from the place of Israel's scriptural history in the Christian and Islamic understanding of the history of revelation and salvation.

Symbols are polyvalent and Jerusalem's meaning as a symbol is determined by the doctrines and traditions of each community. The communities in question derive their theological views from their respective canons of foundational writings, as well as from authoritative sources of interpretation. It is this whole conglomerate of mutually interpreting traditions that I call Scripture. The communities also interact with one another, and they do so not only in their constitutive phases, but also over long periods of time and under specific circumstances involving power differentials and other variables. Thus, Jerusalem's symbolic meaning unfolds in readings of multiple, but related, scriptures that take the city as a preeminent location in the unfolding of the mystery of divine providence.

Remarkably, far from having lost its luster, thinking in terms of divine providence continues to be relevant today. Modern historical consciousness may have dispensed with pre-modern notions of divine agency or governance, but whenever we invest "history" with teleological expectations of outcomes or resolutions, we invoke a notion borrowed from messianic or apocalyptic and hence providential thinking. Rather than a radical departure from the age of Scripture, the modern historical perspective remains indebted to Scripture. In some respects modern Protestant culture has made Scripture more immediately relevant to politics than it was in an age when the church tightly controlled access to biblical writings. I elaborate on this observation in the following section when I consider Jerusalem's configuration in the scriptural religions of Judaism, Christianity, and Islam. Using Scripture as a phenomenon in the history of religion that is shared by Jews, Christians, and Muslims, I divide the history of Jerusalem-*qua*-symbol into three "periods," namely, before Scripture, in Scripture, and since Scripture.

Why Scripture?

Jerusalem's religious character has been decisively shaped by religions that are based on related, though distinct, canonical sacred writings or scriptures. These texts don't exist in isolation but are always approached through authoritative commentary and in the context of institutional means of dissemination established in Jewish, Christian, and Muslim tradition. In the following I refer to Scripture as the sum-total of this type of literary-religious phenomenon, and I take it for granted that Jewish, Christian, and Muslim scriptures have been co-emerging since late antiquity. Scripture in the larger sense is the medium through which these communities have configured Jerusalem as an eminent token of divine providence. Providence itself is not exclusively a concern of "monotheistic" traditions, and it is not always based on sacred text. Rather, it is a fundamental assumption associated with any belief in anthropomorphic divine beings. In this regard, the Torah, the Gospel, and the Qur'an are not exceptional. What sets them apart is the claim to provide particularly *credible* evidence for belief in divine providence, evidence that lends authority to the laws and instructions conveyed in legal, prophetic, and other genres of exhortation on how the chosen community (Hebrew: *am yisrael*; Greek: *ekklesia*; Arabic: *umma*) and its members are to live their political, communal, and personal lives. Jerusalem's role in this system is neither simple nor uniform. Its history, often reduced to a simplified moral tale of disobedience and punishment (i.e., destruction), attests to divine justice. But the memory of Jerusalem as a divinely chosen cult center, enshrined in rabbinic law and liturgy, evokes desire for return, revival, and restoration. In contrast, the holy places of Christendom are objects of meditation on the mysteries of divine transcendence and immanence, and of the incarnation, death, and resurrection of Christ. The holy places of Islam, in turn, signify the connections between earlier and later prophecy and attest to the divinely sanctioned status of Islam as the restoration of the original religion of Abraham. All these are different conceptions of what makes Jerusalem a sacred place, and the list is not complete. But all of these are eminently *scriptural* aspects of Jerusalem's holiness.

Jerusalem attests to the truth of the sacred history (Latin: *storia sacra*) conveyed in Scripture; it constitutes a sacred place and includes sacred places foregrounded in Scripture and thus affirms the truths of Scripture. Scripture prompts the believers to attend to Jerusalem's history as an indicator of past divine intervention, as well as to the holy places as prompts for meditation on the dialectic of transcendence and immanence, divine presence and absence. For as long as Jerusalem has been elevated by Scripture, one of the sustained preoccupations pursued both within the city and from afar has been the study of text. Jerusalem is therefore, in the end, a perpetual prompt to engage with Scripture.

Jerusalem's Ordinary and Extraordinary Holiness

Scripture is what has made Jerusalem what it is to Jews, Christians, and Muslims. But this is true only from a particular point onwards, from a historical moment of whatever duration after which Jerusalem became the city of Scripture. But when did this moment occur, and what was the city before it became decisively shaped by Scripture? In other words, we need to ask what the city was *before Scripture*.

I stipulate that Jerusalem's holiness is not an innate quality of the city, its name, or its sacred landscape, but something that has changed over time and was decisively shaped by the holy text traditions of Jews, Christians, and Muslims. Let me try to state what this means.

Holiness as such may be a universal category in human culture, but scripture-based religions are constitutive of a particular set of civilizations and societies, with a peculiar interest in Jerusalem as a particularly holy place, if not the center of the universe. As a set of related traditions, the scriptural traditions of Judaism, Christianity, and Islam form a religious phenomenon sui generis, even though each of these scriptural traditions is also unique in its particulars. To determine whether, and if so, how, Scripture reconfigured the holiness of this particular city, we must contrast its holiness before and after the rise of the canonical writings of Jews, Christians, and Muslims. Let us first recall what we mean by "holy" in a more general sense.

Generally speaking, holiness is not a substance but a quality conferred on something that might otherwise be perfectly mundane. Holiness establishes a distinction. The holy cave or mountain is like other caves or mountains in every respect except for being set aside or identified as holy, namely, holy *to* someone (a god, a group of people) because of something that occurred there (a theophany), or because of its use for a particular purpose (sacrifice, oracle). The Hebrew word for "holy," *qadosh*, literally means separate, distinct, set aside. It thus carries the connotation of a taboo, a sacred precinct, something dangerous and untouchable, but always in contrast to the mundane, ordinary, harmless. The sacred evokes a sense of vital rather than trivial difference. This is true of every sacred person, object, place, or time. The sacred can be profaned and violated, but it cannot be ignored. One who comes upon the sacred by accident is frightened by the possibility of having incurred divine wrath by inadvertent profanation. A case in point is Jacob's fear upon waking from a dream that made him realize that the ground on which he had slept was "none other but the House of God and the Gate of Heaven" (Gen. 28:10–22). Let us note at once that this definition applies as much to places sacred to the ancient Israelites as to places sacred to any of their neighbors in the ancient world.

What is a "holy city" and how does a city acquire holiness? The ancient city is always a sacred precinct, with the temple of the tutelary deity as the inner sanctum and residence of the god or gods. Usually, the founding of the city is enshrined in a myth that tells of a god, or the gods, as the founders of the city. This is true of the temple cities of the ancient Near East, such as Babylon (the name means "gate of the gods"). But it is also true of a city like Rome, which constitutes a sacred precinct whose boundaries are fixed by the plough drawn by sacred oxen, a fact that was commemorated in an annual ritual. The citizenries of Greek and Roman cities initially consisted of a few families in whose hands remained the sacred duties and priestly functions. In short, every ancient city is in some sense a holy precinct, distinct from its inhospitable or uncivilized surroundings. The Christian term "paganus" still carries with it the ancient distinction of the uncouth villager from the noble citizen.

According to the Hebrew Bible or the Old Testament, and in contrast to the lore about the founding of Rome by Romulus, Jerusalem was found, not founded. According to the Book of Joshua, the conquering Judahites destroyed Jerusalem by fire. According to the Book of Samuel and similar in Chronicles, David took the city by stealth but did not drive out its original inhabitants and the preexisting local elite continued to dwell alongside the Judahites and Benjaminites, on whose territorial boundaries the city was found. Ezekiel 16 depicts the city as a foundling of mixed Amorite and Hittite descent, discarded, found in its blood, and told by

YHWH to live. According to 1 Kings 8:29, Jerusalem was the city chosen by YHWH from among Israel's tribes for his name to reside.

The fact that Jerusalem can be said to have been destroyed, conquered by stealth, or found in its blood by YHWH, and yet be chosen for His name to reside, indicates that, at least *in Scripture*, the ancient Judahites have no sense of an essential connection with the city. Just as the promised land in general was inherited from its earlier inhabitants, Jerusalem, the last city to be conquered, fell to a people waging war in the name of YHWH. Once Jerusalem was theirs, the land had rest; hence the association of the reign of Solomon with a realm at peace. But Judah, and even the kingship of David, preceded Judahite occupation of Jerusalem and Solomonic temple building. Neither the prophetic historians nor the legalists of the Bible speak the language of mythology: there is only a faint and possibly polemical echo of the slaying of Tiamat in Genesis 1:2, and the gods do not extend the favor of building a city as a house for her slayer. Neither Canaanite nor Mesopotamian myths are invoked to explain the building of cities on earth. Instead we have a negative image of cities in general (the first one was built by Cain; the city of Babylon was a sign of human *hubris*), and a set of semi-nomadic herdsmen as Israel's patriarchs. Wanderings and peregrination are the pattern on which the biblical community is based, not city building. Heroic figures are the exception. If there is anything peculiar about the biblical view of the connection between the city and people of Judah it is that peoplehood, kingship, and worship of YHWH are only tenuously related to the place where these institutions eventually alight. To be sure, what I just described is exclusively based on literary evidence; once this literature was canonized and interpreted in light of later Jewish concerns (including destruction, banishment, and the Christian transformation of the holy land), the tenuousness of the relation between the Jews and Jerusalem gave way to an elaborate mysticism of holy place.

We must assume that, for the ancient Judahites, Jerusalem's holiness was more or less like that of other cities. If the city was holy at all, it was, so to speak, an *ordinary* holy city. Jerusalem served as a royal and priestly center since before the Israelite conquest. If the story about Melchizedek in Genesis 14 is anything to go by, the kings of Jerusalem served as priests of the "Most High." This "Most High" (*el elyon*) was not an exclusively Israelite deity but a divinity revered by the elites of various late Bronze Age and Iron Age Canaanite societies. The city's original tutelary deity, reflected in the city's pre-Israelite name, was *shalem* (Salem), the Evening Star of Canaanite mythology. Jerusalem's sacredness was thus easily recognizable from the outside, since the character of this sacredness was akin to that enjoyed by other eastern Mediterranean royal or temple cities. The institutions and personages that shaped ancient Jerusalem thus participated in the *koine*, or common symbolic vocabulary, of the ancient world.

In contrast, the Jerusalem of the past 1,700 years has been an *extraordinary* holy city, a city sometimes shared, sometimes contested, by three extraordinary religious movements. These movements are often referred to as Abrahamic or monotheistic, but the aspect that interests me most is that they are "revealed" or scriptural traditions. The Muslim tradition, in an astute phenomenological recognition of the essence of the matter, speaks of these and other communities as "people of the book," recognizing sacred scriptures as what unites communities and distinguishes them from others.[8] Scripture, in the broadest sense, is what distinguishes a "revealed" tradition from its "pagan" antecedents. What I mean by Scripture in this broad sense is a plurality of related, yet distinct, canons of sacred texts that are inextricably linked to particular histories of reception, including traditions of commentary, embellishment, expansion, and interpretation. Scripture is passed on in well-developed scholarly institutions (the seminary, the yeshiva, the madrasa) where it is learned by heart and diligently studied. I take this complex and integrated cluster of canonical texts and authoritative interpretations as the decisive source of Jerusalem's holiness in the eyes of Muslims, Christians, and Jews. That is, from a religious studies standpoint what matters first and foremost is not the city as such, but the city as a symbol shaped by Scripture.

8. Early Muslims recognized other communities as "people of the book," for example Zoroastrians and Sabians, that are not based on the biblical tradition. To be precise, the phenomenon of "Scripture" that I am referring to here is thus not limited to the three book religions that are related by their common reverence for a particular line of prophetic figures, most significantly the figure of Abraham.

To be sure, in order to understand how Muslim, Jewish, and Christian attachments to Jerusalem are shaped by their respective scriptures, it is not enough to look for particular passages in sacred books that may or may not even refer to the city. We also need to pay attention to other means of dissemination and reinforcement of meaning, such as customs and practices shaped by the desire of connecting with the realities conveyed by Scripture and of living one's life in accordance with its precepts. These practices include rites of pilgrimage but also the representation of the city from afar in any form, including visual art and architecture (including churches and synagogues "oriented" toward the holy city), biblio-drama, hymnic, paraphrastic, and homiletical genres of literature, and sacred landscapes (e.g., stations of the cross).[9] As may be imagined, the economy of representation is frequently affected not just by religious, cultural, and economic factors but also by political interests, such as the exploitation of pious attachments to Jerusalem for the sake of propaganda, especially in times of war or contestation.[10]

The central issue, the essential connection between city and Scripture, is the *storia sacra* or history as the locus of divine providence. More precisely, since the biblical-qur'anic scriptures combine the issuance of divine commands with the story of how those obliged by these commands fared in history, Jerusalem—or rather its history—functions (in Scripture) as an indicator of the truth and seriousness (i.e., the holiness) of the commanding voice of the law. The fate of Jerusalem, as a synecdoche of Jewish history, is paradigmatic for Jews, Christians, and Muslims in that it reveals the logic, justice, and inevitability of divine providence in the form of reward and punishment. Furthermore, since the biblical-qur'anic scriptures are not just a record of the past but an imperative to those addressed by them, Jerusalem's ongoing fate remains implicated in how we apply the scriptural imperative of covenant and obligation to ourselves. To be sure, the

9. The "exportation" of Jerusalem in artifacts and architecture, a vast topic, was first made a comprehensive subject of investigation in Wharton (2006).

10. As an example of aggressive naming, consider the Palestinian Islamic Jihad's Al Quds Brigades.

imperatives that Jews, Christians, and Muslims derive from their respective scriptures differ in many ways. These differences are a major source of inter-community polemics. Believers frequently claim that others derived the wrong imperatives from scripture and condemn one another as *infideles, perfideles,* heretics, *qufr, minim,* etc. (Our traditions love to insult one another, but they love to insult deviants within their own respective traditions even more.)

The transformation of Jerusalem from an ordinary holy city of the ancient southern Levant into the holy city of Jews, Christians, and Muslims, is a significant moment not only in the city's character and function, but also indicates a shift in Roman political theology, which became a model for the early Muslims as well. To the extent that Rome, or rather Byzantium, became the model for a plurality of monotheistic empires—including the Muslim caliphate, as well as the Holy Roman Empire founded by Charlemagne (who is said to have held the keys to the holy city, presented to him upon his coronation by Caliph al-Rashid)—this shift in Jerusalem's function and meaning indicates a significant paradigmatic shift in civilizational history from "paganism" to what I would like to call *biblicism,* a Judeo-Christian-Islamic phenomenon of political theology based on the biblical-qur'anic scriptures. At the very moment when Roman Aelia (the military colony established by Hadrian in place of the earlier Jerusalem) was dismantled and biblical Jerusalem was excavated under the watchful eye of Empress Helena Augusta, Rome—a major non-Jewish civilization and empire—inscribed itself into the providential history of Scripture. To Gibbon, this may have been the beginning of the decline and fall of the Roman Empire. To us, it is an inaugural moment in the political-theological history of an empire shaped by its engagement with Judeo-Christian Scripture, a moment when imperial power was imbued with the sanction of a divine providence conferred by the merger of biblical prophecy and imperial power.

The History of Jerusalem as a Question of Periodization

Historians address the dialectic of continuity and discontinuity by dividing history into periods. In the case of Jerusalem, it is conventional to distinguish between pre-Israelite and Israelite periods; first and second temple periods; Roman and Byzantine periods; early Muslim, Crusader, Mamluk, and Ottoman periods; the period of the Mandate, the time of the divided city, and the current, post-1967 period of Israeli dominance. This seems straightforward enough.

While certainly useful as a first orientation, periodization comes with problems of its own and it often reinforces unstated presuppositions. It obscures continuities that extend from one period to another; it privileges sovereignty and subordinates other more limited kinds of presence; it looks to power as a unifying principle and eclipses subordinate pluralities; it seduces us to assume that there are concrete beginnings and ends to historical processes by associating them with the ascent to power and the deaths of great men, which also has the effect of obscuring processes of longer duration, as has been pointed out by the French *Annales* school.

The device of periodization itself is as ancient as mythology and historiography. The Achaemenid Persians described themselves as the legitimate heirs to the great empires that came before them, going back to Sumer and Agade. The divine sanction of imperial rule remained the same, even as dynasties came and went. While the Persians considered themselves the third and last in a sequence of empires, the authors of the Daniel apocalypse extended the schema to a sequence of four empires: at the appointed time, the entire age of historical rulers will come to an end, giving way to the age of divine governance, the messianic age.

Every historian struggles with the organization of inchoate material into manageable units. To separate historical data into clusters that amount to clearly delimited periods entails interpretation, and every judgment is subject to debate. By foregrounding the question of how Jerusalem became the symbol that it has been for the monotheistic traditions and by making the periodization of Jerusalem's history dependent on this question, I achieve a kind of shift in perspective. Familiar (or at least widely known) material is presented in an unfamiliar chronological framework. This achieves several goals. I make it clear what this history is about. The story I tell is not that of the domination of the city by a sequence of empires, but the history of its meanings, a kind of history of Jerusalem-related mentalities. By proceeding as I do, I remind my students that the division of history into periods is always guided by some sort of antecedent assumptions we rely on as we organize the manifold material of history into manageable and meaningful units. By echoing the tradition of dividing "world-history" into a few periods or stages, I make it evident that even schemata that we normally employ without blinking, such as the division of history into ancient, medieval, and modern periods and notions of historical linearity and teleology, are based on speculative or culturally specific conceptions of history and based on tacit meta-historical assumptions.

The periodization I suggest also has the effect of making visible and relevant the profoundly significant ways in which Jews, Christians, and Muslims are contemporaries. They inhabit the same space in historical terms, rather than simply following one upon the other. Islam may have been formed after Judaism and Christianity, but neither of these earlier communities is identical with "biblical Israel," even though Jews and Christians understand themselves as "Israel" or "the new Israel," respectively. Christianity may have Jewish roots, but all three communities relate to a shared pool of sacred texts and traditions that predate the Judaism that was formed in response to the Roman destruction of Jerusalem. Christianity and Islam may be the daughter-religions of ancient Judaism, but all three have also been competitors and functional contemporaries.

After, before, and in Scripture

If the above is valid (or at least pedagogically useful as a technique of estrangement), then we can state the following: Jerusalem is a city significant to many communities (resident and nonresident) whose fate over the centuries has been determined by certain canons of scripture and their competing authoritative interpretations. It is a point in space where certain "religions of the book" converge and where their concerns with memory, with the presence of the holy, and with the expectation of redemption intersect.

If the current age can be seen as significantly configured by canons of sacred scriptures and authoritative bodies of interpretation (as well as by modes of resistance to the authority of Scripture), then we may also state that there was a time "before Scripture" when Jerusalem was not configured by sacred canons and their competing interpretations, when it simply was not what it has been since Scripture has played a role in the making of Jerusalem's character and history.[11]

For example, the Amarna letters from the fourteenth century BCE testify to the existence of a typical late Bronze Age Canaanite city-state by the name of Urushalim that was a vassal of Egypt, maintained political and economic relations with other Canaanite city-states and was threatened by a class of people called *hapiru*. None of these facts appear in the biblical scriptures exactly as they appear in these letters, although it is possible that some of the historical circumstances that emerge from the Amarna correspondence are nevertheless remembered by the biblical historians and reflected in some aspects of the biblical tradition. Contrasting biblical literature with the evidence from the Amarna letters and from other epigraphic evidence (such as the Egyptian execration texts from the eighteenth century BCE where the city's name is first mentioned) allows us to realize some of the ideological tendencies at work in the biblical texts. Most importantly, however, this juxtaposition helps us to distinguish between the city in Scripture and the city before Scripture.

There is then not only a "before" and a "since Scripture," but also a third period—in chrono/logical terms: the second or middle "period." This is what we might call the period *of* Scripture, or more accurately: the city as it appears *in* Scripture.

Aside from the complicated questions of canon formation, we ought to distinguish between authorial intention or plausible first reception of texts, as far as these are retrievable, and the meanings that these texts attained once they became part of a scriptural canon. The texts have come down to us in edited and contextualized form (each biblical "book" is really an intermediate canon or an archive in the Derridian sense (cf.

11. This insight is based on an idea expressed by Leo Strauss in a 1930 essay titled "Religiöse Lage der Gegenwart" (see Strauss 1997, 377–90). Under the influence of Franz Rosenzweig's concept of revelation, Strauss credits Maimonides with the thought that revelation constituted a further difficulty for philosophers added to the "natural" difficulties of philosophizing known to the Greeks. A similar historical schema appears in a nearly contemporaneous essay by Strauss's friend Gerhard Krüger. I thank Thomas Meyer for drawing my attention to the latter essay.

Derrida 1996), but they may yield insights into radical or contradictory views that, once edited and canonized, became neutralized by integration into more conciliatory or piously conservative contexts. To be sure, the tendency of the earlier strata may be obscured by a history of reception guided by authoritative translations, paraphrasing, retelling, and other strategies of interpretation (midrash, allegoresis, etc.).

The ultimate form of Scripture as a complex artifact constituted by textual traditions, editorial interventions, canonical framing, and interpretation is its complete rewriting in light of the sensitivities of a later age. This is the case with the Book of Chronicles, which—though it appears in the scriptural canon of Jews and Christians—constitutes a pious correction and retelling of Samuel and Kings. It is also the case with the Qur'an, which "restores" the original revelation in form of a polemic against its Christian and Jewish "distortions." The Christian New Testament reflects an intermediate step toward rewriting scriptural revelation in that it lets the original Scripture stand next to new canonical texts that disclose its "true" meaning (in this case: the once and for all "fulfillment" of the prophecies "contained" in Scripture). Further intermediate forms are the numerous pious retellings of biblical stories (such as the Life of Adam and Eve). The Qur'an represents the extreme case where the oral tradition has virtually emancipated itself from the biblical canons so that pious commitment to revelation requires a complete reiteration of the original revelation, purified of the dross accrued by unreliable transmission. To avoid the opprobrium of "innovation," the Qur'an is revered as the exact copy of an "uncorrupted original" that just happens to conform with the established sensitivities of an oral tradition that, indeed, had intervened to deal with a literal sense of *taurat* (Torah) and *injil* (cf. *evangelion*, a Greek and early Christian term for "gospel") that, by then, had become highly problematic and contested.

The period (or phenomena) reflected *in* the texts that became Scripture resembles what is conventionally called the "biblical" period. It seems to me that expressions such as "biblical Jerusalem" or "biblical Israel" are hybrids that are not usually seen for what they are, but are used as if "biblical" signified a historical epoch (such as when God still spoke through his prophets; or the time from David to Jesus). What "biblical" denotes is a literary phenomenon (or a theological doctrine) that is superimposed on historical phenomena that are described and reflected in this literature (or spoken of as significant events in the economy of salvation). But the naïve conflation of the historical and the literary (or theological) is not a reason to dismiss the term altogether. As long as one keeps the historical distinct from the literary, the qualification of a period as "biblical" may still be useful.

What biblical means conventionally, however, is not what I mean by the city *in* Scripture. When referring to something "biblical," the post-biblical traditions—traditions that acknowledge and treat a certain body of texts as canonical, as a binding rule of law or faith—mean something unified in the sense that they make these internally diverse texts appear supportive of later doctrine. Our traditions take recourse to authoritative instruments of interpretation precisely because the biblical canon is internally diverse and full of contradictions. Religious reading inevitably harmonizes even when, as frequently in midrash, it initially raises problems requiring reconciliation. We require text *and* interpretation, Torah *and* midrash, written *and* oral Torah, Old Testament *and* New Testament, Qur'an *and* Hadith, Bible *and* doctrinal authority of the Church, etc. Even the Protestant reformers, who placed vernacular Scriptures into the hands of common believers, could not resist the temptation of helping untutored readers along by reorganizing the canonical order of the books, demoting certain books to the status of Apocrypha, and highlighting certain passages in print.[12] No Bible-based tradition is without its particular ways, means, and methods of interpretation. The term "biblical" usually means this conglomerate of Scripture and interpretation, even where it is used (as in Protestantism) as an attack on someone else's manner of controlling the ambit of biblical meanings. "Bible" and "biblical" are relative terms.

What I mean by the city *in* Scripture is the city as it appears in the writings that attained canonical form and status long after these writings

12. The doctrine of *sola scriptura* was not articulated by Luther but by Lutheran orthodoxy.

came about. I am interested in the diversity of views and in the discernable traces of the intellectual struggles that are generally eclipsed by assumptions shared by the interpretive communities that presuppose Scripture, but do not slavishly follow it. Some of the most important tropes are not even mentioned in canonical texts but first appear in deutero-canonical or post-biblical literature. For example, the notion that city and temple were created before the creation of the word first appears in a text from the late Second Temple period, the Second or Syriac Apocalypse of Baruch 4:1–7, from whence it was absorbed by early rabbinic, Christian, and Muslim theology.

The periodization I propose is sensitive to the connection between the growth and development of Jerusalem as a symbol and the history of ancient Jewish literature. To be sure, our knowledge of the history of early Jewish literature aside from what made it into the canon is sketchy. But given the rich afterlife of the Jewish literary imagination and its impact on Jerusalem's history as a symbol, it seems warranted to foreground the canonical texts as reflections of the concerns of ancient Jerusalemites vis-à-vis the holy city. It requires that we try to distinguish them from the views one finds in the burgeoning apocalyptic and utopian literature of the late Second Temple period that presupposes and augments, or attempts to supplant, the normative works.

The distinction between before, in, and since Scripture corresponds to significant shifts in the conceptual, institutional, political, and cultural realms. In some biblical writings, the Israelites, liberated by Moses, covenanted to YHWH alone, and miraculously given possession of the land, appear as recidivists who, because of their entering into relations with the local populations instead of "putting them to the ban," lose first their distinctiveness and eventually their kingdom. Before and aside from Scripture, where this narrative is the dominant story, Judahite and Israelite society, as far as it can be ascertained, appears as a "normal" aggregation of tribes settled in Canaan's central highland, with village elites that are not as yet the elevated individuals enshrined in sacred texts but players eminent in local and regional spheres of influence, the competitive world of the southern Levant wedged between Egypt and Assyria, Phoenicians and Arameans, and, from a Mesopotamian perspective, "Hatti-land," or the land "beyond the river." Just as before Scripture the people of Israel are unexceptional; so their deity, YHW(H) (Greek: IAO), appears as the member of a pantheon and, though apportioned to Israel, is unexceptional in nature, gendered, coupled (with "his Anat"), and commonplace in his attributes ("rider of the clouds"). In Scripture, this older, unexceptional, and syncretistic, though particular deity rubs against other, more sublime and profound conceptions of divinity, most notably the stark YIIWII monotheism of Isaiah 45 (a Persian-age passage). Before Scripture, Jerusalem is an unexceptional, though certainly feisty and self-assured royal center; in Scripture it attains the status of the city YHWH chose from among all the tribes for his name to reside. Just as "Israel," the idealized covenanted collective, is to worship YHWH alone, so YHWH is to be worshiped in Jerusalem alone. This, too, is a scriptural conceit, a norm and commandment rather than an empirical description of the practice of every Jewish community even as late as the post-exilic age.

The literatures that became Scripture commemorate the unification ("covenant") of tribes under a central authority (charismatic or dynastic kingship) and their struggle to maintain independence in an age of imperial expansion and competition. Assuming a largely exilic/post-exilic provenance, biblical historiography narrates this authentic story of the pre-exilic polity in terms that are meaningful for a community of Persian-age returnees struggling with those who had remained, a nation ruled by priests rather than kings, compelled to function under the tutelage of an empire that, on the whole, remained favorable to the consolidation of a Jewish temple state on the border between Mesopotamia and Egypt, while preventing the reestablishment of an independent kingdom. Biblical history looks back on the emergence of Jerusalem as dominated by the House of David as the legitimate heir of a pan-Israelite heritage. As the prophetically endorsed center of YHWH worship, it mourns the destruction of the city, provides a rationale for its fate, and preserves a variety of competing blueprints for its reestablishment as a city holy to YHWH.

The religious communities founded on this literature as part of their respective Scripture are significantly different from either the Judahite and Israelite societies remembered in this literature, or from the society of those who produced and shaped the literature in which these earlier societies are remembered. While the distinction between pre-exilic and post-exilic "Israel," or between "the Israel of history and the history of Israel" (Liverani 2005), is commonly accepted among Bible scholars, I think it is rather novel to attempt to combine this scholarly reconstruction with an account of the post-biblical world of the scriptural religions. The success or usefulness of this approach to the history of Jerusalem depends on whether our "third period" can be meaningfully described as conditioned by the influence of Scripture.

Toward a Symbolic History of Jerusalem

Four presuppositions underlie the alternative periodization that I propose.

First, Jerusalem is holy to three religious traditions: Judaism, Christianity, and Islam. Why only these traditions and not others? The answer is obvious. Only these religions share with one another the same pool of religious ideas transmitted in Scripture, oral tradition, and authoritative interpretation.[13]

Second, religious meaning and the political history of Jerusalem are intricately linked. The story of Jerusalem cannot be meaningfully told and its development over time cannot be properly understood without considering how people's political desires and behaviors have been shaped by their respective religious traditions. Demography and the economy of the city cannot be understood without taking into account its religious functions and meanings for multiple traditions. International attention to the city at the time of the Crusades, but also in connection with the mid-nineteenth century Crimean War, and the exploitation of its religious status by the Great Powers, cannot be understood without considering religious attachments that extend well into the modern age. The displacement of secular Zionism by Jewish religious nationalism is not merely a political fact, but indicates the continued vitality of a Jewish religiosity devoted

---

13. The Samaritans are the only community that shares the Torah with the Jews but does not recognize Jerusalem as a holy city. In this they are the true successors to the ancient Israelite community, at least if the latter's viewpoint is reflected in 1 Kings 12:28 (minus the Judahite editorial tendency). On the Samaritans more generally, see Crown (1989).

to the redemption of the land, with Jerusalem as its "heart."[14] Religious law shapes the social and economic behavior of religious communities, it plays into public policy, and it influences both intra- and inter-ethnic relations. In sum, religion and the urban reality of Jerusalem are intertwined.

Third, in order to tease out the peculiarities of Jerusalem's religio-political character, its origins, and its development over time, I suggest focusing on Scripture and on the Scriptural traditions. I foreground "Scripture," rather than "God," "religion," or "the Holy" so as to remain open to variations in the pertinent attitudes and formations (some traditions foreground law, others doctrine; some traditions are shared by some or all, others are more idiosyncratic), while being specific enough to speak to what is particular to the traditions in question.[15]

Fourth, the focus on Scripture and the popular and authoritative traditions that relate to it locates my study of Jerusalem in a larger attempt to come to terms with the western "monotheistic" traditions and their pervasive cultural and political influences. This is a complex issue and my contribution here is tentative and limited. In pedagogical terms, I aim to make students mindful of the influence of the "religions of the book" on how members of the monotheistic—or better, the Scriptural—traditions and "biblicate" civilizations perceive themselves in relation to others and how they determine their place in the world. They share a reverence for written prophetic traditions. They honor books as authoritative divine

14. It is an often-repeated topos in the literature on modern Zionism that Jerusalem was peripheral to pre-1948 Zionism, but this claim requires further examination. Jerusalem's geographically peripheral, though politically central, place on the Israeli map from 1949 to 1967 and the characteristics imposed on the city even after 1967 by its de facto division into a Jewish and an Arab city are explored by Klein (2008), who describes Jerusalem as a "frontier city." Another important trope in secular Israeli discourse is the disposition to distinguish between the culture of Tel Aviv and that of Jerusalem. Ram (2005) looks at this matter from the perspective of urban and economic cultural theory.

15. Armstrong (1997) proceeds from a general concept of a sacred mountain that is echoed in biblical literature but the role of Scripture in shaping Jewish, Christian, and Islamic conceptions of the Holy City is not emphasized. Armstrong foregrounds what she considers the prophetic ideal of social justice and measures the behavior of the dominant communities by this standard.

utterings more than they trust the charisma of living prophets. For these communities, "re-ligio" clearly derives from *re-lego*, to read again.

Deciphering Jerusalem: The City as Text

To study the city as a phenomenon shaped by text presupposes that it is a thing that can be read and deciphered. Readability is not a new metaphor. As the philosopher Hans Blumenberg (1986) has pointed out, the "readability" of the world was one of the guiding metaphors in humanism (the age of the book) and the Enlightenment, when the modern conception of science was shaped. Nature was to be deciphered as if it were a book. The presupposition of readability as a metaphor was that nature, like the Bible, had an "author"; in fact, nature was thought to have the same infinitely wise, benevolent, and powerful author as Scripture (cf. Blumenberg 1986).

The etymology of the German word for reading (*lesen*) seems to indicate that the art of deciphering developed independently from writing. It began with the decoding of messages of the gods conveyed in the form of patterns of bones or twigs. Writing originated elsewhere and for different reasons. Cuneiform, for example, which was used widely throughout the eastern Mediterranean as part of the cultural koine of the Bronze Age, seems to have been invented by the Sumerians for the purpose of record keeping. The Phoenician (Punic) alphabet, which is at the basis of Greek and Latin but also of Hebrew, Aramaic, and Arabic scripts, came into being in the early Iron Age and was part of that period's koine. In both cases, the pervasiveness of a single type of writing testifies to the interconnectedness of the eastern Mediterranean, Anatolian, and Mesopotamian regions. Thus we find Bronze Age testimony to the name "Jerusalem" in an Egyptian archive, written in cuneiform by a Syrian scribe whose native language was not the Akkadian in which the Amarna correspondence was conducted and who wrote for a king whose name pays homage to a deity, possibly originating in Aleppo, but most popular in the cities of the Hurrian kingdom of Mittani, in the region of modern Kurdistan.[16] The

---

16. On the deity Hebat, referred to in the theophoric element in the name of the king of Jerusalem (Abdi Heba) mentioned in the Amarna letters, see Trémouille (1997).

earliest reference to Jerusalem is recorded on Egyptian execration texts, in Hieroglyphic (see also Ahituv 1984, 42, and plates XI and XII). The city of Scripture however appears in Hebrew and Greek manuscripts, eclipsing *and* preserving its earlier form. The scribal art was practiced in Jerusalem since before Scripture. Scripture would not have come into being without there being scribes in Jerusalem. But the scribes of Scripture used a different script than the kings of Judah (the so-called Chaldean alphabet, rather than paleo-Hebrew), they represented a different age, and they were committed to a new religious and political ideology that emphasized the foreignness and discontinuity between themselves as the descendants of their patriarchs (hailing from the Chaldean city of Ur) and the people of the land they were to inherit.

After Scripture, Jews, Christians, and Muslims approach the city through the lenses of their respective scriptural and interpretive traditions. Canonization of Scripture and the formation of these "post-biblical" traditions are coeval. Jews, Christians, and Muslims read, decipher, and approach the city through the prism of Scripture.

Pilgrims in particular never really see the city for what it is (if there is such a thing), but for what their scriptures tell them. Examples abound. Pilgrimage reports bear this out. The phenomenon I am referring to is not a simple one. It is partially caused by our natural tendency, when traveling, to latch onto the familiar. ("Look, this is just like. . . .") What is recognized, however, is what is familiar from Scripture. One finds what one expects because it is what one has been looking for (the empty tomb, the Rock from which Muhammad ascended to heaven, the remnants of the Temple). Scripture, liturgy, years of guided religious imagination in Sunday schools, yeshivot, and madrassas program readers to see what they expect to see, although it may take a moment to adjust their mental image to the reality of what is before them. The bridge between the two, which allows mental image and reality to merge in the perception of a place, is the familiar name. Homonymy allows the spatial object to sustain the meanings we bring to it.

Sacred places are not the only objects decoded in light of and by means of Scripture. Religious contemplation in a multi-religious place is marked by the presence of other decoders. The major places of religious veneration are not just frequently crowded, they are located in a living city. Chance encounters provide occasion for the decoding of the behavior of the pilgrims or members of *other* communities, whose place in one's own symbolic world may be predetermined, marking the individual as representative of a group (e.g., as an "infidel," "foreigner," "Jew," "Arab," etc.). Especially in the Byzantine period, when Jews were banished from residing in the city, the Byzantine community interpreted Jewish rites of mourning for the destruction of the temple as signs of their miserable state of existence, confirming that they had been punished by God for the rejection of Christ. Decoding on the basis of Scripture and doctrine applies to the city as a whole, as well. Pilgrims or tourists encounter "Jeru-salem," Yerushalayim, or al-Quds, and gradually synthesize what they see with what they knew in advance. The streets and alleys, houses and *sabils*, shops and churches, smells, signs, and natural features all combine with the names and knowledge each person always already brings to the experience of "the Holy City."

What helps to decode the inevitable discrepancy between expecta-tion and reality, between the familiar mental image and the onslaught of the unfamiliar, is the distinction between an "upper" and a "lower" Jerusalem. This distinction first appeared after city and temple had been restored sometime in the second temple period when, at the peak of its ancient career, Jerusalem was host to hundreds of thousands of visitors who came to celebrate the three annual pilgrimage festivals of Pesach (Passover), Shavuot (Pentecost), and Sukkot (Booths). Reality and expecta-tion must have been at odds especially for the meticulously devout (and sometimes provincial) visitors, such as Jesus of Nazareth.[17] This may explain why, already then, apocalyptists developed the notion of the "two cities," the upper and the lower, the earthly and the divine, the apparent and the real; the real being not what we experience with our senses but what we know to be true because we believe in the truth of a Scripture. Since no mere historical reality can ever approach the heights of utopian

17. Hence the plausibility of the scene of Jesus attacking the moneychangers. See Mark 11:15–17.

perfection envisioned in Scripture, the city always appears twice: as the surface reality perceived by the senses and as the city of Scripture, the ideal, the coming, the upper, the New Jerusalem. To study the city of Jerusalem as a Holy City requires for us to consider this quasi-Platonic duality and make sense of it.

To be sure, some of what has been said here about Jerusalem applies to every city, and much of what is true of other, comparable cities is also true of Jerusalem. Every city is open to an analysis of its symbolic dimensions. Urban theory presupposes that every city can be "read," deciphered, decoded, and examined in the light of theory. Cities can be described, analyzed, compared. Cities differ, but they correspond to ideal types. Until recently, Jerusalem might have been called a typical "Muslim city," a term coined by mid-twentieth-century urban historians.[18] To capture the long-term developmental characteristics of the city, however, I suggest classifying Jerusalem as a scriptural city or, more precisely, as *the* city of Scripture. While in many ways a city like others, with its infrastructure and architectural styles, it is unique because of the ways in which being the city of Scripture distinguishes Jerusalem from all other cities. Urban theory cannot provide the tools needed to describe Jerusalem's uniqueness, but the unique emerges only in comparison with similar ancient, medieval, and modern cities with shared characteristics.

Conclusion

The fundamental core of our Western traditions, the traditions that hold Jerusalem in particular esteem as a holy city, is Scripture. The fact that Scripture, the conglomerate of sacred writings, traditions and normative interpretations of particular communities, predisposes our communities to take Jerusalem rather seriously is not necessarily a bad thing. But it is not necessarily a good thing, either. In the religious studies classroom, Jerusalem—or, rather, attitudes toward the city, the formation of attachments, and the rise of an ordinary royal city of the ancient southern

18. For the difference between Greek *polis* and Muslim town, see Kark and Oren-Nordheim (2001, 21–24).

Levant to the status of the Holy City of three global monotheistic traditions—provides ample occasion to examine the history and dynamics of these traditions of faith. I like to remind my students that religious studies may be one of the few places today where religion is not primarily treated with respect (pause to leave room for an audible gasp), but with curiosity. The study of Jerusalem allows students from different backgrounds to acquire a great deal of religious (and historical) literacy, to hone critical reading skills, to examine contemporary sources for bias, and to engage in discussions on their own position vis-à-vis the conflict in the Middle East, its players, and the factors that have contributed toward the complexity of the situation. In other words, Jerusalem is a terrific topic for instruction in the religious studies classroom, as long as it is treated judiciously. It affords opportunity for critical self-examination (a general goal of liberal arts education), awareness of history, consideration of the role of Scripture (and thus literature) in the formation of our religious beliefs and symbols, and recognition of the complexity of interreligious and international relations.

Jerusalem is also a topic by which we can encounter and consider religious difference and how to live with it. Although students generally acknowledge that they are biased when it comes to deciphering Jerusalem, it is less evident to the students how to subject their biases to an analysis or why it should be necessary to do so.

Christians may be predisposed to read the history of Jerusalem as a sequence of tragically missed opportunities. Their interest in history as a phenomenon in its own right, as a domain of meaning and as phenomena susceptible to rational or moral decoding, can be shown to be inspired by the Christian tradition of an economy of salvation. Given the course material and the standard histories of Jerusalem, the challenge is how not to make the Crusades appear as an aberration and how not to blame the British for making a mess of the Middle East.

Jewish students may find it irresistible to read their own modern story and perspective into the biblical and Second Temple Jewish perspectives, to obliterate the differences between these historical entities and to identify with the ancient Jews. Here the challenge is how not to make a course on Jerusalem into a vindication of Jewish nationalism.

Not a single Muslim student I have had in any of my classes approached the question of Jerusalem in an exclusivist or possessive spirit. Palestinians usually consider the city from a perspective of local patriotism. For me as an instructor, it is difficult not to regard Muslim tradition as the most reasonable and historically most successful in negotiating the differences between communities. Here the problem is really how to avoid an unrealistic idealization of Islam that reduces it to an Orientalist idyll.

4

The City and the Body

Jerusalem in Uri Tsvi Greenberg's *Vision of One of the Legions*

SHAI GINSBURG

Thinking Literary

Participants in this volume were asked to tackle two tasks: to reflect on the place of Jerusalem within their given discipline, and to explore Jerusalem from the perspective of their discipline. It appears, however, that the literary scholar has to do more, for she or he is also asked to defend the merit of literary criticism for an interdisciplinary endeavor such as this one. Whereas studies of Jerusalem from political, social, or religious disciplinary perspectives are received as a matter of course as pertinent to the study of Jerusalem, literary analysis is censured for being of little interest for those who are not specifically interested in poetry or prose fiction. Indeed, one may wonder, what can a close reading of a poem or a work of fiction contribute to a tapestry of work illuminating the political, social, and religious aspects of Jerusalem? What would the niceties of literary analysis contribute to our understanding of the city?

The literary scholar, as we shall presently see, faces an uneasy task. For if she is to compile a list of references to Jerusalem in literature and underscore the importance of the city as a literary topos, she would surely tell her readers little that they did not know or suspect beforehand. Alternatively, if she is to address the place that the city occupies in literature in some broad, general statements, she faces the greater risk of not only reiterating known clichés and platitudes, but of also betraying a literary corpus of such wealth and diversity as to defy any attempt to neatly sum it up. Rather than mystify the reader through the one or the other, I turn to a close engagement with one long poem, following the difficult and complex route it blazes as much as the scope of this paper would allow it.

Indeed, close reading would not provide the reader with any comprehensive view of the topos of Jerusalem in literature; nor would it supply her with some ready-made, simply articulated statements about the topic. It would, however, impart the unique contribution literary analysis may have for a multi-disciplinary intellectual project such as this book. For close reading puts into relief the inherent indeterminacy that haunts Jerusalem as a topos—not only as a literary topos, but also as a historical, a political, a religious, and a social topos—an indeterminacy that challenges the endeavors to account for it critically. Whereas this indeterminacy is commonly glossed over or even suppressed for the sake of a clear and decisive presentation—one that easily lends itself to processes of decision-making, whether by governmental or nongovernmental bodies, whether by national or international institutions—close reading explores it and its consequences for our conceptualization of the subject matter. Indeed, it points to the pitfalls entailed in the failure to account for this indeterminacy, a failure that haunts, I would suggest, such processes of decision-making.[1]

To explore in greater detail the tension between close reading and other approaches to the topos of Jerusalem and, more particularly, between the literary and the political conceptions of the city, I turn to the Hebrew poetry of Uri Tsvi Greenberg. Greenberg's poetic corpus seems apt in this context, for it is habitually deemed central to discussions of modern Hebrew poetry, yet also a key articulation of Zionist right-wing politics. A prime example of how the political imagination of Jerusalem relies quite directly and explicitly on the cooption of the literary imagination, it is often read as a blatant, though poetically magnificent, expression of staunch chauvinism that centers on the city of Jerusalem as its prime

---

1. For an account of the possible contribution of such a literary engagement to an analysis of a given subject as computed by the disciplines of the social sciences, see Spivak (2003).

symbol. It thus asks to be read, so it seems, in between the poetic and the political, as it were, a perspective rarely employed in the discussion of Jerusalem as a literary topos. Yet, a close reading of that poetic corpus will reveal a surprising indeterminacy of the city as a literary topos in Greenberg's poetry. Such an indeterminacy points at the spuriousness of the common literary accounts of Greenberg's poetry, and by implication, of the place of Jerusalem in Hebrew poetry in general. Simultaneously, it also points at the spuriousness of political paradigms, inasmuch as they rely on literary topoi to account for Jerusalem.

Critical History

Surveying the place of Jerusalem in modern Hebrew literature, the pre-eminent scholar of that literature, Dan Miron, wonders what kind of a statement or comment the literary scholar can make, if "Jerusalem in the new Hebrew literature [is] as pervasive as the joint force of religious tradi-tion, the *maskilic* quest for Hebraic origins, and Zionism dictate." And he continues: "At first glance, it seems that only two forums, diametrically opposed, are available: a bulky literary-historical monograph based on an extensive bibliography, focusing on various significant configurations of Jerusalem in as many literary works as possible, or a very short general text that would sum up the self-evident with the help of a few striking illustrations. . . . But what should the scholar do if he or she deems the first of these impracticable and the other intellectually unacceptable? How should one go about looking for a third option?" (Miron 1996, 247–48).

In his search for a third option, Miron directs the literary scholar to search for "a general principle that in itself could be concisely expressed in a relatively short essay. Such a recognition and definition," he assures us, "might raise the critic above the shallow waters of truisms and vacuous phraseology, insofar as his or her general principle entails the discovery of the infrastructure itself" (ibid., 258).

Miron's observations are worth lingering upon. His assertive rheto-ric makes evident that the critical endeavor to comment—not just acci-dentally, but in principle—on the place of Jerusalem in modern Hebrew literature and criticism is inextricably bound with the endeavor to estab-lish one's position of authority vis-à-vis the literary as well as the critical traditions. Yet, the very subject matter—namely, Jerusalem—threatens to undermine that position, and these passages indeed betray Miron's anxiety. For Jerusalem seems to set critics between a rock and a hard place: it forces on them two alternatives that render their discourse trivial and banal. Triviality and banality are all the more patent by the pervasiveness of Jerusalem as a theme in Hebrew literature, for the critical discourse becomes either insignificant under the overwhelming wealth of instances and occurrences of the city in Hebrew poetry and prose fiction, or is rendered self-evident.

In an endeavor to avoid these benumbing alternatives, Miron seeks to substitute the bird's-eye view with a penetrating glance, a glance that would reveal one regulating principle beneath the myriad literary appearances of Jerusalem. Yet, this principle, he asserts, should not be merely recognized; it should also "be concisely expressed in a relatively short essay." In other words, only a disciplinary articulation of a particular kind, only a particular genre and rhetoric, could render significant the endeavor to say something about the appearances of Jerusalem in Hebrew literature. Only such an articulation could save the critic from the banality that endangers her, reinvest critical discourse with meaning, and thus reassert critical (that is, the critic's) authority.

What principle, then, does Miron recognize here? "In the case of the Jerusalem theme in modern Hebrew literature," he writes, "[O]ne must first recognize the fact that it has always evolved within a binary context. Every specific configuration of this theme finds its place along a scale, the two extremes of which point to different directions. Sometimes the locus is closer to one end and sometimes to its opposite, but in the most interesting cases, it is to be found in the middle scale. The nature of the two extremes and the content they represent varies" (ibid., 258).

For all of Miron's dismissive rhetoric, which all but ignores previous critical endeavors to account for subject matter as merely caught in "truisms and vacuous phraseology," the regulating principle he identifies appears at first glance to be neither surprising nor revolutionary. Even a superficial reading of the critical literature would show that most critics in fact chart the appearances of Jerusalem in Hebrew literature in terms of such binary oppositions.

Miron is, of course, correct in identifying "catalogues," that is, lists of as many appearances of Jerusalem in literature, as a prominent genre (see, for instance, Ben-Barukh 1955; Chertoff 1987; and Omer 1987). To this genre also belong anthologies published on the subject (see, for instance, Be'er 1983; Cohen 1937; and Toren 1968). Yet, most critical essays published in the last four decades seem to follow (or precede) Miron in identifying one or another binary opposition as regulating the appearances of Jerusalem in Hebrew literature. A few select examples should suffice here. Boaz Arpali (2006) reads Yehuda Amichai's Jerusalem poems as expressing the tension between the experience of the individual and the metaphysical or collective paradigms—whether religious, historical, or national—that force themselves on humans. Ranen Omer-Sherman (2006) reads these in terms of the tension between heavenly and earthly Jerusalem. Aminadav Dykman (1994) reads Dan Pagis's Jerusalem poems along the same lines. Haviva Pedaya (2007, 162–63) maintains that Greenberg's Jerusalem poems express "a radical dichotomous feeling" and oscillate "between two extremities" (I shall say more on Pedaya's reading of Greenberg later). Indeed, often, the field as a whole is articulated through such oppositions. Ziva Ben-Porat (1987), for example, analyzes the appearances of the city in literature in terms of the binary opposition between historical and ahistorical representations. Dan Miron (1987) and Nurith Govrin (1989) read Hebrew fiction as set within the opposition between Jerusalem and Tel Aviv. Lily Orbach (1993) discusses literary portrayals of the city as oscillating between its representation as a physical space and its representation as a concept. Tova Cohen (2002) portrays the field as polarized between male poetry and female poetry, and Yedidya Yitzhaki (2002) reads poems on Jerusalem as set within the opposition between the destroyed city and its rebuilding. For Irene Zwiep (1998), poems of Jerusalem oscillate between remembering and forgetting. For Gabriel Levin (1982) and Avner Holtzman (1994), the tension between earthly Jerusalem and heavenly Jerusalem is the central characteristic of the manifold appearances of Jerusalem in Hebrew literature. Interestingly, even when Holtzman appears to diverge from the binary scheme, as in his essay on portrayals of Mandatory Jerusalem in Hebrew literature (Holtzman 2003), he falls back on it. He thus maintains that whereas early literary depictions of

Jerusalem in the said period betray a binary infrastructure, between mundane and divine Jerusalem, as well as between Jerusalem and Tel Aviv (or the new Jewish colonies), later portrayals of the city are more nuanced and multi-faceted. Nevertheless, each of the works noted as presenting such nuanced, multi-faceted depictions—with the notable exception of Agnon's novel *Shira*—is still discussed in binary terms: town and country; historical significance and elision of that significance; concrete historical reality and extra-temporal existence; and Mandatory Jerusalem and Israeli Jerusalem. Tellingly, the responses to Holtzman's work, while questioning a number of his guiding principles, never challenge the binary structure of his discussion (Govrin 2003; Gouri 2003; Schwartz 2003). Finally, in one of the most recent and insightful contributions, Sidra DeKoven Ezrahi (2007, 228) reads the city in Hebrew literature between a "Jerusalem whose metaphoric shapes are free, tentative, and self-conscious and an allegorized or literalized Jerusalem reduced finally and fatally to an essential self."[2]

Miron's innovation rests, then, not so much in articulating the field in binary terms as in turning what is often articulated as a thematic opposition into a structural principle.[3] This "structuralization" allows Miron to

2. A couple of exceptions are noteworthy. Gershon Shaked, who, alongside Miron, dominated Hebrew literary criticism of the second half of the twentieth century, presents an evolving historical scheme, where the focus changes with time. He thus argues that modern Hebrew fiction started by portraying Jerusalem at the center of a conflict between "life" and religion. It then moved to represent it as a multi-ethnic city of immigrants, and moved on to focus on the city as embodying the Israeli-Palestinian conflict. It concluded with attempts to represent mundane life in Jerusalem as removed from the symbolic and historical focus (Shaked 1998). In their reading of David Shahar's magnum opus, *The Palace of Shattered Vessels*, Moshe Ron and Michal Peled-Ginsburg set Shahar's mature fiction within a liminal space that is not subjected to the binary modes commonly employed to portray the city in the fiction of such authors as Amos Oz and A. B. Yehoshua, and even in the early fiction of Shahar himself (Ron and Peled-Ginsburg 2003). Last, DeKoven Ezrahi also diverges in a number of important aspects from the binary tradition (see footnote 3).

3. Indeed, Miron seems to follow here the fundamentals of a structuralist analysis; see, for instance, Lévi-Strauss's essays collected in *Structural Anthropology* (1963) and, in particular, the essay "The Structural Study of Myth" (206–31) in which he posits that all myths share a fundamental structure, that of binary oppositions.

tie together the wide range of seemingly disparate themes and tropes that at the opening of the essay seemed to threaten the critical endeavor:

> In many literary works, Jerusalem functions primarily as a receptacle for swelling emotions, a lyrical focal point of intense national sentiment. In others, it is present as pictorial, epic space that calls for detailed mimesis. Often Jerusalem appears as a tragic memory of national and cosmic devastation; it is the core of the myth of *hurban* (destruction), all but a figment of a tearful imagination. Just as often, however, the city emerges as a harsh and blunt reality, an oppressive physical, social, and political entity on which all illusions are bound to flounder. It suggests, alternatively, happiness and tragedy, harmony and discord, peace and war, health and sickness, even insanity, divine grace, and implacable divine wrath. (Miron 1996, 241–42)

All these themes and tropes can now be linked and placed within a framework charted between two binary loci: between reality and myth, "life" and the religious codes, instinctual spontaneity and moral circumspection, Judaism and Hellenism, nationalist particularism and humanistic universalism, old and new, past and present, past and future, truth and illusion, metaphor and metonymy, and so on (Miron 1996, 258–59). Of significance, Miron asserts, is not the attainment of a synthesis between these binary opposites, but the presentation of "a real conflict," of producing "in the reader a feeling of being 'torn'" (259). That is to say, the structure that governs the manifold appearances of Jerusalem in Hebrew literature is that of an unresolved conflict, an unending struggle.

Ironically, notwithstanding Miron's emphasis on conflict, the recovery of infrastructure is in itself closely linked to the critical structure of authority. In other words, the structure as conflict serves to contain and master literature as well as criticism or, more so, to contain and master Jerusalem as "a core element of the Jewish psyche, the hub of its reality and the center of its dreams and visions" (Miron 1996, 243). Ironically indeed, conflict in this discourse is the mark of the *Jewish* psyche, seemingly displacing and eliding the ethnic and national conflict, for the latter is nowhere to be found, as if it is inappropriate for literature and criticism. In this respect, there is only little difference between Miron's structural reading of the literary tradition and other critics' thematic or rhetorical reading of the same tradition.[4] By setting Jerusalem on a well-marked rut that runs between two well-defined extremities, the political conflict over the city is elided and the city is claimed, domesticated, and appropriated for the (Jewish-Israeli) critical imagination.

Uri Tsvi Greenberg and His *Vision of One of the Legions*

To divert the discussion from this rut, I propose in what follows to closely read—an option Miron does not entertain—the portrayal of Jerusalem in one poetic work by one author: Uri Tsvi Greenberg's *Hazon ehad ha-ligyonot* (*Vision of One of the Legions*) published in 1928.[5] Greenberg, asserts Shalom Ben-Barukh (1955, 160) in a book-length study of Jerusalem in Modern Hebrew poetry, "calls himself 'the poet of Jerusalem'—and rightfully so. This sublime name befits and becomes him, for there is no other like him among the poets of our time, whose creation is so completely attached to the City of David and who sees in it the most important thing, so much so that it is for him the alpha and the omega, both a symbol and reality, both a city and a whole kingdom, an absolute blending of earthly corporeality and supreme, divine vision."[6]

What underlies Greenberg's denomination as "the poet of Jerusalem," so it seems, is a binary infrastructure of oppositions: beginning and end, symbol and reality, the earthly and the divine, corporeality and vision. Be that as it may, both poet and work figure prominently not only in literary studies of Jerusalem, but in *historical* and *political* studies, as well. Yet,

---

4. Such critical strategies seem uneasily close to current political strategies that are designed to secure national and political control over the city. DeKoven Ezrahi's (2007) essay significantly diverges from this tradition of critical displacement and elision by explicitly situating questions regarding the political authority over the city at the core of the rhetorical examination of the appearances of Jerusalem in literature. The above, then, is an attempt to take her argument a step further so as to include the critical imagination alongside the literary one.

5. All rights to the works of the poet Uri Tsvi Greenberg are reserved to his estate.

6. All translations from the Hebrew are the author's. See also Shmuel Huppert's (2006, 18–21) comments on Greenberg's self-perception as the poet of the city.

I shall suggest, *Vision of One of the Legions*, both in theme and in rhetoric, does not merely defy the kind of binary scheme that Hebrew critics commonly employ when claiming Jerusalem, but, in fact, prefigures the failure of the poetic as well as political endeavor to claim and appropriate the city.

Greenberg—one of the major figures of Hebrew and Yiddish poetry of the twentieth century—was born in 1896 in Bialykamien in the Austro-Hungarian Empire to a distinguished Hassidic family. Shortly after his birth, his parents moved to Lvov, where he received a traditional schooling and where he began to write in Yiddish and in Hebrew; his first poems were published in 1912. With the outbreak of the First World War, he was drafted to the Austro-Hungarian Army and served on the Serbian front; after he deserted in 1918, he returned to Lvov, where he and his parents survived a Polish anti-Jewish pogrom. After the war, Greenberg continued to publish in Hebrew and in Yiddish, becoming a leading figure of the Yiddish expressionist avant-garde. In December 1923, he immigrated to Palestine and, simultaneously, shifted the gravity point of his work from Yiddish to Hebrew. Throughout the 1920s, Greenberg introduced expressionism to Hebrew poetry and established himself as one of the major Hebrew modernist poets.

Initially, Greenberg affiliated himself with the Zionist Labor Movement, but in the second half of the 1920s, in light of the economic and ideological crisis visited upon Jewish-Nationalist communities in Palestine, he began censuring its leadership in harsh terms. In the wake of the 1929 anti-Jewish Palestinian riots, he joined the right-wing Revisionist party, becoming one of its main spokesmen; with Aba Ahimeir and Yehoshua Heschel Yeivin, Greenberg formed *Brit ha-biryonim* (the Brotherhood of Zealots), a radical group on the extreme right of Zionist-Revisionism that was active between 1930 through 1933. During the 1930s, Greenberg served as a Revisionist delegate to the legislative body of the Jewish communities in Palestine, as well as to the Zionist congress, while spending protracted periods of time in Poland as the editor of the Revisionist Yiddish organ. Whereas for the Revisionist youth Greenberg's poetry seemed prophetic and constitutive, Greenberg's abrasive rhetoric in poems and journalistic pieces alike—he depicted the Labor Movement as deceitful and treacherous, knowingly and willingly undermining the nationalist endeavor in Palestine—outraged and alienated many, and Greenberg and his poetry were boycotted by the Hebrew political and literary establishment.

During the Second World War, in which Greenberg lost all of his family, not a single poem of his appeared, but immediately following the war, he started publishing poems that mourned the murdered Jews and the destruction of European Jewry, and these were enthusiastically received by both critics and the general public. These poems catapulted him, once more, to the center of the Hebrew literary scene. Following the establishment of the State of Israel, Greenberg was elected to the first parliament as a delegate of the right-wing Herut Party, but he declined to be included in the party list of candidates for the following elections. In 1957 he was awarded the Israel Prize for Hebrew Literature. During the last decades of his life, Greenberg wrote avidly, and while he continued to express radical right-wing opinions, he rarely affiliated himself with any of the established parties or movements. He died in 1981 (Arnon 1991; Hever 1977; Huppert 2006; Miron 2002).

Greenberg's poems of Jerusalem are often read doubly, as both a poetic and a political statement: as a poetic articulation of a political claim over Jerusalem, indeed, as a political vision that could only be articulated poetically. The city "trespasses" its "municipal boundaries," for Jerusalem is perceived as embodying both Greenberg's corpus of poetry as a whole and the territorial corpus divinely promised to Jews.[7] As such, Greenberg's Jerusalem now takes part in yet another binary opposition: "a chasm open[s] widely between the poet's vision of Jerusalem delivered, the vision of the great kingdom, and the reality of the small state, the 'coastal plain state'" (Yeivin 1949, 16–17). Greenberg's poetic-territorial corpus, the expression of an ultra-nationalist vision, is contrasted with political reality in a Manichean structure that highlights at its center the struggle over dominion.

---

7. Yeivin (1974, 83) thus asserts, on the one hand, that "the focal point of [Greenberg's] poetry, the point where its heart of hearts beats, is—Jerusalem" and, on the other hand, that it serves as the focal point of his political-territorial vision (Yeivin 1949).

Nonetheless, little has been written beyond such pronouncements on the figuration of Jerusalem in Greenberg's poetry.[8] The following is therefore an initial attempt to map Greenberg's Jerusalem in the *Vision of One of the Legions*. Whereas Greenberg's references to Jerusalem are often read as an assertion of the claim and the right over the city, this long poem manifests a deep-seated anxiety about the city, an anxiety that undercuts the discourse of dominion, both poetically and politically.

Jerusalem Unsettled

Ostensibly, Jerusalem occupies the spatial focal point of *Vision of One of the Legions*, a poem that explicitly raises questions of territorial possession and dominion. The *Vision* seems to literalize and transpose the prevalent rhetoric of Labor as deployed by the various Labor parties—a rhetoric that employed terms such as the "Conquest of Labor" and the "Regiment of Labor," and that underscored physical labor, agricultural labor in particular, as fundamental to any Jewish political claim over Palestine. Greenberg's poem depicts the Jewish-nationalist endeavor in Palestine not as a campaign over labor, but as a true *military* campaign designed to take possession and establish political authority by brute force over the land, a campaign that is expected to reach its climax in the battle over Jerusalem. Such a rhetorical transposition seems to befit the common narrative of Greenberg and his

---

8. In a rare exception, Haviva Pedaya comments on the portrayal of Greenberg's long Jerusalem poem *Eyma gdola ve-yare'a'h* (Great Fear and a Moon) and *Se'if sela' 'eytam* (To the Top of the Rock of Etam). Pedaya underscores the great complexity of Greenberg's poetry: "The break-down into elements is one of the fundamentals of this poetry, which contains so many voices, so many shards and memory fragments, so much movement of coming and going between life segments; a great hurling of being that makes present all times, all possibilities, all the landscapes stored in the soul . . . —and move between them like a merry-go-round" (Pedaya 2007, 162). Yet, she immediately moves to subject it to an overall binary structure: "The movement between the extremities takes place out of a radical dichotomous feeling: impurity versus purity, body versus soul, Europe versus Jerusalem, secularism versus religiosity, childhood versus adulthood, the love of a maiden versus sex with a mistress, childhood versus parenthood, life versus death, the Temple versus destruction, Jewishness versus Arabness. . . . All the noted elements move between two extremities and are set off against their opposites" (2007, 162–63).

poetry, for it seems to foreshadow the poet's political shift and embrace of ultra-nationalist ideology, which was to take place shortly after the publication of the poem. A close reading of the *Vision*, however, would suggest that the poem could not be subjected to such a narrative. Quite surprisingly, in fact, it tells of one's failure to claim city and territory and, moreover, suggests the inadequacy of the military figuration that pervades it.

Indeed, the very title of the poem destabilizes its central figuration. As Dan Miron notes, the title welds nouns from two distinct cultural fields: *hazon*, vision, is a Hebrew term that belongs to the biblical prophetic genre; *ligyonot*, or legions, on the other hand, is derived from Latin and is closely linked in the Jewish imagination to the Jewish-Roman wars, which led to the destruction of Jerusalem and of Jewish life in Palestine and to two millennia of exile (Miron 1999, 216). Notwithstanding the power of its belligerent rhetoric, Greenberg's *Vision of One of the Legions* undercuts itself. For whereas the speaker in the poem proclaims, through *vision*, Jewish sovereignty over Palestine, *legions* suggest that he can only prefigure it as its violent undoing. The poem thus embodies not just a realization that the Jewish nationalist revolution, in its aspiration to appropriate Palestine, should liken itself more to the Roman expeditionary force than to the besieged Jews; rather, as Miron writes, in order "to realize the revolution, the *I* has to internalize the Other. Jerusalem has to be Rome as well and the conqueror also has to be the conquered" (ibid., 220). In other words, quite disturbingly the poem undermines our ability to distinguish the desire to claim the territory as—in the words of the 1917 Balfour Declaration, which had a profound impact over the Jewish imagination—"a national home for the Jewish people" from the frustration of that desire and the destruction of home by the Jews' emblematic Others.

The poem's narrative similarly frustrates claims for possession and authority. Dan Miron argues that these coordinates define a traditional *fabula*, characterized by the unity of its protagonist, as well as of its temporal and spatial dimensions. The protagonist of Greenberg's poem is "one of the legions," the poetic speaker, who is portrayed at times as an individual, and at other times as standing for the collective. Space, Miron contends, is organized around two axes: vertical and horizontal. The horizontal axis follows the route of the Roman legions in their military mission

in Palestine, from Jerusalem to Masada. Vertically, the vision develops as
a movement downwards—with few diversions only—from the heights of
Jerusalem to the depth of Hell. The temporal dimension likewise is organized around two axes. The narrative present time is bracketed between
the legionnaires' sense of desperation as they are camped outside the
walls of Jerusalem and their realization of their ultimate defeat, after
which they withdraw from the city. Into this present, the speaker weaves
scenes from the near past, which portray the present as the climax of a
process of disintegration and unburdening of national values. Against
this near-past, the speaker sets the distant past of besieged Jerusalem and
its destruction in the first century CE (Miron 1999, 222–25).

Useful as Miron's observations are for navigating the poem, they
are also possibly misleading. The poem, I would suggest, does not build
upon spatial and temporal linear progression, but upon its disruption.
The first chapter[9] of the poem begins with the following proclamation
(Greenberg 2:9):

> Vision of one of the legions
> As holocaust comes to the homeland
> And desperation steams
> Facing the walls of Jerusalem

The very setting of the poem as a *vision* should alert the reader to the
disruption of spatial and temporal unity and continuity, for vision cuts
through the time and space, disturbing both the here and the now. Rather
than traditional, linear progression, this first stanza suggests that the
speaker remains *stationary*, unable to avoid or to divert a looming disas-
ter. Indeed, as we shall see, the poem ends where it begins, just outside
the walls of Jerusalem, in a nightmarish vision that elaborates the omi-
nous omens of the first stanza.[10] It is important to note that the poem ends

---

9. On the poem's division into chapters, see Hever (1994, 139–40). I employ Hever's
division throughout. The translation of the poem from the Hebrew into English is mine.

10. The poem ends, in fact, by the Dead Sea, but as even a superficial reading of the
twelfth chapter of the poem shows, the poet still portrays this position as adjacent to Jerusalem, just outside its walls.

neither in Jerusalem, as one may have expected, nor in Masada, the Jewish last stand during the "Great Rebellion" against the Romans, as Miron would have it, but in between the two. Why would the poet choose to bring his poem to a close in such a (non-) place, a place that defies the narrative of the Jewish-Roman campaign, which traditionally concludes either with the destruction of Jerusalem and the Temple or with the fall of Masada? The answer to this question lies, I suggest, in the protagonist of the poem and in his relationship to Jerusalem.

From the very outset of *Vision of One of the Legions*, the poem draws together speaker and city. The motto poem thus states:

> The joys that were like occupation armies in the territory of the *I* have departed——
> Ha, how I likened to a city left by the armies?
> (2:7)

These lines allude to the opening verse of the Book of Lamentations— "How doth the city sit solitary, that was full of people" (Lam. 1:1). Greenberg's poem picks up the central trope of Lamentations, which—within the context of political and military disintegration—anthropomorphizes Judea in general and Jerusalem in particular. Yet, the *Vision* reworks this trope in important ways. For one, it reverses its direction: it is not the city that is personified; rather, the speaking subject is "citified." The resulting internalization of the military-territorial terms of war and occupation to portray the internal world of the *I* is not only unusual, but also quite troubling. Moreover, the poem unsettles the very logic of the Lamentations trope by constructing the metaphor around the equation of *joys* and *occupation armies*. Ordinarily, the withdrawal of occupation armies from a conquered city would be interpreted to mean liberation and re-establishment of sovereignty, a reason for joy; here, however, by equating joys and occupation armies, the poem paradoxically turns the withdrawal of the armies into a moment of grief and great distress (see also Hever 1994, 196–97). Ultimately, then, the metaphor heightens anxiety that is centered on the question of dominion, on the tension between occupation and sovereignty that haunts both the speaking and the city and which can be accounted for only in a conflictual and paradoxical way. It further suggests that neither speaker nor city could be characterized in terms of unity and coherence.

City and Anxiety

To gauge what is at stake in *Vision of One of the Legions*, one has to turn to Greenberg's earlier poetry, and in particular to his second book of Hebrew poetry, *Ha-gavrut ha-'ola* (The Rising Manhood), which was published in 1926, only a few years before *Vision of One of the Legions*. A reading of this earlier work would show how the poet's vision of Jerusalem is pervaded by anxieties that form and shape his conception of his personal body to such an extent that his endeavor to articulate a *political* vision that is centered on the city is not only shaped but also undone by the *poetical* articulation of these anxieties. In the first chapter of *The Rising Manhood*, "For the Epiphany" (*Le-'hag ha-hitgalut*), in the second poem, "Section and Command" ('*Hitukh ve-tsivuy*), the poet introduces his poetic mission:

> The God of Fear of father and mother likewise knows my depth among
>   the cuts of cuts of the being of my manhood that ascends
> To its Jerusalem of Gold, which is still in vision.
> And I shall liken my years to lambs . . . they shall also come with me to
>   the mountain!
> . . . .
> Generations sunk in their pained flesh and blood in some land in the
>   world.
> Command the grandson:
> . . . .
> Do not sing of the glory of Heavens; rather tell of the living man on
>   land:
> Flesh, blood, nerves, cartilages, skin.
> Clothes, bread, water, house, tools.
> Woman, cradle, the good infant in his smallness.
> Land, iron, lantern, machine, steering wheel.
> Day and night: longings, distances, walks.
> Twins are the dream and wakefulness, there is hardly a distinction:
> The one feeds on the other, the one embraces the other
> And both have horns in the middle of times——

> The God of Fear of father and mother sections a tunnel in the thickness
>   of my being, which carries its thirty lambs to live up high,
> And through my two eyes He watches a first radiant year on mother's
>   breast——
>
> *Blessed be He My God in the mother of my shining depth!*
> (1:78)

The poem vacillates between heterogeneous perspectives—between section and command, between divine injunction and the decree of the dead, between phylogenetic memory and the present, between utopian vision and concrete materiality, between deliverance and the mundane. The poetic mission of *The Rising Manhood* depends on the speaker's ability to mediate between seemingly binary injunctions: between a *personal* utopian revelation and the *collective* demand—as uttered by past generations, the demand to focus exclusively on the endeavors of human enterprise and to celebrate the concrete materiality, which, at the time the poem was published, must have been read also as a reference to Zionist colonization endeavors in Palestine. Yet, as we shall presently see, the poem unsettles such unequivocal binarism.

The ascent to Jerusalem, to the locus of revelation, frames the poem. The experience of revelation, however, is anything but unequivocal. The metaphor that forms the opening and the closing lines is of the pilgrimage to Jerusalem, of the three pilgrim festivals. The duty of pilgrimage stems from the injunction in Exodus 23:17: "Three times in the year all thy males shall appear before the Lord God." Yet, if the three pilgrim festivals in Jerusalem are characterized in Jewish literature as a male collective experience of joy, the pilgrimage here is individual and personal, and also ridden with male anxiety. The speaker brings his very self as a lamb for sacrificial slaughter to the "God of Fear." Indeed, revelation carries with it a state of bliss, the memory of "a first radiant year on mother's breast," yet it does so only at a great price, for the speaker's very being, his very manhood, is cut to achieve that vision. Jerusalem as a locus of revelation thus cannot be dissociated from the cut being of the speaker. This cut, I would suggest, cannot be read simply as metaphorical, but has to be read literally.

The literal cut of the body can be found two poems later, in *"Ushpizin"* (Divine Guests). Here the reader finds the cut body of the Jewish male, that is, the circumcised Jewish body:

> My mother had not told me that, as I burst out of her womb, angels
>   sang or much cried by her bedside for my birth.
> Yet, I was once told that gaiety had increased in my father's house.
> People danced on tables and benches;
> And on the eighth day I was so pained in the name of great
>   Judaism——
> (1:80)

Pain, muted in the second poem, is now revealed as the shaping force of the speaker's weltanschauung. Whereas circumcision inscribes the Jewish male as a member of the Jewish collective, just conceived as the pilgrimage to Jerusalem, the speaker's physical pain unsettles the passage from the personal to the collective and serves as the ground for his *alienation* from the latter.

In "Section and Command," then, the demands of poetic revelation are juxtaposed to the memory of the visceral pain of circumcision, a pain whose memory and bodily sign haunt the poet and interrupt the integration of the individual into the collective. This interruption threatens the poetic project of *The Rising Manhood* as a whole, for that project relies on the reconciliation, difficult as it may be, of the personal and the collective, of the spiritual and the material. The poem thus ends with the poet's withdrawal into his memory in search of a moment before pain or, more precisely, of a moment that would recompense him for the pain inflicted on him.

The second chapter of *The Rising Manhood*, "Be-erets ha-nevi'im" (In the Land of the Prophets), however, marks the transformation of the relationship between the personal and the collective and, consequently, of the place of Jerusalem. *"Hizdaharut"* (Shining), the third poem of this chapter proclaims:

> Miraculously, I was saved from the hands of the gentiles, blessed be
>   the God of my father! And I came not to the worms in the land of
>   the Slavs

A cut Jew.

A great shining in the body—I am so Jerusalemite! Even from within
    my ribs the light

Sings to the Messiah.

May the blood that was spilled come and gather in the arteries!

Judea! Samaria! Galilee!

My mountains! My vales!

My deserts and my seas!

Ein Harod, Tel Yossef, and Beit Alfa, two fevering Deganias!

Jerusalem—head tefillin and the [Jezreel] Valley—hand tefillin!

(1:85)

In proclaiming "I am so Jerusalemite," the speaker does not merely persist in his own personal vision, but turns it into a collective one. His
own individual survival, or, rather, resurrection—physical as well as
spiritual—is rendered collective in an appropriating gaze that claims
dominion over a wide and open territory: "*My* mountains! *My* vales!/*My*
deserts and seas!*" Indeed, the reader might have expected that for the
speaker, the transportation from Eastern Europe to Palestine would have
bestowed on Jerusalem a concrete reality: no longer would it be a mere
abstract symbol of revelation and vision. Yet, despite the speaker's proclamation, his gaze focuses not on the city, but on the new Jewish agricultural collective colonies in the northern part of Palestine. The speaker's
gaze reduplicates, in effect, the Socialist-Zionist hegemonic one, which
privileges agricultural labor over religious tradition, the agricultural
colonies over Jerusalem.[11] Labor thus becomes a locus of authentic Jewish religious ritual, in which the personal ritual of the tefillin becomes a
collective ritual. Still, contradicting one's expectations, the poem does not
set an opposition between Jerusalem and the colonies. While Jerusalem
is depicted as the head tefillin, the Jezreel Valley, symbol of Jewish agri-

11. While Shmuel Huppert (2006) argues that Greenberg's messianic rhetoric contrasts
with the socialist rhetoric of the Labor Movement, Hannan Hever (1995) has shown the
prevalence of messianic rhetoric throughout Hebrew literature of the time.

cultural colonization, is depicted as the hand tefillin. Jerusalem and the colonies are thus perceived as complementing each other in one and the same *collective* ritual.[12]

Anxiety and the Political

Vision of One of the Legions, I suggest, re-writes the earlier *Rising Manhood*. The later poem projects the personal pain and anxiety that haunts the first chapter of *The Rising Manhood* onto the collective sphere, while turning the memory of primordial, infantile bliss—which mitigated the pain in the earlier poem—into a nightmarish image that further threatens to undo the speaker. At the center of this radical re-writing lies Jerusalem: the city in its concrete materiality now defines the speaker's gaze and serves to anchor his poetic vision.

It seems, at first, that *Vision of One of the Legions* continues the movement charted in the second chapter of *The Rising Manhood*. The earlier command to sing (as in "Section and Command") is converted into the national command to immigrate to Palestine and to labor, literally, in order to realize *collective* deliverance. At the end of the route to deliverance lies Jerusalem:

> From the podiums at assemblies we were commanded:
> Go *to Sodom*;
> We were commanded to go *to the abyss*
> *And from there*—to Jerusalem
> . . . .
> Do you recall us, God,
> A flock of young men and women,
> Without a father here and without a mother here,
> Like the army at campaign,
> And the spade was cutting
> Like a sword in the landscape of Philistia,

---

12. For an expansive discussion of Greenberg's *The Rising Manhood*, see Abraham Nowersztern (2000). My comments here, however, are not always consistent with Nowersztern's insightful reading.

And the roller was lead,
Like the chariot of the messiah . . .
And Your Jerusalemite rock
We raised like gold
In the blessed hands
To remove the disgrace of the millions?
(2:14–15)

Language here suggests, however, that such a desire for deliverance is never far removed from the *personal* pain and anxiety that shaped the earlier vision of *The Rising Manhood*; indeed, deliverance here is articulated in terms of sections and cuts, now projected from the male body onto the land.[13] Whereas the rhetoric of the second chapter of *The Rising Manhood*, as that of the Labor Movement in general, dissolves personal pain and misery in the transposition from body to territory, *Vision of One of the Legions* reveals this pain and misery to be as potent as they seemingly are in the first chapter of *The Rising Manhood*.

The exteriorization of the pain of manhood structures a central conflict in *Vision of One of the Legions*, one that threatens and, ultimately, undermines the utopian poetical as well as political desire hailed by the speaker. The conflict is between "one of the legions," a representative of the pioneer laborers and their speakers and the workers' political leadership, "who deny/our agony, swindlers of brothers" (2:15). The opening stanzas of the *Vision* depict this conflict in striking terms:

A small house we have erected, pilgrims of the sun in Israel,
And set our youth alight as beacons for conquests
And called the Messiah
From what was immersed in the well,
The well of blood and tears.
And in the shining house of our lives

---

13. For a discussion of how central were metaphors of cutting for the conception of the land for the Jewish immigrants to Palestine in the 1920s—Greenberg's envisioned public of readers—see Neumann (2011).

Rose the ancient serpent,
Rose the many-faceted serpent,
And many recognized him not:
For he rose from going on his belly,
For he put on trousers,
And the pain in his mouth is false.
(2:9–10)

As both Dan Miron and Hannan Hever note, the image of the serpent has mythical-kabalistic sources, and refers to the Supreme Evil, the Messiah's archrival (Hever 1994, 140–42; Miron 1999, 203–4). The poem, then, stages the circumstances in Palestine and the tension between the workers and the leaders of the Labor Movement as a Manichean play, a battle between the followers of the Messiah and his archrival.

This Manichean play is central to Hannan Hever's reading of *Vision of One of the Legions*. Greenberg's poem, he contends, is the first mature political poem to be published in Hebrew (Hever 1994, 139). Hever reads Greenberg's political and poetic route in the 1920s as pointing at a wider poetic shift, namely, from *ideological* poetry to *political* poetry, from *shirat ha-'avoda* (labor poetry), which endeavored "to present itself as an ideological, normative and consensual articulation of Zionist being in *Erets-Yisrael*" to poetry that strove "to expose political polarization and that employs the literary work as a direct political tool" (Hever 1994, 15, originally in Hebrew).[14] The poetic-political act is characterized, then, by *negation*—the negation of the power structure that forms a given cultural field. Political poetry seeks to undermine the poetic strategies that underlie this power structure. *Vision of One of the Legions*, Hever argues, challenges the poetic strategies of Labor Poetry and, consequently, also challenges the political power structure of the Labor Movement, which relied on these poetic strategies. In the *Vision*, the challenge is embodied in what Hever names the "politics of total desperation," by which Greenberg sets

---

14. While Hever's distinction between the ideological and the political poem has been influential, it has encountered challenges. See, for instance, Openhaimer (2003).

a mystical, messianic political-theology against the "concrete" or "pragmatic" politics of the Labor Movement (Hever 2004, 16–17).[15]

In terms of the poems read here, the transition from ideological poetry to political poetry is the transition from chapter two of *The Rising Manhood*—with its emphasis on labor and in which Jerusalem and the colonies complement each other in one ritual moment—to the mythical Manichean rivalry we have just examined. But is this mythical scene merely staging a political rivalry? Is not the serpent—who rises to put on trousers—a sexual image, an image of male sexuality, of manhood that threatens the speaker? Read in this way, the scene turns into an exteriorization of the existential anxiety that haunts chapter one of *The Rising Manhood*, an anxiety that the move to Palestine not only does not resolve, but exacerbates all the more.

City of Despair

The full impact of the exteriorization of the speaker's existential anxiety is revealed in the portrayal of Jerusalem, in the second half of *Vision of One of the Legions*, (chapters eight through twelve). These chapters actually parody the depiction of the poetic mission in the first chapter of *The Rising Manhood*. The speaker's poetic-spiritual ascent, which facilitates his descent—through the cut in the poet's being—to a foundational blissful vision of "a first radiant year on mother's breast" in the earlier poem, are reworked in the later poem into an ascent to Jerusalem and a descent to hell, a route that is accompanied by unsettling nightmarish visions. Jerusalem, that earlier in *Vision of One of the Legions* seemed to bear the promise of deliverance, now becomes a site of utter despair.

The speaker's entrance to Jerusalem marks neither the conclusion of a successful military campaign, nor the realization of a vision of deliverance. On the contrary, Jerusalem now becomes the site of fast decline,

---

15. Interestingly, while Miron rejects Hever's emphasis on the political aspect of the poem (for Miron, the poetic elements of the *Vision* continuously undermine its political message), he still renders the poem in terms of strict binary oppositions (Miron 1999, 201).

death and destruction. Chapter Ten of the *Vision* is central to the re-imag-
ining of *The Rising Manhood*:

> Deeper than death in Titus's vision and still thirsty for blood,
>   deadening Jerusalem!
> In the name of the God on my shoulders, whom I shall carry like a
>   lamb from the Jerusalemite blaze,
> I adjure you to rise, dead mother, from the depths,
> And call me in my name only once and I shall know
> That you have heard my whisper and my cry in Judea.
> . . . .
> You died and delivered me; in our house a blaze occurred; they say:
>   father in heaven
> Wept a weeping into the sea and made swamps out of tears.
> I was thrown into a ship by an officer loyal to Titus and brought as a
>   gift to Rome——
>
> In Rome and in Spain, in Germany and in France, in Russia and Poland
>   I was nursed wormwood-skins,
> And I grew up under their flag and bled under their sword, until I got
>   up and fled
> To the Jerusalemite legions.
>
> Now, dead mother, on city-cemetery I shall walk and talk to the rocks:
> Once there was here mother's house——
>
> Royalty has not departed from the city. In all the lights its glory plays,
>   the gold of its crown and purple.
> (2:26)

In a complex image, the poem conflates Jewish, Roman, and Christian
mythologies, as the destruction of Jerusalem is imagined both as the
destruction of Troy and as Christian deliverance, while also alluding to
Greenberg's own earlier poetry. The speaker—who in *The Rising Manhood*
likens his years to lambs in his ascent to Jerusalem—is likened to Aeneas
who mounts his father, Anchises, on his shoulders as he escapes the blazing
Troy; he too has to flee the blazing Jerusalem with god on his shoulder like
a lamb. Likewise, the image reworks and reverses the traditional Christian

imagery of Jesus as the Good Shepherd, who lays down his life for the sheep. No wonder, then, that the vision of destruction remains ambivalent and is not translated immediately into utter despair, for as the escape from Troy ultimately leads to the establishment of Rome, the great imperial city, and as the parable of the Good Shepherd—even in its reversal—allegorizes the promise of deliverance, so the destruction of Jerusalem bears the hope for its messianic restoration. The speaker's fortune of imprisonment and exile is thus reversed as he escapes his bondage to enlist in the Jerusalemite legions. As he returns as a legionnaire to the destroyed city and witnesses its past glory as still present—attributes of its essence as a locus of inherent sovereignty—it seems that the hope to reinstate his rule over the city, and thus reinstate its full past sovereign glory, is about to be realized.

Yet, this hope is immediately frustrated. While the return to the city is initially perceived as holding the promise of mending history, this promise is now exposed as ephemeral:

Everything is worm-eaten, everything is rusted of old age.

In the Mountain of my Olives, the tombstones are spilled over the slope:
Like teeth spilled from a mouth by Titus's fist——

And only yesterday I held might in my fist like a flint,
In the joyful song new legions sang to you, Jerusalem!——and today:
Here is yesterday's might pouring like sand between my fingers;
And my vision clasps your rocks and is like the red of a setting day
(2:27)

While the speaker celebrates one historical cycle, the cycle of the renewal of Jerusalem of old in its past glory, the city is caught in another vicious cycle of destruction and desolation. The ruined past now threatens to ruin the present. What appears at first to be an escape from death and a beginning of a new life transpires as the reduplication of death and destruction. The very landscape of the city becomes the embodiment of that destruction. Whereas the landscape of Palestine in Chapter Two of *The Rising Manhood* serves to anchor the poetic speaker in space and to guarantee his Jerusalemite vision, here the very concrete Jerusalem threatens the speaker's position. Indeed, in its very corporeality, the city embodies past human tragedy. It becomes a site of a past that refuses to depart, of a past that repeatedly enforces itself on the present.[16]

The speaker thus finds himself trapped within the vicious cycle of national as well as personal destruction embodied by the city. His vision of deliverance is blocked by the very material presence of Jerusalem as a destroyed city. Baruch Kurzweil (1966, 50) celebrates Greenberg's poetry for what he sees as "a wondrous experiential continuity, in which past, present and future are merging"; Greenberg, he continues, "ascertains the One and Only in the myriad phenomena of time and place." It seems, however, that the poet's position vis-à-vis the one principle that shapes history is more ambiguous; in fact, that principle is viewed here as threatening and deadly.

Indeed, the city ensnares the poet in a deadening, horrifying embrace. In the lines that conclude the first stanza of this poem, the speaker adjures his mother to rise from the dead, to counteract the image of material destruction. He thus reiterates the polarization between material reality and revelation that structures chapter one of *The Rising Manhood*, where the vision of "first radiant year on mother's breast" is prefigured as a refuge from the anxiety of adulthood and as the apex of poetic as well as divine vision. When the image of the mother finally appears in chapter ten of *Vision of One of the Legions*, however, it is nothing like the blissful image of the earlier poem:

> At night, I am like an infant in you, not like one of the legions——:
> You give me a teat to suckle in your death—drug, not milk,
> And he who suckles the teat of a dead mother in his manhood shall
>   bitterly cry *and in his body he shall hang in his nights*, or lose his mind
> (2:27)

City and mother are conflated—the ruin of the one becomes the ruin of the other. The blissful vision of the mother turns into a horror

---

16. *Vision of One of the Legions* could thus be read as the articulation of trauma; for discussions of trauma, see, for instance, Laplanche and Pontalis (1973), Caruth (1996), and LaCapra (2001). A full exploration of Greenberg's poems under such a term will have to wait for another opportunity.

picture—deploying images made famous by Bialik's "City of Killing"—of an infant suckling the teat of his dead mother; no longer a comforting promise of refuge and respite, the vision throws into relief how exposed the poet is to the wrath of time and place. Indeed, vision and memory of the mother turn out to be part of a threatening world that endangers the poet's body and soul.

The Landscape of the Apocalypse

Haunted by apocalyptic dreams and terror, the legionnaires leave the city, and the speaker goes down to the Dead Sea:

> That night my sleep wandered. . . . Darkness. Then the cemetery descended from the slope of Mount Olives and came to me in its graves as a frozen herd of goats. And the tomb of Absalom the shepherd stood in front of me and said: I am Absalom the general and these are the armies of my dead. You are the reincarnation of Father David. Why have you escaped me? He then opened his legs wide and I saw the form of a gate and the gate is very dark and from it emerged the gravedigger. . . . Then rose my gravedigger and said: in the thickness of the earth go, His Highness. He decreed—let there be a gap. His Highness shall come in full stature. You, land of salt marshes, yield a gap! And as the cry came out in its length my gravedigger prostrated himself by its length and the shadow was cut like a long knife in the Dead Sea. And I covered my face with my palms. Oh, my father's God of Fear. Neither Yodphat in the Galilee. Nor Beitar in Judea. Nor even Massada. A sea and a salt marsh, and great, distant captivity.
> (2:29)

The poem stages an *Inferno*-like scene, a nightmarish, devilish rendition of the Resurrection of the Dead, the Armageddon and the Last Judgment, in the guise of Absalom's Rebellion (2 Samuel 15). The speaker, who is now identified as the reincarnation of King David, faces Absalom, his rebellious son, the leader of battalions of dead corpses and the personification of Lucifer or the anti-Christ, who approaches to mock the speaker's messianic aspirations to build anew the kingdom of old in the city of Jerusalem. While the Jerusalem chapters climax with the encounter of *mother* and son, the speaker's final descent leads him to a not less horrific encounter between *father* and son. Indeed, *Vision* reverses the biblical story: while the biblical rebellion is suppressed, Absalom is killed and King David returns victorious to Jerusalem; here it is the defeated King David who is shown the way to the netherworld by his victorious son.

At first glance, the scene appears to restage the mythical Manichean rivalry between the pilgrims of the sun and the kabalistic serpent with which *Vision of One of the Legions* opens. A closer reading points, however, to the modes by which the poem destabilizes such a mythical polarization. Indeed, the rivalry here is not between opposing, mutually exclusive forces, but between the speaker and his own flesh and blood son. It is further given clear sexual content, for the father's gravedigger is "born" from between the son's legs. Indeed, the images, as well as the very title of *The Rising Manhood*, seem relevant here. The mythical conflict, clad as it is in nationalist-messianic terms, is thus revealed to be yet another articulation of a personal, existential, male anxiety that cuts through and binds together what seems initially to be polarized images. I employ the word *cut* advisedly, for it appears here once again at a key moment as, following the gravedigger's edict, the shadow cuts the land to allow the speaker to descend to the dead. The cut that enabled the blissful vision, which is revealed to be the cut of the circumcision in chapter One of *The Rising Manhood*, as well as the cut of the pioneers' spade in the landscape earlier in *Vision of One of the Legions*, are now revealed as the cut of a bleak apocalypse, as well. No longer can one tell visions of bliss from those of despair, the messianic aspiration to take possession of the land from its apocalyptic undoing. As the distinctions between these dissipate, it is no wonder that the speaker is despairing. No longer can he tell the difference between Yodphat, Beitar, Massada—hailed in Zionist texts as the last Jewish stands during the two anti-Roman rebellions and as the last beacons of Jewish sovereignty—and exile.

Such an overdetermination of the images and figures of this apocalyptical scene suggests that Hever's reading of Greenberg's *Vision of One of the Legions* as political has to be re-thought, inasmuch as political poetry is understood as striving to "expose political polarization," inasmuch as Greenberg's poem in particular is taken to posit messianic resolution to what it perceives to be the impasses of pragmatic politics. For as my reading of the apocalyptic scene of *Vision of One of the Legions* suggests, the tropes and figures of the text point at their mutual contamination and indeterminacy rather than at their mutual exclusion; and inasmuch as they are contaminated, they cannot be subsumed under a binary structure. And just as importantly, *Vision of One of the Legions* does *not* conclude with a messianic resolution of tensions and conflict, nor with a promise to alleviate the speaker's existential anxiety. On the contrary, it points at the *failure* of messianic thinking.

Yet, what is more striking from our perspective is the absence of Jerusalem from these concluding lines of the chapter and from the two final poems of *Vision of One of the Legions*. In the closing poem, as the messianic aspiration to reassert dominion over the land has come to naught, the speaker dreams himself once again in Europe, the subject of Christian persecution:

> I dreamed a dream. There was blood and mist. Stupefied flesh
>   suspended from doors
> And sections of skulls were presented to my nostrils so I could smell
>   the cadavers of death——
> From whence came a journey to rattle in my temples, from whence
>   burst-out the blazing train-engine,
> That takes condemned Jews to the gallows?
> . . . .
> And the ancient fear closed on me: I am in exile, back under crosses.
> Condemned outside and groans of scalding——
> (2:31)

Under the impact of the apocalyptic vision, when aspirations for dominion and sovereignty are rendered chimerical, Jerusalem is displaced and disappears. Ultimately, it seems, the city sustains its place only as long as its ambiguity is maintained; that is, only as long as the tension between the realization and the frustration of aspirations for dominion and sovereignty, between blissful personal memories and their undoing, is retained. Once this tension is rendered false—when the speaker discovers that all terms are collapsed into each other in *in*difference, when the city yields a vision of demise that leaves no space for desire and hope—Jerusalem fades away from the poem. What is left is a non-place, a dream of the inferno, and images that eerily anticipate those that within fourteen years would become associated with the reality of the Jewish Holocaust.

How is one then to think of Jerusalem in Greenberg's *Vision of One of the Legions,* both poetically and politically? If, on the one hand, Jerusalem embodies the happy conflation of poetry and politics, as so many political and literary critics have noted, inasmuch as both are construed in terms of authority and dominion, on the other hand, it also stands for their horrendous disunion inasmuch as it cannot overcome the voice of anxiety of the cut Jewish man, a voice that ultimately silences whatever political vision one may entertain. Jerusalem as a topos thus vacillates between assertion of authority and dominion and their denial, forever haunted by anxiety, indeterminate and incommensurable with itself, as it were. One may now wonder at the impact this disturbing image of Jerusalem had on the politics and ideology of the Zionist Revisionist movement, which raised Greenberg and his Jerusalem poetry on a banner. This, however, must await a future discussion.

5

Contested Ignominies and Conflicting Sacralities

The Changing Faces of Zionism's Jerusalems

ARIEH SAPOSNIK

REFLECTING ON THE transformation that seemed to be taking place in his home city of Jerusalem in the first decade of the twentieth century, Hebrew writer Kadish Yehuda Silman recounted a conversation he had had with "one of the important tourists," as he identified him, whom he asked what he had seen that had been tourist-worthy in the city. "Two things," the tourist answered, "The dead Western Wall and the living Bezalel; the remembrance of the past and the harbinger of the future" (Man 1910).

These, indeed, were the two Jerusalems of the Zionist imagination. Many Zionists evinced a marked ambivalence toward that city that had been described by Theodor Herzl (1960, 745–46), after his 1898 visit to the city, as "the musty deposits of two thousand years of inhumanity, intolerance, and uncleanliness . . . in . . . foul-smelling alleys." It was also Jerusalem, however—the focal point of traditional Jewish longing for generations—that had given the modern Jewish nationalist movement its name. The city consequently served at the same time as a powerful symbol in the movement's budding national liturgy, as Herzl himself would discover when, at the conclusion of the stormy "Uganda Congress" in 1903, he ceremoniously (in faltering Hebrew) quoted the psalmist, proclaiming "if I forget thee, O Jerusalem, let my right hand wither" (Laqueur 2009, 129).

If Herzl's single (and rather brief) visit to the city, and his meager familiarity with traditional Jewish imagery and tropes could arouse such duality, for Zionists in Palestine—whose familiarity with Jerusalem was much more concrete, and many of whom had a much more intimate (if correspondingly more troubled) relationship with traditional Judaism— the city engendered what was perhaps an even sharper ambivalence. This equivocality in the Palestinian arena would have concrete ramifications for the construction there of a budding national entity's culture, collective identity, and the organizational structures that would serve as its infrastructure. Indeed, among the central discursive and symbolic axes around which the Hebrew national culture would form—often even in its most purportedly "secular" undertakings—Jerusalem seemed in many ways to represent the twin poles of a national ignominy that lay, after all, at the very root of the Zionist impulse on the one hand, and a sense of sanctity that appeared to be stubbornly attached to the city on the other.

This duality in Zionist perceptions of the city is worth stressing, particularly given the standard presentation of the attitude of the Jewish national movement to the ancient city as one of all but unequivocal aversion. "A negative attitude toward Jerusalem," as one scholar has written, "became increasingly prominent with the crystallization of a secular national consciousness which placed [the creation of] a new society and a new culture at its center" (Aharonson 1989, 63).[1]

In fact, however, this framing of the place of Jerusalem in Zionist national consciousness and praxis ignores the tensions that were inherent to that national consciousness, and assumes an unproblematized understanding of the "secularization" that it entailed. The Zionist relationship with the city that had provided traditional Judaism with many of its most cherished defining symbols and which, since the early nineteenth century

---

1. Bernard Wasserstein (2002, 49) echoes this view, writing that, due to the predominance of the Orthodox "old Yishuv," the city was "regarded, particularly by secular Zionists, as the home of all that was primitive and backward-looking in Judaism. Far from viewing Jerusalem with affection, they despised it and all it stood for, particularly the traditional dependence of Jews there on haluka [a system of alms distribution on which a significant portion of Jerusalem's Orthodox community subsisted]."

had been making its way progressively to center stage in an international struggle for political and cultural-religious-symbolic dominance in the modern world (Bovis 1971; Wasserstein 2002), was far more complicated, and would undergo many changes over the decades. Some turning points in this dynamic relationship are clearly identifiable, as in the ambivalence of some of the Zionist leadership to Jerusalem during the fighting of 1947 to 1949 (Golani 1995), or in the (not unrelated) refiguring of the imagery of the Western Wall surrounding the 1929 riots and once again, some four decades later, after 1967 (Saposnik 2009).

What follows is an attempt to shed some light on this multi-hued and evolving Zionist relationship to the city, and on Zionist praxis in it. My argument here is rooted in a particular understanding of the makings of Zionist culture in Palestine, based in turn in an argument relating to the nature of nationalism itself and the shaping of nationalist liturgies. In my book *Becoming Hebrew* (Saposnik 2008), I have argued that a close look at the ways in which Zionist culture was produced in Palestine shows that the picture of modern Zionism and of nationalism generally as products of an unqualified and largely one-directional process of secularization is overly one-dimensional. Based in an historical understanding of culture as a broad interweaving of a wide range of human activities, and a corre-lated methodology that seeks to synthesize a literary-like study of imager-ies and discourses with a more anthropological examination of observable cultural practices, I argue instead that the relationship between the Zion-ist cultural undertaking and traditional Jewish culture is far more com-plicated and nuanced. Like other nationalisms—as a relatively new, but growing corpus of scholarship is recognizing (see, e.g., Smith 2003; Bell 2003)—Zionism emerges in a complex and dialectical relationship with the religious cultures and traditional societies out of which it grows, and its attempt to create an unprecedented—indeed, revolutionary—Jewish national culture maintained a delicate balance between continuity and innovation.

Although it had a palpable presence in much of the material that went into the making of my book and my arguments in it, Jerusalem itself did not figure as a distinct focus. The invitation to contribute to this volume provided me the opportunity to reflect on the role of that city—both its concrete reality of people and stones, and its status as a locus of symbolic and iconic importance—in the making of a national culture. Jerusalem emerges from this examination of a "history of culture" as a central arena of internal struggle in the formative period of Zionist cultural activity that occurred in the closing decade and a half of Ottoman rule.[2] As it turns out, the ambivalence that the nascent nation evinced toward Jerusalem would be both a catalyst in shaping some of its foremost cultural institutions and undertakings, and a window into the complicated and dialectical nature of that culture's dialogues with innovation and tradition and the inherent tensions within it between secularization and re-sacralization.

If religion and politics stand as central pillars in virtually any study of Jerusalem, this is due not to a mutual interpenetration of religious discourse and political praxis, or to the mutual interference of religious and political institutions and entities in the other's sphere, but rather, I hope to suggest, to a congenital and indissoluble twinning of the "religious" and the "political," the sacred and the profane, in Jerusalem's history. If this is true in the many struggles that have taken place over Jerusalem between religious and national groups, it is no less the case in the internal Jewish and Zionist struggles over political power and spiritual hegemony in the holy city. Indeed, in these formative years of the Zionist cultural project in Palestine, Jerusalem emerges as a critical fulcrum in Zionism's attempt to appropriate political power in the city's growing Jewish community and, in the process, to redefine the sources of holiness and to claim authority over them.

To be sure, as earlier historical and political science studies have argued, the very earliest organizational bodies of Hibbat Zion (the proto-Zionist "Lovers of Zion" movement) and of the Zionist Organization alike were often established in Jaffa or in other centers of the emerging "New Yishuv,"[3] where they might avoid the "quarrels and discord among

2. It was during those years, as I argue more extensively in the book, that a wide variety of Zionist activities began to visibly produce the kernel of a national entity in Palestine (see Saposnik 2008).

3. The term "Yishuv" is used generally to designate the pre-state Jewish community of Palestine. Members of the Hebraist and Zionist segment of that community, which began

our brethren in the Holy City," as Zalman David Levontin put it after his arrival in 1882 (Levontin 1924). But Zionist ambivalence toward the city—indeed, even the revulsion at Jewish life there and at much that the city seemed to represent—did not always lead to flight from it. It could in fact have the very opposite effect—of lending particular weight to Zionist work in the city as a means of transforming it from a center of reviled exile in the very heart of the land of would-be redemption, and hence reclaiming it from the clutches of what to many Zionists was the gravest of national desecrations, and elevating it to the centerpiece of a new national sacrality.

This was an undertaking that sought at once to wrest the mechanisms of power out of the hands of the leaders of the Orthodox "Old Yishuv" in Jerusalem, but which ran much deeper, seeking to undermine their very claim to represent the sacred, and the authentic, in Judaism. The national sacrality that Zionists would establish in Jerusalem, so as to expunge the calumny that the city represented in their eyes, would come face to face, in other words, with the city's holiness and with its guardians. This would pit the Zionist bid to claim Palestine and Jerusalem for Hebrew culture against the existing power bases of Jerusalem's "Old Yishuv," and against the cultures and mentalities that served as its ideological foundation, and for whom in turn it was the Zionist attempt to re-sacralize the city that constituted a profanity and an abomination.

An increasingly bitter and irreconcilable struggle between these two communities coincided with palpable lines of continuity in their conflicting notions of the city's holiness, and in the praxis each adopted so as to shape the city in its own image. One place where this becomes evident is in the establishment of Jewish neighborhoods outside the walls of the

---

to emerge as a distinct sociological group in the late nineteenth century, drew a distinction between themselves—the "New Yishuv"—and the traditionalist Orthodox Jews of the country, who were concentrated in the four "holy cities" of Jerusalem, Hebron, Tzefat, and Tiberias—the "Old Yishuv." This terminology has been bequeathed to the historical literature, as well, although a significant body of literature has also pointed to the problems inherent in it (e.g., Bartal 1977; Ettinger and Bartal 1981). The work of Yehoshua Kaniel (1981, 1982) has also been definitive in this regard.

Old City first, beginning in the mid-nineteenth century, by the Orthodox "Old Yishuv," and later as a part of the Zionist project. Although they have often been considered early harbingers of a budding national sensibility and a modernizing impulse, Israel Bartal has shown that the first Jewish neighborhoods were in fact part of a process of "orthodoxization" of the city's "Old Yishuv"—its transformation from a traditional society to an Orthodox enclave, in which the new neighborhoods emerged in part as a defense against the winds of modernity that had begun to blow even in this ancient city (Bartal 1977, 1989).

By the early twentieth century, corporate groups similar to those that had established the new Orthodox enclaves, now motivated however by Hebraist and Zionist ideologies, came together in Jerusalem to initiate similar residential projects. Based on competing conceptions of sacred and profane, the goals of the new Hebrew-oriented neighborhood corporations differed markedly from those of their Orthodox predecessors, even as much of their praxis is strikingly similar. When one group of Hebrew educators and activists came together in 1902 with the aim of "creating a Hebrew city" out of Jerusalem's then very non-Hebrew reality, they conceived of the process as one that would create a definitively Hebrew public space. Hebrew in this new "city" would not only be the spoken language, as the bylaws stipulated (replacing Mea Shearim's halakhic law as the central pillar and rationale), but would be given a new status as a sacred tongue in a way that would transform the language itself and the very notion of sacrality associated with it. Hebrew, of course, holds the status of sacred tongue in Orthodox Jewish understandings as well, where it is reserved largely for liturgical use. In the projected new Hebrew neighborhood, however, it was precisely the removal of the language from the heavenly sphere and its transformation into a language of the mundane, an instrument of daily speech, that was to give Hebrew a liturgical dimension of a new kind as it becomes the central pillar of new nationalized rituals and in performances of a reshaped public sphere. Central to the creation of the new neighborhood's "Hebrew" character, the charter stipulated, would be the establishment of "Hebrew children's festivals . . . , evenings of entertainment" and such public performances as "children's plays in Hebrew" (Protocol 1902). Speaking Hebrew with one another, the new neighborhood's founders would not only be residing in a Hebrew neighborhood, but living a Hebrew life in this kernel of a new "Hebrew city," as they had already taken to calling it.

Ultra-Orthodox neighborhoods such as Me'ah She'arim (established in 1874) had served both as tools for self-segregation and as a defense against the winds of modernity that had begun to penetrate even this bastion of Jewish tradition (Bartal 1989, 31). Self-segregation and isolation—the attempt to create cultural and even legal islands—emerge here in tandem with an implicit claim on behalf of a universalizing orthodox vision of Jewishness and the sacred character of Judaism's holiest city. The image of Jerusalem as a city besieged—primarily by other Jews intent on destroying the traditional world—had been "an important element in the collective consciousness of the 'Old Yishuv.'" New neighborhoods were posited as "battle positions in a global front whose defenders are the Ultra-Orthodox loyalists to Jewish values" (Bartal 1989, 22).

Here too, we find overlapping lines of continuity and rupture in the later Zionist initiative. Like the Orthodox neighborhoods before them, this was on the one hand a tool for self-segregation through which these Hebraist modernizers—still an embattled minority among the city's Jewish population—could create for themselves a micro-Jerusalem reflecting their own spirit and conceptions of Jewish culture; an island in a hostile "Old Yishuv" sea. Such self-segregation, however, would serve in equal measure as a power base from which the Hebrew character of the island microcosm could be pushed outward in a bid for a reshaping of Jerusalem through the instruments of its new language and its corresponding liturgical style and rituals. The modernizing, Hebraizing neighborhoods evinced a similar tension between an isolationist and a universalizing impulse—based, of course, on a competing notion of "Jewish values" and the nature of the sacred that was being besieged. They too would use the new neighborhoods as a foothold from which to spread outward into other parts of the city, which they would then transform in such a way as to clean it of its impurity and re-establish a newly recast spiritual cleanliness and ritual purity.

The clash between these communities and their competing sacralities would grow louder during the final years of Ottoman rule in Jerusalem, as this Hebraizing agenda of the city's "New Yishuv" appeared increasingly poised to make a serious bid for greater political power and cultural hegemony. The polemics that shook Jewish Jerusalem again and again as early Hebrew and Zionist cultural institutions were established in the city gave powerful voice to this sacral character of the escalating struggle.

Hebrew Education for a New Jerusalem

One of the first of these was the Hebrew kindergarten that was established in the city in the spring of 1903. This was not the very first kindergarten of its kind in Palestine—its earliest predecessor had been founded five years earlier in the colony of Rishon LeZion (Elboim-Dror 1986). The attempt to open such a school in Jerusalem was deemed to be of particular importance, however, given precisely this struggle for the city's sacrality. The city's status as the stronghold of the Orthodox "Old Yishuv" and hence as the site of exile in the heart of the Promised Land made it a particularly compelling and important front on which to prosecute this campaign for the transformative power of Hebrew. The kindergarten was conceived in this context as an instrument in a far-reaching national transformation that would begin with a dramatic makeover of the Jews and Judaism of Jerusalem. Not surprisingly, the city's Ashkenazi rabbis immediately identified the new initiative as a veritable existential threat, and promptly issued a strict prohibition against it. Whatever the purposes of the children's center, they wrote, the kindergarten would surely not produce "holy fruit of praise [to God]." What it clearly *would* do was to "turn the children's hearts away from the ways of Torah and lead them to walk in tortuous paths" (Ben-Yehuda 1903a, 211).

In an open letter to the rabbis, the kindergarten's founders fervently protested the imprecation, objecting that in no way had they intended a challenge to the sacred core of Judaism. The school, they wrote, was being established in order to "teach our young children prayers and blessings . . . so that, from their very childhood, they might be good Jews, loyal to our laws and our Holy Torah." Indeed, the Hebrew language that was to be the language of instruction had been chosen so as to ensure that "our children might be immersed all day long in our holy tongue," an imperative for which they produced a series of classic rabbinic proof texts (Yellin, Press, and Levi 1903, 212–13).

Whether this tacit acceptance of traditional notions was meant in earnest or whether it was merely tactical,[4] it remained a lone voice of would-be moderation in the polemical storm that followed, in which competing conceptions of holy and profane came to full fledged blows. The establishment of the kindergarten now emerged clearly as a front in the struggle for political power within a changing Jewish community in Jerusalem, and for the power to delineate sacred and profane. As most of its supporters would now present it, the kindergarten would act as powerful tool not for bringing the children closer to "prayer and blessings," as the founders' letter suggested, but on the contrary, for transforming them into a new kind of Hebrew who would likely have little, at best, to do with such traditional rituals. The children who would emerge from this school would bear hardly any resemblance at all to the "gaunt and feeble" children of exile, but would instead constitute a new generation of strong, robust, and natural Hebrews. The rabbis, in other words, as one scathingly sarcastic editorial had it, were in fact correct in identifying the kindergarten as a threat to their Judaism. The hygienic sensibilities of a Hebrew kindergarten, for one—the fact that it would be well ventilated and open to the outdoors—stood in marked contrast with the traditional heder, where "the children sit crowded together, creating their own gusts of wind, and providing the heder with its own unique odor." The organized curriculum would strike a blow to the unsystematic approach of the traditional autodidactic melamed. In contrast with the aged and constricted children

---

4. There is abundant reason to take it with a grain of salt, given that the question of Hebrew literacy and instruction had long been an arena of struggle between traditionalists and modernizers in the Jewish world. For traditionalists in Europe and Palestine alike, dissemination of Hebrew grammatical education, and certainly Hebrew speech, was in itself deemed a threat to the traditional social and theological order, and to their own mechanisms of social control (see, e.g., Parush 2004). Given this, the open letter ought probably to be seen as an attempt to use the language of tradition as a reproof of the city's would-be guardians of tradition rather than as an earnest attempt to mollify them.

of exile, in a Hebrew kindergarten, the children will play, "stroll in the gardens and gather roses . . . and sing about the trees and flowers, about goats and dogs, God forbid." Finally, they will learn to engage in physical exercise, "and their arms—heaven forbid—will be like the arms of Esau." All of these, according to the commentary, were indeed a threat to the Judaism of exile, which the Orthodox rabbis represented, and were designed to be just that. "Combing one's hair," after all, the editorial commented wryly, "is the beginning of *heresy*; a clean nose—the spark of *sacrilege*" (Petachia 1903, 213, emphases added).

Another commentator, a Zionist visitor from abroad who happened to arrive in Jerusalem just in time to witness the controversy, recalled being cautioned by friends before his departure that he would find many distasteful things in Palestine due to the "depressed spiritual state of our brethren here." Having seen the rabbinic prohibition on the kindergarten—"a villainous abomination," as he wrote—he understood what they had meant (Friedman 1903, 214). A response by a pseudonymous "Pilgrim" played on the imagery of traditional ascent to Jerusalem and served witness to the changing character of the city, which although still barely perceptible, had been made more evident by his time away from the city. A generation was now clearly emerging, he wrote, that was casting off its *streimels*, snipping off its sidelocks, and relinquishing the indolence of halukkah—the system of alms dispensation that, according to a virtual Zionist consensus, was a leading source of national debasement in Jerusalem. Jerusalem was beginning to open "windows onto [its] darkened alleyways, to eradicate its stench and to purify its air" with the breath of Hebrew breezes now blowing in the city, bringing with them "light, life, and progress" (Oleh Regel 1903, 217).

A seemingly unrelated piece in that day's issue of *Hashkafa*—Eliezer Ben-Yehuda's militantly Hebraist, Zionist, and Jerusalem-based paper—sheds a further ray of light on the reconfiguration of sacrality that was implied by the kindergarten as the new front line in the campaign to Hebraize Jerusalem. The polemical pieces were followed by a report on scientific advance the likes of which was a common feature of the Ben-Yehuda papers. Science, for this nationalized *maskil* (proponent of the

Jewish Enlightenment), was the path not only to a new truth, but to a form of holiness recast. In this vein, an earlier report on Marconi's advances with the telegraph had made an explicit case for science as a replacement for magic and religion in approaching the wonders of the world. Had Marconi appeared in an earlier age, Ben-Yehuda wrote, "people would have [either] treated him as a holy man of God, and bowed down to him in prayer, [or] seen him as a magician who uses the forces of evil, and would have feared him and put him to death" (Ben-Yehuda 1903c, 1). Now, in the issue devoted to the kindergarten, the polemical pieces were followed by a report on Marie Curie's discovery of radium and radiation. Titled *Hom ha-Ganuz la-Adam la-Atid Lavo* (A Heat Concealed from Men for the Future), the report played on the traditional kabbalistic notion of the *Or ha-Ganuz*, the hidden light of the divine that had to be reduced for human consumption, but which, in the messianic age, would once again shine with full divine splendor. Soon, Ben-Yehuda promised, balls of *orit*, as he dubbed the new substance, would be hanging from our ceilings "and the light will never darken or cease." Indeed, this step forward for the human mind, this wonder of the natural world, would provide light and heat together "for the future yet to come" in a language that was adopted directly from the mystical tale of the *Or ha-Ganuz* (Ben-Yehuda 1903b, 214).

Other reports in *Hashkafa* took no less pleasure relishing in the sense of blasphemy aroused in the city's Orthodox Jews at the sight of the invading armies (such as they were) of Hebrew language and culture. One witness to a small procession that followed on the heels of a meeting of the recently established *Tze'irot Yerushalaim* (Young Women of Jerusalem) reported being transported to "visions of ancient times, when we were a nation settled on its own land, and young Hebrew maidens danced in gardens, dressed in white dresses. . . ." For other Jerusalemites, however, the sight seems to have been somewhat less inspiring. Upon hearing the young women's Hebrew speech, according to the account, "a hasid with long sidelocks" who was standing nearby "fled like a dog catching scent of stick, and I could hear him muttering 'Oy vey! The abomination! The abomination has penetrated into here, as well. Heaven forbid!' And he spit a few mouthfuls of spit at the young women" (Ben-Uri 1904, 286).

Art and the New Jerusalem

If the scientism of Ben-Yehuda's *maskilic* Zionism seemed to offer one path to a new light, for Boris Schatz it would be art and artisanship that would constitute a new Torah. The Bezalel art museum and school he established in Jerusalem in 1906 was conceived as its holy sanctuary, a veritable Third Temple. The scope of the new Bezalel's undertaking was consequently a broadly defined one, and included the ingathering of Jewish cultural possessions, the creation of a new Jewish art, aesthetic and culture, and finally, the training of Palestine's Jewish community, and the impoverished Jews of Jerusalem in particular, in a variety of crafts that would help wean them away from the halukkah economy. Bezalel was envisioned as the site in which a number of seemingly distinct national projects in the realm of the arts, artisanry, and crafts, and even labor economics, would be fused together to give new shape not only to the Jewish community of Jerusalem and Palestine, but to Jewishness itself and to Jewish life throughout the world.[5] The opposing poles of holiness and profanity were pivotal in this ambitious recasting of Jewish life, which placed Jerusalem at its very center—as both a locus of the profane and the site of a future renewed sacrality. Indeed, Schatz's vision for Bezalel was for a sweeping revival that he conceived in terms of a literal national redemption that would spring forth from a revitalized and re-sanctified city.

Shortly before his arrival in 1906, accompanied by the Zionist movement's star artist, Ephraim Moshe Lilien, Eliezer Ben-Yehuda's *Hashkafa* proclaimed the national significance of the upcoming event. "For Beauty will issue forth Out of Zion and Art from Jerusalem," the paper's lead headline declared in its translation of the traditional "Torah will issue forth out of Zion and the Word of the Lord from Jerusalem." Bezalel, as the new aesthetic and artistic expression of the national imperative,

---

5. On the influence of then-current German political discourse in this conceptualization, and the differences in the ways in which this was understood by the figures involved, see Bertz (2004). Dalia Manor (2005, 29) stresses the eastern European models on which this conception was based. For additional discussion of the early Bezalel, see Shilo-Cohen (1983) and Saposnik (2008).

would replace the religious dimension of Torah and the covenant with God that it embodied, and would exert a powerful spiritual influence on the lives of Jews in Palestine and throughout the world. Its commitment to establishing workshops and to providing training in various crafts, Ben-Yehuda proclaimed, will help bring about an end to "the life of shame through 'charity,' which so degrades one's soul and spirit," and would usher in "salvation to the colonies." No less important than this economic salvation, Schatz's new undertaking would serve as the basis for an aesthetic-spiritual transformation of "the masses of Jews here who are slowly perishing in a life lacking in hygiene and cleanliness." Among them, he projected, "there will gradually emerge a generation that will be more attuned to feelings of *beauty, cleanliness and purity*" thanks to the work that Bezalel would soon undertake (*Hashkafa* 1905, 1–2, emphasis added).

In his own first programmatic statement, Schatz framed what he expected to be Bezalel's importance as part of a modern nationalist movement in terms of a traditional religious act of constructing a home for sacred national treasures in Jerusalem. The creation of a Jewish art institute in Jerusalem, he wrote, was first and foremost an expression of the Jewish people's return to life. Jerusalem, after all, "has remained holy to us throughout our extended period of exile." While it was true, he conceded, that in the past centuries, "we have not constructed glorious temples" in the city, the lingering bond to the land and to the city had inspired Jews to continue to build "many houses of prayer and of burial . . ." (Schatz 1906a, 1). Indeed, for centuries, Jews had maintained customs such as burial with small packets of soil from the Holy Land, and some had immigrated there in old age with the intent to be buried in its soil. While burial rites had been important in maintaining a bond between the Jews and their land, this very link, Schatz argued, was too exclusively associated with death. Now, in the era of national rebirth, it must be given new form. Bezalel's presence in Jerusalem would renew the Jewish people's link to the vitality of their distant past in the land, thus prompting a profound transformation in the Jewish people and infusing their death-bound link to the land with a stream of new life. "Gradually," Schatz wrote, "our people will learn to look to the Holy Land not as a . . . place where one hopes to be buried, but rather as a living land, in which one can live a pleasant life today as well, and to return it to that distant time when the Mount of Olives was covered in olive trees and an echo responded from within that grove to the voices of the daughters of Israel and to their song" (Schatz, 1906a, 1).[6]

The transvaluation that Schatz envisioned in the reality of the Mount of Olives and in its national-spiritual significance evinced precisely the kind of interplay between traditional tropes and radical innovation that characterized much of Zionist discourse and cultural praxis in Palestine. While excoriating the traditional Jewish relationship to the Mount of Olives, echoes of that very tradition continue to resonate in Schatz's vision of the transfigured bond between nation and land. Of course, the death associated with the Mount of Olives traditionally had itself been interwoven with a vision of renewed life: it was from there that the messianic resurrection of the dead was to begin. Schatz interlaces an echo of this traditional sentiment within his very attempt to supplant it, and it is precisely this use of traditional imagery that, rather than mitigating the revolutionary nature of his message, serves instead to further radicalize it. This underscores Bezalel's transvalued messianic presumption that it would effect a redemptive resurrection of the dead nation in the Land of Israel and upon the Mount of Olives.

These messianic expectations were but one facet of the religious tone that permeated much of the discourse surrounding the new school. Bezalel was named, after all, for Bezalel Ben-Uri, who had been charged by Moses with designing and building "a temple in the wilderness," in Schatz's words, for a people heading toward the Promised Land (1911, 64). Schatz viewed himself and the art he would create as a veritable renewal of prophecy in modern form, and often cast himself as the modern equivalent of Moses, traditionally the first and greatest prophet of Israel, once again appointing the artists and directing the art that would create a modern tabernacle to lead a wandering nation to its Promised Land. "I looked upon art," as Schatz wrote, "as a temple and upon artists as its priests" (1911, 60).

---

6. For a rich and insightful discussion of the relationship between Jerusalem, redemption, and death, see DeKoven Ezrahi (2000). See also Saposnik (2005).

Since it was only in "the cradle of our nation," as Schatz put it that the *"holy spirit* of art [might] descend upon the Jewish artist," considerations of Bezalel's location came to be of prime importance. The site Schatz initially chose for his new artistic tabernacle, in the eastern part of Jerusalem and in close proximity to the Old City, was selected as a spatial marker of particular evocative force. Its most salient feature—and one that Schatz repeatedly highlighted in his efforts to obtain the necessary funding to purchase it—was the view it offered of the Temple Mount. It was "of prime importance," he wrote to one of his supporters in October of 1906, that so vital a national institution as his own be erected *"near the location of the Holy Temple"* (Schatz 1906b, emphasis in the original). And a religious-national possession of this kind in a Palestine experiencing intense struggle between the European powers would have a profound importance in altering the Jews' political position in the country and their relations with other nations. "Every nation," Schatz wrote, "can boast a house of prayer, a monastery, [or] a school [in Jerusalem]." It was "only by a miracle," he added, "that this land has remained in Arab hands rather than having been purchased by Christians, who already own everything in its proximity. . . . And we—if we purchase this land—will secure for ourselves a national institution near the walls of our city" (Schatz 1906c).

The significance of the site was echoed by the Zionist Movement's official representatives in Palestine. Menahem Sheinkin, director of the Hovevei Zion Information Bureau in Jaffa, and Zalman David Levontin, who directed the Anglo-Palestine Company (the Zionist bank) wrote to Zionist Organization president David Wolffsohn in support of Schatz, stressing the importance of the site as one that offered a view of "the historical Mount Moriah," and the "Makom-Mikdasch" [site of the Temple]." Confirming the sense that the site offered to provide the Jews with a combined religious-political foothold in the city, they went a step further than Schatz himself, urging Wolffsohn to have the National Fund "purchase the entire plot," explaining that "aside from the Jews, every nation has national land and national buildings in Jerusalem and its surroundings" and that "only the Jews, who now lay claim to Palestine, have nothing" (Levontin and Sheinkin 1906).

This redemptive anticipation was not enough, however, to spare Schatz protracted negotiations with the Zionist Bank under Levontin's directorship, at the end of which the purchase of the plot failed to materialize—a fact that could surely only have served to deepen his sense of his own likeness to the original Ben-Uri, constructing a tabernacle for a nation still wandering in the wilderness. Notwithstanding his disappointment, however, Schatz would soon complete the purchase of a building in the developing western part of Jerusalem, and although the view it offered of the Old City and its eminent religious and historic sites was not quite as compelling, the new site quickly emerged as a site of pilgrimage to the "new" Zionist Jerusalem and as a national icon in its own right. Adorned with a seven-branch Menorah, Bezalel's building would become one of the most important and recurrent symbols of national rebirth in Zionist depictions of Jerusalem, where it was often contrasted with such traditional sites as the Western Wall, deemed at this point as too much of a symbol of destruction and exile to fit comfortably into the national liturgy (Saposnik 2009).

In the years before the war, the Wall, and much that was Jerusalem, often continued to be deemed outposts of *galut* (that is, exilic life) within the land of rebirth, while Bezalel was the spearhead and the leading symbol of its transformation into the land of Hebrew redemption. Little more than a year after its establishment, Schatz could write to a supporter abroad that "I have succeeded in bringing together around Bezalel all those who strive for life, for a human heart and a Jewish soul. And they have all come to see that Bezalel is the nation's home and *the very heart of the Holy city*" (Schatz 1906c, emphasis added).

As in the case of the kindergarten three years earlier, however, Schatz's appropriation of the city's holiness did not go unopposed, and soon his new tabernacle would stand accused of outright heresy. An exchange of correspondence between Schatz and the (then) American Hebrew writer Ephraim Deinard provides a particularly telling instance of the struggles over national sacrality embodied in the new national art. Identifying himself as a supporter of Bezalel, Deinard wrote that he was reconsidering his backing after reading in "a Yiddish journal . . . that the image of Jesus of

Nazareth and pictures of his apostles are being created in your school," a possible echo of the prominent exhibition of Shmuel Hirshenberg's painting of "The Wandering Jew." Admittedly, Deinard wrote, as a Hebraist and Hebrew writer himself, he might have been skeptical of this particular source—the organ of a competing vision of Jewish culture—but a visitor from Jerusalem had recently brought with him reports that were even more disquieting. Not only did he speak of an art that displayed forbidden images, but of a range of new customs that surrounded it, which evinced a heretical bent that seemed to lend the Yishuv's emerging culture the tenor of a pagan cult. Further transgressing the traditional prohibition on the forging of images, Deinard's letter quotes his guest's report that "a statue of Dr. Herzl was formed, and a procession marched with cries of joy to a colony where the deceased had planted a tree." Supporters of Zionist work were deeply disconcerted, Deinard reported, and now found no answer to their opponents' charge that the Zionists were *"defiling the land with statues and images"* (Deinard 1906, emphasis added).

In its substance this was not, of course, an inaccurate depiction of the new holidays and styles of celebration that were coming together in Palestine to constitute a budding national culture—one that aimed at the transformation of the Jews, of the Holy Land, and the Holy city, and through them, of the Holy itself. In his reply to Deinard, Schatz implicitly acknowledged all this but argued not only that such a transformation was not a desecration, but that the charge itself showed the accuser to be "one of the indolent Jerusalemites who see Bezalel as a threat to their halukkah livelihood" and who themselves, therefore, constituted the true blemish on the city's holy character. Bezalel's efforts to create avenues for the "productivization" of Jerusalem's Jewish community, inseparable from its reclamation of a lost national aesthetic sensibility, was in fact a reclamation of a Jewish holiness and the sacredness of a Jerusalem defiled. Those who opposed these efforts, he wrote, were consequently "of the clan of Korach"—the leader of a group of biblical rebels who, motivated by greed and corruption, attempted to challenge the leadership of Moses in the desert (and who were punished accordingly). Bezalel (and Schatz himself) were cast once again in this context in the role of Moses, the messengers of a new Torah that would indeed issue forth from Zion, but not from that of the traditional, corrupt and exilic "Old Yishuv." Sacrality itself was being contested and refigured, as differing visions of Jewish culture, and of Palestine's place in that culture, increasingly competed for centrality and legitimacy in a changing Jewish world. In many senses, of course, Zionist cultural work did represent an effort to secularize the land—to transform a Holy Land into a homeland. At the same time, however, this stress on a 'this-worldly' Jerusalem was in itself (at least much of the time) an effort to re-sanctify Jerusalem and the Land, ostensibly defiled by a holiness long since perverted. This was sanctity reconceived—one that would stand not in opposition to the lived-in city of stones and buildings, but which inhered in its very mundaneness, itself revitalized and reclaimed. It was a sacrality drawn down from the celestial spheres and re-imposed onto a this-worldly Jerusalem.

The Zionist Anti-Missionary Campaign

It was in the name of precisely this re-sanctification that another front developed in the struggle for Jerusalem and which, in the first years of the twentieth century, pitched the city's increasingly ascendant Hebraist-Zionist "New Yishuv" against the Orthodox "Old Yishuv" in a surprising way. The drive to eradicate the influence on Jerusalem's Jews of Christian missionary institutions had roots extending back to the early nineteenth century, when missionary schools and hospitals had begun to proliferate throughout the city, and had set their sights on the city's Jews as a particularly important (and safely available) target for proselytizing (Wasserstein 2002, 50–53; Okkenhaug 2002). Orthodox Jewish resistance was quick to follow, but by the early twentieth century a shift had occurred in the leadership of Jewish anti-missionary resistance from the ultra-Orthodox community to the "New Yishuv" Zionists, and with this shift in the struggle's demographic spearhead came a change in the nature and goals of the struggle itself.

The Zionist anti-missionary campaign, much of which was centered on Jerusalem as a missionary stronghold, began to gain momentum around 1910 and reached a fever pitch by 1912, when it seeped in palpable ways into the budding national liturgy and became a building block in the construction of the emerging national culture. The struggle also happened to coincide and overlap with the internal Jewish political struggle that was taking place in the city. Making the anti-missionary campaign an important instrument in this intra-Jewish struggle for dominance in Jerusalem, the Hebrew press repeatedly focused on the Jewish students in missionary schools who came from within the Orthodox "Old Yishuv."[7] Indeed, more than a struggle against the missionary institutions themselves (which enjoyed the protection of powerful governments) the Zionist anti-missionary campaign was in fact arguably more a battle against the Orthodox Jewish establishment and "an entire system of unconscious assimilation," of which they were taken to be guilty, along with certain Orthodox Zionists (*Ha-Po'el Ha-Tza'ir* 1912, 19–20). Cast in these terms, it was an all but eschatological battle for the very soul of the nation against what many commentators referred to as the *avoda zara*—foreign worship, or idolatry—of missionary education.

The play on the multi-valenced Hebrew word *avoda*, which became pivotal in the largely rhetorical campaign, helped cast the anti-missionary front as an integral component in a broader struggle to reshape the Jewish Yishuv of Palestine and Jewishness itself, and served to deepen the religio-cosmic dimension of the general struggle against all that was deemed national abomination. In the socio-economic struggle being waged primarily by the young Labor-Zionists of the period, *avoda Ivrit* was often similarly posed as the counterpoint to another *avoda zara*, in this context referring to the employment by Jewish employers of "foreign" (i.e., Arab) labor, itself now seen as a form of idolatry. With the use of this terminology in the anti-missionary, or anti-Orthodox, struggle in Jerusalem, Hebrew labor and Hebrew education merge to form a united front in the campaign for national culture, in which all things Hebrew now become the new guardians of a true sacrality, at war with the many false idols arrayed against it. "The very same youngsters who are doing battle against avoda

7. Reasons for this seem to have included the absence of frameworks for the education for young girls within the Orthodox community and the general poverty of much of the "Old Yishuv," for whom the meals and the extended school day that the missionary schools offered the children who attended were an often irresistible windfall. See Saposnik (2008).

zara in the colonies," as the Labor Zionist Ha-Po'el Ha-Tza'ir argued, "can and must take up arms against the avoda zara that exists in the field of education as well" (Ha-Tzofeh 1912, 21–22). To the writer Yehuda Burla, Jewish parents who chose to send their children to missionary schools were the modern day equivalent of those of their ancient forebears who chose to sacrifice their children in the rituals of various idolatrous cults. Like those ancients, segments of the Yishuv today, he wrote, are similarly worshiping false idols by "happily and blindly handing our children over to . . . a new avoda zara—the missionary and Jesuit schools in our country" (Burla 1912, 1).

At a time when new Hebrew educational institutions were jockeying for primacy in the Yishuv—indeed, on the eve of the climax of this educational battle, which came in the form of another educational-political struggle that would come to be known as "the language war"—this struggle against missionary educational influence in the Yishuv was at its core a battle for the social and political dominance of Jerusalem's emergent nationalist elite. Its principal goal was the creation and inculcation of a particular type of national consciousness that involved a new valuation of the sacred and the profane, and that would replace the competing and heretofore regnant theological conception. The central thrust of the anti-missionary campaign, as one writer put it, was to open the eyes of Jerusalem's Jews to see "the filth in which their children are mired" (Yisraeli 1913, 34) and to pave the way for the Zionists' purifying educational institutions and their new cult of the Hebrew nation.

Placing it firmly in the heart of that new cult, in the spring of 1913 the anti-missionary campaign became the centerpiece and the defining theme in the celebration of the traditional, but transformed, holiday of Lag Ba-Omer, which was fused with the newly instituted "Flower Day." During the previous year's festivities, one commentator noted, the "Jerusalem crowd [had] stood by passively and hardly participated in the purchase of flowers." Now, however, the fusion of the new festival and the religio-national campaign helped to further the Zionist re-shaping of Jerusalem's public space, and to inspire the growing crowd with a sense that "it had an obligation to support our treasury so that we will be able to fight against the mission—the purpose to which the proceeds of this year's "Flower Day" were devoted." Bestowing added significance on the event, the report added, "the flowers were sold by the boys and girls of the Hebrew schools" (Ha-Po'el Ha-Tza'ir 1913, 15–16)—the youth of the new Zionist sacred, contrasted with those children who, as the language of the campaign would have it, were being sacrificed to the Moloch of the missionary schools. The flower sales, processions, and gymnastics demonstrations that colored the celebrations were punctuated by speeches that all protested "against the mission and against those who send their children to that inferno" and by the crowd's responses of "down with the mission" (ibid.).

Central though it was to that moment in the construction of the Yishuv's national culture and to the shaping of its nationalized Jerusalem, the anti-missionary campaign would soon give way to other concerns. Indeed, it seemed to be all but forgotten[8] as Palestine's Zionists soon took aim at their next critical front as the "Language War" raged through Jewish Palestine, followed by a World War that would end, of course, in a British conquest that would redraw the battle lines in the holy city, and seemingly change forever both the physical contours and the symbolic faces of Jerusalem.

Challenging Historiography

This rapid succession of events, and the dramatic changes that Jerusalem has undergone while maintaining its status as a center of multiple battlegrounds, highlight one of the defining challenges of any historiography—the elusive line between continuity and change that is at the very root of the historical enterprise. Historians of Jerusalem, like visitors to the city, meet with physical, tangible traces of that ancient past immediately abutting the latest asphalt, concrete, and barbed wire of the new and very recent. With its ancient archaeological relics and the antiquity of its symbolisms on the one hand, and the discernible evidence of the many competing claims, wars, and changes of regime that have shaped its

8. So much so that there is scant mention of it in the historiography, having been largely overlooked by historians as well.

history on the other, there are few places that more acutely confront one with the tension between history's *longues durées* and its deep fissures and discontinuities. Indeed, in contemporary Jerusalem, defining the lines between old and new, separating continuity from discontinuity, has in itself become one front in the intense struggles taking place both between Israelis and Palestinians and within Israeli society.

The repeated reconfigurations of Jerusalem in Zionist thought and praxis begins with the late nineteenth century twinning of rejection and embrace, and continues through to the city's changing physical and symbolic terrain during the British Mandate years, after 1948, again in the wake of 1967, and repeatedly since 1987, the first Palestinian uprising, and the negotiations between Israelis and Palestinians that ensued. It would reach a symbolic apex during Ehud Barak and Yasser Arafat's negotiations in summer 2000 that were designed to demarcate terrestrial and subterranean spheres of sovereignty, re-articulating in starkly literal terms the traditional Jewish distinction between a Jerusalem *shel ma'ala* (above) and a Jerusalem *shel mata* (below). Each of these Jerusalems have now been pulled down a few notches on the continuum leading from the celestial to the earthly—and in this case, subterranean—as conflicting claims to the city's ancient past and to the very heart of its holiness have been translated into the language of international diplomacy and (sadly, unsuccessful) conflict resolution. Indeed, these diplomatic episodes stand as final manifest illustrations that the story of the struggle for Jerusalem is not one in which rational, self-interested political calculations camouflage themselves in religious and sacral language. In Jerusalem, another of the seam-lines that remains indistinguishable—if indeed it is a line at all—is that which serves not so much to separate, but rather to fuse and blend the political and the sacred, whether in the struggles between national-religious groups or in those that take place within them.

With its latticework of crisscrossing seam-lines—both literal and figurative—Jerusalem thus emerges as a seductive peephole in the search for the subtle and elusive threads that stitch together continuity and change in the making of modern nationalisms. Nationalism, Anthony Smith (2003, 6) argues, ought to be understood in part as a selective adoption, adaptation, and re-interpretation of "pre-existing symbolisms, mythologies, attachments, and beliefs of traditional religions and outlooks." This type of cultural history reveals that Zionism's ambivalent discourses regarding Jerusalem, its often rocky relationship with the city that gave it its name, combined with its attempt to reclaim that city's purportedly lost sacredness, come together to paint a revealing picture of the dynamic nature of a nationalist hermeneutics as the ongoing process of selection, re-selection, and adaptation that it entailed.

The story of Zionism's Jerusalems here connects to a longer *durée* history of Jewish imaginings. As literary scholar Sidra DeKoven Ezrahi (2002, 49) has argued, one can look at least as far back as the eleventh and twelfth century poetry of Yehuda Halevi to find Jerusalem at the central axis in a "struggle between the metaphorizing and the concretizing imagination, and between body and territory, undertaken in the service of a reclamation of political-historical or mystical access to holiness." One is reminded of Eric Hobsbawm's contention that "no historical continuity whatever [exists] between Jewish proto-nationalism and modern Zionism" (Hobsbawm 1990, 76) and of his conception of nationalism as so novel a phenomenon that "even historic continuity had to be invented . . ." (Hobsbawm and Ranger 1983, 7). The histories of Zionist Jerusalem's sacrality and re-sacralization, I am arguing, militates against Hobsbawm's notion of nationalism, which is implicitly based in a sense of absolute fissure between the modern and all that came before, and of a one-directional and unequivocal process of secularization that helped carve out that chasm. In "constantly redefining and reenergizing itself by reference to outworn religious traditions," secularization—even in its most extreme ideologically-committed forms (as in the type that appears in some versions of the Zionist project)—is finally "a way of preserving, at a more rarified and rationally persuasive level of awareness, precisely what it seeks to destroy" (Pecora 2006, 20).

Ben-Yehuda's language of redemption through science and human progress and Schatz's use of a language and imagery of prophecy and revelation—as well as his own self-image as a latter-day Moses or Bezalel Ben-Uri devoted to the task of bringing a new Torah to a revived Israel and to a Jerusalem awakened from the dead—serve as vivid illustrations of this duality in which innovation and preservation, secularization and sacralization, intertwine in Zionist culture-making in Palestine. In his *Sacralizing the Secular*, Stephen McKnight (1989, 15) has argued for an understanding of modernity not in terms of an unproblematized process of secularization, but rather as a series of reconceptualizations that ultimately blur the distinctions between the sacred and the secular. Although his book has been the target of considerable criticism, much of it pointing to the limited body of evidence for an argument of such sweeping implications (Gosselin 1990; Dumm 1990), the broad outlines of his argument for a modernity in which secularization and re-sacralization are intertwined and act as twin poles of the same processes we tend to call "modernization" is compelling. Taken together, McKnight and his critics point to the knotty problems involved in attempting to balance the *longue durée* against the historical event, and the impact of lingering, and at times reemerging, subterranean processes and ideas at specific historical moments. A study of the multifaceted recasting of Jerusalem in Zionist imagination and praxis around the turn of the century can hardly claim to represent material for a thorough reevaluation of modernity. It does, however, seem to suggest at least some broad outlines of an argument for a more Janus-faced character of the modern, in which secularization and re-sacralization are conceived as twinned and as engaged—however uneasily—in a dialectical tango that, in at least some very important instances, would prove to be a formative historical force.

6

Changing Research Perspectives on the Changing City

MENACHEM KLEIN

FOR THREE REASONS Jerusalem is the focus of a great deal of research in history, archeology, religion studies, and politics.[1] First, it is one of the oldest cities in the world, containing in its subterranean layers a rich and dramatic history. Second, Jerusalem is holy for many millions that see it as the place where earth links heaven. Third, Jerusalem is the stratum where Israeli and Palestinian nations contest over sovereignty and legitimacy. Yet, much is lacking in academic studies on Jerusalem, as Rashid Khalidi (2005, 14, 15, 16) notes: "Perhaps what is most lacking in the existing histories that deal with Jerusalem are good general books on the subject[,] ideally ones covering a broad historical sweep and accessible to a wide audience.... [A]nother need is for a basic history of Jerusalem as an urban or municipal area . . . to address myths that need to be deconstructed as part of a serious agenda for writing the history of Jerusalem." Obviously, as in any academic field of research, students of Jerusalem use different disciplines and make individual choices. They are called to successfully neutralize any national or religious bias and use their national and reli-

1. A selected bibliography of titles in Israeli academic libraries is maintained by the Israel Palestine Center for Research and Information (http://ipcri.org/httpdocs/IPCRI/R -PolicyPapers.html). For a database on historic Jerusalem, including photos and maps, see the Jerusalem Virtual Library (http://www.jerusalem-library.org). Researchers can also use the Israeli National Photo Archive (http://147.237.72.31/topsrch/defaulte.htm).

gious belongings to enrich their research perspectives. In this essay I aim
to pinpoint neglected subjects and to focus on what we do not know about
the city. Rather than discussing in detail why and for what reasons those
subjects are fully or partly neglected, I prefer to stay positive and suggest
instead the methods in history, political geography, and sociology that
will help fill in our current gaps of knowledge.

History

Salim Tamari (2005, 2009) and Rashid Khalidi (1998) use Palestinian
written documents and photographs to explore how the local identities
of Jerusalem and Palestine were constructed and reproduced in the late
Ottoman period by the entry of nationalism, colonialism, and imperialism. Following Edward Said's *Orientalism* (1978) and Benedict Anderson's
Imagined Communities (2006), this direction is popular among the younger
students of Tamari and Khalidi, for example, Issam Nassar (2006) and
Abigail Jacobson (2001, 2011, and calls for further study.

Salim Tamari's (2002) research on Jerusalem in the late British Mandatory period raised a subject that still is a socio-historical taboo in both
Israeli and Palestinian societies: the social interaction of Arab Palestinians, Jewish Palestinians, and the British in a time of an escalating ethno-
national conflict. Further research is needed to reveal the social origins
of those individuals whose paths crossed in Jerusalem, including their
social boundaries, the size and depth of their mutual relations, and the
impact left by them. How often were these crossings made? Did these
engagements create a community even as their respective compatriots
engaged in fighting? Was the impact of the Second World War on Jerusalem similar to that of Cairo (see, for example, Cooper 1989)? How were
plans for partitioning Palestine and constituting an international regime
in Jerusalem in the years 1945–48 rooted in the city's inter-communal
relations? These are questions that only further research can answer. It
will be interesting to compare the findings of this suggested study on
the mid-twentieth century interaction with Jerusalem's inter-communal
identity eighty to fifty years earlier, at the late Ottoman period, or with
the Israeli-Palestinian interaction in the city since 1967. I hope to answer
some of these questions in my next research project where I compare

Jewish-Arab interactions in Jaffa, Jerusalem, and Hebron since the late nineteenth century.

To the best of my knowledge, very little has been written on divided Jerusalem in the years 1949–67. The "new historians" publish extensively on how the division of Israel/Palestine was planned and how it operated before and during the 1948 war. But there has been little research done on how the western and eastern parts of the city managed urban life under the 1949–67 division. Indeed Kimberly Katz's (2005) book is one of the few works devoted to this period. However, she looks at Jerusalem from the perspective of the central authority in Amman. Katz deals with the ways that the Hashemite establishment used Jerusalem to obtain legitimacy for its rule over the East and West Bank. The Hashemite administration presented itself as the custodian of the holy places and displayed Jordan as central to the Holy Land. Yet, the view from Jerusalem is absent even from this work, which does not focus on the city itself or its inhabitants (ibid.). How the Israeli and the Jordanian border cities managed the lives of their citizenry remains an unanswered question. No less interesting is to find answers to the following questions: What remained in the Israeli and Jordanian-Palestinian collective memories from the time during which they were one entity? What were the components of each side's local identity? Presumably, studying divided Jerusalem was not attractive and was even illegitimate after the 1967 war when, on the one hand, the Israeli concept of a united and open Jerusalem ruled over city life, and on the other hand, the Palestinian Liberation Organization contested Jordan on the right to rule Jerusalem when the Israeli occupation ended. Such sentiments carry less weight today, thus facilitating renewed study of this time period.

Another uncultivated field of research is a "bottom-up" history of the Israeli annexation of Jerusalem from the Palestinian-Jerusalemite perspective. There is considerable research on the "top-down" effect of Israeli occupation, that is, how Israel confiscated land and properties, built settlements, and discriminated against the Palestinian population (see, for example, Nitzan-Shiftan 2006). But no research tells the history through the eyes of Palestinian residents. Theoretically, an occupied people can choose between the following strategies: be loyal to the system enforced on it; accommodate and enjoy the limited benefits that the new system offers, while maneuvering to survive as long as possible; reject the imposition either by acts of protest or by managing a revolt; and exiting the city. What were the strategies used by the Palestinians in Jerusalem? Did different neighborhoods or social classes react differently to Israeli occupation or use different types of strategies? Related to this set of questions is the following one: In what ways have the Palestinians in Jerusalem changed their everyday life since 1967 as a consequence of their interaction with Israel in an "open city"? Following Foucault (1977), Braverman (2006) sees illegal building in East Jerusalem as Palestinian spatial rejection of Israeli housing and building laws and their enforcement. But her innovating and pioneering study is limited to the subject of house construction and demolition. Her interest is in exposing methods and agencies that the Israeli hegemonic power uses in order to maintain and reproduce its power relations with the weaker Palestinian actor. Only in a very few pages does Braverman deal with the Palestinian bottom-up reaction in the way that I have been describing it.

A brief historical review of a small Palestinian village on the outskirts of Jerusalem underscores how limited our historical knowledge is. The place is Nu'man, also known as Khirbet Mazmuria.[2] In 2003, Nu'man had some two hundred residents, who lived in twenty-five houses. The village is located on the southeastern border of the Jerusalem Municipality, a few hundred meters north of Bait Sahur, a town that lies adjacent to Bethlehem. Northeast of Nu'man are the Palestinian neighborhoods Umm Tuba and Tsur Baher; the Jewish Israeli Har Homa settlement was built there in 1996. In the 1967 census, the residents of Nu'man were mistakenly recorded as residents of the West Bank and were given West Bank identity cards rather than the Israeli identity cards given to most Palestinians who lived in areas annexed by Israel. How this mistake occurred remains unclear. According to Jamal Dir'awi, head of the village committee, the census takers ignored the fact that all the families were living in their homes at Nu'man at the time of the census (B'Tselem 2003). Notwithstanding this, they registered them as residents of the West Bank because

2. The information below on Nu'man draws from a B'Tselem (2003) status report.

the mukhtar of their clan was living in neighboring Umm al-Tal'a at the time. It is also possible that, because of Nu'man's proximity to the Jerusalem Municipality's border, the census takers mistakenly believed that the houses were not located in the territory annexed by Israel.

Until the early 1990s, the failure to register residents of Nu'man as residents of Jerusalem had almost no effect on them. Although Nu'man was formally annexed into Israel in 1967, the Israeli authorities completely ignored the village for many years. Israel's police had not enforced law in the village, and had never considered the question of whether the residents have been residing lawfully within Jerusalem's borders. The Jerusalem Municipality has not supplied any services to the residents and has not required the residents to pay municipal taxes. It is worth noting that this was also the case in other border villages such as Wallageh, north of Bethlehem and Beit Jalah, near the Israeli settlement of Gilo.

Following the annexation of East Jerusalem in 1967, Israel nullified the Jordanian master plans that were prepared for these areas, thereby creating a policy vacuum. This vacuum prevented the issuing of building permits, and almost completely froze the development of East Jerusalem. In the early 1980s, the Jerusalem Municipality decided to prepare master plans for all of the Palestinian neighborhoods in East Jerusalem. Most of these plans have been approved. In preparing the master plans, the municipality ignored Nu'man, and the village is still classified as "white land." Under this classification, building permits may not be issued, regardless of the status of the residents.

Because the Israeli authorities ignored the village, it is unclear if the residents were aware of the legal and other ramifications of the Israeli annexation. Over the years, residents of Nu'man developed various connections with Jerusalem and with the villages surrounding it, in some cases even prior to 1967. Many residents worked in the city and children from the village studied in Tsur Baher and Umm Tuba, which are in East Jerusalem. Residents of Nu'man also maintained social and commercial relationships with the residents of these villages.

In 1991, the Israeli government decided to require Palestinian residents of the occupied territories to obtain individual permits to enter Israel. The decision was reinforced in 1993, when Israel imposed a general closure on

Gaza and the West Bank. Because most residents of Nu'man have West Bank identity cards but live within Jerusalem's borders, residing in their own homes became an illegal act. Leaving their village for other areas of Jerusalem, including the villages annexed to the city, entailed the risk of arrest by the Israeli police or IDF. Since the outbreak of the al-Aqsa intifada, in late September 2000, the IDF and the Border Police have further restricted the movement of Nu'man's residents. These restrictions affect all aspects of their lives. For example, the Israeli restrictions have caused a sanitation crisis in the village. Lacking a sewage system, the village relies on cesspools, which are emptied by a pump and tanker. Israel's blockage of the road to al-Khas has prevented the cesspools from being emptied and removed from the village. A second example centers on the village's children and their access to education. Since there are no schools in Nu'man, from the 1960s until 1995 the village children studied in schools in the East Jerusalem communities of Umm Tuba and Tsur Baher. In 1995, the Jerusalem Municipality decided that, because Nu'man's residents have West Bank identity cards, they would not be entitled to study in the Israeli school system. The children then transferred to schools in al-Khas for primary school and to Beit Sahur for high school. But the blocking of Nu'man's roads caused many problems for the children on their way to and from school.

As holders of West Bank identity cards, Nu'man's residents are not allowed to stay in Jerusalem or in the villages annexed to the city (including their own homes!) without a special permit issued by Israel's Civil Administration. In May 2000, the Ministry of the Interior noted to the residents that "clarifications that we made with the Jerusalem building inspection department indicate that these two places [Nu'man and an adjacent village] lie in Judea and Samaria and not within the municipal jurisdiction of Jerusalem." Simultaneously, the building inspection department of the Ministry of the Interior accused three village residents of building houses without permits.

In June 2002, the Israeli government decided to establish a barrier that cuts into the West Bank and is meant to prevent the uncontrolled entry of Palestinians into Israel. The barrier's route passes between Nu'man and Beit Sahur, thereby completely blocking the road linking the two communities. The only road open from Nu'man to the West Bank now is the road leading to al-Khas. In late March 2003, the residents learned for the first time that the road to al-Khas would also be blocked as part of Israel's ongoing plans for continued construction of the separation barrier. Blocking the only road left to the residents of Nu'man to reach the West Bank effectively imprisons the residents—who are also forbidden to enter Jerusalem—in their village. Isolation, and the impossibility of having a normal life, may lead the residents of Nu'man to consider leaving their village. In so doing, Israel will then be in a position to realize its plan to extend the Jewish Har Homa neighborhood.[3]

This narrative tells us what a powerful state has done to villagers residing on the border of a desert and a metropolitan city. But we know much less about the development of Nu'man from a semi-nomadic society to a suburb of blue collar workers. Beyond its occupational blindness to local patterns of life while exercising its power, we know almost nothing about Israel's interaction with Nu'man on a daily basis: What did the occupied population adopt and reject? How did the residents of Nu'man build relations with their nearest cities, and how did they maintain a communal identity while experiencing such dramatic changes? The Palestinian voice in this and similar places has still not been heard.

Political Geography

The case of Nu'man shows the importance of border areas. According to MacGregor (1994), there is a need to pay special attention to the edges, the dividing lines within and between cities. In reconstructing a sense of political community there is a need to also reconstruct public space and unite these social and spatial divides. These include reconstructing public services, full employment, development plans, giving equal opportunities, and imposing fair wages. Unity means also providing full citizenship rights, solving the acute problems of housing, social incorporation and full integration, agreeing on shared fundamental values, shaping public

---

3. Sheikh Sa'ad is an East Jerusalem neighborhood close to Nu'man that suffers from similar problems of access and underdevelopment (see Issacharoff and Harel 2010).

education to enhance these values, and launching open political life by allowing the full and equal representation of socially different groups in a wider political system. In other words, to bridge the divide means building a multicultural, nonethnic democracy in the city. There is no doubt that this state of affairs does not exist in today's Jerusalem. Worse, the Israeli-Palestinian conflict shifted in 2000 from a border struggle to an ethnic conflict that is centered in Jerusalem (Klein 2010).

Divided City

In the academic literature, Jerusalem is considered to be a divided and frontier city (Dumper 1997; Kliot and Mansfield 1999; Cheshin, Hutman, and Melamed 1999; Bollens 1998a, 1998b; Hasson 1996; Klein 2001). According to Kotek (1999, 228), "three elements characterize any frontier-city: sovereignty quarrel, double legitimacy and conflict." However, according to the new political geography, frontiers, boundaries, and borders are a more rich and multidimensional phenomenon. As Newman (1999), Ackleson (2000), and Paasi (1999) argue, the conflict in the frontier city is not only over sovereignty, but also about collective identity and narrative, social control, the spatial division of labor, economics, and the control of resources, culture and administration.[4] Similarly Falah and Newman (1995) conclude in general, and regarding the Israeli-Palestinian conflict in particular, "in addition to horizontal territorial structures, boundary concepts also relate to social, ethnic, gender, and class vertical structures."

Ackleson (2000) sees territory relating to and representing collective identity in three ways. First, the representation changes as the territory and borders change. Second, borders and issues of collective identity such as nationalism directly impact how members of bounded communities understand their separateness. Borders drive right to the heart of the bonds between citizen and state, creating a distinction against the other. Borders establish the limits of state sovereignty, which encapsulates citizens' legal rights by demarcating territory and encouraging the national

---

4. On identity and narrative conflict in the Holy Basin of Jerusalem, see Ir Amim (2008).

idea within it. Third, border zones are places where the state is not the sole "power container," but is in fact a "leaking container."

There is, indeed, little difference between a frontier and a boundary. A boundary marks the point up to which each collective reaches, while the frontier directs its gaze to the other side of the boundary, to encounter and confront an opposing entity or culture. Each of the contending groups seeks to control or defend its territory against being physically taken over by the "other," the "invader." Moreover, drawing the boundaries of the "other" and excluding her is essential to defining an "us." In the framework of the conflict, territory has a symbolic value that mobilizes group members to defend against the enemy that threatens them. According to this view, in East Jerusalem there is a confrontation between two cultures and communities, between two national identities that are competing for a single space. Moreover, being the Israeli capital and capital-in-the-making for Palestine, Jerusalem contains a reciprocal relationship between micro-local divisions and macro ones (Hasson 1996; Kotek 1999; Falah and Newman 1995; Klein 2001; Stotkin 1996; see also M. Klein 2005).

According to MacGregor (1994), divided cities face problems of legitimacy because of the exclusion of parts of their residents from full citizenship as expressed in political participation, fair and equal treatment in law, distribution of goods, access to social benefits, and allocation of state services. For pluralism to be effective it must operate within a wider system where all accept the rules of decision-making and the settlement of disputes, and accept certain fundamentally shared values. Divided cities are no-go and stateless areas, where the rules and values of the wider state and society do not apply. Since the division in Jerusalem is multifaceted and has several dimensions, further research is needed in order to conclude which border areas fall under these classifications of stateless and "leaking containers." The Shou'afat refugee camp in the northeast of Jerusalem seems to be a good place to start such a study. This would complement the above-mentioned studies on the interaction that exists in Jerusalem's border zones.

In addition, an interesting comparative study might be done on divided Jerusalem and Berlin. According to Lamont and Molnar (2002), West Germany has successfully constructed a narrative of prosperity as a basis of positive national identity, whereas East Germany largely failed to provide its citizens with a similarly coherent competing narrative. Germany's unification left this deep divide almost intact. Differences continue to be reproduced through symbolic boundaries such as rhetoric and identification. Further research is needed to expose the similar types of division in Jerusalem. Related to this is the need to enlarge the comparative study on Jerusalem by moving beyond comparisons of it to Belfast, Brussels, Berlin, and Nicosia to other cities in Europe. Europe is known by its numerous divided cities and border areas, where people share daily life while holding allegiance to two (or more) sovereign systems. Italy's Institute of International Sociology in Gorizia (ISIG), under the direction of Professor Alberto Gasparini, has a database of 1,060 towns in Europe situated within twenty-five kilometers of the borders separating two states. Those border towns range from villages of 2,000 to 5,000 inhabitants to Copenhagen, which has over 1.6 million residents. ISIG has completed a number of research projects on European cross-border cooperation that can be relevant to the study of Jerusalem. Learning the European experience in trans-border cooperation will be particularly relevant for understanding the types of relationships and tensions likely to develop after the implementation of a comprehensive final status agreement between Israel and Palestine. After all, an Israeli-Palestinian peace agreement will establish an international border in, or next to, Jerusalem (Klein 2007). Therefore, these studies will be essential to the Israeli-Palestinian case in general, and to Jerusalem in particular.

Two of Bollens's (1999) conclusions on urban peace-building in Belfast and Johannesburg seem relevant to Jerusalem and call for a special investigation. Bollens concludes that a redistributive and equitable policy that would favor the disadvantaged ethnic group is needed in order to build peace. The powerful party must be aware of its biases and its previous discriminatory policies that were implemented on the "other." However, such equitable policies are impossible where inter-ethnic relations are formed as a zero-sum game and basic political parameters remain contested. Bollens's second conclusion is about the relationship between local (micro) politics and national (macro) politics. Urban policymaking cannot address the ethno-national base of the urban conflict. Yet local politics can connect the daily issues of urban living to unfair national governance structures, and can increase national politicians and negotiators' understanding of how the roots of urban polarization can be addressed and reconciled without sacrificing the "soul" of the city or urban life. Urban peace-building principles can contribute to national-level negotiations dealing with overarching political claims, basic social structures, and power relations.

Types of Territories and Models of Walls

MacGregor (1994) notes that cities are in constant change; they rise and fall. But not only are cities changing constantly, so too our research methods and perspectives are in constant flux. Multidisciplinary approaches on boundaries and borders can enrich our understanding of Jerusalem as a living city. Lyman and Scott (1968) classify territory into four categories: private, home, public, and a platform of interaction. Private territory is the body itself, and is thus manifestly intimate. It is rarely breached, and any kind of contact with it requires prior consent. The territory's owner cannot leave it and remain alive. A home territory also has a sense of intimacy and freedom, but its occupants may come and go as they please. Strangers can enter only with permission and under restrictions. Public territory is open to all, but often stricter and more binding rules of behavior apply there than in a private home. A platform of interaction is territory in which different social groups come into contact. In the context of Jerusalem, Jewish Israelis and Arab Palestinians encounter each other to a certain extent on platforms of interaction such as the labor market, tourist routes and sites, taxicabs, hospitals, malls, main traffic arteries, and restaurants and hotels located along the seams between the city's neighborhoods. Social boundaries are easily breached in this territory. A platform of interaction is fragile because it is not homogeneous, yet it is a basis for connections among the different groups that pass through it. The borders of this kind of territory are both porous and mutable. To apply Lyman and Scott's (1968) approach to Jerusalem and go beyond impressionist conclusions we need to develop a database on modes of interaction in the city.

Lyman and Scott classify territories first along the tension between public and private, second along the tension between personal freedom and binding rules, and third according to the possibility for breaching these rules. They emphasize tensions, but ignore the necessity of characterizing the walls and dividers that separate different kinds of territories. However, it should be noted, Lyman and Scott stress the kinds of interaction that take place in a particular territory. In this way, they recognize the dynamic dimension of a given territory, a dynamism that is absent from many other studies of divided cities, such as that of Peter Marcuse.

Marcuse (1995) defines five distinctive types of residential areas along a socio-economic scale, and a similar scale of five economic activities in any big city. According to Marcuse, each of the two scales has its own dividers, or walls. Accordingly, the concept of a "wall" in the urban context has more than one meaning. Walls are multifunctional and multidimensional. Some cities, such as Nicosia (Kliot and Mansfield 1997), Berlin from 1945 to 1991 (Kliot and Mansfield 1999), and Jerusalem from 1949 to 1967 (Dumper 1997; Benvenisti 1976; Israeli 2002) contain physical barriers that divide them. Residents of the cities cannot pass through these barriers from one side to the other. The only exceptions, if any, are limited numbers of tourists and pilgrims. The walls in other cities, however, do not totally seal each side off from the other; the physical barriers may exist but they allow for passage between the two sides.

Marcuse defines five types of walls, according to their functions. The first two models of walls are protective, sheltering those inside them. The third model is aggressive, aiming to make an impression on those outside. The fourth is exclusive; this kind of wall serves as a checkpoint and helps control and filter movement between the two sides. The fifth kind of wall aims to dominate by combining elements of all of the four other models. Accordingly, the five kinds of walls may be defined as follows:

1. *Prison walls* define and preserve enclaves or ghettos. They are physical, social, or economic walls designed to ensure the preservation of a group's identity and self-determination through isolation and segregation.

2. *Barricade walls* function for a community's protection, cohesiveness, and solidarity, not through physical means but by way of symbols and expressions of community identity, such as the languages of street signs and national-flag colors on sidewalks.

3. *Walls of aggression*, such as fences and patrols in military bases and police compounds, aim to express domination and force.

4. *Sheltering walls* of exclusiveness protect privilege and wealth, and select and control those admitted within them; these walls' presence is necessary for the dirty work of maintenance and repair. Walls of this type provide privacy by limiting access from the outside to the sheltered area, but do not limit movement from inside to outside.

5. *Castle walls* of domination, such as prime ministerial/presidential offices and homes and government compounds, express economic, social, or political superiority.

In applying this model to Jerusalem, one should take into account that Marcuse's framework depicts ideal types. In reality, most cities are made up of several of these distinct types. In addition, Marcuse describes a city with a single center, whereas there are two cities in Jerusalem, each of which has its own center. Moreover, the overlap between Jerusalem's two cities is limited. When a resident of East Jerusalem and one of West Jerusalem refer to themselves as "we," it is rare for that pronoun to be grounded in the reality of their lives and consciousness. Marcuse's model also lacks a dynamic dimension. He describes a static situation, not a dynamic one in which there can be entrance and exit between one wall and another. Finally, Marcuse does not deal with the interaction that takes place next to walls or in the places in which they are low or porous. In contrast to Lyman and Scott, Marcuse does not deal with no-man's-lands or public areas used by the residents of different "cities." However, Marcuse's types are nevertheless useful in that they provide us with multiple points of view in our analysis of the walls that divide East from West Jerusalem.

Identity, Representation, Border, and the Other

Jerusalem is the center of spiritual identity for millions of people worldwide. The Holy City represents for them God's eternity. For others, Jerusalem is the focus of national identity and aspiration. Hence a review of recent studies suggesting a method for understanding the relationship between the spatial unit and its meaning is necessary. Indeed it is impossible for any writer to ignore the symbolic aspect of the city. However, only rarely are studies of "Holy Jerusalem" systematically based on the concepts of political geography, including social and identity borders/

boundaries that divide "us" from the "other" (whoever this "other" is: a divine or religious entity, a nation, or a social sector).

As noted by Newman and Paasi (1998), since the late 1980s much research has been done on the relationship between space and territory to identity. Critical geographers began to challenge the idea of fixed boundaries, and raised questions about inclusion/exclusion within a given territory. According to Newman and Paasi, boundaries are connected to national identity and to the constitution of the nation-state. They are constructed by social, political, and discursive forces, and are not simply objective, material factors. Boundaries have deep symbolic, historical, cultural, and religious meanings for different communities. Boundaries are perceived as the embodiment of implicit and explicit norms, values, moral, and legal codes. They manifest themselves in numerous social practices. Some geographers argue that attention should be paid to boundary-producing practices. Hence, new conceptualizations and representations of space have emerged at the conjunction of cultural studies and political geography. Newman and Paasi identify four major themes within the interdisciplinary field of boundary studies. All four connect between territoriality and identity:

1. The disappearance of boundaries experienced in multi-identities on a shared space. Permeable boundaries and cultural lines replace the previous sovereignty boundaries. Conflict resolution can create new states with their own new boundaries.

2. Boundaries are made by identity and create it. Some approaches prefer to deal with boundaries between social collectives rather than between states. Accordingly, cultural and identity boundaries create patterns allowing cooperation between identity group members that cross over state borders. They play major roles in the construction of socio-spatial identities by making cultural and social distinctions, and by expressing power relations aimed at achieving the "purification of space" as a means to secure socio-spatial ethnic hegemony and to achieve exclusive control of the space.

3. Boundary narratives and discourse on exclusion and inclusion: studies on "us" against "them," "domestic" versus "foreign" that take narratives and places in narratives very seriously. Territory is part of

wider socialization narrative, often used to justify territorial claims. The discussion is on the boundaries of the imagined communities, the narratives constituting collective identity, and the construction of identity narratives. Attention is placed on who dominates these narratives, inclusion/exclusion relations in the narratives, and how they are reproduced. Boundaries are part of the discursive landscape of social power, control and governance, which are produced and reproduced in social practices. School textbooks, ceremonies, and national celebrations are the main arenas where such socialization is implemented through the iconography of boundaries in which space is made uncontestable. Thus boundaries are part of the discursive landscape of social power. The boundary does not limit itself merely to the border area but manifests itself in social and cultural practices and legislation, and public events. These tools create "literary landscapes" that shape the mindset.

4. The different spatial scales of boundary construction. Boundaries and territoriality are contextual, moving from the global down to the everyday life experience of an individual. Administrative boundaries have a far greater impact on the daily behavioral patterns of most individuals then do national and international borders.

Lamont and Molnar's (2002) perspective is broader than that of Newman and Paasi. Lamont and Molnar review the study of boundaries in social science in general, and not only in political geography. Research on boundary work and community, Lamont and Molnar argue, can be grouped to four categories. First, research on internal symbolic boundaries emphasizes labeling categorizations, or deals with boundaries within specific institutional spheres such as religious community boundaries with the secular public. Social identity theory has been particularly concerned with the permeability of symbolic and social boundaries. Group boundaries and collective identities generating shared definitions of us/them, and the constitution of social actors through boundaries as a central process of contentious politics—all are subjects for study.

Second, researchers tie communities, networks and meaning systems together. For example, the nation-state is a producer of differences and acts as an internal homogenizer through ethnic classifications. Third, there is research on communities that do not involve face-to-face contacts. Their symbolic and social boundaries put clear distinctions between the pure and the impure in defining the appropriate citizen. Lastly, there are studies on political inclusion and exclusion in a political-symbolic community. Bourdieu (1984) wrote on the reproduction of inequality, through managing cultural capital, and controlling symbolic class markers/boundaries and cultural practices. Symbolic violence is used to impose a specific meaning as legitimate or to mark cultural distance and proximity (disposition), as well as to monopolize privileges.

Contrasting with Bourdieu's approach is research on permeability and the relative importance of boundaries. Models of knowledge are diffused across countries and impact local institutions and identities. Instead of treating boundaries as markers of difference, here boundaries facilitate knowledge production by enabling communication across communities. Boundaries are conditions not only for separation and exclusion, but also for communication, exchange, bridging, and inclusion.

Lamont and Molnar (2002) suggest alternative strategies to integrate these existing studies. They suggest studying a boundary's property, such as its permeability, salience, durability, and visibility. Boundaries may generate new levels of tolerance; other territorial borders produce differentiation and categorization. Much more needs to be done in order to delineate the conditions that produce each of these two types of boundaries. Lamont and Molnar also suggest building a catalogue of the key boundary mechanisms: activation, maintenance, transportation, bridging, crossing, dissolution, expansion, expulsion and protection of autonomy, and accumulation. Finally, they suggest a focus on the theme of cultural membership, that is, how social actors construct groups as similar and different; how group classification is made; how individuals think of themselves as equivalent to, or compatible with, others; and the hidden assumptions that drive the creation of high and low status groups.

For Lamont and Mulnar, borders provide a concrete and powerful experience of the state, where citizenship is strongly enforced. Borders are nationalized and national identity overlaps other differences such as race, gender, or sexuality. Yet states do not simply impose the boundary on the nation. Local communities also make use of the nation and its boundaries in pursuit of local interests. Border societies have indeed produced a range of multiplex and translational identities moving beyond the more monolithic categories. Borders became not sites of division and opposing identities but sites of interaction, hybridization, and negotiation. In border zones, the construction of "otherness" takes place on both sides of the border. The social experience of borders encompasses formal and informal ties between the local community and larger politics, and micro and macro dimensions of national identity. Further research along these lines should be done in Jerusalem in order to find out when, where, and why these dynamics are practiced.

States and Societies as Borders and Boundary Creators

In spite of globalization, Paasi (1999) concludes that boundaries still function as territorial limits for state sovereignty. Contemporary boundaries are complicated social processes and discourses rather than fixed lines. Boundaries are therefore not merely lines on the ground, but above all manifestations of social practice and discourse. The production of boundaries is linked effectively with the social and spatial division of labor, the control of resources and social differentiation. He also argues that social action, discourse, and ideologies produce diverging, perpetually changing meanings for boundaries and that these are used as instruments of social distinction and control. Boundaries are not constant but mean different things for different actors and within different contexts. Boundaries are institutions, but they exist simultaneously on various spatial scales in a myriad of practices and discourses included in culture, politics, economics, administration, or education. The meaning of sovereignty and territoriality are also perpetually changing, which suggests that territoriality is not just a static, unchanging form of state behavior.

Paasi suggests two important conclusions on border construction. First, he sees a link between boundary construction and the creation of identity narratives. The construction of meaning occurs through narratives connected to the nation, state, and territory. Boundaries between "us" and "others" are critical elements in establishing "us" and excluding "others." A boundary manifests itself in many institutions such as media, education, memorials, ceremonies, and the like. Therefore Paasi attaches a great deal of importance to examining how boundaries become a part of everyday life. Second, he sees a link between boundaries, both as symbols and as a specific form of institution, and state power. By excluding the "other" through a border the powerful state can institutionalize identities. In other words, border construction is an expression of both physical and normative power relationships. The narratives attached to boundaries change perpetually along with developments in international socio-political relations and the internal relations within specific states. For example, we face the challenge to further study the changing interpretations given to Jerusalem's boundaries and how these express inter-state ideologies and links with the international geopolitical landscape.

Another conclusion made by Paasi allows us to improve our studies on the subject. Boundaries, Paasi argues, not only separate groups and social communities from each other, but also mediate contacts between them. As symbols, boundaries are mediums and instruments of social control. Boundaries are expressions of power relationships, parts of the discursive landscape of social power that produces and reproduces boundaries and their meaning.

Duncan (1993) also deals with the relationship of place, identity, and power—how "we" and "they" are represented in a certain place. He focuses on why the other is put in his "own" and "natural" place, or in a place that is strange and hostile. In order to understand how sites are represented and articulated we must understand how they were colonized and constructed socially and temporally as sites of desire, power, and weakness. The major tool of this colonizing is the discourse of the Other. The binary opposition of "us" against "them" serves the dual purpose of reinforcing and defining group identity and hegemony. Placing and representing the Other is an act of power, part of symbolizing the site in time and space. By analyzing power relations we can see how interests play a constitutive role in vision and representation. The powerful side claims to represent accurately and objectively the nature of the place. Moreover, the powerful side tries to assimilate the site being represented to the site from which the representation emerges by putting both sites along a continuum. Indeed, identity politics is not played only by the powerful side. The deprived party has also its own Other. However, we lack studies of the Otherness of Israel (and of Jewish Israelis in Jerusalem) from the perspective of the Palestinians similar to my study on the Otherness of the Palestinians in the eyes of the Israelis (Klein 2004).

The last study I will review here is that of Migdal (2004). Migdal argues that boundaries enclose people in an alliance of belonging. Identity binds people together beyond their material interests and creates communities of belonging. Since no one has just one set of operative boundaries, people face constant tensions regarding their identities. As a political sociologist, Migdal emphasizes the construction of boundaries and barriers. Beyond simple separation, boundaries have two elements, checkpoints and mental maps. Checkpoints refer to the sites and practices that groups use to differentiate members from others, and enforce separation and categorization. They can be physical or virtual, such as dress or language. Mental maps incorporate elements of meaning that people attach to spatial configurations, the loyalties they hold, the emotions that a grouping evokes, and their cognitive world order. Beyond state borders, multiple sets of boundaries can exist. While state borders create single units, mental boundaries can have differential and discontinued spatial experiences and different divisions of space. Most of the time multiple maps coexist, but at other times they clash. Boundaries change, leak, and carry different meanings for different people. Different social groups make contradictory demands on them, complicating both the placement of a certain boundary and its precedence. People navigate between boundaries demanding different, competing, or even contradictory practices in terms of behavior, emotions, and cognition. Mental images are constantly being contested and transformed, creating dissonance. To some extent, people can accommodate multiple boundaries, even ones with radically different underlying principles. They make such accommodations by activating different mental maps, but this sort of accommodation has its limits. Contradictory mental maps can force people to create hierarchies, inducing them to choose which boundaries, practices, and principles to submit to—and which to resist, reject, and violate. It is in such situations that we find the sites of social struggle and social change.

The contemporary nation-state faces the paradox of being simultaneously a part of society and apart from it. State officials act sometimes to blend the state into society; at other times they act to mark the state clearly as different, as the ultimate source of authority above society. Yet, the state can do little more than rhetorically assert its authority and control over people who have a distinct language or customs. There are times when ordinary citizens do not reinforce the image of the state and its boundaries, and they create a different set of boundaries. Questions that this approach puts in relation to Jerusalem are: Under what circumstances will the Palestinian "other" succeed in its demands for full membership? Which identity will command their loyalty? How are Jerusalem's boundaries constructed and maintained, and how do they function in excluding and including particular people? What are the sites and practices that constitute Jerusalemites' mental maps and virtual checkpoints?

Further Research Agenda for Political Geography

There is no doubt that political geography provides very rich theoretical approaches and research tools to study Jerusalem, either within the framework of divided cities or in comparison to other divided cities. Klein (2001) takes the first track, and Kliot and Mansfield (1999) and Bollens (1998a, 1998b) take the second. Jerusalem is one of the major subjects of the project "Conflict in Cities and the Contested State—Everyday Life and the Possibilities for Transformation in Belfast, Jerusalem, and Other Divided Cities," a joint study program of the University of Cambridge, Exeter University, and Queen's College, Belfast. Based on field work and theories from the field of urban studies, its working papers and publications follow the above-mentioned two tracks. Yet much more research is needed on border types in past and present Jerusalem, and on East Jerusalem as a stateless place.

Political geography's starting point in researching polarized cities are divisions and borders. Separation is the guiding principle for these studies. Interactions and cooperation between the sides dividing the place came later as subjects of interest. Jerusalem as a hybrid place and hybrid places in Jerusalem are subjects waiting for further scholarship. The same is true for other issues such as: Which public spaces are in use by both Jews and Palestinians in Jerusalem? What is the perspective of those who cross the divide back and forth, such as taxi drivers? What are the rules of interaction and engagement in inter-community activism, such as in *Solidarity*

Sheikh Jarrah, a joint Israeli-Palestinian organization that opposes Israeli settlement in the Sheikh Jarrah neighborhood of East Jerusalem?

Conclusion

Two of the most famous Israeli writers, A. B. Yehoshua and Amos Oz, were born in Jerusalem. Both left it to live in other places. Jerusalem simultaneously attracted and repelled them.

In Yehoshua's (1992, 151) novel *Mr. Mani*, a British soldier portrays Jerusalem as "a small and shabby place and after a few months there I'm quite prepared to say that it's a frightfully dull one as well. The population is extremely mixed, a hodgepodge of small unsociable communities that are as indigent and ignorant as they are endowed with a messianic sense of superiority. As usual, there seems to be no relation between the reputation of the place[,] which it owes to the great books written in and about it, and the sordid reality." Jerusalem in these lines is the "Other place" that borders our reality. And it is a city in which a contradiction exists between its reality and its many representations and productions.

Like Yehoshua, Oz (2006, 42–43) focuses on the people of Jerusalem:

> Jerusalem of my childhood back in the 1940's was full of self-proclaimed prophets, redeemers, and messiahs. Even today every other Jerusalemite has his or her personal formula for instant salvation. . . . [E]ven in today's Jerusalem, in every line waiting for a bus, conversation is likely to spark and turn into a fiery street seminar with total strangers arguing about politics, morality, strategy, history, identity, religion, and the real purpose of God. Participants in such street seminars, while arguing about politics and theology, good and evil, try nevertheless to elbow their way to the front of the line. Everyone screams[;] no one ever listens. Except for me. I listen sometimes; that's how I earn my living.

Oz sees the otherness of Jerusalemites and the city's many social, religious, and political boundaries. Yet, as I have suggested in this essay, he also advises us to look and to listen—to open our eyes and ears to its many faces and dynamics, and to the interactions that occur at the seams of the city's divisions.

7

Viewing the Holy City

An Anthropological Perspectivalism

GLENN BOWMAN

I STARTED MY investigation into the question of Jerusalem and disciplinary foci by looking at a couple of classic analyses of the anthropology of the Middle East, specifically Michael Gilsenan's (1990) "Very Like a Camel: The Appearance of the Anthropologist's Middle East" and Lila Abu-Lughod's (1989) "Zones of Theory in the Anthropology of the Arab World." Interestingly, but not surprisingly, I discovered that the models they sketched out, both historical and contemporary, did not really encompass the anthropology of "the Holy City"[1]; whilst there might be occasionally appropriate characterizations, focused on particular approaches to Jerusalem's populations and their habits, the city in general did not appear particularly to fit the topoi of the anthropologists' Middle East. This may,

1. Gilsenan (1990) argues that the village and the tribe, conjugated around the issue of a disappearing traditionalism, have marked traditional anthropological studies of the Middle East, and notes that the historical—as an active force in shaping identities rather than just a corrosive displacement—has virtually been excluded. Abu-Lughod's (1989) contention is that segmentation, the harem, and Islam have been the dominant tropes in the (largely male-dominated) anthropology of the Middle East, and that while Middle Eastern women have been the focus of many texts, these women have been oddly "haremized" and insulated from the wider currents of Middle Eastern life (rather in the same manner as the Middle East, except when the focus of policy studies has been itself secluded in orientalist isolation). Lindholm's (1995) "The New Middle Eastern Ethnography" reviews six recent anthropology texts relating to the region, but none are here more than incidentally relevant.

of course, be largely a matter of the anthropological study of the Middle East having been, until recently, largely an engagement with rural, rather than urban, communities (see Bowman 2012b; Deeb and Winegar 2012; and Hafez and Slyomovics 2013). It will, of course, also have much to do with the fact that Jerusalem is not only a city on the ground but as well—and more than most—a city of multiple imaginings, not only national and nationalistic, but also global and transcendental. Nonetheless, disciplinary training does provide its students with conceptual toolboxes, and it is interesting to observe what has been—and can be—drawn from past anthropological traditions to apply to contemporary Jerusalem.

While Gilsenan's observation that much of Middle Eastern anthropology focused on the village or tribe might seem apt for characterizing those studies that carve out for attention particular communities from the urban congeries, isolation from currents both of history and of the surrounding milieu does not generally characterize the study of particular Jerusalem communities. This, of course, is in part because urban anthropology generally problematizes such isolation and in large part because Jerusalem, both in pre-modern and modern terms, has been and is profoundly compounded and transnational. Abu-Lughod's assertion that Islam, the harem, and segmentation have focused the discourse of Middle East anthropology has resonance in Jerusalem, although it does not quite work for a situation in which Islam, contested by the co-presence of both Judaism and Christianity, is generally presented—at least by Western commentators—as a "problem" rather than as a socio-cultural determinant, in which the harem is generally seen as having disappeared with the death of Solomon (although some work on ultra-Orthodox Jewish communities is tinged with an "haremic" concern with the sexual, albeit tempered by psycho-medical discourse), and in which segmentation, while serving as a model for understanding inter-communal and intra-communal divisions, has also been critiqued as an inadequate tool for encompassing the complexities of processes of political and cultural definition.[2]

2. See the debate between Jonathan Webber and me in the pages of *Anthropology Today* in which Webber (1985, 5) argues that "the business of each of the old native populations of

Furthermore, the "absence" of history in Middle East societies—or rather the "stranding" of Middle Eastern societies in an atrophied traditional past—is far from the case in perspectives on Jerusalem, although the role of history is there rather complex and problematic. Jerusalem has, if anything, *too much* history, and one result of this has been a problematic bifurcation of anthropological studies of the city. On the one hand, one finds an anthropology of an historical past; there is a wealth of material, both literary and archaeological, on the many Jerusalems of the biblical and post-biblical pasts, and this draws scholars to apply to it "anthropological" methods. Thus a brief scan of Google Scholar for references to texts treating Jerusalem anthropologically reveals that a significant proportion of those found are anthropologies of biblical or ancient history.[3] On the other hand, "history"—in the sense of politically significant developments—constitutes another Jerusalem for anthropologists. Here we discover a political anthropology that seems dedicated less to the close observation and analysis of social and cultural configurations than to setting out political problems and proposing solutions to them, or at least suggesting means of accessing alternative futures to those dire futures that conditions seem to predict. The products of such endeavors appear either as current event reports in more journalistic disciplinary outlets such as *Anthropology Today*[4] or as contributions, often not publicly evident,

---

Jerusalem is to manufacture and maintain its set of holy places, and to codify and organize perceptions of events and the existence of other communities according to that fundamental principle. . . . [R]eligious communities in Jerusalem talk past each other [and] refuse to take each other into account[.]" My understanding (Bowman 1986, 4), to the contrary, was that "Jerusalem . . . is neither as 'oriental' nor as holy as Webber's; it is deeply, often brutally, involved in contemporary history, and is populated by two national groups (Palestinians and Israelis) that, intensely aware of themselves and of each other, are consciously engaged in overcoming religious divisions so as to participate most effectively in a nationalist struggle for the control of the land of Palestine/Israel."

3. For instance, see Matthews (1995) or Zias (1983).

4. I note here articles from the past ten years on Jerusalem from the same "Google Scholar" search: Efrat Ben-Ze'ev and Eyal Ben-Ari (1996) and Ulf Hannerz (1998), not to mention articles by Jonathan Benthall, Emmanuel Marx, and others that refer to the "problem" of Jerusalem.

to "think tank" work around the issues. Here anthropologists are at risk of becoming simply one cadre in a phalanx of experts engaging with the "issue" of Jerusalem or the wider issue of "the Middle East," abandoning wider perspectives to focus on specific problems. As Gilsenan (1990, 229) warns, discussing an earlier emergence of "Area Studies" (one seemingly being revisited with current US and UK strategies on developing Middle East "security expertise"), "the emergence of 'the expert' is central here. Knowledge of contemporary events and the structures or systems held to underlie them became critical. . . . Such an evolution tended to direct students away from anthropological theory and more towards the idea of expertise. . . . Debates tended to become internalized to Middle Eastern studies, and it was all too easy to find oneself in a ghetto."[5]

The question then becomes one of whether or not one is doing "anthropology" in the sense of close ethnographic observation and analysis brought into productive conjunction with comparative insights, or whether one is engaged in journalism, policy studies, or a combination of the two. The question also surfaces of what of Jerusalem itself is visible if it is approached as simply the setting of contestation or the plum to be fought over in a vicious war of civilizations.

~

In writing the above I have found myself troubled by a failure to bring to mind many notable examples of what I would consider contemporary anthropologies of Jerusalem,[6] whether these be in article or book form.

---

5. I would stress that I am not in any way questioning the vital necessity of political analysis of the situation, especially insofar as anthropological work—which usually entails a more sustained face-to-face relation between researcher and researched—is likely to make visible conundrums and brutalities more positivist research effaces. I am, however, implying that the focus of such studies excludes information that may, in the less immediate term, be vital to understanding fundamental characteristics and underlying structures of the site.

6. Because of my own field research I tend to think of Jerusalem's Old City when I speak of Jerusalem, but as Laurie King-Irani pointed out in comments on a draft of this chapter, such a delineation is somewhat artificial: "Why just the Old City? Does it not articulate economically and politically with the rest of the city, and now, thanks to Israeli expansionism, a huge swath of territory never considered to be part of 'Greater Jerusalem' until about two decades ago? And if we want to take the Greater Jerusalem idea to its maximal

Earlier work like Azarya's (1984) study of the Armenian Quarter is good, and there are anthropological elements in other interdisciplinary projects (for instance, Romann and Weingrod 1991, and Spolsky and Cooper 1991) that are useful despite being essentially surveys rather than ethnographies, but material is sparse. When I was a Lady Davis Fellow at the Hebrew University in 1983–84, I would hear anthropologists in the Sociology and Anthropology Department telling me that, apart from Azarya, no anthropologist worked in Jerusalem, either the Old or the New City. Possibly this was because it was too close (one looked down on the Old City from the Senior Common Room at Mt. Scopus) and the "anthropology at home" paradigm had not yet caught on, and possibly it may have been because any "anthropological" study of Israelis would be seen to demean them (see Dominguez 1989). Research on Palestinians was politically problematic either because leftists didn't want to denigrate them by separating them out as objects of study or, more likely, because Israeli academics—with the exception of an earlier generation's, such as Abner Cohen, Emmanuel Marx, Henry Rosenfeld—were simply nervous about working with the enemy. Generally, the anthropology of Palestinians by Israelis is a deeply murky area (see Rabinowitz 2002) and it may be that many simply wanted to stay clear—or to appear to be staying clear. In the meantime, excellent work was being done, and continues to be done, by Palestinian academics I would describe as anthropological, such as Salim Tamari (1983, 1991, 1992a, 1992b, 1999, 2004a, 2004b, 2009), but this work tends to be either archive-centered or social demographic. Frankly, problems of access (far worse now than in 1983–85 when I first worked out there) have made Jerusalem an impossible object of research for Palestinian academics and, then as now, the demographic and social work of charting the impact of occupation is more important than seemingly more arcane ethnographic research. Here the issue of "too much history" is very much to the fore.

---

expression, then it encompasses the entire Muslim, Jewish and Christian worlds, in terms of collective representations." Perhaps the remainder of the chapter will explain why my vision is so delimited, and why such delimitation may be linked to processes of carrying out field research.

Curiously, however, Jerusalem has also not seen the kind of interest from foreign anthropologists that its salience would lead one to expect. I was involved a few years back, at the Van Leer Institute and later at the American Anthropological Association meeting in New Orleans, in a for-the-most-part anthropological series of seminars on Palestinian-Israeli mixed towns organized by Daniel Monterescu and Dan Rabinowitz (this is the context in which I first met Madelaine Adelman). The seminars heard excellent papers on Haifa (2), Jaffa (2), Acre, Nazareth, and Lydda, but the one paper on Jerusalem (presented by Tamari) was archival and demographic. This gap—this empty center—seems somehow indicative, and, although I am aware of two anthropologically trained scholars of Jerusalem currently producing valuable work,[7] I would like to see more work—and more diverse work—being carried out.

~

As readers here are undoubtedly beginning to note, I have a quite specific criterion for judging whether or not work is suitably anthropological. Unsurprisingly this is one very central to the tradition of British Social Anthropology—that initiated by Branislaw Malinowski—and has at its core an insistence that good anthropology depends on an extended period of intensive participant observation research amongst the people or peoples one studies. Such work, which usually entails learning local languages and living amongst (and in the same conditions as) your subject population, is intended to ensure that the anthropologist becomes aware not only of the quotidian habits and assumptions of the people he or she works with, but also of the central concerns and conditions of their life. Anthropologists, or at least those of this particular "school" of anthropology, contend that other methods of social research—such as those based on questionnaires and surveys—predetermine the researcher's findings insofar as all directed questions delineate a particular range of reply and

---

7. Tom Abowd (2002, 2007, 2014), who finished his Ph.D. at Columbia in 2002 and is publishing in *Middle East Report* and the *Journal of the Institute of Jerusalem Studies,* and Rochelle Davis (2003), who also completed her Ph.D. in 2002 and who has published extensively on Jerusalem history.

also because informants—be they nervous, accommodating, or desirous of reward—are very often likely to tell the researcher what they think he or she wants to hear.

   Essential to the process of anthropological fieldwork is, strangely, the necessity of getting lost—lost not so much in place (although we, too, are good at that, and learn from finding our ways back out), but lost in terms of not knowing precisely what one is doing. I can do little better here than to relay a story that Godfrey Lienhardt, one of the central figures at the Institute of Social Anthropology in Oxford, where I did my postgraduate work, told about fieldwork. He would tell aspiring anthropologists that they would, after a year or so of lecture, seminar, and library preparation, head to their respective fields (his had been the Sudan) with their brains full of theories, of hypotheses, and of scholarly descriptions of their peoples and their contexts. For the first six months of fieldwork, he would say, everything would seem tremendously exciting and satisfying; what informants would relay would tie in beautifully with expectations, offering strong support for the theses one was intent on demonstrating. Then, one day, someone would say or do something odd and—Lienhardt would say—"if you were good" you would take note of it. Once sensitized to such inconsistencies, you would become aware of them popping up more and more often, and as you noted them down—and tried to think them through—they would begin to erode your assumptions until, somewhere in the second six months of field research, you would find yourself sitting in your tent profoundly depressed that you knew nothing, that you understood nothing, that all of the theories you'd carefully packed along with your luggage seemed unworkable, and that you just wanted to go home. This, Godfrey would say, was the moment real anthropological work could start as, over the next year or so, you reconfigured your assumptions more in line with what you were seeing and hearing around you, reconnected (and rethought) the theories you'd brought out with you with the materials you were now trying to explain, and put together something that provided real insight into the lives of the people you were living with. I've tried to analyze in some detail the implications of this anecdotal rendition of fieldwork in two articles (see Bowman 1997, 1998), but actually the story itself is hard to fault as a guide to issues of anthropological observation.

Let me briefly expand upon it with reference to my own experience doing research in the Old City in the early to mid-eighties.[8] I, like many anthropologists of my and previous generations, had come to anthropology from literature; in my particular case I had been drawn to the study of Jerusalem by an interest in two coexistent and ideologically incompatible forms of literary travel—pilgrimage and mercantile—popular in the late Middle Ages. Invited to move from literary to literal Jerusalem pilgrimage by Erik Cohen, an anthropologist at Hebrew University, I came out in 1983 and, after three months of living in West Jerusalem, managed to move into the heart of the Old City, taking up residence in a housing compound populated by Christian Palestinians who had been driven from West Jerusalem in the 1948 war. Certainly I worked on pilgrimage practices during the sixteen months I lived over the Eighth Station of the Via Dolorosa—I travelled across the country with a number of different pilgrim groups from different nations and different Christian denominations, attended the many feasts of the plethora of Christian sub-communities who celebrated the place, and spent countless hours sitting, watching, and interviewing in the *Anastasis* (also known as the Holy Sepulchre) and numerous other churches and institutions (see Bowman 2011, 2014)—but I also perched in the houses and shops of my neighbors, hearing them speak of their pasts, their family problems, their relations with tourists and soldiers, and their dreams and nightmares while they drew me out about who I was and what I thought. I also spent hours walking the streets of the Old City, accompanied or alone, day and night, coming to see it as a very different place than I'd read about or even perceived on my first visits. Although I certainly ended up writing about Jerusalem pilgrimage (Bowman 2013), I also found myself drawn—through identification with informants and neighbors and through psychological investment in the terrain we shared—into an involvement with the dilemma of Palestinian tourist guides (Bowman

8. An account of my experience of "coming into the field," with all the complexities of losing and finding one's way, is available as "At Home Abroad: The Field Site as Second Home" (Bowman 2008).

1992), as well as, amongst many other things of which it has proved the most notorious, a bemused fascination with why street merchants were obsessed with stories about sex with foreign tourists (Bowman 1989 and Bowman 1996).[9] Fundamentally, long-term engagement with a population in place brought me close to being able to see the place as they did without occluding the "other view" with which my scholarship and my origins in a different place and culture provided me.

I stress here the importance of integrating the two perspectives the anthropologist builds up on a place—that of local vision based on engaging, and engaging with, as wide a portion of the local community as one can, and the analytical knowledge of a "stranger" who compares and contrasts what he or she is learning to see with a broad repertoire of theoretical and comparative materials pertaining not only to the social setting studied, but as well to societies more generally. I say this in part because I am not trying to promote a naïve and romantic view of the anthropologist as someone who, shedding the baggage of his or her cultural past, "goes native" and is thus offered access to a magical alterity undiscerned by the rest of the world. Anthropological knowledge builds both on ethnographic awareness of the particularities of the specific cultures studied and a learned ability to see those particularities in terms of structures, functions, and relations that are analogous to, or variations on, those operating in the other cultures of the world. The "conceptual toolbox" I referred to in the opening paragraph of this chapter empowers the anthropologist, through measuring and evaluating a "play" of difference and similarity, to make sense of what he or she sees or is told in terms of theories and models other anthropologists know, share, and use to communicate. The tools in that toolbox are sufficiently stable to allow common usage but simultaneously manipulable enough to allow them to be put to uses not precisely those for which their fabricators imagined

9. These papers examined the way Palestinian merchants selling goods to tourists in the markets of Jerusalem's Old City countered their apparent passivity in the face of the vacillating demands of groups of foreigners endowed with economic and social superiority with the development of an aggressive sexuality focused on females of the tourist populations.

they would be used; observers of the histories of anthropological theories note a perpetual process of adaptation and transformation of those tools as anthropologists—whom Lévi-Strauss (1966) would refer to as *bricoleurs*—work with and on them to make them serve to make sense of new encounters or perspectives (see Moore 1999). Disciplinary involvement (which entails common access—and the occasional contribution—to its conceptual toolbox) means that the anthropologist, "lost" in the field, needs to work on the one hand on translating what he or she sees into something similar to what he or she has been trained to recognize, and on the other to adapt the models and theorems learned so as to be able to incorporate the novel situation without doing it violence. This labor results in a dialectical relation between the known and the novel; one sees the everyday illuminated against a backdrop of theory, and theory evidenced in the setting of the everyday.

In my case I came to Jerusalem looking to investigate foreign pilgrims intent on finding on the ground a palpable rendering of a city they knew in song, text, and prayer. I found them—many of them—but I also found not only the complex social, economic and psychological structures of close-packed communities variously shaped by living in a city held sacred by others but as well structures of acquiescence and resistance thrown up in response to barely masked intercommunal warfare. The "scene" was far more complex than anything I had imagined while reading about Jerusalem in Oxford (or in my first few months in the city), and that complexity was one of the inseparable interaction of a number of elements rather than simply one of multitudinousness. Thus the work I ended up doing on, for instance, Palestinian street merchants and foreign women involved observing and interconnecting the disparate workings of tourism and family life in the Old City, the ways merchants worked and competed in the everyday tension of a market economy dominated by buyers rather than sellers, gossip about male competition in situations where local women were rendered inaccessible, the not always subtle signs that marked the differential power of Israelis and Palestinians (and the gender symbolism of that differential), and the vagaries of language use in conversations between merchants, pilgrims, tourists, and Israeli shoppers. This was not research I carried out by delineating a problem, determining to study it, setting out my methods and parameters, and collecting data; it was work I came to find myself driven to engage after several months of sitting with close friends in their shops, listening to their competitive banter, lusting with them after women whom we could envisage as available to us, observing—and hearing stories of—interactions with tourists as well as Israeli guides and shoppers, and watching the way sexual politics were both imbued by and overturned by a barely spoken national politics. The material—descriptions of bargaining sessions, sordid stories of small conquests and angry failures, descriptions of mythic Israeli seductresses and boys shamed for "taking what was not offered"—collected in my notebooks, but also in my memories; this, via my connection with my friends, my growing anger at the occupation, my dismay at the sublimation of politics in the discourse of the market traders, and my own sexuality became a situation I needed to understand, and my anthropological knowledge enabled me—in time—to do so.[10]

In another melding of moments and concerns, in this case giving rise to my "Nationalizing the Sacred: Shrines and Shifting Identities in the Israeli-Occupied Territories" (Bowman 1993; see also Bowman 2012a), my original project of working on Christian pilgrimages morphed into a study of local Muslim-Christian interaction around holy sites mutually revered in the period leading up to the First Intifada. Observations of the central role of Christian Palestinian scout troops in religious festivals led me to follow a group on the feast day of the Prophet Elijah to Mar Elyas, an ancient Greek Orthodox monastery between Jerusalem and Bethlehem. There, in a milieu denuded of foreign pilgrims, I discovered a site where local Christians and Muslims gathered to picnic together and access thaumaturgic articles, presaging, in that sharing, the sorts of national collaboration that would make itself evident in the intifada. Again, my own life in a place, living over an extended period of time in close communion with

10. Interestingly, and I suspect somewhat analogously, a close friend raised in the Christian Quarter by poor Catholic parents, and eventually sent off by the Franciscans to study psychoanalysis in Paris, also found himself working on and through the issue of "fucking tourists" when unemployment stranded him back in the *suq* of the Old City.

a people whose practices and concerns I came to share, drew my attention to, and emotively involved me in, activities I had not planned to look
into. These called on the scholarship I had prepared in anticipation of my
planned work on Jerusalem pilgrimage, but drew that scholarship into
new relations that threw light on structures of interrelation that were not
visible to the local eye. My current work on "shared" or "mixed" shrines
in Macedonia (FYROM) and West Bank Palestine has grown out of this
work, and the resonances I could perceive of it in my subsequent experience of driving through war-torn Yugoslavia (Bowman 2010, 2012a).

This "binocular" (as distinct from schizophrenic) vision is, I believe,
particularly anthropological, but failures to bring its two lenses into alignment will produce particularly symptomatic faults in anthropological
commentators. One fault is that of "over identification," a fault to which,
particularly in war zones such as that which has engulfed Jerusalem over
the past few decades, one can easily succumb. Here one commits completely to the position taken by the community one has adopted through
one's research to the extent of uncritically accepting its assumptions about,
and positions on, its dilemmas.[11] I want to stress that I am not criticizing
positioning oneself politically in activist terms in alignment with a community one has "adopted" in the course of research; knowing, better than
most outside that community, the situations it faces may in many cases
call on a scholar to struggle against those depredations. I have certainly, in
relation to the position of the Israeli state towards the Palestinian people,
taken sides. I am instead criticizing an unwillingness to be critical of the
strategies and assumptions of the community one works with when those
appear counterproductive or simply wrong-headed.[12] An outside scholar

11. See here the debate between Moshe Shokeid (1992) and Ted Swedenburg (1992)
sparked by the latter's earlier "Occupational Hazards: Palestine Ethnography" (Swedenburg 1989).

12. "Fucking Tourists," given to my mates on the street, was "therapeutically" critical
(and taken as such), while my "Exilic Imagination" (Bowman 1999), presented one year earlier at Birzeit University in 1998, attacks the nationalist mythification of Palestinian history
as well as the condescension of "returnee" Palestinians in their relations with those who'd
remained under occupation. The response to the latter paper at a conference on "Landscape

brings into particular situations knowledge drawn from other sites and situations that may be of value in working through conflicts or contradictions in the "native" position, and a self-abasing celebration of the rightness of the "local" that forbids one from contributing those insights to internal debates damages not only the anthropologist's integrity, but also that community's own possibilities for self-assessment.

The other fault, probably less overt (and more masked) in these days of reflexive anthropology than it was when it appeared in its original form, is the insistence on seeing the subjects with whom one works as the objects of a detached and "objective" knowledge. This is a failure of identification and, whereas in other locales of anthropological study it has often been evident in the "modern" anthropologist's disdainful distance from the "primitives" he or she studies, it can easily be found in less scientific guises in work around Jerusalem where scholars take an orientalist, or even racist, "distance" from communities of "Arabs," "Jews," *mizrahim*, "Orthodox," "Bedouin," or the like (Furani and Rabinowitz 2011). Said's (1978) comments on the politics of orientalist academia need no elaboration, but their application to "scientific" objectivity when it serves to mask ethno-nationalist or communitarian disdain is not always so obvious.

You will note that I have not at any point cited "partiality" as a fault. Fieldwork entails working closely in a particular setting, and the description I have provided in the preceding pages makes it clear that identification with the inhabitants of that setting in the specificities of their situation is an essential part of the work. I will allow that settings can be occupied by a number of different groupings and would note that, in my own work, I was brought into frequent, and often close, contact with diverse groups of people—pilgrims, priests, tour groups, and locals of various faiths and political allegiances. Many of these groups shared little if any overlap, and I moved variously amongst all of them. I would also note that situational identifications are characteristic of our social lives, and that some ethnographic work may depend precisely on limning out

---

Perspectives on Palestine" was itself bifurcated, with the rage of some Palestinians countered by the appreciation of others.

and closely describing the experiential world of a group one shares for a relatively brief period of time. In my article in the *Contesting the Sacred* volume (Bowman 2013) I looked, for instance, at the very different ways three denominationally distinct pilgrim groups (Greek Orthodox Cypriots, British Catholics, and American Christian Zionists) I travelled with conceptualized and approached a number of religious sites.

In this chapter, however, I have been describing longer immersions, and stressing the benefits of being engaged with a community for a sufficient time to enable one to begin seeing differently, and more complexly. In that immersion one is likely to identify predominantly with a circle of persons with which one is most closely integrated on a daily basis in one's relations, in sharing their surroundings—public and private, and in engaging with and imbuing their perspectives and concerns. That group might be diffused and might conjoin persons or groups that would be considered, in academic terms, categorically distinguished (for instance Christian and Muslim Jerusalemites). Categorical borders are not the salient issue however; ethnographic life consists in large part of following local networks—often across what seem to be boundaries—and observing the ways in which those networks stitch together individuals, groups and small communities. Such networks however are unlikely, except when necessity intervenes (in the form of events such as demands for the payment of taxes or calls to the cells for interrogation), to carry their inhabitants into the domains either of strangers or of those I would call "antagonists" (see Laclau and Mouffe 1985, 92–148; Bowman 2006, 33–34 passim). As a consequence, the ethnographer, while *knowing of* those on the "outside" of the community he or she cohabits (whether they be enemies or just "others"), is not likely to engage in any depth with their everyday lives and concerns. Close fieldwork with a community will teach an ethnographer much about the ways the members of his or her community characterize those beyond the border of the community, but it will not— unless the anthropologist breaks away from his or her primary group to live with the others—give any sort of access—intimate or otherwise—to the lifeworld of the outside community.

Ethnographic knowledge is by its nature perspectival, and profoundly partial; the wider theoretical and anthropological knowledge the anthropologist carries in the aforementioned tool kit may allow that partial knowledge to be contextualized, and even juxtaposed with the similarly partial lifeworlds of other groups cohabiting the place studied,[13] but it cannot produce an image of the "real" city all of these groups share. This is because, at least in the experiential sense, there is no "real" Jerusalem that can be caught in any single representation; Jerusalem is the compound setting of the lifeworlds of the peoples that cohabit in it whilst engaging it, and each other, differently.

~

I have here criticized some of my colleagues in anthropology for predetermining their findings by restricting the queries they direct towards Jerusalem and Jerusalemites. This is a danger all disciplines, by their nature as disciplines, are prone to, and I have tried to suggest that extended participant observation may suggest ways other scholars in other fields might escape the deductivism that lurks at the heart of most if not all of our methodologies. Some close forms of archival work, in history in particular, have begun to reconstitute what appears to be the lifeworlds of previous inhabitants of the city, although that work is of course held to account by questions of differential access to language and of how much language can carry of the implicit shapes of the times and lives it seems to body forth. I have also regretted that so few anthropologists have worked on Jerusalem and its environs; there is a feeling, I suspect, that certain field sites belong to those scholars who have laid claim to it and that others should not seek to work there, unless to seek to prove the precursor wrong.

Perhaps I can close with a lesson taken from the struggle between Margaret Mead and Derek Freeman over the real character of Samoan sexuality and society (see Shankman 1996; Côté 2000) that illustrates the role of perspective in constituting the "truth" of a place or situation. Freeman dedicated his life to proving that Mead was an opportunist and a liar

---

13. Friedland and Hecht's (1996b) book comes as close as anything I know to doing this convincingly and, while it is not an anthropological text in the formal sense, its authors' methods, involving intensive interviews, approximate one.

in what she said she had learned about Samoan life from a circle of young girls in the 1920s; he had worked on Samoa, largely in the 1950s and 1960s amongst a circle of male tribal elders, and collected from them very different versions of sex and life on the island. Freeman's error, and to a lesser degree that of Mead, was to assume that there was *a* Samoa on which all persons accorded their ways to *a* moral code. His attack was in part misdirected because three decades of rapid modernization had changed Samoa inexorably, but also more significantly because he circulated with, and imbued the ethos of, a group of individuals profoundly different in age, gender, and status from those Mead had earlier communicated with in the course of women's work and play. In retrospect we can see that both Mead and Freeman were right, and wrong. Both saw aspects of Samoan society that were truths in their own context, and partial truths in the larger context of an island culture in history. Had Freeman not devoted himself single-mindedly to destroying what he saw as Mead's unfairly garnered reputation, he would have—as later anthropologists have—been able to work out how the two apparently incommensurate worlds could inhabit the same small place within a small span of time. Samoa, like Jerusalem, is a place "compacted together," and the more partial views of the sites we gather the better an understanding we can derive of how the lives lived there fit, and sometimes clash, with each other. Only through a gathering of multiple views, carefully and painstakingly gathered and collated, can we begin to get a sense of the singular multiplicity that is Jerusalem.

I can do no better than to close with a wonderful passage by the master of perspectivalism: "There is only a perspectival seeing, only a perspectival 'knowing'; and the more affects we allow to speak about one thing, the more eyes, different eyes, we can use to observe one thing, the more complete will be our 'concept' of this thing, our 'objectivity'" (Nietzsche [1887] 1994, 92).

8

Sex and the City

The Politics of Gay Pride in Jerusalem

MADELAINE ADELMAN

ONE OF THE first large-scale public events hosted by Israel's gay community was held in Tel Aviv's Sheinkin Garden in 1993 (Walzer 2000). Five years later, 10,000 people gathered in the city for Wigstock, a drag queen festival held in Independence Park. That same year, 1998, Israel's first gay pride parade was held in Tel Aviv. Supporters gathered in Rabin Square, a national site for protests and rallies, and marched to Independence Park, a popular location in Tel Aviv for gay men.

Over the years, the city has responded affirmatively to the gay community. Since 2002, it has offered discounts and benefits to same-sex couples (Yehoshua 2002). The LGBT Pride Center, situated in the city's centrally located Meir Park, is underwritten by the municipality (Feldinger 2008). The country's first memorial to gay victims of the Holocaust, which is located in the same park, also was established by the municipality (Aderet 2013). Front-running candidates for recent municipal elections were described as trying to "out-pink" each other (Halutz 2013). It makes sense that Tel Aviv has been the center of gay life in Israel: the city is resolutely youthful, multicultural, and secular. It is Israel's cultural capital, where fashion, art, music, and dance compete with the Mediterranean beach and its shopping districts, cafés, and clubs for the leisure time of local residents and tourists, gay and straight.

This reflects early Zionist visions for the first Hebrew city: to be the "New York of the Land of Israel," the "wonder city," or as Mayor Dizengoff called it, the "city of [entrepreneurial] dreams" (Azaryahu 2009). From the beginning, the new, modern city of Tel Aviv intentionally distinguished itself from the past-tense orientation of the old city of Jerusalem. In the 1980s, Tel Aviv mimicked New York City's image by branding itself as "the city that never stops" (Azaryahu 2006). Its growth into a global city is due in large part to the embrace of Tel Aviv by gay men, lesbians, and transgender people, the same people largely rejected by the decidedly particularistic city of Jerusalem.

Israel's business leaders are banking on Tel Aviv's gay-friendly reputation. Tourism industry heads have pledged to transform Tel Aviv, also known as the "White City," into the "Pink City." According to an Israel Hotel Association official, "Tel Aviv and gay people are a perfect fit"; Israel Tourism Ministry Director-General Eli Cohen has said he would offer any financial assistance necessary to turn Tel Aviv into the gay capital of the world (Sadeh 2005). Israel's national airline, El Al, offers travel packages to gay tourists in Europe. The municipality's Association for Tourism also seeks to attract gay tourist dollars through targeted marketing, such as the prominent link to "Gay Tel Aviv" on its website, and by co-sponsoring a gay city tour during Tel Aviv's Pride Week. The mayor appointed openly gay city councilman Itai Pinkas, and Adir Steiner, coordinator of Tel Aviv's Pride Parade, to showcase the city at the quadrennial worldOutGames, an LGBT multisport event (Laufer 2008). Together with the Israel Tourism Association, the municipality hosted the 2009 Annual Symposium of the International Gay and Lesbian Travel Association. Such efforts paid off when Tel Aviv recently was named the world's "best gay city" (*Ynet* 2012).

While business leaders and others seek to capitalize on Tel Aviv's reputation as Israel's gay-friendly pink city, opposition to public expressions of support for gay rights permeates Jerusalem. When the first gay pride parade was held in the streets of Tel Aviv in 1998, the Gay and Lesbian Student Association (GLSA) at the Hebrew University in Jerusalem also celebrated. They hosted a party, held indoors, which drew about 200 people. At the time, GLSA Chair Sa'ar Nathaniel noted the contrast between the two cities: "I can't have anything in a park, or anywhere outdoors. People live in the closet here"; Nathaniel planned to leave Jerusalem for Tel Aviv as soon as he completed his studies (Eaves 1998).

The contrast in 1998 between the gay pride celebrations in the two cities inspired Menachem Shezaf, president of the oldest gay rights organization in Israel, Agudah, to promise "This year we took Tel Aviv; next year we take Jerusalem" (Ilan 2006). Ten years later, the contrast between the two cities remained: "In Jerusalem, the mayor invests all his power in attempts to stop the parade . . . while in Tel Aviv, the mayor recognizes the political power of the LGBT community and is a speaker at the parade" (Udasin 2009).

The distance between Tel Aviv and Jerusalem is recognized both by those who object to gay pride and by those who support it. Many secular Israelis avoid Jerusalem, whether out of respect or distain for its self-identified religious orthodoxy. As an effect of secular Jewish out-migration, and the displacement and political marginalization of Palestinian residents, Jerusalem is governed now largely by the ultra-Orthodox contingent of the city's Jewish majority (Dumper 1997; Shabbaneh 2006). Leaders in Jerusalem opposed to gay pride have basically ceded Tel Aviv to the secular world in order to protect the sanctity of Jerusalem (Sela 2006a). This non-negotiated stalemate not only increases the social distance between Tel Aviv and Jerusalem, it also sets up Tel Aviv as the modern and secular face of Israel, rendering Jerusalem as the embattled embodiment of its traditional and religious future.

As a result, Jerusalem's treatment of the gay community has become the object of a kind of endgame battle over the religious and national identity, as well as the democratic and modern nature of the state. Those who reject the legitimacy of homosexuality stand in a defensive posture against the threat of gay visibility on Jerusalem's streets, the extraordinary growth of gay rights within the Israeli legal system, and the ongoing call for the inclusion of the LGBT community within the social fabric. Jerusalem's former mayor Uri Lupolianski and City Manager Yair Ma'ayan have argued in a letter to the High Court of Justice that the gay pride parade should be banned because it is a "desecration of the holy city" (Lis 2008). At the same time, gay Jerusalemites, religious and secular, Palestinian and Jewish, who wish neither to leave the city nor to become invisible in it, continue to push for a more inclusive Jerusalem. According to former Jerusalem resident Avigail Sperber, who is an Orthodox Jewish lesbian, "It's more important to hold a gay pride parade in Jerusalem than in Tel Aviv because being gay in Tel Aviv is not much of a problem" (Sheleg 2006).

Why does being gay in Jerusalem constitute a problem for supporters and opponents alike? How have supporters and opponents of gay rights sought to secure their vision for the city of Jerusalem? What can be learned about the city of Jerusalem and its role in forming religious and national identity, and determining the meaning of democracy, by studying the unfolding story of its annual gay pride parade? Below I address these questions, and in doing so, offer some clarity about the relationship between sex and the city of Jerusalem. First, I will describe my intellectual approach to the topic as a justice studies scholar. Second, I will introduce readers to gay pride festivals. I then will present chronologically and analyze thematically the story of gay pride in Jerusalem, indicating how the fight over it in Jerusalem reveals the "difficulties of managing cities where residents have contradictory needs and identities" (Elman and Adelman, this volume).

Justice Studies

Justice studies, first developed in the 1980s at Arizona State University (ASU) by faculty from its Center for the Study of Justice, is an interdisciplinary field of study pursued in universities around the world (Jurik and Cavender 2004; Lauderdale and Cavender 1986). What faculty in justice studies hold in common is our commitment to place the contested notion of "justice" at the center of our research questions, and to draw from a diverse methodological toolbox to answer them. Our scholarship is guided by three research imperatives (*Justice and Social Inquiry* 2012). First, justice studies scholars reveal intersecting forms of injustice. We do this by identifying the often competing meanings of justice and trace how dynamics of inequality are built into the social fabric, body politic, economic practices, and public policies in ways that perpetuate intersecting forms of injustice. Second, justice studies scholars engage multiple visions of justice. We assess how local and global processes have hindered or engendered visions for a just society, and reflect on how communities are shaped by contested visions of justice. Third, justice studies scholars analyze and help transform pathways to justice. We consider how people have organized for justice in past and contemporary periods, and how justice efforts in one historical moment, location or issue area affects the lives of people who might have parallel, intersecting or distinct justice concerns. We also participate in the design and implementation of new justice movements for the twenty-first century.

Justice studies scholars vary in how they produce knowledge. Most continue to draw on their home disciplines for intellectual guidance, while also being informed by the limits of their own and the opportunities afforded by disciplinary approaches to scholarship they adopt. Others craft interdisciplinary research questions, individually or within team-based projects. A number of justice studies scholars conduct transdisciplinary research. Transdisciplinary research has been defined as scholarship that begins with a social problem that requires the input of not only multiple disciplines working in tandem, but also the expertise of those most affected by the social problem, who are best suited to help identify and/or implement the solution (Messing, Adelman, and Durfee 2012).

This study of the politics of gay pride in Jerusalem grows out of research, teaching and social justice advocacy efforts related to gender violence in Israel and elsewhere that I have been engaged in for two decades. It also is inspired by over a decade of "safe schools" efforts to integrate LGBT issues into K–12 education (see e.g., Adelman and Woods 2006; Adelman and Lugg 2012; Lugg and Adelman forthcoming). In my research I ask how and why the "political" is felt so very personally in everyday life. The "political" is a socially constructed notion that generally refers to the national collective, state government, economic market, and public streets. The "personal," also socially constructed, refers to the individual self, gender and sexuality, cultural norms, the home and family. Critics suggest that the political is valued over the personal, that the distinction between the political and the personal is actually a false one, and that the personal should be considered a political arena, as well. My work on the politics of gender violence (e.g., Adelman 2000, 2003, 2004, 2010; Adelman, Erez, and Shalhoub-Kevokian 2003; Adelman, Cavender, and Jurik 2009; Adelman, Haldane, and Wies 2012; Erez, Adelman, and Gregory 2009; Morgan, Adelman, and Soli 2008) reflects my interest in turning around the now classic feminist slogan "the personal is political" in order to explore how the "political is personal." Here, I conduct a justice studies inquiry about the political and personal through an analysis of the gay pride march in Jerusalem. To do so, I draw on my ethnographic experience in Israel, while building an interdisciplinary-based argument.

Gay Pride

Gay pride festivals and parades were organized originally to commemorate the Stonewall Riots, a turning point in the gay and transgender liberation movement in the United States (Duberman 1993). The Stonewall Riots occurred in and around the Stonewall Inn, a bar located in Greenwich Village, New York City, frequented by lesbian, gay, bisexual, and transgender (LGBT) customers. One night in late June, 1969, as was typical during the time period, law enforcement entered the bar. Stonewall Inn patrons, soon joined by community members on the street, fought back rather than acquiesce to this discriminatory pattern of police harassment. This local instance of LGBT resistance to heterosexism and forced gender conformity, replicated in other cities, became a symbol of the gay liberation movement, as did the gay pride parades and festivals soon organized to commemorate the Stonewall Riots.

Gay pride marches, organized in June 1970 to observe the first anniversary of the Stonewall Riots, were held in major cities across the United States. The anniversary also was commemorated at gay bars around the world (Hogan and Hudson 1998, 642). Since its inauguration, gay pride events—or "Pride," as they have come to be known—have become a visible expression of gay life, and constitute a political effort to secure acceptance and social change for LGBT people and their families. Pride events have been held in cities such as New York, London, Montreal, Sydney, Shanghai, Guadalajara, San Paolo, and Budapest. International Pride events also have been organized in cities that are perceived as being particularly unwelcoming for LGBT people. The inaugural WorldPride was held in Rome in 2000, during the Vatican Jubilee. WorldPride 2006, originally scheduled for 2005, was awarded to Jerusalem. Similarly, EuroPride 2010 was held in Warsaw, in solidarity with eastern Europeans who face violent opposition to LGBT rights in general and Pride parades specifically.

Gay pride parades typically take place in the city center in order not only to draw the highest possible number of participants, but also to reclaim "queer" public space for a stigmatized and invisible community. The parade and its associated festival-like activities are an opportunity for individuals to literally "come out" to proclaim their same-sex sexual orientation, gender nonconformity, and/or support for the LGBT community. Some consider attendance at gay pride a "rite of passage" that confers belonging within the gay community. Others look to Pride as an opportunity to subvert heteronormativity and gender norms, accomplished through music, dance, dress, public displays of same-sex affection, signs, symbols, and slogans, or as an opportunity to practice "strategic public visibility" (Currier 2012) as a gay and/or transgender person or ally.

Attendees come to Pride events for networking purposes; others come from near and far to party. Gay pride also offers politicians, celebrities or other notable guests the chance to identify with or show their support for the LGBT community. Travel agencies and municipalities include signature Pride events in their gay tourism marketing plans in an effort to capture the global flow of disposable income. Indeed, forty years after Stonewall, in gay-friendly cities, Pride has become a marketing venue and revenue stream for individual artists and entertainers, nongovernmental organizations, local businesses, host cities, and international corporations (Johnston 2005; Kates and Belk 2001). In this way, Pride events enact multiple meanings: a social stage where creative performances take place in front of an audience (Goffman 1959); a liminal social space where norms can be collectively resisted and transgressed (Markwell and Waitt 2009); a political protest where marginalization and violence are contested, oftentimes through invocation of an international human rights framework (Pearce and Cooper 2014); and, an economic endeavor in which elites benefit from the popular carnivalesque atmosphere.

Gay pride events are covered by the media, attracted in part by the mass of humanity that typically participate in the parade and in part by the spectacle nature of festivals. The media also are drawn by protestors who object to the parade's so-called normalization of homosexuality. These sorts of conflicts over gay pride parades have been observed around the world. In some cities, state agents, such as law enforcement and other opponents, have harassed, physically assaulted, left unprotected, and/or arrested gay pride participants (Nielsen 2013). In other cities with widespread opposition, outspoken individuals, nongovernmental groups, or state agents have persuaded courts and parliaments to ban public celebrations of gay pride (Clemons 2012; Matthews 2012), often breaching an established right to assembly (Holzhacker 2013). In those cities most supportive of gay pride, smaller groups of opponents have protested on the sidelines while law enforcement protect participants. Over time, the city of Jerusalem has reflected this range of responses to its gay pride parade.

The Politics of Gay Pride in Jerusalem

Jerusalem has been the site of a contested annual gay pride march since 2002. The struggle over gay pride in Jerusalem is made all the more meaningful when set within the larger context of the recognition of LGBT legal rights in Israel, a country where personal status law remains largely under the control of religious courts (Adelman 2000). For the most part, "the political agenda of the international gay and lesbian civil rights movement has progressed further, and more quickly, in Israel than in almost any other country in the world" (Fink and Press 1999, 9). According to The Agudah, and other Israeli advocacy organizations, since 1988, when the state officially decriminalized sodomy, Israel has banned harassment and employment discrimination based on sexual orientation, including within the military; approved domestic partner benefits; allocated survivor benefits for same-sex relationship widows or widowers; defined same-sex couples as families for purposes of issuing domestic violence orders of protection; legalized same-sex parental adoption of nonbiological children; and recognized same-sex marriages conducted abroad (Dahan 2008). At the same time, LGBT advocates are quick to point out that these rights have been primarily acquired through judicial rather than legislative means. This was demonstrated bluntly by the current parliament's failure to pass anti-discrimination legislation, notwithstanding overwhelming support of full and equal rights for gay men and lesbians among Israelis (Lior and Lis 2013; Lis 2013b). Because of this political tension, supporters and opponents alike view Jerusalem's gay pride parade as a (welcome or unwelcome) means to further advance the visibility, legitimacy, and rights of the LGBT community in Israel.

From its first step, the gay pride festival in Jerusalem has served as a referendum on the legitimacy of the LGBT community in Israel. As such, the parade also has been inextricably linked to politics: international, national, and domestic. Jerusalem's Pride event intends to transcend the multiple political, religious, social, and physical borders its organizers claim segregate the city. Below I analyze the politics of the Pride parade, addressing the international conversation about LGBT rights more generally; national politics of the Pride parade in Jerusalem, such as how Israel's relationship to Palestinian territories has shaped the meaning and practice of the parade; and attending to the domestic politics of the parade, including how inter-religious, intra-religious, and religious-secular tensions have played out in Jerusalem's parade. I acknowledge that it is at times difficult to tease apart international, national, and domestic politics, both due to how they overlap chronologically and their substantive linkage. Where possible, I note these intersections or disjunctures. Before I turn to this analysis, I provide a brief chronological overview of gay pride in Jerusalem in table 8.1.

"Make Jerusalem more open, more pluralistic, more tolerant"

The main organizational sponsor of the gay pride parade, the Jerusalem Open House (JOH), the LGBT Center in Jerusalem, describes itself as a crossroads where Jews and Palestinians, religious and secular, young and old, gay and straight can be together in one place. Along similar lines, openly gay city councilman Sa'ar-Ran Nathaniel, then the municipality's advocate for the gay pride parade, opened Lulu, a bar in Jerusalem where he hoped to attain his vision for Jerusalem: in his words, a place with "everyone together" (*Jerusalem Is Proud to Present* 2007).

JOH organized the first Pride march in Jerusalem in June 2002, which they called a "March for Pride and Tolerance." The theme selected for Jerusalem's Pride festival was "Love without Borders," reflecting organizers' desire to "make Jerusalem more open, more pluralistic, and more tolerant" in terms not only of sexual orientation but also religion and nationality (Hazan 2003). One of the event's organizational participants, Black

TABLE 8.1

Pride Parades and Marches in Jerusalem

Date of Event	Type of Pride Event	Politics
June 7, 2002	Jerusalem's first Pride march	Second Intifada
June 20, 2003	Jerusalem Pride march	Postponed one week from June 13, 2003 to mourn victims of bus bombing
June 30, 2005	Jerusalem Pride march	Interfaith coalition against Pride; three participants stabbed
August 19–28, 2005	WorldPride Jerusalem	Festival cancelled after Gaza disengagement is pushed back to August 16
August 6–12, 2006	WorldPride Jerusalem	Rescheduled festival held, but parade cancelled due to Israeli war with Hezbollah in Lebanon.
November 10, 2006	Jerusalem Pride march	Rescheduled parade transformed into stadium rally due to riots in Jerusalem and fear of retaliation to Israeli airstrikes in Gaza.
June 21, 2007	Jerusalem Pride march	10,000 security personnel line parade route
June 26, 2008	Jerusalem Pride march	Many opponents avoid public protests
June 25, 2009	Jerusalem Pride march	Many opponents avoid public protests
July 29, 2010	Jerusalem Pride march	First parade route to end at Knesset building.
July 28, 2011	Jerusalem Pride march	Scheduled to commemorate Tel Aviv shooting; social justice activists join parade
August 2, 2012	Jerusalem Pride march	Tenth annual parade, returned to original parade route.
August 1, 2013	Jerusalem Pride march	Most gay-friendly Knesset in history, and rise of "pink-washing" critique

Laundry, whose formative slogan, "No Pride in Occupation," emphasized the connection between gay pride and national politics through their signage printed in Hebrew, Arabic, English, Yiddish, Russian, and Amharic that read, "Transgender not Transfer," and "Jerusalem: One City, Two Capitals, All Genders" (Katz 2002). Noting the link between sexual and national liberation by referencing Palestinians in the West Bank, JOH Executive Director Hagai El-Ad argued just prior to the first parade that he felt personally that "[t]he struggle for our rights is worthless if it's indifferent to what's happening to people a kilometer from here" (El-Ad 2002).

The first gay pride parade in Jerusalem took place during the Second Intifada and its associated downturn in the economy. The parade was scheduled in the midst of a dramatically violent period, which deterred many locals and most tourists from doing business in West Jerusalem. Still, the event attracted approximately 4,000 participants who marched through Jerusalem, from Zion Square through the city center to Independence Park, a popular rendezvous in Jerusalem for gay men (Fink and Press 1999). Organizers and local business people were equally surprised at the crowds that were drawn to the parade, given the concern about political violence, and the overall level of everyday homophobia in the city. One parade organizer announced to the assembled crowd, "It wasn't simple, but there are people here for whom this is their first day out of the closet to get out of the dark and into the light" (*BBC News World Edition* 2002). Ofer Ben-David, the owner of a souvenir shop along the parade route, shared the parade organizers' positive assessment: "People can do what they like. . . . Live and let live. They're colorful and they're livening up downtown, which was dead" (Greenberg 2002). The city's first parade drew protestors, but in relatively small numbers, perhaps due to the support of—if not endorsement from—then mayor of Jerusalem Ehud Olmert, a decidedly secular Jewish Israeli who soon became prime minister.

Jerusalem's second Pride parade, scheduled for June 13, 2003, was held just after the election of the city's first ultra-Orthodox mayor, Uri Lupolianski. At first, Lupolianski nominally defended the existence of a gay pride parade in the city, saying "Everyone has his own parade. I myself will be marching in another parade" (Advocate.com 2003). His putative neutrality received severe rebuke from his religious constituents. Ultimately, the parade was postponed for a week until June 20, 2003, not because of any political or religious opposition, but in order to allow Jerusalemites to mourn the victims of a bus bombing in the city center, which killed seventeen people (including one of the Pride parade organizers) and injured more than 100. Despite ongoing political violence, and lukewarm reception from its city leader, Jerusalem's first and second gay pride parades were considered successes by its organizers. The Jerusalem Pride parade

did not fare as well a couple of years later when organizers were confronted by a combination of domestic and national political challenges:
threats of violence stemming from an interfaith coalition of religious leaders, and from Israel's relationship to the Palestinian territories.

"This is not the homo land, it is the Holy Land"

Mayor Lupolianski, joined by similarly minded members of the Jerusalem
municipality, sought to halt the fourth annual local Jerusalem gay pride
parade, scheduled for June 30, 2005. The Pride parade clashed with their
vision for the city of Jerusalem. Allowing the gay pride parade to move
forward would affirm a worldview they rejected: universal secularism,
homosexuality, civil marriage, and sexualization of public space; at the
same time, the parade would explicitly reject the core values they cherished: religiosity, the traditional family and procreation, the status quo of
personal status law, and sexual modesty. Because the event would take
place on the open streets of Jerusalem, they were concerned that young
people would be exposed to what they defined as abhorrent, and would
be witness to the desecration of the city. The mayor argued that a Pride
parade would incite violence among Jerusalem's religious residents and
harm the city. However, parade organizers turned to the justice system
where the Jerusalem District Court ordered the city to treat this festival as
it would any other, and the Israel Supreme Court required that the parade
be held as planned. The police concurred, stating, "We will protect this
demonstration and that one [the counter-demonstration], so that there
won't be violence between them" (Stahl 2005).

On the day of the parade, approximately 10,000 participants were met
by about 700–1,000 protestors, primarily members of *haredi* communities. At one point in the parade, a group of protestors pushed through the
police line that had been protecting the participants. One of the protestors,
thirty-year-old Yishai Schlisel, stabbed one man and two women, telling
police he wanted to kill homosexuals in the name of God for parading in
the holy city. At the culmination of the parade in Liberty Bell Park in Jerusalem, organizers read a statement from the Israeli interior minister, Ophir
Pines-Paz: "Jerusalem Pride is part of the struggle for human rights and
freedom for all sectors of society. The heads of the Jerusalem Municipality

should self reflect on their contribution to the incitement leading up to today's violence" (International Lesbian and Gay Association 2005). Ultimately, Schlisel was convicted of attempted murder, given a twelve-year jail term and fined $30,000 as compensation to the victims. At about the same time, Judge Yehudit Tzur ordered the Jerusalem municipality to pay organizers of Jerusalem Gay Pride $77,000 for refusing for three years to recognize the event, which would have entitled organizers to receive public funding (*365gay.com Newscenter* 2006).

Efforts to halt the annual, local gay pride parade were amplified by an unprecedented interfaith coalition of Jewish, Muslim, and Christian leaders from within Israel and across the world. They came together to oppose the ten-day WorldPride festival, an international Pride event held every five years, which had been awarded to the city of Jerusalem, and was scheduled to be held August 18–28, 2005.

Lupolianski reportedly stated he would do "everything in his power" to stop WorldPride Jerusalem, describing it as a "parade of abominations" (Coyne 2005). The mayor was joined by individual Christian Zionists and their organizations (e.g., International Christian Embassy in Jerusalem, Christian Friends of Israel, Bridges for Peace, and Jerusalem Prayer Team), who were concerned with how the city—"where heaven and earth met and will meet again"—would be defiled (Klein 2005). American Jews such as Yehuda Levin of the Rabbinical of Alliance of America, who helped galvanize anti-Pride efforts, described WorldPride Jerusalem as the "spiritual rape" of the city (Chabin 2005), arguing "[t]his is not the homo land, this is the Holy Land" (Goodstein and Myre 2005).

Within Israel, an interfaith coalition against WorldPride Jerusalem temporarily unified Israel's Sephardic and Ashkenazi chief rabbis, the patriarchs of the Roman Catholic, Greek Orthodox, and Armenian churches, and a group of Muslim clerics, who publicly condemned the festival (Goodstein and Myre 2005). Speaking to their commonly held concern about the threat of violence should the parade take place, Archbishop Pietro Sambi, the Vatican's ambassador to Israel and representative to the Palestinians, stated that "no one can assure that this parade will go on in a peaceful way and will not provoke reaction from the faithful" (Greenberg 2005). On the global level, Israel's Sephardic chief rabbi

Shlomo Amar requested support from Pope Benedict to halt the parade. His counterpart, Ashkenazi chief rabbi Yona Metzger, argued in front of a group of interfaith leaders gathered in Moscow from forty countries, including Iran, Saudi Arabia, and Syria, that "political disputes should be left behind" and that "countries must stand united around their belief in one God" (Sela 2006e).

Organizers of WorldPride Jerusalem responded to critics: "What brings an American Evangelical leader, a Sephardi *haredi* Knesset member and a New York rabbi together? No, this is not the beginning of a joke. Rather it is the manifestation of how powerful a coalition fear and prejudice can be. A coalition of fundamentalist Christians and Jews has joined hands in an attempt to yet further monopolize their interpretation of the meaning of Jerusalem" (El-Ad 2005). Organizers countered what they saw as an overly narrow definition of religion by arguing that WorldPride Jerusalem "will make history in one of the world's most historic cities, bring a message of reconciliation to people troubled by conflict and claim dignity and acceptance in a city holy to three of the world's great religious faiths. . . . All this we can do—and we can do it only in Jerusalem" (Coyne 2005). WorldPride organizers insisted that theirs was an inclusive event, intended to honor religious people, gay and straight.

This claim was echoed by another rare but different show of unity. Representatives from three major non-Orthodox streams of Judaism in Israel (i.e., Reform, Conservative/Masorti, and Reconstructionist) spoke out in support of WorldPride. Soon after, however, Rabbi Ehud Bandel, president of the Conservative/Masorti Movement, clarified that they would not participate in the parade and were not endorsing the festival, per se, but rather "the community's right to hold this event in the face of so much hatred . . . in the name of free speech and tolerance" (Chabin 2005). The situational unity of non-Orthodox streams with regard to World-Pride Jerusalem sharpened the ongoing intra-religious power struggle within Judaism in Israel between Orthodox and non-Orthodox streams of thought. At the same time, the common enemy of homosexuality generated never-seen-before inter-religious unity in Jerusalem and around the world when Jerusalemites and others fought to secure from endangerment their vision for the city. The place of religion in the national identity of the Israeli state was the most common frame found in the fight over gay pride, serving as a proxy for a particular vision of Jerusalem. Jews, Christians and Muslims drew together based on a shared sense of morality and justice, either in protest or in support of the festival.

"Why does Israel look like paradise to gay Palestinians?"

Religion and nationalism also were woven into the fight over WorldPride Jerusalem with regard to Palestinians. The Palestinians were taken up in a variety of ways in the debate over gay pride in Jerusalem, which received criticism and support from both the right and the left. Positions on gay pride from the left ranged from those who opposed the parade to those who endorsed the parade. Aswat, a Palestinian gay women's organization, spoke out against the parade and decided not to take part in WorldPride Jerusalem. Instead, Aswat helped to organize an alternative event called "Parade to the [Separation] Wall" (Aswat 2006). Aswat also joined other organizations from the left who called for global non-participation in WorldPride Jerusalem, based on the South Africa divestment/boycott model. Leading the boycott was the San Francisco-based organization Queers Undermining Israeli Terrorism (QUIT). QUIT argued that "Palestinian queers who live just 10 minutes away . . . will be stopped at military checkpoints from joining this celebration. . . . [T]he government of Israel is not building a wall around an entire country because it is attempting to create a queer safe space" (QUIT 2005). QUIT also rejected the WorldPride theme "Love without Borders," in light of the Separation Wall, which physically divided the city, and their understanding of Jerusalem as a politically occupied city. QUIT and its boycott coalition members argued that it was hypocritical to participate in a Jerusalem-based event that pitted LGBT and Palestinian freedom against each other.

Leftist organizations did not all agree about how to handle the relationship between Israeli military policy, the Palestinians, and WorldPride Jerusalem. Many recognized how Jerusalem Open House, the event's primary organizer, provided critical resources to Palestinian gay people, both inside and outside of Israel's contested borders. Black Laundry, a social justice group in Israel organized against the occupation and other forms of oppression, did not endorse a full boycott, but critiqued the overall de-politicization and commercialization of the gay rights movement: "[W]e've been outspoken in opposing the occupation and homophobia in Palestine. But we also trust the organizers and the activities of the Jerusalem Open House, one of the only places where Palestinian gay men have any sort of visibility and community. . . . We don't actively encourage anyone to visit Israel to take part in WorldPride events, or in any kind of global consumerist gay culture, but we will organize events and present radical alternatives to international queers who do decide to visit" (*Black Laundry* 2005). According to this logic, it was appropriate to recognize at WorldPride Jerusalem the development of a safe space and specific services for Palestinians.

Organizers of gay pride in Jerusalem similarly echoed the importance of JOH services for Palestinian gay people. Additionally, they argued that gay pride parades in Jerusalem, including WorldPride Jerusalem, would help reclaim the city for those who had given up on it "as a place where different communities can coexist, but it's actually one of the few places in Israel where Jews and Arabs, and secular and religious people come together precisely because of their sexual orientation" (Friedman 2006). As noted above, from its conception, gay pride in Jerusalem was envisioned as an event that focused on both sexual and national liberation for all participants, regardless of religious identity (El-Ad 2002).

From the right, uncommon expressions of concern for the safety and well-being of gay Palestinians entered the debate in a number of ways. The idea of Jerusalem and Tel Aviv as a welcoming oasis in a hostile Middle East has been used by non-LGBT Zionist individuals or groups as a point of pride for Israel, to associate Israel with the United States or Europe, and to differentiate Israel from what they identify as the homophobic and violent Middle East or Muslim World (Maikey and Ritchie 2009). For example, Israel's gay-friendly status has been incorporated into a campaign called iPride, sponsored by StandWithUs, a US-based Israel advocacy organization whose members hope to counter negative conflict-focused images of Israel and to "show that Israel is a liberal country, a multicultural, pluralistic country" (Bezelel 2009; and see Kraft 2009). StandWithUs participants argue that "Israel advocacy needs to come from the gay community and it needs to come from the most liberal, leftist parts of society" (Liphshiz

2009). A spokesperson for the organization explained that gay people are generally liberal who "identity with the Palestinian," but "we find it a bit ironic because you can't really be gay in the Palestinian territories" (Bezelel 2009). A flyer from their campaign builds on this worldview by asking viewers, "Why does Israel look like paradise to gay Palestinians?" and then answering the question: "Israel respects life," imputing a presumption of death for openly gay Palestinians (StandWithUs n.d.). Israel's Foreign Ministry also has helped to sponsor efforts to publicize abroad the state's liberal approach to gay rights.

Critics on the left labeled such state branding public relations efforts as a form of "pinkwashing," noting the intent to distract or dissuade the public from an anti-Israel or pro-Palestinian perspective with claims of LGBT equality in Israel (Gross 2012; Gurtler 2012). The concept of pinkwashing is part of a larger argument against "homonationalism," understood as the (mis)alignment of neoliberal politics and state violence with the pursuit and promise of LGBT rights. Homonationalism is secured through patriotic silence, and "homonormativity," where LGBT people strive for acceptance through assimilation within heteronormative institutions such as the military and marriage, and via mainstream engagement in the market as consumers (Duggan 2002; Gross 2010). In Israel, queer activists opposed to pinkwashing commonly boycott or refuse to participate in Pride, organize alternative Pride activities (including solidarity events with Palestinians), and/or participate in or endorse a multi-issue social justice approach to Pride.

Still other critics of the gay pride parade from the right focused less on boosting Israel's image, and more on protecting the nation-state from its putative Arab enemies. For example, Jerusalem city councilwoman Mina Fenton, argued that the political violence associated with Arabs, who reject the legitimacy of the Jewish state of Israel, takes precedence over any potential discussion of social issues such as gay rights. Fenton said that holding WorldPride during wartime was "disgusting" and that "gays should be put to better use helping soldiers in Lebanon or bringing food to families living in bomb shelters" (Luongo 2006). Parade opponents sought to maintain a sense of unity in the face of what they perceived of as a national threat. Ashkenazi chief rabbi Yona Metzger stated, in reference to the public conflict over disengagement from Gaza, "We have enough tensions in our small country. . . . Adding tension to tension and creating a new provocation will inflame all the religions of the world" (Greenberg 2005). Government support of gay pride in Jerusalem also has been used to explain national threats to Israel, including military losses in Gaza and Lebanon (Traiman 2006). Other opponents used the legal system's affirmation of the gay community's freedom of expression to assert their sense of nationalism by hosting more than a dozen "Jewish pride parades" in Palestinian Arab towns in Israel (*Jerusalem Post* 2009).

From the right, as well, critics of gay rights have suggested that hosting a large-scale event such as WorldPride Jerusalem would provoke violent responses from Muslims. During an interfaith press conference of Pride opponents on June 21, 2006, Sheikh Ibrahim Sarsur, member of parliament, warned that if homosexuals "dare to approach" the Temple Mount "they will do so over our dead bodies" (Chibbaro 2006). Others integrated the "clash of civilizations" model, in which "Islam" and the "West" are at war with each other, into their explanation as to why World-Pride Jerusalem should be cancelled: "In their eyes, the parade is part of a whole chapter where Israel brings the defilement of the United States and the West into the holy land and Jerusalem . . . [a]nd they react to it with bloodshed" (Chibbaro 2006). Labor Minister Eli Yishai (Shas) sought to banish gay pride events not only from Jerusalem, but also from all of Israel, by arguing, "There is no such thing as restricting the abomination. . . . This march will lead to world-wide social destruction" (Stoil and Izenberg 2006). The specter of Palestinian violence against gay people has been used to oppose the (West) Jerusalem site of the annual Pride parade. Deputy mayor of Jerusalem Eli Simchayof and Shas representative Yair Lari both suggested disingenuously that the Pride parade should be moved to East Jerusalem. Lari commented, "we will see what they [Palestinians] will do to them" (Sela 2006b).

Supporters thought that WorldPride Jerusalem offered the State of Israel a number of unintended benefits, in addition to the pursuit of justice for LGBT people. Embracing gay pride was good for business because it would enhance economic development and tourism. Publicizing gay pride was good for Zionism because it would showcase Israel as a modern and democratic state, which confers legal rights to gay Israelis and serves as a safe harbor for gay Palestinians in the Middle East.

In contrast, opponents anticipated that WorldPride Jerusalem would create a host of problems. Some were concerned that it would bring thousands and thousands of people to Jerusalem, whose travel to the city and participation in the festival would signal at least tacit support for Israel's military policies and the Separation Wall. Others were more concerned about how WorldPride and its normalization of homosexuality would defile the home and defy the values of three monotheistic religions; an event that affirmed gay pride, supported with city dollars, would sully the streets of its religious inhabitants and corrupt its youth. Opponents worried that WorldPride Jerusalem would trigger violent responses that might lead to the destruction of the city, nation or state.

"This is bigger than gay rights"

The theme of WorldPride Jerusalem, scheduled for August 18–28, 2005, remained "Love without Borders" to "show that human rights transcend cultural and ethnic boundaries." Organizers anticipated the need for a thorough security plan, due to the potential for political violence associated with the Second Intifada. They understood that security would be their biggest expense. They had not anticipated that the festival would take place during the Israeli government's unilateral evacuation of its settlements and redeployment of its military from the Gaza Strip. However, the pullout was pushed back from July 25, 2005, to mid-August so as to not coincide with the three-week mourning period preceding the Jewish holiday Tisha b'Av.

The government's disengagement plan was vociferously challenged, with members of Israeli settlements in Gaza threatening to refuse to evacuate, and Palestinians protesting increased limits on their mobility. Nevertheless, JOH Director Hagai El-Ad argued that "the parade will be an alternative to overdosing on disengagement mania. It will also serve as a reminder of the many post-disengagement issues we must face, on the path towards building a more democratic, civil society" (El-Ad 2005). From his perspective, if Israel's disengagement from the Gaza Strip cancelled the gay pride parade in Jerusalem, then it would reinforce how Israeli domestic concerns such as women's rights, environmentalism or poverty, among others, often are subordinated to national politics. However, after discussing it with police, WorldPride organizers agreed to postpone the festival for a year, and re-scheduled it for August 6–12, 2006.

Opponents of the festival, who had been relieved when WorldPride did not take place in August 2005, returned to their local, national, and international efforts to halt the now-rescheduled parade. By early summer, two-thirds of the Jerusalem city council members had signed a petition to cancel the march. Yair Gabbai (National Religious Party) suggested to the "mayor that the police should forbid the parade as a disturbance, just like they forbid Jews from visiting the Temple Mount" (Derfner 2006). Women began to speak out as well against WorldPride Jerusalem, emphasizing their rejection of the sexualization of culture in general, and homosexuality in particular (Fendel 2006). Interfaith gatherings took place where speakers urged the government to cancel the parade or the organizers to move the parade to Tel Aviv. The police also suggested the parade be moved to Tel Aviv where they are "more used to such events" (Sela 2006a). The parliament hosted a meeting of the Internal Affairs Committee to which were invited opponents of the parade ranging from Orthodox Jewish and Muslim members of parliament to the Vatican's ambassador to Israel; supporters included members of parliament and parade organizers (Marciano 2006).

Extralegal efforts to halt the parade emerged as well. Hundreds of denunciation posters were affixed to buildings, and letters were circulated in mailboxes in the Jerusalem neighborhood of Mea She'arim that offered a reward of NIS 20,000 for "whoever causes the death of one of the people of Sodom and Gomorrah" (Ettinger 2006). The letter included details about how to make Molotov cocktails, nicknamed the "Shliesel Special," in honor of the man who stabbed three people at the June 2005 gay pride march (Sela 2006d). Additional threats of violence emerged when Sheik Taissi Tamimi, head of the Islamic court in the West Bank and Gaza, called on Palestinians to take to the streets to prevent WorldPride participants from entering East Jerusalem (Nessman 2006).

These efforts to halt the parade were partially successful. WorldPride Jerusalem took place as scheduled in mid-August, but the parade itself, the festival's symbolic event, was cancelled. Officially, it was the war between Israel and Hezbollah in Lebanon that summer that persuaded the police to cancel the parade. According to the police, the escalating conflict had left them unable to ensure the parade's security, particularly because they feared violence threatened by the opposition during the parade (Sela 2006c). However, officials admitted using this concern as a cover in order to cancel a controversial event; tellingly, a week before the scheduled parade, Jerusalem police allowed a rally in the Old City, marking the one-year anniversary of the Gaza Disengagement (Sela 2006c). WorldPride organizers called the cancellation "anti-democratic" and urged the police to "protect freedom of expression . . . [and] not to surrender to violence in advance" (Sela 2006c). However, they cooperated with the Jerusalem police, and announced that the parade would be re-scheduled, again, when the fighting in the north ceased. When the war in Lebanon ended, the parade eventually was returned to the city calendar and slated to kick off on Friday, November 10, 2006.

Between the end of the war in Lebanon in August, and the new date for the parade in November, the debate continued as to whether the parade should or would ever occur. As the parade date drew nearer, the conflict over the gay pride parade intensified, and by the end of October, it was unclear whether the police would issue a parade permit to World-Pride Jerusalem. On October 31, 2006, in anticipation of the November gay pride parade, Jerusalem's police chief placed his force on "Emergency Alert." Soon thereafter, opponents within ultra-Orthodox Jewish communities began public protests that quickly escalated into riots around the city and in other *haredi* towns such as Bnei Brak. Posters again were affixed to buildings, announcing a reward for killing parade participants. A poster also was erected in Mea She'arim that called Jerusalem police chief Ilan Franco the grandson of a Nazi SS officer because he appeared to be willing to issue a permit for the parade. Because of death threats, the director of JOH was assigned a twenty-four-hour bodyguard. These tactics were particularly alarming because they occurred during the week of the eleventh anniversary of the assassination of Prime Minister Yitzhak Rabin, who similarly had been labeled a Nazi and a traitor of the Jewish people.

The riots went on for days, with hundreds of mostly young *haredi* men hurling food and rocks at motorists and police, setting garbage cans and cars on fire, burning tires, placing spikes in the street and blocking traffic (Lefkovits 2006).[1] Parts of the city looked and smelled like a war zone. In the meantime, a group of individuals, including the minister of labor, petitioned the High Court of Justice to cancel the parade, based on their claim that opponents had threatened to protest the parade with violence, and that such protests would endanger the lives of the protestors, marchers, and security personnel (Stoil and Izenberg 2006). Although the number of participants in the riots was relatively small, the riots were widespread, publicly visible, seemingly without end, and attracted significant national attention. In response to the riots, and the attempt to force cancellation of the parade based on them by representatives of the groups behind the riots, Elena Canetti, a JOH spokeswoman stated, "This is bigger than gay rights. It's now about whether we respect the rule of law in Israel, or give in to threats of violence" (McGirk 2006). Indeed, the attorney general turned down a police request to ban the parade and urged the parties to find a compromise that would enable the parade to move forward securely.

However, when an Israeli military strike killed nineteen Palestinian civilians in Beit Hanun, Gaza on Wednesday, November 8, 2006, police in Jerusalem feared retaliatory violence in the city. As a result, the police said they did not have sufficient personnel to protect both the parade and the city. On Thursday, a day before the parade had been planned to take place, the police, organizers, and opponents agreed that the parade would not be held. Instead, it was announced that the parade would be replaced by a celebratory rally at the Givat Ram campus of Hebrew University in Jerusalem. Approximately 4,000 participants enjoyed the festive "All the Colors of the Rainbow" rally in the university stadium, protected by 3,000 security personnel.

---

1. In response to Haredi anti-gay pride riots in Jerusalem, an unidentified group of gay rights activists were suspected of smashing the windows of the Geula Synagogue in Tel Aviv, and spray-painting the walls with the message, "If we can't march in Jerusalem, you won't walk in Tel Aviv" (A. Cohen 2006). This further emphasized the territorial "ownership" of Tel Aviv and Jerusalem by their respective secular and religious communities.

Over a period of two years of planning to either host or halt the WorldPride parade, it had been postponed a year, then cancelled, and then rescheduled again, transformed from a public expression of visibility and belonging, into a heavily policed, private indoor party. Opponents appeared somewhat satisfied with this outcome, pointing to their success at delaying and ultimately forcing the removal of the symbolically important parade from the streets of Jerusalem and its containment in the stadium as a closed event. They declared victory in the ongoing battle over how Jerusalem is envisioned and experienced. Organizers also seemed somewhat satisfied that despite the long-term and last minute changes, the celebratory event was neither eliminated nor moved to Tel Aviv. Rather, it was held in Jerusalem when and how its stakeholders ultimately agreed upon.

Nevertheless, Pride supporter and Jerusalem city councilman Sa'ar Nathaniel expressed his concern with the process that led up to the final agreement. He described Jerusalem as being caught in a tug-of-war, unsure of its future character: "We are struggling with something that is much deeper than gay rights. . . . We are struggling about the image of Jerusalem: Will it be pluralistic and tolerant and democratic, or a twin city of Tehran or Kabul?" (Nissenbauma 2006). With this comment, Nathaniel created a snapshot of the politics of gay pride in Jerusalem, where perceptions of competing notions of justice and identity continue to form the city.

After WorldPride Jerusalem

Ten days after the "All the Colors in the Rainbow" parade substitute was held in Jerusalem in 2006, the Supreme Court ruled 6–1 that same-sex couples married outside of Israel could be registered by the state as married couples. The ruling actualized a significant component of the gay community's pursuit of justice in Israel: "This is an historical day for the [gay] community and for democracy. This is our real pride parade" (Yoaz 2006). As such, the ruling irreparably undermined the vision for the city of those who opposed the parade. It did so by further marginalizing the relevance of Orthodox religious authority over personal status law, whose jurisdiction over the years has been narrowed, although certainly not eliminated, with regard to heterosexual marriage. The ruling in support of the recognition of same-sex marriage also advanced the possibility of civil marriage in Israel, which is understood by opponents as a deathblow to Israel's intertwined formation of religious and national identity.

The next year, in 2007, Jerusalem again was the site of a contested gay pride parade. Based on their experience of the 2006 riots, and the additional protests and threats aimed at the 2007 parade, Jerusalem police posted around the parade route a security force of close to 10,000 persons, which represented more than half of the active duty personnel in the country. In 2008, opponents shifted strategies and turned to the parliament in an attempt, albeit unsuccessful, to legislate through an amendment to the Jerusalem Basic Law an outright ban on the parade. Beginning in 2008, leaders of the *haredi* communities also decided to not orchestrate large-scale public demonstrations, wanting instead, they argued, to shield their community from the event. As a result, participants in the 2008 and 2009 gay pride parades in Jerusalem encountered opposition, but no large-scale rioting.

Subsequent gay pride events in Jerusalem in 2010 and 2011 were scheduled to commemorate the then still-unsolved shooting that caused two deaths and fifteen injured at an LGBT youth gathering in Tel Aviv (Cohen 2009). Given the growing visibility of both the victimization and collective influence of the LGBT community, Jerusalem Pride organizers continue to emphasize through the design of their event the need for political change, further distinguishing the city of Jerusalem from Tel Aviv. This was accomplished symbolically in 2010 by routing the Pride march to culminate for the first time in front of Israel's parliament building (Hasson and Kyzer 2010). The Pride event in Jerusalem in 2011, again scheduled to commemorate the mass shooting, drew thousands of participants, some of whom marched in solidarity with the LGBT community as members of that summer's nascent social justice movement whose focus was primarily economic justice issues such as housing and food costs (Hasson 2011b). This shift may portend future opportunities for cooperation, if not collaboration, across various social justice movements in Israel.

A combined sense of history and success permeated Jerusalem's gay pride parade in 2012. In anticipation of the event, supporters spray-painted the city's iconic "Hollywood"-esque welcome sign, positioned at the western entrance to Jerusalem, in rainbow colors. Organizers returned the parade to its original route to mark ten years of Pride, to physically stand where three people were attacked during the fourth annual parade in 2005, and to commemorate the third anniversary of the then still-unsolved Bar Noar shooting in Tel Aviv. Elinor Sidi, the director of the Jerusalem Open House explained that Jerusalem "has changed a lot in the past ten years, following a decade of repeated petitions" from the community (Hasson 2012). She observed that Jerusalem seems to have "accepted its gay community members" (Hasson 2012).

A year later, a local producer of weekly gay dance parties in Jerusalem, twenty-nine-year-old Sarah Weil, agreed with Sidi's assessment that "[t]here is also a gay awakening in Jerusalem. . . . Of course, I'm not talking about the ultra-Orthodox. But the secular and modern Orthodox Jewish communities do accept us, and I feel I don't have to hide who I am" (Keissar 2013). Yet, Nadja Rumjanceva, another participant in Jerusalem's 2013 gay pride parade, noted the dogged distinction between it and the party in Tel Aviv: "in Tel Aviv the Pride Parade would be sending out booming decibels; here it was more like a whisper of positivity among the other noises of the city. . . . No mind-boggling torsos, no skimpy speedos, no confetti, no alcohol stalls along the road, but an intimate and laid-back atmosphere . . ." (Rumjanceva 2013).

Jerusalem's more modest atmosphere reflects the consistent political message of their March for Pride and Tolerance. In 2013 the theme was "We Want Change." According to organizers, "We Want Change" referred to frustration over the passing of decades with minimal legislative intervention to protect and include the LGBT community in Israel. Dissatisfied with narrow and precarious court-based social change, and faced with the friendliest Knesset ever, JOH director Elinor Sidi emphasized that "[w]e in the gay community have had enough of talks and promises" (Hasson 2013).

Today, inspired by Jerusalem's persistence, and Tel Aviv's unfettered growth, Pride events are hosted by organizations across the country, not only in the "third city" of Haifa, but also in smaller locales such as Ashdod, Be'er Sheva, Eilat, Hadera, Petah Tikva, Ra'anana, and Rishon LeZion. Each locale's Pride activities reflect the personality and politics of place.

With this proliferation of Pride activities, the LGBT community continues to take to the streets to call for statewide legislative recognition, protection, and rights. At the same time, Prime Minister Netanyahu continues to champion LGBT rights in Israel around the world, to critique Iran, and to burnish the state's reputation. This attracts applause from those on the right, who are proud of the distinction and the liberal basis of the Israeli state, and who wonder why such equality is dismissed by many on the left (*Jerusalem Post* 2011), who point to the state's discriminatory stance toward African asylum-seekers, Palestinians, and human rights organizations (Gross 2103). Meanwhile, those traditionally opposed to the gay pride parade in Jerusalem as the incarnation of LGBT rights in particular, and the incursion of secularism more generally, have gained support from the more centrist religious Zionists and nationalists in the government coalition, as well as from several parties in the opposition, to continue to successfully reject same-sex marriage and thus any further encroachment upon the status quo of religion-based marriage and divorce (Lis 2013a).

Conclusion

Gay pride in Jerusalem continues to differentiate itself from the Pride parade and festival in Tel Aviv, their respective styles and substance reflecting the particularities of place. The Jerusalem parade attracts more opponents, who use legal and extra-legal attempts to halt it in order to protect what they understand as the sacred nature of the city; in Tel Aviv, the opposition, already marginalized socially and politically, is sidelined. Jerusalem Pride tends to attract a smaller number of participants, some of whom travel from Tel Aviv or other parts of the country to support the contested parade. In contrast, the Pride parade in Tel Aviv attracts a significant number of tourists from outside the country for whom the appeal primarily lies in its open Mardi Gras atmosphere and exotic but familiar location. Because Jerusalemites have distinct social and political needs, and perhaps in deference to the dominant sensibility of its residents, gay pride in Jerusalem focuses on community affirmation and social change rather than just celebration.

In this way, Jerusalem also continues the Stonewall tradition of the parade as a means of political engagement. Participants in Jerusalem still fight for freedom of expression and unfettered access to public space, while Tel Aviv's mayor exuberantly welcomes the annual event. Given the larger proportion of gay, religious residents in Jerusalem, organizers build its Pride activities around the inviolable nature of the two identities. The Tel Aviv parade, while not ignoring the ongoing fight for LGBT rights of its secular or religious residents, is an extension rather than an instance of the public expression of gay life in the city. And, in light of Jerusalem's geographic, economic, political, and personal ties to the struggle over the Palestinian state, the city's Pride intentionally incorporates this national struggle for human rights. The emergence of an economic justice movement in Israel that has at least informally extended support for the local Pride march offers a potential new pool of Jerusalem constituents whose vision for the city includes the visible legitimacy of its LGBT residents.

It is unclear what the politics of Jerusalem Pride will be like in the future. The capacity of the LGBT movement in Israel is growing, as is the social and legal acceptance of LGBT rights more broadly, most recently declared succinctly by US Secretary of State Hilary Clinton (Capehart 2011) and echoed several months later by UN Secretary General Ban Ki-moon (Ban Ki-moon 2012). International pressure to join the community of states who support LGBT rights—expressed either rhetorically, or expressed by states seeking to join entities such as the European Union—has already been felt in Israel, which has officially expressed at least partial identification with this now commonly-accepted indicator of enlightenment. Israel is also not alone in tapping liberal acceptance of LGBT people as a "way of distinguishing 'us,' the good native folk, from 'them,' the [so-called] bigoted Muslims" (Buruma 2009, 36). At the same time, rejection of LGBT rights marks those states whose leaders wish to defend against the anticipated imperialism and homogenization of so-called Western values, even when those anti-gay politics have been imported from the United States (Kaoma 2012).

The tension between these two views is embodied in the struggle over the gay pride march in Jerusalem. For supporters, a viable gay pride event moves Jerusalem toward their vision of an inclusive and multicultural city. For opponents the successful silencing or at least marginalization of the march would help protect their vision of a sacred Jerusalem controlled by religious interests. Much will depend on the shape of the city's shifting population and the status of its political boundaries. Today, the demographic profile of the city is moving rapidly in favor of the ultra-Orthodox Jewish religious community and away from Palestinian and non-ultra-Orthodox Jewish influence. Governance of the city will be determined by the geographic outcome of any future peace process. Taken together, these factors will determine the configuration of support for and opposition to public expressions of LGBT rights such as the Pride parade in Jerusalem. The outcome of this struggle will align politically with the overall nature of the city. In this way, a study of the status of gay pride events becomes a way to measure the identities and values of a city's residents and those who govern the everyday life of a city.

The protracted contest over gay pride reveals the centrality of Jerusalem both for those who wish to highlight its timeless sacrality, and for those who wish to strengthen its multicultural or progressive political landscape. For both sides of the debate, Jerusalem has become a tipping point in the fight over the future of the state. Should gay pride advance successfully, Jerusalem may become more like Tel Aviv. Or, the LGBT community in Jerusalem, perhaps in cooperation with a range of supporters, may be able to generate new ways to share the city with those who oppose LGBT rights (Curtis 2013). Whether this outcome is assessed positively or negatively depends upon one's aspirational desires for the city. Jerusalem's struggle over gay pride illustrates how contested notions of justice and identity literally and figuratively form cities. Its future is not unlike other cities where the place of gay pride continues to mark struggles among competing visions for the body politic.

9

Jerusalem in Java[1]

MARK WOODWARD

ANTHROPOLOGY COUNTS RELIGION as one of the discipline's constitutive domains. In turn, religious studies draw on anthropological theory to help explain how religion is taken up and given ever changing meanings by human actors on an everyday basis. As an anthropologist in a religious studies department, I have moved my research on Islam beyond disciplinary boundaries. Here, I analyze how storytelling (or legends) and the everyday use of religious sites help to establish the legitimacy of Javanese territories and communities. I focus on the Javanese city of Kudus, where believers have replicated their vision of Islamic Jerusalem. Kudus is a shrine city in Indonesia with a population of 135,000, an important pilgrimage site, and a center of Islamic learning since the sixteenth century. In Kudus, Javanese Muslims attempt to link conceptions of Java as a Muslim

1. This paper is based on ethnographic research conducted in Kudus in 2006 supported by the Directorate of Islamic Education of the Indonesian Ministry of Religion and elsewhere in Java between 1978 and 2006. I have lived and worked among Javanese Muslims of almost all theological and political orientations. Field work conducted in the late 1970s serves as a baseline. It was supported by the Council for the International Exchange of Scholars, the Social Science Research Council, and the Graduate College Research Board at the University of Illinois. I would like to thank the Center for Asian Research and the Center for the Study of Religion and Conflict for financial support for more recent research. I would like to thank Madelaine Adelman and Miriam Elman, the organizers of the conference at which an earlier version of this paper was presented, for providing me with the opportunity to develop my thinking about the Jerusalem-Java connection and for many editorial suggestions.

land with the Islamic symbolism of Jerusalem. Kudus is not unique in its architectural symbolism. Replications of Jerusalem can be found, for example, in the Holy Land Park in Orlando, Florida. However, Kudus is unique in how the architectural symbolism of Jerusalem achieved legitimacy for its local Muslim community by becoming a "celestial archetype" (Eliade 1959).

The historian of religion Mircea Eliade, and many others concerned with the study of mythology, ritual, and sacred geography, have noted a tendency for sites such as temples, cities, and empires to be constructed as replicas of what he terms "celestial archetypes" (ibid.). Palaces, realms, and temples replicate the structures of the cosmos, and particular those of the "symbolism of the center." This establishes the religious legitimacy of political entities and is widely believed to be responsible for their economic, military, and political success (ibid.). Eliade also argues that in traditional societies events are meaningful only to the extent that they repeat or participate in mythological archetypes (ibid., 34). He describes portraying social conflict in terms of cosmic conflict between heroes and demons, and cyclic theories of time in which the universe moves from creation to destruction or from order to chaos, as being among the strategies traditional peoples employ to explain misfortune and to ameliorate suffering—which he refers to as "the terror of history" (ibid., 142–51). Equally significant is his demonstration that the epistemological shift from description of events to mythic representation of them can occur with remarkable speed (ibid., 44–45).

Using Eliade's notion of the mythic representation of social conflict within celestial archetypes, this chapter concerns the replication of the Islamic symbolism of Jerusalem in the Indonesian city of Kudus. It is based on ethnographic fieldwork conducted in Kudus and elsewhere in Indonesia over the past three decades, and on the analysis of contemporary Indonesian writings that are as much mythological as they are historical. These texts, which circulate widely, are contemporary retellings of tales included in eighteenth century Javanese texts and are also preserved in oral tradition, told daily to thousands of pilgrims who visit the city's shrines.

It is important to note that it is Islamic Jerusalem that is replicated in Kudus, while Jewish and Christian themes and motifs are totally absent.

In doing so, the Indonesian city of Kudus links the mythology of Kudus with Indonesian Islamic discourse about contemporary world affairs. Surprisingly, despite his significance in Indonesian Islam, there is very little scholarly literature on Sunan Kudus, for whom the city is named, and his shrine in European languages. In this chapter, I highlight how elements of myth, ritual and architecture are expressive of the tension between Islam as a Middle East-centered tradition and Islam as it is understood and practiced in the context of Javanese culture. To do so, I examine the sacred biography of the founder of the city, the Javanese *wali* (saint) Sunan Kudus, along with its shrine, which consists of the mosque, the stone minaret, the cemetery where the Sunan and members of his family are buried, and the rituals associated with them.

Java, Kudus, and Islam

Indonesia is an archipelago of more than 17,000 islands straddling the equator in Southeast Asia. It is the world's most populous Muslim nation. Islam came to Indonesia from south India and Arabia. The first Muslims appeared to have arrived in the eleventh century. By the end of the thirteenth century there was a well-established Islamic kingdom in north Sumatra. The faith spread rapidly in the fifteenth and sixteenth centuries and came to dominate the major population centers other than those on the island of Bali, whose Hindu inhabitants resisted conversion. Indeed the percentage of Muslims in the Islamic regions of Indonesia exceeds that of most Middle Eastern countries. Indonesia is approximately 88 percent Muslim. The non-Muslim, primarily Christian, minorities are geographically concentrated. The vast majority of Christians in the region are ethnically Chinese. The percentage of Javanese who are Muslim clearly exceeds the percentage of those who are Arab. The overwhelming majority of Indonesian Muslims are Sunni. There are very small Shi'ah and Ahmadiyah minorities in the region.

Indonesian Muslims have maintained relationships with the Middle East for many centuries. They have journeyed to Mecca and Medina on pilgrimage and to study. It is not known how common pilgrimage to Jerusalem was in the sixteenth century, but it is clear that Indonesian Muslims have long been aware of its religious significance. The anniversary of

the Prophet Muhammad's Night Journey, which Islamic tradition maintains was from Mecca to Jerusalem, is an important religious holiday for
Indonesian Muslims. There are also symbolic references to the city in the
architecture of the Yogyakarta palace, which is an iconic representation
of a variant of the Sufi mystical path (Woodward 1998). However, prior to
the advent of steam navigation in the nineteenth century, the journey to
Mecca and Medina was long and fraught with danger—so much so that
many pilgrims did not expect to survive the journey. In the nineteenth
century there was a substantial Java colony in Mecca that included some
of the city's most important scholars (Hurgronje 1970).

The city of Kudus, founded in the mid-sixteenth century, today hosts
a population of approximately 135,000. Kudus is located in the eastern
quadrant of the Island of Java, a region long known for a Sufi mode of
Muslim piety in which the veneration of saints (wali) and their tombs plays
a central role (Woodward 1989; Ricklefs 2001). Its tomb of Sunan (saint)
Kudus, after whom the city is named and by whom it was founded, is
central to the city's political and economic life. Sunan Kudus is one of the
legendary wali songo (nine saints) who are said to have been instrumental
in the Islamization of Java (Bashah 1993; Ringkes 1996). Their tombs are of
particular importance as pilgrimage sites. Many traditional Javanese Muslims believe that visiting all of their tombs is the equivalent of perform-
ing the hajj pilgrimage to Mecca. As a result, the Sunan Kudus tomb and
mosque are important pilgrimage sites for Muslims from throughout the
country. However, a distinction can be drawn between conservative traditionalist Muslims, associated with the organization Nahdlatul Ulama,
who maintain that pilgrimage to holy graves is an efficacious devotional
act, and modernist Muslims, associated with Muhammadiyah, who consider it to be among the worst forms of shirk, the sin of associating other
beings and powers with Allah. The city of Kudus is among the strongest
bastions of conservative traditionalism.

The symbolism of Kudus is exemplary of the ways in which Javanese
Muslims have sought to link conceptions of Java as a Muslim land with the
symbolism of Muslim centers in the Middle East, including Mecca as well
as Jerusalem. The replication of Islamic archetypes associated with the
Prophet Muhammad was among the means through which early Javanese

Muslims sought to define Java as Muslim space and to legitimize Islamic political authority. Kudus is perhaps the clearest example of this variety of religious thought in that it is the only major Javanese site to have an Arabic name. Kudus is a Javanese transliteration of *al-Quds*, the Arabic name for Jerusalem. It is also known as Baitulmukadis, which is the Javanese form of the Arabic term for the Temple. The principal mosque is named for the al-Aqsa Mosque on the Temple Mount in Jerusalem. It is also known as Mesjid Menora because it is one of the relatively small numbers of pre-modern Javanese mosques to have a minaret. Minarets are increasingly common in contemporary Indonesia, reflecting the continuing development of variants of Islam oriented towards the Middle East and the fact that mosque construction is funded by donors from Saudi Arabia and the Gulf states.

Sunan Kudus

A recent biography of Sunan Kudus begins with a discussion of the Sufi concept of sainthood as it is understood by traditional Javanese Muslims. It states: "The *wali* are described as the heirs of the Prophet. They are the ones who continue the missionary work of the Messenger of God. The lives of the *wali* were filled with challenges. Their stories provide lessons in ethics and devotion to God and Truth" (Arrosi 1992, v). All of the available biographical information on the life and career of Sunan Kudus is tinged with such hagiography. It is difficult to sort fact from legend, but for understanding his role in contemporary Javanese Islam, this is unimportant because for millions what modern scholars would deem legend is simply fact.

Description of the *wali* as the heirs of the Prophet Muhammad establishes a direct mytho-historical link between Indonesia and Arabia, and between the seventh and twenty-first centuries. It collapses the eight centuries between the time of Muhammad and those of the *wali*, whom Javanese tradition and chronicles place in the fifteenth century. The veneration of saints occupies a central position in conservative Muslim piety. As a result, this imagined configuration of time and space also buttresses the dominant theological position of the conservative Muslim community in Kudus represented by Nahdlatul Ulama (NU). NU scholars, *kyai*, consider themselves to be, and are generally recognized as, the heirs of the *wali*. In contrast, modernist Muslims represented by Muhammadiyah, and Islamists influenced by the Saudi Arabian Wahabi sect, denounce this practice as a combination of *bidah* (sinful innovation in religious matters), *kufarat* (unbelief), and *shirk* (polytheism).

Sunan Kudus was born "Ja'far Shadiq." This has led some Indonesian and Western scholars to suggest that there was a Shi'ah dimension to early Javanese Islam because this is also the name of the sixth Imam. There is, however, nothing in his biography or in the ritual complex associated with his mosque and tomb to suggest that this is the case. It is more likely that the name is linked to the fact that in addition to being an Imam, Shadiq was also an important figure in the Nashqabhandi Sufi order, which has long been the most popular in Java and throughout South East Asia.

The Javanese Ja'far Shadiq is said to have come from a family of *ulama* and to have been of Arab descent. As do many Javanese, he studied first with his father and subsequently with other prominent *ulama* of the day. He was a brilliant student, rapidly mastering the traditional Islamic subjects of theology, law, and quranic exegesis. He also is said to have mastered Javanese history and literature, much of which concerned the island's pre-Islamic past, and in the case of Javanese literature, is based on the Hindu epics Ramayana and Mahabharata.

Like many Sufis, Ja'far Shadiq held a number of official positions. On completion of his studies he was appointed pilgrimage master for the kingdom of Demak. He also was a military commander and played a significant role in the defeat of Majapahit, the last major Hindu kingdom in Java, in part, through his use of magical power. He also is said to have led an unsuccessful campaign to drive the Portuguese from the port of Malacca on the western shore of the Malay Peninsula. At the time, Malacca was an important seaport and center of the Southeast Asian spice trade. The fall of Malacca to the Portuguese, and subsequently the Dutch, contributed significantly to the expansion of European power in the region and to what Indonesians refer to as three centuries of colonial rule.

The text (Shiddiq 2000, 43–44) begins with a conversation between the saint and military commander Sunan Kudus and Sultan Patah of the early Javanese Muslim kingdom of Demak:

"What is it Commander?" asked Sultan Patah. "Here is a guest from Malacca" replied Sunan Kudus as he presented the visitor. "The letter he brings explains the Malacca has been seized by the Portuguese." "Apparently the colonizers intend to come here. This cannot be tolerated. We must take action" replied the Sultan.

The text next explains:

In the year 1453 Portugal was occupied by the Turks who established an Islamic government.[2] Because of this the Portuguese hated Islam with a passion. They did not distinguish between ethnicity and Islam or between Islam and ethnicity.

Keep in mind the fact that at that time Indonesia was known as a fertile and prosperous Muslim land that the Portuguese wanted to attack. Killing the Muslim saints was the means through which they intended to expand their influence in Indonesia. In 1511 they succeeded in occupying Malacca. All of the inhabitants fled to Sumatra, Sulawesi or Java.

Sultan Patah ordered his Commander Ja'far Shadiq [Sunan Kudus] to assemble a fleet of tens of vessels. They were ordered to sail from Jepara to the sound of *takbir* [calling on God]. The fleet arrived at Malacca on January first 1513. Ja'far Shadiq initiated a naval battle. But at that time the Dutch came to the aid of the Portuguese with troops and modern weapons. Because of this the Demak fleet was easily defeated and was forced to retreat. Ja'far Shadiq had no choice other than to order his fleet to disengage.

Only a small number of ships survived the journey home. Most of the fleet was sunk by the Portuguese naval forces. Most of those who had struggled died as heroes.

This text is remarkably contemporary and resonates strongly with recent world events. The text was written in 2000 prior to the September 11, 2001 attacks on the United States and the subsequent US wars in Afghanistan and Iraq. When asked about it in 2006 and 2007, many Indonesians

---

2. This statement is inaccurate. Portugal was not conquered by the Turks. It is probably a reference to the Turkish capture of Constantinople in that year.

volunteered that the Crusades, colonialism, and current conflicts are fundamentally similar. Christians who hate Islam and all Muslims launch wars of aggression to seize the lands and wealth of innocent Muslims. Western military alliances and superior technology make it impossible for the Muslims to defeat the colonialists and large numbers die as martyrs or become refugees. This enables many Javanese Muslims to use the colonial past and even the Crusades as archetypes for understanding contemporary affairs. None of the Indonesians I have spoken with in recent years support foreign occupation of Muslim territory. Even the most moderate believe that control of oil resources was the actual motivation for the Iraq war. Many do not believe that Muslims were involved in the September 11 attacks. In an interview during which he described the peaceful nature of Indonesian Islam, Hasyim Muzadi, the general chairman of the traditionalist *Nahdlatul Ulama*, stated, "All religious followers have to be vigilant about efforts to use religion for non-religious purposes. For example, in the war in Iraq [US president George W. Bush] made a 'Crusade' the theme while the actual motive was the control of oil. Fortunately, both Muslims and Christians know this very well. It should never happen that people use religion in a war for oil" (Boediwardhana 2006).

In the context of Indonesian and broader Muslim discourse, Muzadi's description of the Iraq war as a "war for oil" must be considered moderate. Indonesian radicals think of it as a war against Islam, with the goal of killing Muslims. Indonesian radicals believe that there is an international conspiracy between Christian Crusaders and Zionist Jews dedicated to the destruction of Islam. The Gulf War, along with the occupation of Iraq, the West Bank, and Gaza Strip, are cited as illustrations of the effort to destroy Islam, as are the US inclusions of Iran and Iraq in the "axis of evil." The recent Israel-Lebanon War, the more recent conflict in Gaza, and threats against Iran's nuclear program are understood as just other parts of this global conspiracy. The popular Islamist magazine *Sabili*, available for purchase on newsstands and in mainstream and Islamic bookstores, describes the "invasion" of the Islamic World, liberalism, ridicule of the Prophet Muhammad (a reference to the Danish cartoon crisis), conversion to Christianity, and pornography as efforts to destroy the morality of the Muslim community by colonialist Crusader forces, against whom it is necessary to conduct jihad (*Majalah Islam Sabili* 2006). Those who hold such views place themselves and their action within a tradition of epic struggle against sworn enemies of Islam. For them, Sunan Kudus is one in a series of Muslims to suffer defeat at the hands of the infidels.

Ja'far Shadiq was subsequently one of the *Penghulu* (judges, ritual officiants) of the kingdom Demak, the first Islamic state in Java. He is said to have left Demak and established Kudus in 1549. There are at least two traditions concerning his decision to strike out into undeveloped territory. The first is that he had a great desire to build a "holy city," and to live a more purely religious life. The second is that he left because of a dispute concerning the proper date for the beginning of the fasting month of Ramadan.

Additional legends concerning Ja'far Shadiq's travels in the Middle East are the foundational myths of the new city. There are two versions of the core myth: one locating it in Mecca, the other in Jerusalem. In both the city is devastated by plague. Ja'far Sadiq recommends that a *do'a* (intercessionary prayer) be added to each of the five daily prayers, and that through the sincerity (*ikhlas*) of his prayer God causes the plague to recede. In return, Ja'far Shadiq is offered many valuable gifts but will accept only a stone. Some say this offering is a portion of the black stone said to have fallen from heaven and currently located in the Kaaba in Mecca. Pilgrims to Mecca strive to touch or kiss this stone. Others suggest the stone was taken from the al-Aqsa Mosque in Jerusalem. Given the name of the city, the latter version seems more reasonable. Regardless of its origin, the stone is now located in the *mimbar* (niche from which the imam leads prayers) at the front of the Sunan Kudus Mosque.

The Architecture of Islam in Kudus

The mosque, the minaret, and legends concerning the now Sunan Kudus's career are based on two basic themes: the first is the integration of Islam and local culture, and the second is the often violent suppression of heresy. The mosque and the minaret are architecturally Javanese. Among the distinctive features are the split gates. The minaret which is still used for the call to prayer, is said to be built over a well the local Hindus believed to be a source of Holy Water so powerful that it could bring the dead back to life. One myth recounts that Sunan Kudus chose this site to establish continuity between the old and new religion; another that he chose this site to block access to the well, and consequently, to prevent new converts from lapsing into unbelief.

The present Middle Eastern Arab-style structure of the mosque is a twentieth century addition. Indeed, the contrast between Javanese and Middle Eastern motifs in the architecture of the shrine is an example of how architecture can be what Kusno (2003, 57–67) describes as sites of negotiation between global Islam and local culture. In Kudus the Middle East and global Islam are symbolically brought to Java. Inscriptions found inside the mosque are in Arabic, and give its name and date of its construction, as well as a statement to the effect that Sunan Kudus is a caliph. This statement is ambiguous as regional leaders of Sufi orders as well as rulers are referred to as *khalifah*. Either reading is possible because Javanese sultans continue to use the title to the present day. The inscription also refers to Sunan Kudus as a devotee of the *sunnah* of the Prophet David. Some suggest that this is evidence that the authors of the inscription had somehow confused David and Solomon (Guilot and Kalus 2002, 27–56). This is not necessarily the case because, as is well known in Kudus, the term *Sunnah Nabi Daud* refers to the practice of fasting for two days every week throughout the year.

The belief that a particular shrine offers a direct connection to the holy lands is not unique to Kudus. Two of these resemble Kudus in that they bring the holy lands to Java. Sultan Agung of the seventeenth-century Central Javanese kingdom of Mataram is said to have flown to Mecca every Friday for the congregational prayer. It is also said that he requested permission to be buried next to the Prophet Muhammad in Medina, but that his request was denied so that he could be the great saint (*pepunden*) of Central Java. He was, however, allowed to bring soil from the vicinity of the Prophet Muhammad's grave, which was deposited at the royal cemetery Imo Giri. There is also a "black stone" on one corner of the palace wall in the Sultanate of Yogyakarta in Central Java.

Here it is interesting to contrast myths concerning the construction of the Great Mosque in Kudus with that of the neighboring territory of Demak, where another of the most important Javanese shrines is the

Grand Mosque of Demak. The Grand Mosque of Demak is said to have been the first constructed on the island. In this instance the mythic logic is quite different. The holy lands are not brought to Java; rather, Java is oriented to the holy lands. The Demak mosque architecture is distinctively Javanese with a three tiered roof instead of a dome. According to myth, after the mosque was constructed, it refused to orient itself toward Mecca and spun in circles. Another of the nine *wali*, Sunan Kaligaga, is said to have fixed the direction of the *kiblat* (direction of prayer) by holding one hand to the center post of the mosque and by reaching out with the other and touching the Kaaba in Mecca. In contrast to how the Kudus mosque brought Islam to Java, this myth of the Demak mosque bends Java towards Mecca and global Islam.

For the remainder of his career, Sunan Kudus is said to have devoted himself to *dakwah* (the propagation of Islam) in a region where there were still many *kafir*. His strategy was to infuse local culture with Islamic meanings and to bring elements of Hindu Javanese religion including the Hindu epics into Islam. He is said to have invented the *wayang golek* (plays performed with wooden puppets) through which the epics are told.[3] The most striking example of his efforts to localize Islam is reflected in the tale that he once tethered a cow at the mosque to attract Hindus, since he understood that they loved cows, and forbade the slaughter of cattle in the city. This custom is maintained to the present day. Even today in Kudus, water buffalo meat is a local substitute for beef. The meanings of this substitution are complex because the water buffalo is regarded as one of most important symbols of Javanese culture, and is used as a campaign symbol by numerous political parties. The Surakarta palace counts a "family" of albino buffalo as one of its most important heirlooms, and its leader is named *Kyai Slamet* (Lord Tranquility). Interestingly, people from Kudus find the notion of sacred buffalo to be utterly absurd. When I told colleagues in Kudus about it, they made innumerable jokes about eating him.

---

3. These are three-dimensional wooden puppets in contrast to the more common two dimensional leather *wayang kulit* puppets.

In contrast with what is often termed a "gentle" approach to *dakwah*, Sunan Kudus was exceptionally harsh with Muslim "heretics," especially those teaching the doctrine of *whadat al-wujud* or the unity of the divine essence (*zat*) and the human soul. He executed such teachers on more than one occasion, and in one case the bodies of a husband and wife were transformed into black dogs when they were buried, a very common theme in Javanese religious texts (Soebardi 1975).

Taken as a whole, these accounts place Sunan Kudus well within the mainstream of Javanese Islam. He is depicted as a pious and learned Muslim scholar, but at the same time as one sensitive to the cultural context in which his teaching was delivered. He was, in fact, more tolerant of Hindus than of Muslims he considered to be heretical. This remains a central theme in the conservative Islam of *Nahdlatul Ulama* and stands in sharp contrast with the tendency of modernists and Islamists to denounce elements of Javanese culture, especially the rejection of *wayang* theatre as polytheism and unbelief.

Ritual

In Java, major shrines define both a territory (*wilayah*) and a community (*ummah*), which exhibit highly distinctive variations on common ritual themes. In addition to the Friday prayers, the most important rituals conducted in the Kudus shrine complex center on *ziyarah*, the visitation of the graves located behind the mosque, the *haul* or *urs*, commemorating the death of Sunan Kudus, and the celebration of the fast of Ramadan.

There are more than a hundred graves in the cemetery behind the mosque. Tens of thousands of pilgrims visit them annually seeking blessing (*barakah*). Some seek blessing in a general sense, others come with specific requests: healing, jobs, children, success in business, and educational endeavors being among the most common. Before entering the cemetery complex, pilgrims remove their shoes and perform the *wuduh* or purification rites required before prayer. Knowledgeable pilgrims visit several of the graves, but most visit only that of Sunan Kudus. Unlike other graves in the cemetery, it cannot be approached directly except by the caretakers of the shrine. It is surrounded by a white gauze curtain. Pilgrims sit on all sides and recite or read from the Qur'an, usually *Surah Yasin*, which in Java is strongly associated with mortuary rituals, holding their palms upright to receive the descending blessing.

Many of the pilgrims are from the Kudus area and visit the grave on a regular basis. Others come on commercially organized pilgrimage tours. Some of these are very basic, while others offer luxury accommodations, including air-conditioned buses offering food service and video programming. Generally they are comprised of groups of relatives, friends, neighbors, or co-workers. Most are guided by an experienced pilgrim or *sheik*, who, if the shrine is so crowded that entry is impossible, will perform the *ziyarah* on behalf of the entire community. Pilgrims often shop in the many stores located in the area for a wide variety of religious paraphernalia and Arab style clothing. Most sample traditional Kudus cuisine, which usually includes water buffalo stew. Many, particularly the elderly who remember the days when pilgrimage was far more arduous than it is today, explain that increased commercialization has led to decreasing religious value of *ziyarah*.

The *urs* or *haul* is celebrated annually on the tenth of the Islamic month of Muharram. This holiday also commemorates the martyrdom of Imam Hussein, the grandson of the Prophet Muhammad. Although it is the most important Shi'ah religious festival, it is widely celebrated in Java. On this occasion the curtain that surrounds the grave of Sunan Kudus is removed and cut into small squares. These are given to "important people," including politicians, businessmen, and religious leaders who, in turn, give them to their followers. This custom is typical of traditional Javanese Islam in which blessing is thought to flow downward through social and political hierarchies. Prior to the Second World War, similar practices were observed in the palace rituals of the central Javanese kingdoms of Surakarta and Yogyakarta. Its rituals, celebrating the two *Ids* and the birth of the Prophet Muhammad, consisted of gifts of food transmitted to the general public through the kingdoms' political hierarchy. In an effort to democratize the rituals, the gifts are now given directly to the people in the courtyards of the great mosques of the kingdoms (Woodward 1991).

Prior to these ceremonies mosque officials solicit contributions of food. In 2006 they collected twelve tons of rice, eleven water buffalo, and thirty-seven goats. The goats and buffalo are slaughtered in the court-yard of the mosque and prepared in special dishes cooked only at this time of the year. In 2006 only six tons of rice was cooked for the *haul*. The remainder was divided into fifty-kilogram parcels and distributed to the poor (*fakir miskin*) as charity (*sadakah*). Cooked food was distributed to the assembled pilgrims and to residents of the neighborhoods surrounding the mosque. In this sense, the *haul* with its combination of prayer and the distribution of food resemble the *slametan*, the prayer meal commonly per-formed by traditional Javanese Muslims (Woodward 1988).

The *keris* (ceremonial dagger) belonging to Sunan Kudus is also ritu-ally cleansed or "bathed" on the occasion of the *haul*. Almost every Java-nese man has at least one *keris*, which are considered to be heirlooms and thought to preserve some of the magical power their previous owners possessed. The magical power of Sunan Kudus is believed to transmit the ability to defeat heresy because it is the weapon he used to kill those whom he was unable to convince to renounce their false teachings.

At the beginning of Ramadan, residents of Kudus assemble at the mosque to await the beginning of the Holy Month. This is in keeping with the more general Javanese belief that one should visit the graves of family members at both the beginning and the end of the month. All of these rites are particular to Kudus, though they resemble those performed at other major Javanese shrines and in mosques and cemeteries known only to their local communities. The symbols and rituals unique to Kudus define the territory and the community as distinctive sub-units of the large land and culture of Java.

Conclusion: Why Is Jerusalem in Java?

The religious legitimacy of Javanese Muslim communities, territories, and states were built up through legends surrounding their direct contacts with sacred centers in the Islamic Middle East. Kalus and Guilot (2004) have suggested that Ja'far chose to call his city (and himself) "Kudus" because his act of founding a holy city was analogous with that of the Prophet David who was the founder of the holy city of Jerusalem, or alternatively with the nearly contemporaneous actions of the Ottoman Sultan Suleiman the Magnificent who did much to restore Jerusalem at approximately the same time. The association of Javanese sites with their religious counterparts in the Middle East continues to motivate local pilgrimage traditions.

There is, I think, more to be said regarding Eliade's insights concerning the importance of the "axis mundi" in that traditional religions are important for furthering our understanding of the Javanese Jerusalem. Eliade has observed that traversing the axis mundi is the means through which shamans, saints, and other religious *luminatae* mediate between the sacred and the profane. Of the world's religions, Islam is perhaps unique in that it has not one, but two cosmic axes. While it is believed that the Kaaba in Mecca is directly beneath the throne of God and it is from there that blessing descends in response to prayers, Jerusalem is an axis mundi. It was from Jerusalem that Muhammad ascended to heaven to receive instruction from God, and it was in the al-Aqsa Mosque that he led the assembled Prophets in prayer prior to his ascent. Consequently, in replicating the celestial, the architects of Javanese Islam confronted a choice. In Demak Sunan Kalijaga's choice was to align the mosque directly with Mecca, but in Kudus, only a few miles away, Sunan Kudus chose Jerusalem as an alternative—hence the two versions of the legend concerning the Middle Eastern stone that is the mosque's, the city's, and the community's palladium. Recent retellings of the foundational myth of Kudus suggest parallels between sixteenth century conflicts in Southeast Asia and those in the contemporary Middle East, bringing the two together in a coherent narrative of sacred struggle against seemingly insurmountable odds. Viewed from this perspective, the tale of Jerusalem in Java is not merely one of the replication of celestial archetypes in the construction of a local variant of a "world religion." It is also a theodicy, the branch of Abrahamic theology that explains why the people of God suffer despite their faith.

10

Jerusalem, Tourism, and the Politics of Heritage

DALLEN J. TIMOTHY AND CHAD F. EMMETT

JERUSALEM IS AMONG the world's premier tourist destinations. Each year, thousands of religious tourists (pilgrims)—Christians, Jews, and Muslims—gather to the Holy Land to venerate a sacred urban space that has been pivotal in the development of their religious associations. Heritage (the modern-day use of the past) and tourism are fundamentally political by nature, beset with power struggles, unbalanced hegemonic control, disunity and discord, and societal amnesia. Because Jerusalem shares many parallel spatial and temporal heritages, it experiences a great deal of "heritage dissonance"—a discord or lack of agreement between populations and their heritages (Creighton 2007; Olsen and Guelke 2004; Tunbridge and Ashworth 1996). This results largely from the power relations at play inside and outside Jerusalem, as various religious and cultural groups lay claim to their rightful inheritance of the holy city (Cohen-Hattab 2010). In this regard, each group claims Jerusalem for itself, and in so doing, concurrently disinherits other claimant parties. Perhaps no other heritage city in the world is as hotly contested as Jerusalem in political terms, but also from the perspective of tourism. This chapter probes these concepts of power and heritage contestation as they pertain to Jerusalem, examining the successes and problems associated with the growth of heritage tourism (including pilgrimage) and its various manifestations in the city.

Heritage Contestation and Politics

The cultural past has long been an important resource upon which tourism is based. Even in ancient days, people traveled to see the great cultural wonders of the world. Historic places and relics are among the most pervasive and best-known tourist attractions today, and each of these has a story to tell, or more accurately, several stories to tell. However, it is commonly acknowledged that the accounts most typically interpreted to visitors represent perspectives of the parties in power, or the winners of war. Thus, when a site is selected for conservation and interpretation, it tends to represent biased perspectives of the past. In doing this, other pasts are disinherited, especially when sites to be preserved and interpreted are located in the territory of an opposing group (Krakover 2002; Timothy 2011; Timothy and Boyd 2003).

Claims to heritage spaces have resulted in many violent conflicts throughout the world, and the more ancient the claims, the more belligerent the discord tends to be. Likewise, the more ancient it is, the more disregarded the narrative of the "other side" will be (Scham and Yahya 2003, 400). These tensions or dissonances are among the most fundamental problems (and opportunities) in the development of tourist-historic cities (Ashworth and Tunbridge 2000; Bruce and Creighton 2006).

There are many political uses of heritage and tourism (Cohen-Hattab 2004b; Graham 1996; Hall 1997; Timothy 2007), although only a few will be highlighted here. Even at one specific site, different groups will interpret a location's heritage values in different ways. They are typically in agreement with regard to significance but may disagree with regard to scale of significance or just what comprises the significance (Aplin 2002). Oftentimes such an exclusionary practice is intended as a way of suppressing difficult pasts or precluding histories that might question political legitimacy; this is often referred to as collective amnesia or the excluded past. Similarly, heritage is often purposefully used to spread nationalist propaganda to foreign visitors, perhaps to build solidarity for a cause or to downplay opposing views. Finally, domestic heritage tourism, and tourism targeting diasporic peoples in particular, plays on the loyalist nerve of like-minded people to build patriotism and nationalism within a country's population or its diasporic peoples abroad (Kim, Timothy, and Han 2007) to develop ideologically coded landscapes that are endowed with national soul and memory (Raivo 2000; Timothy and Boyd 2003).

Contested Jerusalem

Jewish, Christian, and Muslim scriptures all identify Israel/Palestine as a Holy Land, today venerated because of its deity-cherished status, the sacred events that occurred there, and its stark political symbolism (Peters 1985; 1989). The territory is claimed holy by Muslims as the home of ancient and ancestral prophets, including their father, Abraham, who with his wife Hagar and their son, Ishmael, represent the founding family of the Arab people. Christian and Jewish traditions also proclaim the land holy due to its being divinely ceded to the Israelites—the progeny of Abraham and Sarah. The centerpiece of this dissonance is the city of Jerusalem, which, while hotly contested itself, remains the unchallenged, supreme capital of the Holy Land. Jerusalem, according to Albin (2005, 344), is a source of major conflict because it is the focus of a battle waged at many levels: locally between people living in Jerusalem, who have different visions of the future; nationally between Palestinians and Israelis; regionally between the State of Israel and its Arab neighbors; and globally between adherents of three major religions.

Rivaling powers have long sought to control Jerusalem. Since David's rule, through Roman destruction and medieval crusades, to the modern-day struggle between the Palestinians and Israel, various parties have desired to own, "preserve," or demolish Jerusalem. Other prominent, multi-religious cities in the region have not seen even a fraction of this level of malevolence and discord (Emmett 1995; Sulzberger 1978; Uriely, Israeli, and Reichel 2003). As the undisputed capital of the Holy Land, Jerusalem has functioned throughout history in a variety of capital-city roles. Perhaps the most pertinent today, however, are the concomitant functions as a divided and an eternal capital. Since the birth of the State of Israel, Jerusalem has frequently been named the ancient and everlasting capital of Israel and the Jewish people. For Jews, this is undisputable and exclusive of any claims by Muslims or Christians anywhere else in the world, because "The Christians have Rome and Canterbury and even Salt Lake

City; Muslims have Mecca and Medina. Jerusalem has great meaning for them also. But the Jews have only Jerusalem. . . . This beautiful golden city is the heart and soul of the Jewish people. You cannot live without a heart and soul. If you want one simple word to symbolize all of Jewish history, that would be Jerusalem" (former Jerusalem mayor Teddy Kollek (1977, 715). This and similar declarations by David Ben-Gurion, Yitzhak Rabin, and other Israeli leaders have provoked prominent Palestinians to make similar claims. In response to Prime Minister Benjamin Netanyahu's recurring declarations that Israel would never give up control of any part of the city, Palestinian leader Yasser Arafat declared Jerusalem to be "the capital of Palestine forever" (Emmett 1996, 238).

Even though Muslims have Mecca and Medina, they (particularly the Palestinians) have equally strong feelings about Jerusalem. From their perspective, Jerusalem is

> the navel, the pivotal link between Nablus . . . and Hebron. . . . It is the site of the holiest Muslim shrines on Palestinian soil. Muslims first turned to it in prayer before they turned to Mecca. Toward it the Prophet Mohammed journeyed on his mystical nocturnal flight and from it he ascended to within "two bow-lengths" of the Throne of God. . . . Within its precincts are buried countless generations of Muslim saints and scholars, warriors and leaders. . . . It contains the oldest religious endowments of the Palestinians, their most prestigious secular institutions—the cumulative and priceless patrimony of a millennium and a quarter of residence. . . . It is the natural capital of Arab Palestine. (Khalidi 1978, 705)

Thus, both sides hold legitimate claims to possession of the city, and therefore heritage experts must confront a highly complicated situation with many contending "and perhaps equally valid stories of the past" (Scham and Yahya 2003, 403) having formed an overlapping spatio-temporal narrative. However, some people maintain that because of the Jewish diaspora and the subsequent replacement of a Hebrew footprint by an Arab one in Holy Land space, Jerusalem is now more Arab and Muslim than Jewish. For instance, little in Old Jerusalem denotes a Jewish distant past. Nearly all of the city's old buildings were Arab built, and its main tourist attractions are Christian. "Israel's panacea for this is the ubiquitous

ancient diorama, where models and simulations of ancient Israelite buildings appear in the most unlikely places. A new Israeli museum, opened
during the current Intifada, shows a virtual Jewish Temple rising above
the actual ruins of an Islamic palace" (Scham and Yahya 2003, 404).

While Jerusalem lies at the heart of the Israeli-Palestinian conflict, at
the center of the heart is the Temple Mount, or Haram al-Sharif (Noble
Sanctuary). This hill on the eastern end of the Old City has, for millennia,
been a hub of contention, zealotry, and intolerance (Silberman 2001). There
is an overwhelming sense in Israel that the Temple Mount is much more
important for Jews than it is for Muslims, owing to its politico-religious
centrality in Jewish administration and as the foundation of the Temple of
Solomon. Such sentiments are typically accompanied by declarations that
the site is referenced hundreds of times in Jewish sacred scripts. When
Israel gained control of East Jerusalem and the Temple Mount in 1967,
Israeli leaders opted not to wrest control of the Temple Mount from the
overseeing Muslim waqf. Instead the government demolished the large
Arab-inhabited Maghrebi Quarter that surrounded the narrow access to
the Wailing/Western Wall—Judaism's most holy site. On the rubble of
Arab homes a large plaza was created that now facilitates safe and easy
access for large numbers of Jewish pilgrims and worshippers (Cohen-Hattab 2010).

Palestinians, while contending the supremacy of their claim, sometimes downplay the Haram al-Sharif's direct religious role, instead focusing more on its pivotal function in the legitimization of the Palestinian
state and the crucial connection it makes between Palestinian Muslims
and their co-believers throughout the Islamic World. For example, the
foray of Israeli leader Ariel Sharon and his large entourage onto the sacred
precincts of the Haram al-Sharif in 2000 was protested not only by local
Palestinians in the al-Aqsa Intifada, but also by Muslims in far off Indonesia as well. Overwhelmingly, Muslims need to control the sacred mount
"for the same reason that Israelis do—because it represents a religious
and historical affirmation of their right to be there" (Scham 2001, 64).

In July 2000, for the first time since 1967, Israel demonstrated a degree
of willingness to negotiate with the Palestinians over the sovereignty of
Jerusalem, suggesting that Palestine could rule the Old City's Muslim and

Christian quarters and the outer Arab districts and villages. Yasser Arafat, the Palestinian leader, was willing to contemplate Israeli control over the Old City's Jewish Quarter, the Western Wall, and Jewish settlements in East Jerusalem, but each party was adamant in retaining exclusive sovereign power over the entire Temple Mount/Haram al-Sharif (Albin 2005, 348). While a glimmer of hope for cooperation shined through, this experience reaffirmed the Temple Mount's position as "the most intractable issue in the conflict" (ibid.).

Heritage Tourism and Jerusalem

There are many subcategories of heritage tourism, based on attraction type and the experiences it affords. The primary resources for heritage tourism include museums, places associated with war/defense, industrial complexes, religious sites, heritage festivals, living cultures and traditions, literary places, and archaeological sites in rural and urban contexts. Heritage-based tourism is one of the most prominent tourism types, and many countries base their service economies almost entirely on this sector.

As already noted, Jerusalem is a pivotal sacred space for three major world religions: Judaism, Islam, and Christianity. Thus,

> Jerusalem presents a singular case among all sacred places, in that it attracts pilgrims from diverse religions, nations, and cultural traditions. The significance of Jerusalem to followers of these three religions, and their many denominations, has created spatial and organizational competition and fierce ongoing conflicts over rituals, sites, and itineraries. Whereas Rome, Mecca, and Varanasi . . . are associated with only one religion, Jerusalem is a multireligious center of unique character, spiritual meaning, and universal appeal. (Shachar and Shoval, 1999, 199)

Jerusalem has long been a center of pilgrimage and cultural tourism. Evidence of the city's importance in this regard dates to 333 BCE with the publication of the oldest known guidebook (Poria, Biran, and Reichel 2007). Modern equivalents of tourism began as pilgrimage to the Holy Land following the death of Jesus, although with the collapse of the Roman Empire, much of this began to wane until the Crusades, and then the Renaissance saw increased international travel between Christian Europe and the Middle East. Pilgrimage travel to the Holy Land grew rapidly between the sixteenth and twentieth centuries, and the change from individual pilgrimage tourism to organized tour participation occurred in 1869 with Thomas Cook organizing a tour for thirty people to Egypt and the Holy Land (Shachar and Shoval 1999, 200).

From a heritage perspective, for Jews, the city represents a stable identity in a world rocked by forced migration and targeted destruction. The Western Wall, the only remaining vestige of the Second Temple, the Temple Mount, and the Jewish Cemetery on the Mount of Olives are the most sacred spaces in the city for them (Albin 2005; Ioannides and Ioannides 2006). Among Christians, Jerusalem's hallowed space derives from the city's role as the birthplace (in nearby Bethlehem) of Jesus Christ and the location of much of his earthly ministry, as well as the scene of his crucifixion, burial, and resurrection (Cohen-Hattab 2004a; Olsen 2006; Vukonić 2006). Many sites abound that relate to the life of Jesus. For Muslims, the holy city resonates as an important venue of events in the life of Muhammad and as the home of ancient biblical prophets. The holiest space, the Haram al-Sharif, with its Dome of the Rock and al-Aqsa Mosque, was said to be the site of Abraham's near-sacrifice of Ishmael and the site of the ascension of Muhammad into heaven. These associations make Jerusalem the third holiest space on earth for Muslims, after Mecca and Medina (Emmett 2001; Timothy and Iverson 2006). These holy places for Jews, Christians, and Muslims are the primary sites that draw visitors to Jerusalem.

Brin (2006) suggests two primary types of tourism in Jerusalem: political and pilgrimage. Politically-oriented tourism, according to Brin, is a relative newcomer to the city. This form of heritage tourism focuses on the sites associated with the Palestinian-Israeli conflict. Tours to sites of conflict are an important part of this, as visitors explore the city's tenuous political landscape. Having been barraged by local tensions in the global media, many people set out to experience it for themselves. "Eventually, these tourists come to the city not just *despite* its troubled reality, but sometimes even *because* of it" (Brin 2006, 215). This resembles tours in northern Israel where people travel to see the Lebanese border or to look across the military installations into the Golan Heights at Mount Bental (Gelbman 2006; Timothy 2001).

Private tour operators (Palestinian and Israeli) and the Israeli government are involved in providing these services to "political tourists." Aside from financial gain, one of their main motives is to spread their message to a captive audience. Most agents promote a political agenda in the hope of spreading political messages to the visitors' home countries. Brin (2006) suggests that political tourists in Jerusalem are either just curious about the extant tension ("intrigued tourists"), or they are "solidarity tourists," who come to the city to show unity for Israel or Palestine. Shachar and Shoval (1999) noted similar sentiments as tourists carry a message of support to members of their chosen group residing in the city. Most pro-Israel visitors are European and North American Jews and evangelical Christians who desire to promote the cause of Zionism. Pro-Palestinian solidarity tourists are less common, but nonetheless exist. They typically participate in one of several pro-Palestinian tours in the West Bank and Gaza, and around Jerusalem. The tours take visitors through East Jerusalem neighborhoods and refugee camps to demonstrate alleged injustices perpetrated by Israel. Palestinian religious and political institutions are also highlighted. The new wall separating Jerusalem from the West Bank also features prominently on tours since its inception in 2002, and visitors are given opportunities to speak with Palestinian families who have been brutalized by the Israeli military (Brin 2006).

Dissonant Jerusalem: A Tripartite Religious Destination

Jerusalem has long been a center for religious tourists, or pilgrims, from the three major religions already discussed. Also, as a center of the world's three monotheistic religions and its position as the disputed capital of two nations, Jerusalem has become a place of segmented tourist spaces. These "well-demarcated zones have been created by distinct groups with distinct programs and activities" (Shachar and Shoval 1999, 210), and according to Ashworth (2003), these tourist spaces have led to the physical displacement of local people who no longer feel at home.

Christian pilgrims are among the largest tourist segments in Israel. They come from all denominations to feel the spirit of the Holy Land and to "walk where Jesus walked." The most visited sites include the Galilee area, but in Jerusalem they are the locations associated with the miracles of Jesus and his death and resurrection. Even within the realm of Christian tourism, however, there is dissonance. Several places are specific to the denomination. Perhaps the most common of these is the contested space of the death and burial of Jesus Christ. For Catholic and Orthodox tourists, the most important place is the Church of the Holy Sepulcher. For Protestants, who do not believe this to be the place of Jesus's burial, the Garden Tomb is the main attraction (Collins-Kreiner et al. 2006; Gatrell and Collins-Kreiner 2006; Poria, Biran, and Reichel 2007). Individual denominations also tend to have their own tours and guides that cater specifically to the individual beliefs and mores of each sect. Likewise, many sites have overlapping or parallel spaces where pilgrims can pray and worship together with other members of their particular denomination.

In recent years there has been a widening schism between the pilgrimage approaches to Jerusalem and the Holy Land among Christians—particularly Protestant pilgrims. This divide is based on differing political beliefs and agendas: one that is very supportive of Israel and one that is very supportive of the Palestinians. Christian Zionists and many Evangelical Christians who participate in pilgrimages see their journey to Jerusalem as one of politically affirming their support for the political state of Israel. In 2008, pro-Israel organizations, such as Christians United for Israel (CUFI) offered solidarity tours to the Holy Land, which included attendance at a two-day Jerusalem Summit that sponsored a Night to Honor Israel and a Middle East intelligence briefing at the Jerusalem Convention Center (CUFI 2008). These events were followed by a Jerusalem Unity Rally Walk in which American Christian pilgrims paraded in support of Israel through the streets of West Jerusalem. Similar processions are held by Christian Zionists in Jerusalem each year during the Feast of Tabernacles (*Succoth*).

Several advertised tours on the CUFI website held in conjunction with the April 2008 conference took pilgrims to an interesting selection of pilgrimage sites with obvious political overtones. Noticeably absent from the listed itineraries were visits to the usual pilgrim destinations of Nazareth (an Arab city in Israel) and Bethlehem (an Arab city in the West Bank).

Stops however did include such places as the strategic Golan Heights and the West Bank Israeli city of Ariel where they met with the Jewish mayor. Stops in Jerusalem included Christian sites such as the Garden Tomb and Gethsemane, along with the Holocaust Museum (Yad Vashem), but did not include the Church of the Holy Sepulcher. These tours seem to have avoided visits to tourist sites in Arab municipalities even though they are in safe areas, and they avoided contact with local Christian Arabs.

At the other end of the spectrum is a growing interest in what has been referred to as Living Stones' pilgrimages (Prior 1994, 189). Participants in these pilgrimages are from more traditional Protestant sects, including Anglicans, Presbyterians, and Lutherans. These pilgrims seek to support local Arab Christians (the Living Stones) by visiting their churches and by meeting with the local parishioners (Ron 2009). Many of these pilgrimages are supported by Sabeel (an ecumenical grassroots liberation theology movement among Palestinian Christians). A description of these tours at the Friends of Sabeel website states: "Alternative travel in the Holy Land provides an added benefit for pilgrimage by connecting you with the Living Stones of Palestine who live under military occupation. Visit the holy Christian sites, worship in ancient Palestinian Christian churches, walk where Jesus walked and bear witness to the realities of occupation—military checkpoints, refugee camps, Israel's Apartheid Wall, bypass roads, illegal settlements and more." (Friends of Sabeel 2012, n.p.).

Long-standing rivalries between Ethiopian and Coptic Christians over competing claims in the sacred Church of the Holy Sepulcher have adversely affected Coptic pilgrimages from Egypt to the holy city. Both communities have competing claims to a monastery on the rooftop of the Church of the Holy Sepulcher. On Easter Sunday, 1970, Ethiopian monks changed the locks on doors leading from the monastery down into the church. This prevented Coptic monks from an adjacent monastery from easily entering into the church. The Egyptian government (which is not usually very supportive of its Coptic citizens) took up the cause of Jerusalem's Copts and strongly discouraged Egyptian Copts from undertaking a pilgrimage to Jerusalem until Coptic access to the church via the Ethiopian monastery was restored (Emmett 1997).

With a recent growth in religious tours by members of the various Orthodox churches of the former Soviet Union and Eastern Europe, there has also been an increase in anxiety between several churches, as they try to reclaim sacred spaces in Jerusalem that were built by them originally but are now occupied by other sects. For instance, there is a growing desire within the Georgian Orthodox Church to recognize true Georgian ownership of a number of holy buildings in Jerusalem, which are currently under the control of the Greek Orthodox and Armenian Churches of Jerusalem (Metreveli and Timothy 2010). While these contentions are not as overt as those between the Copts and Ethiopians, there is a degree of underlying tension.

While Judaism requires no formal pilgrimage, many Jews travel to the homeland to visit the lands of their forebears and the center of their religion. In addition to religious sites, Jews from the diaspora tend to visit places associated with Israeli nationalism and undertake so-called Mitzvahs of Nostalgia (Ioannides and Ioannides 2002), which solidify their identities as Jews and lend solidarity to the State of Israel. Jewish tourists to Jerusalem would be most interested in the scale model of Herod's Temple, the Wailing Wall, museums, Holocaust memorials, and the graves of famous leaders (Ioannides and Ioannides 2006; Poria and Gvili 2006; Scham and Yahya 2003). One contentious spot meant for the view of Jews is a museum in the shadow of the Temple Mount, which depicts the mount devoid of the Dome of the Rock and al-Aqsa Mosque. Such a place, in the words of Scham and Yahya (2003, 63), would "hardly be noteworthy were it not for the fact that the museum was constructed within the walls of an Umayyad palace."

A significant trend is also developing in Israel for building solidarity among the Jewish diaspora. In cooperation with several Jewish associations around the world, the government of Israel has recently initiated two programs to bring young Jews "home" to educate them about the State of Israel and experience language training, cultural awareness building, visits to sacred sites, and participation in religious ceremonies. Israel Experience and Birthright Israel have seen considerably success in the past ten years (Cohen 2006). The cost of Birthright, for instance, is covered by the government of Israel and supporting international agencies and nonprofit organizations. So far, more than 260,000 Jewish youth have participated in Birthright since it began in 2000 (Birthright Israel 2011).

Pilgrimage to Mecca is required in Islam, but Muslims throughout the world also undertake less-obligatory pilgrimages (*ziarat*) that are seen to bless their lives and make their prayers more effectual. In addition to Mecca and Medina, Jerusalem is a potentially favored site for these ziarats (Timothy and Iverson 2006). While Muslim travel to Jerusalem has significant ebbs and flows, typically comprising about one percent of the total arrivals (Shachar and Shoval 1999), depending on political conditions, Muslims are an important segment of Jerusalem's tourist base (Mansfeld, Ron, and Gev 2000). Almost all of the Muslim pilgrims are from non-Arab countries (e.g., Indonesia or Malaysia) or from those few Arab countries that no longer boycott travel to Israel. According to Shachar and Shoval (1999), the most popular sites for Muslim tourists are the Haram al-Sharif, the Mount of Olives, Mount Zion, the suq (market), the Jerusalem shopping mall at Malcha, and the Orient House—the informal office of the Palestinian Authority. Mansfeld, Ron, and Gev's (2000) decade-old study suggested that Israel receives approximately 100,000 Muslim visitors each year. While the government of Israel does not provide current and accurate detailed data on Muslim travelers, it does provide numbers of arrivals by country of citizenship. With this as a tentative indicator, some 78,335 tourists arrived in Israel in 2010 from countries where the majority of the populations are Muslim, with the largest waves coming from Indonesia, Turkey, Jordan, Kazakhstan, and Morocco (Central Bureau of Statistics 2011). This number does not, however, take into account that many of these arrivals are likely to be Christian or Jewish citizens of those countries who might also visit the Holy Land for various religious or personal reasons. Nonetheless, it does illustrate that that there is potential for Islamic travel to Jerusalem owing to its sacrosanct status for Muslims (Mansfeld, Ron, and Gev 2000; Timothy and Iverson 2006), particularly those from non-Arab states.

One interesting and rare Muslim Arab pilgrimage to Jerusalem illustrates the political underpinnings of such journeys. In 1993, 192 Muslim pilgrims from Libya traveled by bus across Egypt and into Israel. The US-led embargo on air flights out of Libya prevented pilgrims from flying to

Mecca, so they chose to drive to Jerusalem, instead. They were greeted at the Gaza border by Israeli tourism minister Uzi Baram. The pilgrimage was seen by Israel as a hopeful sign of greater acceptances by its Arab neighbors, while Libyan president Muammar Qaddafi hoped that his international standing might improve by supporting the pilgrimage. One of the first stops for the pilgrims was the Haram al-Sharif with prayer at the al-Aqsa Mosque. While in Jerusalem some of the pilgrims issued a statement calling for an overthrow of the "Zionist leadership," the "liberation" of Jerusalem, and the establishment of a democratic state of Palestine for Arabs and Jews. Outrage in Israel at this political grandstanding led to a quick retreat out of the country by the Libyan pilgrims (Greenburg 1993; Mark 2005).

Other Politics

The manipulation of the past as a propaganda tool is another important and overlapping use of heritage in Jerusalem. Following the creation of Israel, the Israeli government established several monuments and government sites creating tourist spaces that were highly symbolic and influential. The Knesset building and the nearby Israel Museum are two prime examples. The archaeological artifacts in the museum were carefully selected to illustrate the links between contemporary Israel and its long association with Jewish settlement. The museum intentionally excludes the history of Arabs in the region (Shachar and Shoval 1999). Thus, artifacts and sites are commonly used in Jerusalem to justify one heritage, but exclude another. Similarly, the Yad Vashem Museum, which receives some 1.5 million visitors per year, has been imbued with deep nationalist meaning and acts as a uniter of Israelis and Jews of the diaspora (Krakover 2005). Yad Vashem is also always on the itinerary for visiting US and other foreign dignitaries, who are touched by their visit and reminded of the horrors in Europe that led to the establishment of the State of Israel.

Another interesting political twist is the notion of UNESCO-designated World Heritage Sites (WHS). When a state acknowledges a heritage site as being of universal value, the state party can approach UNESCO to have the site inscribed on the World Heritage List. In doing so, the state party assures UNESCO that it will preserve and protect the location and maintain its heritage integrity. The Old City of Jerusalem, including its ancient walls, were designated a WHS in 1981. What is particularly unusual is that the inscription was requested by Jordan, which held sovereignty over the Old City until 1967. This is the only example of a UNESCO proposal being made and accepted for a property lying outside the borders of the sponsoring state (Bruce and Creighton 2006; Creighton 2007) and demonstrates the multi-stratified nature of this contested city. Old Jerusalem is the only WHS not listed under a "host" country.

The 1967 Israeli occupation of East Jerusalem brought both positive and negative changes to tourism development. The one main advantage of a united Jerusalem under Israeli control was the easy and fluid access between eastern and western sectors of the city. From 1948 to 1967, tourists to the divided city had to navigate border controls at the Mandelbaum gate as they traveled between Israeli West Jerusalem and Jordanian East Jerusalem. Tourists were only allowed to make the crossing one time and in one direction. The aftermath of Israeli occupation meant that many extant hotels and tour operators in the Arab sector went bankrupt. These adverse conditions have begun to improve, and benefits have begun to accrue to East Jerusalem as tourism has grown since 1967. Unfortunately each new political upheaval leads to drops in tourism, which hurts tourist providers on both sides of the divide. In conjunction with the 1967 occupation, the Israeli government has used tourism to assert sovereignty over East Jerusalem, encouraging the development of hotels and other tourism-related infrastructure and encouraging entrepreneurs to initiate tourism businesses and promote pro-Israel sites to the neglect of Palestinian heritage (Dumper 1997).

Conclusion

In the current rounds of Israeli-Palestinian peace negotiations, Jerusalem represents the most intractable of issues. So fervent are feelings for Jerusalem that discussion of its control is always relegated to the final phase of peace negotiations, for both sides know that this one issue alone could derail every other compromise and agreement. Current proposals for the final status of Jerusalem usually focus on either continued Israeli control of the unified city (with perhaps limited autonomy for the Arab sectors) or some sort of shared sovereignty between Palestinians and Israel.

In thinking about the future political status of Jerusalem from the perspective of tourism, two keys thoughts emerge. First, for Jerusalem to reclaim its true essence as a center of pilgrimage, there needs to be a recognition that the city is sacred to all and that no one group has exclusive rights to the city or to its various holy sites. There needs to be a peaceful sharing of the city not only between Israelis and Palestinians, but also between such antagonistic groups as Copts and Ethiopians, Evangelical and mainstream Protestants, and Muslims and Jews. Each group has its own view of the city and each deserves unencumbered access to holy sites. Second, to ensure access for religious pilgrims to Jerusalem, there not only needs to be peace, but there also needs to be a depoliticization of the city. Another choice could be if the Israelis and Palestinians would drop their political claims to the city and retreat to other capitals, then Jerusalem could be anointed a religious capital under the sovereignty of no single state. Instead, a religious council of Jews, Christians, and Muslims could work together to ensure open access to the holy sites within the Old City and surrounding Mt. Zion and the Mount of Olives. By allowing Jerusalem to return to its religious roots, the city might once again fulfill its role as a center of religious devotion and pilgrimage, void of political distractions.

Internet Sources

Maps

Jerusalem is a city in constant flux. Its borders, neighborhoods, and access routes are routinely contested, re-drawn, and re-negotiated. Printed maps can provide information about some of these spatial changes in the city's past.[1] However, various websites currently capture the contemporary city far better than do printed maps. It is for this reason that we do not provide a printed map in this book. Not only would such a map become quickly obsolete, but the nuances of the city's private/public and secular/religious spaces are poorly depicted in a single map. Useful web sources for maps include:

Foundation for Middle East Peace at http://www.fmep.org/
International Peace and Cooperation Center at http://home.ipcc-jerusalem.org
    /en/ipcc/4?tpl=11843
Jewish Virtual Library at http://www.jerusalem-library.org/frameset.php
Terrestrial Jerusalem at http://www.t-j.org.il/
United Nations Information System at http://unispal.un.org/unispal.nsf/udc
    .htm

Organizations and Centers

Many nongovernmental organizations and research institutes provide comprehensive and timely coverage of ongoing developments in Jerusalem. See especially:

Association for Civil Rights in Israel at http://www.acri.org.il/en/
B'Tselem at http://www.btselem.org/topic/jerusalem

---

1. An excellent resource for annotated maps on Jerusalem from antiquity until the mid-2000s is Martin Gilbert's (2008) *The Routledge Historical Atlas of Jerusalem*.

Centre for Jerusalem Studies at http://www.jerusalem-studies.alquds.edu/
Conflict in Cities, UK at http://www.conflictincities.org/Jerusalem.html
International Crisis Group at http://www.crisisgroup.org/en/regions/middle
-east-north-africa/israel-palestine.aspx
Ir Amim at http://eng.ir-amim.org.il/
Israel-Palestine Center for Research and Information at http://www.ipcri.org
/IPCRI/Home.html
Jerusalem Center for Public Affairs at http://jcpa.org/
Jerusalem Fund at http://www.thejerusalemfund.org/ht/d/sp/i/189/pid/189
Jerusalem Institute for Israel Studies at http://www.jiis.org/
Palestinian Academic Society for the Study of International Affairs at http://
www.passia.org/
Sheikh Jarrah Solidarity at http://www.en.justjlm.org/

Newspapers and News Magazines

Israel's flagship daily newspaper, *Haaretz*, provides continuous, up-to-date information on Jerusalem along with opinion essays (see http://www.haaretz.com/).
For additional coverage of the city, see:

Jerusalem Post at http://www.jpost.com
Jerusalem Report at http://www.jrep.com
Jewish Virtual Library at https://www.jewishvirtuallibrary.org/jsource/Peace
/jerutoc.html
Ma'an News Agency at http://www.maannews.net/eng/Default.aspx
Times of Israel at http://www.timesofisrael.com/
Ynet at http://www.ynet.co.il
+972 magazine at http://972mag.com/

Blogs

Blogs offer some of the richest and most personal accounts of Jerusalem's people and places. See especially:

Gershom Gorenberg and Haim Watzman at http://southjerusalem.com/
Hagit Ofran at http://settlementwatcheastjerusalem.wordpress.com/
Reports on the West Bank at http://www.mahsanmilim.com/thoughts.htm
Michael Zank at http://unholycity.blogspot.com/

References

365gay.com Newscenter. 2006. "Jerusalem Ordered to Pay Gay Group $77,000 for Pride." May 29.

Abowd, Tom. 2002. "Landscapes of Exclusion: The Politics of Difference and the Production of Space in Contemporary Jerusalem." Dissertation, Department of Anthropology, Columbia University.

———. 2007. "National Boundaries, Colonized Spaces: The Gendered Politics of Residential Life in Contemporary Jerusalem." *Anthropological Quarterly* 80:997–1034.

———. 2014. *Colonial Jerusalem: The Spatial Construction of Identity and Difference in a City of Myth, 1948–2012.* Syracuse, NY: Syracuse University Press.

Abu El-Haj, Nadia. 1998. "Translating Truths: Nationalism, Archeological Practice and the Remaking of Past and Present in Jerusalem." *American Ethnologist* 25 (2): 166–88.

———. 2001. *Facts on the Ground: Archaeological Practice and Territorial Self-Fashioning in Israeli Society.* Chicago and London: University of Chicago Press.

———. 2006. "Archeology, Nationhood, and Settlement." In *Memory and Violence in the Middle East and North Africa*, edited by Ussama Makdisi and Paul A. Silverstein, 215–33. Bloomington: Indiana University Press.

Abu-Lughod, Lila. 1989. "Zones of Theory in the Anthropology of the Arab World." *Annual Review of Anthropology* 18:267–306.

AbuZayyad, Ziad, ed. 2001. "Focus on Jerusalem." Special issue of the *Palestine-Israel Journal of Politics, Economics and Culture* 8 (1): 1–66.

———, ed. 2007. "Jerusalem: Forty Years Later." Special issue of the *Palestine-Israel Journal of Politics, Economics and Culture* 14 (1): 1–96.

Ackleson, Jason M. 2000. "Discourse of Identity and Territoriality on the US-Mexico Border." In *Geopolitics at the End of the Twentieth Century: The Changing World Political Map*, edited by Nurit Kliot and David Newman, 155–79. London: Frank Cass.

Adelman, Madelaine. 2000. "No Way Out: Divorce-Related Domestic Violence in Israel." *Violence Against Women: An Interdisciplinary and International Journal* 6 (11): 1223–54.

———. 2003. "The Military, Militarism and the Militarization of Domestic Violence." *Violence Against Women: An Interdisciplinary and International Journal* 9 (9): 1118–52.

———. 2004. "The Battering State: Towards a Political Economy of Domestic Violence." *Journal of Poverty: Innovations on Social, Political and Economic Inequalities* 8 (3): 55–74.

———. 2010. "Anthropologies of Domestic Violence: Studying Crime in Situ." In *International Handbook of Criminology*, edited by Shlomo G. Shoham, Paul Knepper, and Martin Kett, 183–209. Oxford, UK: Taylor and Francis.

Adelman, Madelaine, and Catherine Lugg. 2012. "Schools as Workplaces: The Queer Gap between 'Workplace Equality' and 'Safe Schools.'" *Legally Gay, The Symposium Issue, Arizona State University Law Journal for Social Justice* 3:27–46. http://ljsj.files.wordpress.com/2012/09/adelmanqueergapschoolsfall2012final.pdf.

Adelman, Madelaine, and Kathryn Woods. 2006. "Recognition without Intervention: Transforming the Anti-LGBTQ School Climate." *Journal of Poverty: Innovations on Social, Political & Economic Inequalities* 10 (2): 5–26.

Adelman, Madelaine, Edna Erez, and Nadera Shalhoub-Kevorkian. 2003. "Policing Violence against Minority Women in Multicultural Societies: 'Community' and the Politics of Exclusion." *Police and Society: An Interdisciplinary Journal of Law Enforcement and Criminology* 7:105–33.

Adelman, Madelaine, Gray Cavender, and Nancy Jurik. 2009. "The Haunting of Jane Tennison: Investigating Violence against Women in 'Prime Suspect.'" In *Women, Violence and Media*, edited by Drew Humphries, 175–96. Boston: Northeastern University Press.

Adelman, Madelaine, Hillary Haldane, Jennifer Wies. 2012. "A Transdisciplinary Effort to Mobilize Culture as an Asset against Gender Violence." *Violence Against Women* 18 (6): 691–700.

Aderet, Ofer. 2013. "Memorial to Gay Holocaust Victims Inaugurated in Tel Aviv Park." *Haaretz*, December 11.

Advocate.com. 2003. "Jerusalem's Ultra-Orthodox Mayor Backs Gay Rights Parade." Website of *The Advocate* magazine. June 17. http://www.advocate.com/news/2003/06/18/jerusalems-ultraorthodox-mayor-backs-gay-rights-parade-8999.

———. 2011. "Antigay Attacks Mar Croatian Pride Event." Website of *The Advocate* magazine. June 13.

Agha, Hussein, and Robert Malley. 2001. "Camp David: The Tragedy of Errors." *New York Review of Books*, August 9.

Aharonson, Ran. 1989. "Yerushalayim be-Einei Anshei ha-Aliya ha-Rishona." In *Yerushalayim ba-Toda'ah u-va-Assiya ha-Tzionit*, edited by Hagit Lavsky, 47–65. Jerusalem: Zalman Shazar Center and the Center for the Study of Zionism and the Yishuv at The Hebrew University of Jerusalem.

Ahituv, Shmuel. 1984. *Canaanite Toponyms in Ancient Egyptian Documents*. Jerusalem: Magnes Press, Hebrew University of Jerusalem.

Albin, Cecilia. 1997. "Securing the Peace of Jerusalem: On the Politics of Unifying and Dividing." *Review of International Studies* 23:117–42.

———. 2005. "Explaining Conflict Transformation: How Jerusalem Became Negotiable." *Cambridge Review of International Affairs* 18 (3): 339–55.

Algazy, Joseph. 1999a. "Church: Nazareth Ruling Discriminates against Christians." *Haaretz*, October 19.

———. 1999b. "PA Opposes Mosque in Nazareth." *Haaretz*, October 31.

Allegra, Marco. 2011. "From Partition to Reunification to . . . ? The Transformation of the Metropolitan Area of Jerusalem since 1967." *Palestine-Israel Journal of Politics, Economics and Culture* 17 (1/2): 12–20.

Amirav, Moshe. 2002. *The Palestinian Struggle for Jerusalem*. Jerusalem: Jerusalem Institute for Israel Studies.

———. 2009. *Jerusalem Syndrome: The Palestinian-Israeli Battle for the Holy City*. Eastbourne, UK: Sussex Academic Publishers.

Anderson, Benedict. 2006. *Imagined Communities*. New York: Verso.

Anderson, John Ward. 2005. "Israelis Act to Encircle East Jerusalem." *Washington Post*, February 7.

Aplin, Graeme. 2002. "World Heritage: A Complex Web of Scales and Interests." Paper presented at the UNESCO Virtual Congress, Paris, France, October 15–17.

Armstrong, Karen. 1997. *Jerusalem: One City, Three Faiths*. New York: Knopf.

———. 1998. "The Holiness of Jerusalem: Asset or Burden." *Journal of Palestine Studies* 27 (3): 5–19.

Arnon, Yohannan. 1991. *Uri Tsvi Grinberg: Ta'hanot Be-'hayav: Miv'har Ma'amarim*. Tel-Aviv: 'Eked.

Arpali, Boaz. 2006. "Yerushalayim 'Hatranit: Yerushalayim Ke-tsomet Mefarek Mitosim Be-shirat Yehuda 'Ami'hay." *Dapim Le-me'hkar Be-sifrut* 14–15:293–320.

Arrosi, Arman. 1992. *Sunan Kudus Pewaris Ulama Cina The Ling Sing*. Bandung, Jawa Barat, Indonesia: Pemaja Rosdakarya.

Asali, Kamil J., ed. 1997. *Jerusalem in History: 3000 BC to the Present Day*. London: Keegan Paul.

Ashworth, Gregory J., and J. E. Tunbridge. 2000. *The Tourist-Historic City: Retrospect and Prospect of Managing the Heritage City*. Amsterdam: Pergamon.

Ashworth, Gregory J. 2003. "Heritage, Identity and Places: For Tourists and Host Communities." In *Tourism in Destination Communities*, edited by S. Singh, D. J. Timothy, and R. K. Dowling, 79–97. Wallingford, UK: CAB International.

Aswat Palestinian Gay Women. 2006. "Aswat Statement on World Pride 2006: Parade to the Wall." http://www.aswatgroup.org/.

AudioEnglish.org. 2005. Princeton, NJ: Princeton University. Accessed December 21, 2013. http://www.audioenglish.org/dictionary/symbolisation.htm.

Azarya, Victor. 1984. *The Armenian Quarter of Jerusalem*. Berkeley: University of California Press.

Azaryahu, Maoz. 2006. *Tel Aviv: Mythography of a City*. Syracuse, NY: Syracuse University Press.

———. 2009. "The New York of the Land of Israel, the City Without Gentiles." *Haaretz*, April 3.

Azoulay, Ariella. 2008. "Save as Jerusalems." In *Postzionism: A Reader*, edited by Laurence J. Silberstein, 165–92. New Brunswick, NJ: Rutgers University Press.

B'Tselem. 2003. *Nu'man, East Jerusalem: Life Under Threat of Expulsion: Status Report*. September 1. http://www.btselem.org/.

Ban Ki-moon. 2012. "Message to Human Rights Council Meeting on Violence and Discrimination Based on Sexual Orientation or Gender Identity," Geneva, March 7, 2012. http://www.un.org/apps/news/infocus/sgspeeches/statments _full.asp?statID=1475.

Bar-On, Mordechai. 2006. "Conflicting Narratives or Narratives of Conflict: Can the Zionist and Palestinian Narratives of the 1948 War be Bridged?" In *Israeli and Palestinian Narratives of Conflict: History's Double Helix*, edited by Robert I. Rotberg, 142–73. Bloomington: Indiana University Press.

Bar-Tal, Daniel, Eran Halperin, and Neta Oren. 2010. "Socio-Psychological Barriers to Peace Making: The Case of the Israeli Jewish Society." *Social Issues and Policy Review* 4 (1): 63–09.

Bartal, Israel. 1977. "'Yishuv Yashan' ve-'Yishuv Hadash'—ha-Dimuy ve-ha-Metzi'ut." *Kathedra* 2:3–19.

———. 1989. "Ha-Yetzi'ah min ha-Homot—Hitpashtut ha-Yashan O Reshit he-Hadash?" In *Yerushalayim ba-Toda'ah u-va-Asiyah ha-Tzionit—Kovetz ma'amarim*, edited by Hagit Lavsky, 17–33. Jerusalem: Zalman Shazar Center and the Center for the Study of Zionism and the Yishuv at Hebrew University of Jerusalem.

Bashah, Abdul Halim. 1993. *Wali Songo dengan Perkembanngan Islam di Nusantara* [The Nine Saints and the Spread of Islam in Indonesia]. Selangor, Malaysia: Pustaka Al Hijaz.

Baskin, Gershon. 2001a. "The Jerusalem Problem: The Search for Solution." *Palestine-Israel Journal of Politics, Economics and Culture* 8 (1): 6–11.

———. 2001b. "What Went Wrong." Jerusalem: Israel/Palestine Center for Research and Information (IPCRI). http://www.ipcri.org.

BBC News World Edition. 2002. "Gays March through Jerusalem." June 7. http://news.bbc.co.uk/2/hi/middle_east/2031817.stm.

Be'er, Haim. 1983. *Tsipor Ha-even: Yerushalayim Ba-shira Ha-'ivrit Ha-hadasha: Antologya*. Tel Aviv: Sheva.

Begin-Sadat Center for Strategic Studies. 2008. "Israelis Overwhelmingly Reject Division of Jerusalem," *Begin-Sadat Center for Strategic Studies Bulletin* 23 (September 1): 3. http://besacenter.org/news-bulletin/bulletin-23-september-2008/.

Bell, David. 2003. *The Cult of the Nation in France—Inventing Nationalism, 1680–1800*. Cambridge, MA: Harvard University Press.

Bell, Michael, Michael J. Molloy, John Bell, and Marketa Evans. 2005. *The Jerusalem Old City Initiative Discussion Document: New Directions for Deliberation and Dialogue*. Toronto, Canada: Munk Centre for International Studies, University of Toronto.

Ben-Ami, Shlomo. 2006. *Scars of War, Wounds of Peace: The Israeli-Arab Tragedy*. New York: Oxford University Press.

Benari, Elad. 2012. "Statistics: 64% of Jerusalem's Population Is Jewish." *Arutz Sheva*, May 18. http://www.israelnationalnews.com.

Ben-Arieh, Yehoshua. 1984. *Jerusalem in the 19th Century*. New York: St. Martin's.

Ben-Barukh, Shalom. 1955. *Yerushalayim Be-shiratenu Ha-hadasha, Mi-tkufat Hahaskala Ve-'ad Yameynu*. Jerusalem: R. Mas.

Benjamin, Walter. 1996. "One Way Street." *Walter Benjamin: Selected Writings*. Vol. 1. Cambridge: Harvard University Press.

Ben-Josef Hirsch, Michal. June 2007. "From Taboo to the Negotiable: The Israeli New Historians and the Changing Representation of the Palestinian Refugee Problem." *Perspectives on Politics* 5 (2): 241–58.

Bennett, Andrew, and Colin Elman. 2007. "Case Study Methods in the International Relations Subfield." *Comparative Political Studies* 40 (2): 170–95.

Ben-Porat, Ziva. 1987. "History in Representations of Jerusalem in Modern Hebrew Poetry." *Neohelicon* 14 (2): 353–58.

Ben-Uri. 1904. "Ha-Tum'a." *Hashkafa* 5 (32) (5 Sivan 5664/May 19 1904): 286.

Benvenisti, Meron. 1976. *Jerusalem: The Torn City.* Jerusalem: Isratypeset.

———. 1983. *Jerusalem: A Study of a Polarized Community.* Research Paper No. 3. Jerusalem: West Bank Data Base Project.

———. 1996. *City of Stone: The Hidden History of Jerusalem.* Berkeley: University of California Press.

———. 2007. *Son of the Cypresses: Memories, Reflections, and Regrets from a Political Life.* Berkeley: University of California Press.

Ben-Yehuda, Eliezer. 1903a. "ha-Issur al Gan ha-Yeladim ha-Ivri." *Hashkafa* 4 (27) (26 Nissan 5663/April 23): 211.

———. 1903b. "Hom ha-Ganuz la-Adam le-Atid La-vo—Od Pesi'ah." *Hashkafa* 4 (27) (26 Nissan 5663/April 23): 214.

———. 1903c. "Kidmat ha-Mada'im—Od Pesi'ah," *Hashkafa* 4 (15) (24 Tevet 5663/January 23): 1.

Ben-Ze'ev, Efrat, and Eyal Ben-Ari. 1996. "Imposing Politics: Failed Attempts at Creating a Museum of 'Co-Existence' in Jerusalem." *Anthropology Today* 12 (6): 7–13.

Benziman, Uzi. 2008. "Dividing Jerusalem." *Haaretz,* June 7.

Berkovits, Shmuel. 2006. *"How Dreadful is This Place!" Holiness, Politics and Justice in Jerusalem and the Holy Places of Israel* [in Hebrew]. Jerusalem: Carta.

Bertz, Inka. 2004. "Trouble at the Bezalel: Conflicting Visions of Zionism and Art." In *Nationalism, Zionism, and the Ethnic Mobilization of the Jews in 1900 and Beyond,* edited by Michael Berkowitz, 260–61. Leiden, The Netherlands: Brill.

Bezelel, Mel. 2009. "Gay Pride Being Used to Promote Israel Abroad." *Jerusalem Post,* June 7.

Bigelow, Anna. 2010. *Sharing the Sacred: Practicing Pluralism in Muslim North India.* Oxford: Oxford University Press.

Birthright Israel. 2011. "Taglit, Birthright Israel: Your Adventure, Your Birthright, Our Gift." Accessed March 19, 2011. http://www.birthrightisrael.com.

Black Laundry. 2005. "Black Laundry Statement on World Pride." July.

Bloom, Mia M. 2004. "Palestinian Suicide Bombing: Public Support, Market Share, and Outbidding." *Political Science Quarterly* 119 (1): 61–88.

Blumenberg, Hans. 1986. *Die Lesbarkeit der Welt*. Frankfurt: Suhrkamp.

Boediwardhana, Wahyoe. 2006. "Politicization of Religion Sparks Conflicts: NU Chief." *Jakarta Post*, September 11. http://www.thejakartapost.com/news /2006/09/11/politicization-religion-sparks-conflicts-nu-chief.html.

Bollens, Scott A. 1998a. "Urban Planning Amidst Ethnic Conflict: Jerusalem and Johannesburg." *Urban Studies* 35:729–50.

———. 1998b. "Urban Policy in Ethnically Polarized Societies." *International Political Science Review* 19:187–215.

———. 1999. *Urban Peace-Building in Divided Societies: Belfast and Johannesburg*. Boulder, CO: Westview.

Bourdieu, Pierre. 1984. *Distinction: A Social Critique of the Judgment of Taste*. London and New York: Routledge.

Bovis, Eugene. 1971. *The Jerusalem Question, 1917–1968*. Palo Alto, CA: Stanford University Press.

Bowman, Glenn. 1986. "Unholy Struggle on Holy Ground: Conflict and Its Interpretation." *Anthropology Today* 2 (3): 4–7.

———. 1989. "Fucking Tourists: Sexual Relations and Tourism in Jerusalem's Old City." *Critique of Anthropology* 9 (2): 77–93.

———. 1992. "The Politics of Tour Guiding: Israeli and Palestinian Guides in Israel and the Occupied Territories." In *Tourism and the Less Developed Countries*, edited by David Harrison, 121–34. London: Belhaven.

———. 1993. "Nationalizing the Sacred: Shrines and Shifting Identities in the Israeli-Occupied Territories." *Man: The Journal of the Royal Anthropological Institute* 28 (3): 431–60.

———. 1996. "Passion, Power and Politics in a Palestinian Market." In *The Tourist Image: Myths and Myth Making in Tourism*, edited by Tom Selwyn, 83–103. New York and London: John Wiley & Sons.

———. 1997. "Identifying vs. Identifying with 'the Other': Reflections on the Siting of the Subject in Anthropological Discourse." In *After Writing Culture: Epistemology and Praxis in Contemporary Anthropology*, edited by Alison James, Jenny Hockey and Andrew Dawson, 34–50. A.S.A. Monographs 34. London: Routledge.

———. 1998. "Radical Empiricism: Anthropological Fieldwork after Psychoanalysis and the *Année Sociologique*." *Anthropological Journal on European Cultures (Special Issue: Reflecting Cultural Practice: The Challenge of Fieldwork)* 6 (2): 79–107.

———. 1999. "The Exhilic Imagination: The Construction of the Landscape of Palestine from Its Outside." In *The Landscape of Palestine: Equivocal Poetry*, edited by Ibrahim Abu-Lughod, Roger Heacock, and Khaled Nashef, 53–78. Birzeit: Birzeit University Publications.

———. 2000. "Christian Ideology and the Image of a Holy Land: The Place of Jerusalem Pilgrimage in the Various Christianities." In *Contesting the Sacred: The Anthropology of Christian Pilgrimage*, edited by John Eade and Michael Sallnow, 98–121. Chicago: University of Illinois Press.

———. 2006. "A Death Revisited: Solidarity and Dissonance in a Muslim-Christian Palestinian Community." In *Memory and Violence in the Middle East and North Africa*, edited by Ussama Makdisi and Paul Silverstein, 27–49. Bloomington: Indiana University Press.

———. 2008. "At Home Abroad: The Field Site as Second Home." *Ethnologia Europaea* 37 (1–2): 140–48.

———. 2010. "Orthodox-Muslim Interactions at 'Mixed Shrines' in Macedonia." In *Eastern Christians in Anthropological Perspective*, edited by Christtann Goltz and Hermann Goltz, 195–219. Berkeley: University of California Press.

———. 2011. "'In Dubious Battle on the Plains of Heav'n': The Politics of Possession in Jerusalem's Holy Sepulchre." *History and Anthropology* 22:371–99.

———. 2012a. "Nationalizing and Denationalizing the Sacred: Shrines and Shifting Identities in the Israeli-Occupied Territories." In *Sacred Space in Israel and Palestine: Religion and Politics*, edited by Yitzhak Reiter, Marshall Breger, and Leonard Hammer, 195–227. London and New York: Routledge.

———. 2012b. "Refiguring the Anthropology of the Middle East and North Africa." In *The Sage Handbook of Social Anthropology*, edited by Richard Fardon and John Gledhill, 678–710. London: Sage.

———. 2012c. "Identification and Identity Formations around Shared Shrines in West Bank Palestine and Western Macedonia." In *Sharing Sacred Spaces in the Mediterranean: Christians, Muslims, and Jews at Shrines and Sanctuaries*, edited by Dionigi Albera and Maria Couroucli, 11–30. Bloomington: Indiana University Press.

———. 2013. "Christian Ideology and the Image of a Holy Land: The Place of Jerusalem Pilgrimage in the Various Christianities." In *Contesting the Sacred: The Anthropology of Christian Pilgrimage*, edited by John Eade and Michael Sallnow, 98–121. Eugene, OR: Wipf and Stock. First published 1991 by University of Illinois Press (Chicago).

———. 2014. "The Politics of Ownership: State, Governance and the Status Quo in the Anastasis (Holy Sepulchre)." In *Choreographies of Shared Sacred Sites,* edited by Elazar Barkan and Karen Barkey. New York: Columbia University Press.

Brading, David A. 2001. *Mexican Phoenix: Our Lady of Guadalupe: Image and Tradition across Five Generations*. Cambridge: Cambridge University Press.

Brady, Henry E., and David Collier, eds. 2004. *Rethinking Social Inquiry: Diverse Tools, Shared Standards*. Lanham, MD: Rowman & Littlefield.

Braverman, Irus. 2006. *Powers of "Illegality": House Demolitions and Resistance in East Jerusalem* [in Hebrew]. Tel Aviv: Tel Aviv University–Tami Steinmitz Center for Peace Studies.

Brecher, Michael. 1978. "Jerusalem: Israel's Political Decisions, 1947–1977." *Middle East Journal* 32 (1): 13–34.

Breger, Marshall J. 2002. "Introduction." In *Jerusalem: A City and Its Future*, edited by Marshall J. Breger and Ora Ahimeir. Syracuse, NY: Syracuse University Press.

Breger, Marshall, and Thomas A. Idinopulos. 1998. *Jerusalem's Holy Places and the Peace Process*, Policy Paper No. 46. Washington, DC: Washington Institute for Near East Policy.

Breger, Marshall, Yitzhak Reiter, and Leonard Hammer, eds. 2010. *Holy Places in the Israeli-Palestinian Conflict: Confrontation and Coexistence*. New York: Routledge.

Brin, Eldad. 2006. "Politically-Oriented Tourism in Jerusalem." *Tourist Studies* 6 (3): 215–43.

Brinkley, Joel. 1990. "Israel Says It Helped Finance Settlers in Christian Quarter." *New York Times*, 23 April.

Bronner, Ethan, and Isabel Kershner. 2009. "Parks Fortify Israel's Claim to Jerusalem." *New York Times*, May 10.

Bronner, Ethan. 2009. "Mayor's Vision of a Unified Jerusalem Also Divides." *New York Times*, March 2.

Bruce, David M., and Oliver Creighton. 2006. "Contested Identities: The Dissonant Heritage of European Town Walls and Walled Towns." *International Journal of Heritage Studies* 12 (3): 234–54.

Bruck, Connie. 1996. "The Wounds of Peace." *New Yorker*, October 12.

Bucken-Knapp, Gregg, and Michael Schack, eds. 2001. *Borders Matter: Transboundary Regions in Contemporary Europe*. Aabenraa, Denmark: Danish Institute of Border Region Studies.

Burla, Yehuda. 1912. "Al ha-Avoda ha-Zara." *Ha-Herut* 5 (9) (September 24): 1.

Buruma, Ian. 2009. "Letter from Amsterdam—Parade's End: Dutch Liberals Get Tough." *New Yorker*, December 7, 36–41.

Byman, Daniel. 2006. "Do Targeted Killings Work?" *Foreign Affairs* 85 (2) (March/ April).

Capehart, Jonathan. 2011. "Clinton's Geneva Accord: 'Gay Rights Are Human Rights.'" *Washington Post*, December 7. http://www.washingtonpost.com /blogs/post-partisan/post/clintons-geneva-accord-gay-rights-are-human -rights/2011/03/04/gIQAPUipcO_blog.html.

Carroll, James. 2011. *Jerusalem, Jerusalem: How the Ancient City Ignited Our Modern World*. Boston and New York: Houghton Mifflin Harcourt.

Caruth, Cathy. 1996. *Unclaimed Experience: Trauma, Narrative, and History*. Baltimore: Johns Hopkins University Press.

Central Bureau of Statistics. 2011. "Visitor Arrivals by Country of Citizenship, 2010." Accessed March 23, 2011. http://www.cbs.gov.il/www/tourism_q/t03 .pdf.

Chabin, Michele. 2005. "Pro-Gay Backlash in Jerusalem." *Jewish Week*, April 22.

Chapman, Colin. 2004. *Whose Holy City? Jerusalem and the Future of Peace in the Middle East*. Oxford, UK: Lion Hudson.

Chertoff, Mordecai S. 1987. "Jerusalem in Song and Psalm." In *Jerusalem, City of the Ages*, edited by A. L. Eckardt, 226–40. Lanham, MD: University Press of America; New York: American Academic Association for Peace in the Middle East.

Cheshin, Amir, Bill Hutman, and Avi Melamed. 1999. *Separate and Unequal: The Inside Story of Israeli Rule in East Jerusalem*. Cambridge, MA: Harvard University Press.

Chibbaro, Lou. 2006. "World Pride's Jerusalem Plans Sparks Outrage." *Washington Blade*, June 29.

Choshen, Maya, Michal Korach, Inbal Doron, Yael Israeli, and Yair Assaf-Shapira. 2013. *Jerusalem: Facts and Trends 2013*. Jerusalem: Jerusalem Institute for Israel Studies. http://www.jiis.org.

Clemons, Steve. 2012. "Not the Onion: Moscow Bans Gay Pride for Next 100 Years." *The Atlantic*, June 8. http://www.theatlantic.com/international/archive/2012 /06/not-the-onion-moscow-bans-gay-pride-for-next-100-years/258296/.

Cline, Eric H. 2004. *Jerusalem Besieged: From Ancient Canaan to Modern Israel*. Ann Arbor: University Michigan Press.

Cohen, Avi. 2006. "Synagogue Vandalized as Gay Parade Controversy Picks Up Steam." *Ynet*, November 2. http://www.ynetnews.com/articles/0,7340,L-332 2809,00.html.

———. 2009. "2 Killed in Tel Aviv Shooting." *Ynet*, August 2. http://www.ynet news.com/articles/0,7340,L-3755400,00.html.

Cohen, E. H. 2006. "Religious Tourism as an Educational Experience." In *Tourism, Religion, and Spiritual Journeys*, edited by D. J. Timothy and D. H. Olsen, 78–93. London: Routledge.

Cohen, Raymond, and Raymond Westbrook. 2000. *Amarna Diplomacy: The Beginnings of International Religions*. Baltimore and London: Johns Hopkins University Press.

Cohen, Tova. 2002. "'Ha-'ir Rovetset 'Al 'Hayay': Yerushalayim U-migdar Ba-shira Ha-'ivrit." In *Isha Bi-yerushalayim: Migdar, 'Hevra Ve-dat*, edited by Tova Cohen and Joshua Schwartz, 192–229. Ramat Gan, Israel: Merkaz Ingeburg Renert Le-limudey Yerushalayim, Bar Ilan University.

Cohen, Yaakov. 1937. *Yerushalayim Be-shir Ve-'hazon*. Tel Aviv: 'Hevrat Omanut.

Cohen-Hattab, Kobi. 2004a. "Historical Research and Tourism Analysis: The Case of the Tourist-Historic City of Jerusalem." *Tourism Geographies* 6 (3): 279–302.

———. 2004b. "Zionism, Tourism and the Battle for Palestine: Tourism as a Political Propaganda Tool." *Israel Studies* 9 (1): 61–85.

———. 2010. "Struggles at Holy Sites and Their Outcomes: The Evolution of the Western Wall Plaza in Jerusalem." *Journal of Heritage Tourism* 5 (2): 125–39.

Collier, David, and Colin Elman. 2008. "Qualitative and Multi-Method Research: Organizations, Publication, and Reflections on Integration." In *Oxford Handbook of Political Methodology*, edited by Janet M. Box-Steffensmeier, Henry Brady, and David Collier, 779–95. Oxford: Oxford University Press.

Collins-Kreiner, Noga, Nurit Kliot, Yoel Mansfeld, and Keren Sagi. 2006. *Christian Tourism to the Holy Land: Pilgrimages during Security Crisis*. Aldershot, UK: Ashgate.

Conflict in Cities. N.d. Cambridge, UK: New Centre for Urban Conflicts Research. http://www.conflictincities.org/aboutus.html.

Consulate General of Israel in Los Angeles. 1990. "Excerpt from an Interview of the Greek Patriarch in Jerusalem." *Policy Background*, May 29.

Cooper, Artemis. 1989. *Cairo in the War 1939–1945*. London: H. Hamilton.

Côté, James, ed. 2000. *Journal of Youth and Adolescence (Special Issue on the Mead-Freeman controversy)* 29:5.

Coyne, Katie. 2005. "World Will See Pride in Jerusalem Despite Mayor´s Fighting Talk." *The Pink Paper*, February 4.

Crawford, Neta C. 2000. "The Passion of World Politics: Propositions on Emotion and Emotional Relationships." *International Security* 24 (4): 116–56.

Creighton, Oliver. 2007. "Contested Townscapes: The Walled City as World Heritage." *World Archaeology* 30:339–54.

Crown, Alan D. 1989. *The Samaritans*. Tübingen, Germany: Siebeck Mohr.

CUFI (Christians United for Israel). 2008. Israel tours. Accessed December 3, 2008. http://www.cufi.org.

Currier, Ashley. 2012. *Out in Africa: LGBT Organizing in Namibia and South Africa.* Minneapolis: University of Minnesota Press.

Curtis, Jennifer. 2013. "Pride and Prejudice: Gay Rights and Religious Moderation in Belfast." *Sociological Review* 61 (2): 141–59.

Dahan, Tal. 2008. "The State of Human Rights in Israel and the Occupied Territories." Translated by Arthur Livingstone and Gila Svirsky. Jerusalem: Association for Civil Rights in Israel (ACRI).

———. 2013. *The State of Human Rights in Israel and in the Occupied Territories 2013.* Tel Aviv: Association for Civil Rights in Israel (ACRI). http://www.acri.org.il.

Davis, Mike. 2001. *Magical Urbanism: Latinos Reinvent the U.S. City*. New York: Verso.

Davis, Rochelle. 2003. "Commemorating Education: Recollections of the Arab College in Jerusalem, 1918–1948." *Comparative Studies of South Asia, Africa and the Middle East* 23 (1–2): 190–204.

Deeb, Lara, and Jessica Winegar. 2012. "The Politics of Middle East Anthropology." *Annual Review of Anthropology* 41:537–58.

Deinard, Ephraim. 1906. Letter to Boris Schatz [in Hebrew]. L42, file 57, November 12, Central Zionist Archive.

DeKoven Ezrahi, Sidra. 2000. *Booking Passage: Exile and Homecoming in the Modern Jewish Imagination*. Berkeley: University of California Press.

———. 2007. "'To What Shall I Compare You?': Jerusalem as Ground Zero of the Hebrew Imagination." *PMLA—Publications of the Modern Language Association of America* 122 (1): 220–34.

Derfner, Larry. 2006. "Whose Pride?" *Jerusalem Post*, June 15.

Derrida, Jacques. 1996. *Archive Fever: A Freudian Impression*. Translated by Eric Prenowitz. Chicago: University of Chicago Press.

Desch, Michael C., and Daniel Philpott, eds. 2013. *Religion and International Relations: A Primer For Research*. Unpublished report of the Working Group on International Relations and Religion, Mellon Initiative on Religion across the Disciplines, University of Notre Dame, Notre Dame, IN.

Dever, William. 2003. *Who Were the Israelites and Where Did They Come From?* Grand Rapids, MA and Cambridge, UK: William B. Eerdmans.

Dever, William G., and Seymour Gitin, eds. 2003. *Symbiosis, Symbolism, and the Power of the Past: Canaan, Ancient Israel, and Their Neighbors from the Late Bronze Age through Roman Palaestina*. Winona Lake, IN: Eisenbrauns.

Dominguez, Virginia. 1989. *People as Subject, People as Object: Selfhood and People-hood in Contemporary Israel.* Madison: University of Wisconsin Press.

Dowty, Alan. 1999. "Is Israel Democratic: Substance and Semantics in the 'Ethnic Democracy' Debate." *Israeli Studies* 4 (2): 1–15.

———. 2008. *Israel/Palestine.* 2nd ed. Cambridge, UK: Polity.

Droge, Arthur J. 1989. *Homer or Moses? Early Christian Interpretations of the History of Culture.* Tübingen, Germany: Siebeck Mohr.

Duberman, Martin. 1993. *Stonewall.* New York: Penguin.

Duggan, Lisa. 2002. "The New Homonormativity: The Sexual Politics of Neoliber-alism." In *Materializing Democracy: Toward a Revitalized Cultural Politics*, edited by Russ Castronovo and Dana D. Nelson, 175–94. Durham, NC: Duke University Press.

Dumm, Thomas L. 1990. "Book Review: *Sacralizing the Secular: The Renaissance Origins of Modernity* by Stephen A. McKnight." *American Political Science Review* 84 (3): 972–73.

Dumper, Michael. 1997. *The Politics of Jerusalem Since 1967.* New York: Columbia University Press.

———. 2002. *The Politics of Sacred Space: The Old City of Jerusalem in the Middle East Conflict.* Boulder, CO: Lynne Rienner.

Duncan, James. 1993. "Sites of Representation: Place, Time and Discourse of the Other." In *Place, Culture, Representation*, edited by James Duncan and David Ley, 39–56. London and New York: Routledge.

Dykman, Aminadav A. 1994. "A Poet in the Eternal City: The Case of Dan Pagis." *Compar(a)ison: An International Journal of Comparative Literature* 2:41–56.

Eade, John, and Michael J. Sallnow, eds. 1991. *Contesting the Sacred: The Anthropology of Christian Pilgrimage.* London and New York: Routledge.

Eaves, Elizabeth. 1998. "Gays in Israel Demand Equal Rights." *Reuters*, June 30.

El-Ad, Hagai. 2002. "Gay Israel: No Pride in Occupation." Translated by Lee Walzer. Independent Media Center, February 12. http://www.indymedia.org.il.

———. 2005. "Jerusalem: An Open House?" *Jerusalem Post*, March 26.

Elad-Bouskila, Ami. 1999. *Modern Palestinian Literature and Culture.* London: Frank Cass.

Elboim-Dror, Rachel. 1986. *Ha-Hinuch Ha-Ivri be-Eretz Yisra'el.* Vol. 1. Jerusalem: Yad Yitzhak Ben-Zvi Press.

Eliade, Mircea. 1959. *The Myth of Eternal Return or Cosmos and History.* New York: Harper.

Elizondo, Virgilio. 1997. *Guadalupe: Mother of the New Creation.* London: Orbis.

Elizur, Yuval. 2003. "Israel Banks on a Fence." *Foreign Affairs* 82 (2).

Ellis, Mark. Fall 1996. "Jerusalem and the Broken Middle: Reflections on Jews and Arabs After Oslo." *Arab Studies Journal* 4:133–48.

Elman, Colin, and Miriam Fendius Elman. 1997. "Diplomatic History and International Relations Theory: Respecting Difference and Crossing Boundaries." *International Security* 22 (1): 5–21.

———. 2001. "Negotiating International History and Politics." In *Bridges and Boundaries: Historians, Political Scientists, and the Study of International Relations*, edited by Colin Elman and Miriam Fendius Elman, 1–36. Cambridge, MA: MIT Press.

———. 2008. "The Role of History in International Relations." *Millennium: Journal of International Studies* 37 (2): 357–64.

Elman, Miriam Fendius. 1997. "Israel's Invasion of Lebanon, 1982: Regime Change and War Decisions." In *Paths to Peace: Is Democracy the Answer?*, edited by Miriam F. Elman, 301–34. Cambridge, MA: MIT Press.

———. 2005. "International Relations Theories and Methods." In *Palgrave Advances in International History*, edited by Patrick Finney, 136–60. New York: Palgrave MacMillan.

———. 2000. "Unpacking Democracy: Presidentialism, Parliamentarism, and Theories of Democratic Peace." *Security Studies* 9 (4): 91–126.

Elman, Miriam Fendius, Oded Haklai, and Hendrik Spruyt, eds. 2013. *Democracy and Conflict Resolution: The Dilemmas of Israel's Peacemaking*. Syracuse, NY: Syracuse University Press.

Elon, Amos. 1989. *Jerusalem: City of Mirrors*. Boston: Little Brown.

Emmett, Chad F. 1995. *Beyond the Basilica: Christians and Muslims in Nazareth*. Chicago: University of Chicago Press.

———. 1996. "The Capital Cities of Jerusalem." *Geographical Review* 86 (2): 233–58.

———. 1997. "The Status Quo Solution for Jerusalem." *Journal of Palestine Studies* 26 (2): 16–28.

———. 2001. "Jerusalem's Role as a Holy City for Muslims." *BYU Studies* 40 (4): 119–34.

Entrikin, Nicholas. 1991. *The Betweenness of Place: Towards a Geography of Modernity*. Baltimore: John Hopkins Press.

Eretz. 2008. "Jerusalem: A Special Issue." http://www.eretz.com/NEW/Jlm Contents.shtml.

Erez, Edna, Madelaine Adelman, and Carol Gregory. 2009. "Intersections of Immigration and Domestic Violence: Voices of Battered Immigrant Women." *Feminist Criminology* 4 (1): 32–56.

Ettinger, Shmuel, and Israel Bartal. 1981. "Shorshei ha-Yishuv he-Hadash be-Eretz Yisra'el." In *Sefer ha-Aliya ha-Rishona*, edited by Mordechai Eliav, 1–24. Jerusalem: Yad Yitzhak Ben-Zvi Press.

Ettinger, Yair. 2006. "Police Probe Reward Offer for Killing Gay People." *Haaretz*, July 12.

Eusebius. 2005. *Onomasticon: A Triglott Edition with Notes and Commentary*. Edited by R. Steven Notley and Ze'ev Safrai. Leiden, The Netherlands: Brill.

Falah, Ghazi, and David Newman. 1995. "The Spatial Manifestation of Threat: Israelis and Palestinians Seek a 'Good' Border." *Political Geography* 14:689–706.

Falasca-Zamponi, Simonetta. 1997. *Fascist Spectacle: The Aesthetics of Power in Mussolini's Italy*. Berkeley: University of California Press.

Falk, Richard. 2011. "Israel and Palestine: Obama's Flawed Approach." *AlJazeera.net*, May 21.

Feldinger, Lauren Gelfond. 2008. "Pinking Tel Aviv." *Jerusalem Post*, May 15.

Feldman, Daniel. 2008. "Jerusalem Yesterday, Today, and Tomorrow: A Halachic Perspective." *Jewish Action: The Magazine of the Orthodox Union* 68 (4): 57–61.

Feller, Irwin. 2007. "Interdisciplinarity: Paths Taken and Not Taken." *Change* 39 (6): 46–51.

Fendel, Hillel. 2006. "Working to Stop Gay Pride Event in the Holy Land." *Arutz Sheva*, June 19. http://www.israelnationalnews.com/News/News.aspx/1056 73#.Ur-gcWRDvSg.

Fenster, Tovi. 2005. "Identity Issues and Local Governance: Women's Everyday Life in the City." *Social Identities* 11 (1): 21–36.

Ferrari, Silvio. 2002. "The Religious Significance of Jerusalem in the Middle East Peace Process: Some Legal Implications." In *Jerusalem: A City and Its Future*, edited by Marshall J. Breger and Ora Ahimeir, 223–34. Syracuse, NY: Syracuse University Press.

Fink, Amir Sumaka'i, and Jacob Press. 1999. *Independence Park: The Lives of Gay Men in Israel*. Stanford: Stanford University Press.

Finkelstein, Israel, and Neil Asher Silberman. 2001. *The Bible Unearthed: Archaeology's New Vision of Ancient Israel and the Origin of Its Sacred Texts*. New York, London, Toronto, Sydney, Singapore: Free Press.

Fiore, Stephen. 2008. "Interdisciplinarity is Teamwork: How the Science of Teams Can Inform Team Science." *Small Group Research* 39 (3): 251–77.

Fiske, Gavriel. 2013. "Capital Home to 804,000, Jerusalem Day Stats Reveal." *Times of Israel*, May 7.

Foucault, Michel. 1977. *Discipline and Punish*. New York: Vintage.

Fox, Jonathan. 2001. "Religion as an Overlooked Element of International Relations." *International Studies Review* 3 (3): 53–73.

Fox, Jonathan, and Shmuel Sandler. 2004. *Bringing Religion into International Relations*. New York: Palgrave.

Fraser, T. G. 2004. *The Arab-Israeli Conflict*. New York: Palgrave Macmillan.

Friedland, Roger, and Richard D. Hecht. 1991. "The Politics of Sacred Space: Jerusalem's Temple Mount/*Haram al-Sharif*." In *Sacred Spaces and Profane Places: Essays in the Geographics of Judaism, Christianity, and Islam*, edited by Jamie Scott and Paul Simpson-Housley, 21–61. Westport, CT: Greenwood.

———. 1996a. "The Power of Place: The Pilgrimage to Nebi Musa and the Origins of Palestinian Nationalism." In *The Persistence of Religions: Essays in Honor of Kees W. Bolle*, edited by Sara J. Denning-Bolle and Edwin Gerow, 337–59. Malibu, CA: Undena.

———. 1996b. *To Rule Jerusalem*. Cambridge: Cambridge University Press.

———. 1998. "The Bodies of Nations: A Comparative Study of Religious Violence in Jerusalem and Ayodhya." *History of Religions* 38 (2): 101–49.

———. 2006. "The Power of Places." In *Religion, Violence, Memory, and Place*, edited by J. Shawn Landres and Oren Stier, 17–36. Bloomington: University of Indiana Press.

Friedman, Ina. 2006. "Jerusalem Will Be No More Holy If Gays Are Distanced from It." *The Jerusalem Report*, August 7.

Friedman, Menachem. 2002. "Haredim and Palestinians in Jerusalem." In *Jerusalem: A City and its Future*, edited by Marshall J. Breger and Ora Ahimeir, 235–55. Syracuse, NY: Syracuse University Press.

Friedman ["Dr. Friedman"]. 1903. "Letter to the Editor" [in Hebrew]. *Hashkafa* 4 (27) (26 Nissan 5663/April 23): 214.

Friends of Sabeel. 2012. "Alternative Travel Opportunities." http://www.fosna.org/content/alternative-travel-opportunities.

Fundamental Agreement between the Holy See and the State of Israel. Signed in Jerusalem, December 30, 1993 (Tevet 16, 5754). http://www.vatican.va/roman_curia/secretariat_state/archivio/documents/rc_seg-st_19931230_santa-sede-israele_en.html.

Furani, Khalid, and Dan Rabinowitz. 2011. "The Ethnographic Arriving of Palestine." *Annual Review of Anthropology* 40:475–91.

Fyler, Boaz. 2010. "Tel Aviv: Thousands Mark Year since Gay Club Murder." *Ynet*, July 31. http://www.ynetnews.com/articles/0,7340,L-3927635,00.html.

Gaddis, John Lewis. 1997. "History, Theory, and Common Ground." *International Security* 22 (1): 75–85.

———. 2001. "In Defense of Particular Generalization: Rewriting Cold War History, Rethinking International Relations Theory." In *Bridges and Boundaries: Historians, Political Scientists, and the Study of International Relations*, edited by Colin Elman and Miriam Fendius Elman, 301–26. Cambridge, MA: MIT.

Gagnon, V. P. 1994–95. "Ethnic Nationalism and International Conflict: the Case of Serbia." *International Security* 19 (3): 130–66.

Gal, Sharon, and Akiva Eldar. 1999. "Nazareth Mosque to Be Built Despite Court's Decision." *Haaretz*, October 11.

Gatrell, Jay D., and Noga Collins-Kreiner. 2006. "Negotiated Space: Tourists, Pilgrims, and the Bahá'í Terraced Gardens in Haifa." *Geoforum* 37 (5): 765–78.

Gavriely-Nuri, Dalia. 2007. "The Social Construction of 'Jerusalem of Gold' as Israel's Unofficial National Anthem." *Israel Studies* 12 (2): 104–20.

Gelbman, Alon. 2006. "Border Tourism in Israel: A Profile of Conflict, Hope and Peace." Paper presented at the conference "Border Tourism and Regional Development at the Frontier of Israel and Its Neighboring Countries," Tiberias, Israel, March 21.

George, Alexander L., and Andrew Bennett. 2005. *Case Studies and Theory Development in the Social Sciences*. Cambridge, MA: MIT Press.

Gerber, Haim. 2008. *Remembering and Imagining Palestine: Identity and Nationalism from the Crusades to the Present*. New York: Palgrave Macmillan.

Gerring, John. 2004. "What Is a Case Study and What Is It Good For?" *American Political Science Review* 98 (2): 344–45.

———. 2007. *Case Study Research: Principles and Practices*. Cambridge: Cambridge University Press.

Gieryn, Thomas F. 1998. *Cultural Boundaries of Science: Credibility on the Line*. Chicago: University of Chicago Press.

Gilbert, Martin. 1996. *Jerusalem in the Twentieth Century*. New York: John Wiley & Sons.

———. 2008. *The Routledge Historical Atlas of Jerusalem*. 4th ed. New York: Routledge.

Gilloch, Graeme. 1996. *Myth and the Metropolis: Walter Benjamin and the City*. Cambridge, UK: Polity.

Gilsenan, Michael. 1990. "Very Like a Camel: The Appearance of the Anthropologist's Middle East." *In Localizing Strategies: Regional Traditions of Ethnographic Writing*, edited by Richard Fardon, 220–39. Edinburgh: Scottish Academic Press.

Goddard, Stacie E. 2010. *Indivisible Territory and the Politics of Legitimacy: Jerusalem and Northern Ireland*. New York: Cambridge University Press.

Goertz, Gary. 2006. *Social Science Concepts: A User's Guide*. Princeton, NJ: Princeton University Press.

Goffman, Erving. 1959. *The Presentation of Self in Everyday Life*. New York: Routledge.

Golan, Galia. 2009. "The Peace Process." In *Israel Studies: An Anthology*, edited by Mitchell Bard and David Nachmias. Chevy Chase, MD: Jewish Virtual Library. http://www.jewishvirtuallibrary.org/jsource/isdf/text/golan.pdf.

————. 2011. "Prospects for the Israeli-Palestinian Peace, after September." Public talk delivered at the Maxwell School of Syracuse University, Syracuse, NY, October 6.

Golani, Motti. 1995. "Zionism without Zion: The Jerusalem Question, 1947–1949." *Journal of Israeli History* 16 (1): 39–52.

————. 1999. "Jerusalem's Hope Lies Only in Partition: Israeli Policy on the Jerusalem Question, 1948–1967." *International Journal of Middle East Studies* 31:577–604.

Golani, Motti, and Adel Manna. 2011. *Two Sides of the Coin: Independence and Nakba, 1948: Two Narratives of the 1948 War and Its Outcome*. Dordrecht, Netherlands: Republic of Letters Publishing.

Gold, Dore. 2007. *The Fight for Jerusalem: Radical Islam, the West, and the Future of the Holy City*. Washington, DC: Regnery.

Goldhagen, Daniel Jonah. 2013. *The Devil that Never Dies: The Rise and Threat of Global Antisemitism*. New York: Little, Brown.

Goldhill, Simon. 2008. *Jerusalem: City of Longing*. Cambridge, MA: Harvard Belknap.

Gonen, Amiram. 2002. "Widespread and Diverse Neighborhood Gentrification in Jerusalem." *Political Geography* 21:727–37.

Goodman, Hirsh. 2011. *The Anatomy of Israel's Survival*. New York: Public Affairs.

Goodstein, Laurie, and Greg Myre. 2005. "Clerics of Three Faiths Protest Gay Festival Planned for Jerusalem." *New York Times*, March 31.

Gorenberg, Gershom. 2000. *The End of Days: Fundamentalism and the Struggle for the Temple Mount*. New York: Free Press.

————. 2006. *The Accidental Empire: Israel and the Birth of the Settlements, 1967–1977*. New York: Times Books.

———. 2000. "The Real Blunder." *Jerusalem Report*, November 20.

Gosselin, Edward. 1990. "Book Review: *Sacralizing the Secular: The Renaissance Origins of Modernity* by Stephen A. McKnight." *American Historical Review* 95 (5): 1521–22.

Gouri, Haim. 2003. "Yerushalayim Ve-tel-aviv Ba-sifrut Ha-'ivrit: Hagigm Ishiyim." In *Yerushalayim Bi-tkufat Ha-mandat: Ha-'asiya Veha-moreshet* edited by Yehoshua Ben-Arieh, 397–401. Mishkenot Sha'ananim, Jerusalem: Yad Yitzhak Ben-Zvi.

Govrin, Nurith. 1989. "Jerusalem and Tel-Aviv as Metaphors in Hebrew Literature." *Modern Hebrew Literature* 2:23–27.

———. 2003. "Yerushalayim Bi-r'i Ba-sifrut Ha-'ivrit." In *Yerushalayim Bi-tkufat Ha-mandat: Ha-'asiya Veha-moreshet*, edited by Yehoshua Ben-Arieh, 393–97. Mishkenot Sha'ananim, Jerusalem: Yad Yitzhak Ben-Zvi.

Graham, Brian J. 1996. "The Contested Interpretation of Heritage Landscapes in Northern Ireland." *International Journal of Heritage Studies* 2 (1): 19–22.

Greenberg, Joel. 2002. "The First Gay Pride Parade Ever in Jerusalem." *New York Times*, June 8.

———. 2005. "Opposition to Gay Pride Event in Holy City Unites Diverse Faiths." *Chicago Tribune*, March 31.

Greenberg, Uri Zvi. 1990. *Kol Ktavav*. 16 vols. Jerusalem: Mosad Byalik.

Greenburg, Joel. 1993. "Libyans Cut Short a Visit to Israel." *New York Times*, June 2.

Gross, Aeyal. 2010. "Israeli GLBT Politics between Queerness and Homonationalism." *Bully Blogger* (blog), July 3. http://bullybloggers.wordpress.com/2010/07/03/israeli-glbt-politics-between-queerness-and-homonationalism/.

———. 2012. "Michael Oren Pinkwashes the Truth about Israel and Gay Palestinians." *Haaretz*, May 9.

———. 2013. "After a Global Tour, Pinkwashing Comes Home." *Haaretz*, January 11.

Guilot, Claude, and Ludvik Kalus. 2002. "La Jérusalem Javanaise et sa Mosquée al-Aqsâ. Texte de Fondation de la Mosquée de Kudus Daté 956/1." *Archipel* 63:27–56.

Gurtler, Yehoshua. 2012. "The Pink Elephant and the Israeli-Palestinian Conflict." *Haaretz*, May 13.

Gutmann, Stephanie. 2005. *The Other War: Israelis, Palestinians and the Struggle for Media Supremacy*. San Francisco: Encounter Books.

Ha-Po'el Ha-Tza'ir. 1912. "Me'ora'ot u-Ma'asim." *Ha-Po'el Ha-Tza'ir* 5 (7): 19–20.

Ha-Po'el Ha-Tza'ir. 1913. "Ha-Shavu'a. Ha-Shavu'a." *Ha-Po'el Ha-Tza'ir* 6 (32) (May 30): 15–16.

Hadi, Madhi Abdul. 1998. "Negotiating Intractable Issues—Jerusalem." In *Dialogue on Jerusalem: PASSIA Meetings 1990–1998*, edited by Mahdi Abdul Hadi, 96–97. Jerusalem: Palestinian Society for the Study of International Affairs (PASSIA).

Hadorn, Hirsch, Gertrude, Holger Hoffmann-Riem, Susette Biber-Klemm, Walter Grossenbacher-Mansuy, Dominique Joye, Christian Pohl, Urs Wiesmann, and Elisabeth Zemp, eds. 2008. *Handbook of Transdisciplinary Research.* New York: Springer.

Hafez, Sherine, and Susan Slyomovics, eds. 2013. *Anthropology of the Middle East and North Africa: Into the New Millennium.* Bloomington: Indiana University Press.

Haklai, Oded. March 2006. "Religious-Nationalist Mobilization and State Penetration: Lessons from Jewish Settlers' Activism in Israel and the West Bank." *Comparative Political Studies* 20 (10): 1–27.

Hall, C. Michael. 1997. "The Politics of Heritage Tourism: Place, Power, and the Representation of Values in the Urban Context." In *Quality Management in Urban Tourism*, edited by Peter E. Murphy, 91–101. Chichester, UK: Wiley.

Hallward, Maia Carter. 2008. "Situating the 'Secular': Negotiating the Boundary between Religion and Politics." *International Political Sociology* 2:1–16.

Halper, Jeff. 2011. "The Policy of House Demolitions in East Jerusalem: What It Is, How It Is Done and to What End." *Palestine-Israel Journal of Politics, Economics and Culture* 17 (1/2): 74–82.

Halpern, Baruch. 2003. "Late Israelite Astronomies and the Early Greeks." In *Symbiosis, Symbolism, and the Power of the Past: Canaan, Ancient Israel, and Their Neighbors from the Late Bronze Age through Roman Palaestina*, edited by William G. Dever and Seymour Gitin, 323–52. Winona Lake, IN: Eisenbrauns.

Halutz, Avshalom. 2013. "Tel Aviv Candidates Vie to 'Out-Pink' Each Other in Gay Mecca's Local Election." *Haaretz*, October 21.

Hammami, Rema, and Salim Tamari. 2000. "The Battle for Jerusalem." *Jerusalem Quarterly* 10:3–9.

Hannerz, Ulf. 1998. "Reporting from Jerusalem." *Cultural Anthropology* 13(4): 548–74.

Harb, Ahmad. 2004. "Representations of Jerusalem in the Modern Palestinian Novel." *Arab Studies Quarterly* 26 (3): 1–23.

Harvey, David. 1985. "Monument and Myth: The Building of the Basilica of the Sacred Heart." In *Consciousness and the Urban Experience: Studies in the History and Theory of Capitalist Urbanization*, edited by David Harvey, 221–50. Baltimore: Johns Hopkins University Press.

Hashkafa. 1905. "Bezalel: Ki mi-Zion Yetzeh Yofi ve-Omanut mi-Yerushalayim." *Hashkafa* 7 (19) (28 Kislev 5666/December 26): 1–2.

Hassner, Ron E. 2003. "'To Have and to Hold': Conflicts over Sacred Space and the Problem of Indivisibility." *Security Studies* 12 (4): 1–33.

———. 2009. "The Pessimist's Guide to Religious Coexistence." In *Holy Places in the Israeli-Palestinian Conflict: Confrontation and Co-existence*, edited by Marshall J. Berger, Yitzhak Reiter, and Leonard Hammer, 145–57. New York: Routledge.

Hasson, Nir. 2011a. "Jerusalem City Council Member Fired after Opposing Gender Segregation." *Haaretz*, October 21.

———. 2011b. "Annual Gay Pride Parade Draws Thousands in Jerusalem." *Haaretz*, July 28. http://www.haaretz.com/news/national/annual-gay-pride -parade-draws-thousands-in-jerusalem-1.375772.

———. 2012. "More Than 1000 March in Jerusalem's 10th Gay Pride Parade." *Haaretz*, August 2.

———. 2013. "Jerusalem Holds 12th Annual Gay Pride Parade." *Haaretz*, August 1.

Hasson, Nir, and Liel Kyzer. 2010. "In a First, Jerusalem's Gay Pride Parade to End Opposite Knesset." *Haaretz*, July 30. http://www.haaretz.com/print-edition /news/in-a-first-jerusalem-s-gay-pride-parade-to-end-opposite-knesset-1.30 4686.

Hasson, Shlomo. 1996. "Local Politics and Split Citizenship in Jerusalem." *International Journal of Urban and Regional Research* 20:116–33.

Ha-Tzofeh. 1912. "Michtav mi-Yerushalayim." *Ha-Po'el Ha-Tza'ir* 6 (12–13) (December 12): 21–22.

Haynes, Jeffrey. 2005. "Religion and International Relations After 9/11." *Democratization* 12 (3): 398–413.

Hazan, Jenny. 2003. "Jerusalem of Pink." *Jerusalem Post*, June 9.

Herzl, Theodor. 1960. *The Complete Diaries of Theodor Herzl*. Vol. 2. Edited by Raphael Patai, 745–46. New York and London: Herzl Press and Thomas Yoseloff.

Hever, Hannan. 1977. *Uri Tsui Grinberg Bi-mlot Lo Shmonim: Ta'arukha Be-vyet Ha-sfarim Ha-le'umi Veha-oniversita'i*. Jerusalem: Bet Ha-sfarim.

———. 1994. *Paytanim U-viryonim: Tsmi'hat Ha-shir Ha-politi Ha-'ivri Be-erets-Yisra'el*. Jerusalem: Mosad Biyalik.

———. 1995. *Bi-shvi Ha-utopya: Masa 'Al Meshi'hiyut U-folitika Ba-shira Ha-'ivrit Be-erets-yisra'el Beyn Shtey Mil'hamot Ha-'olam.* Kiryat Sedeh-Boker, Israel: Hamerkaz Le-moreshet Ben-Guryon, Ben-Gurion University of the Negev.

———. 2004. *Moledet Ha-mavet Yafa: Estetika U-folitika Be-shirat Uri Tsvi Grinberg.* Tel Aviv: 'Am 'Oved.

Hobsbawm, Eric. 1990. *Nations and Nationalism Since 1780.* Cambridge: Cambridge University Press.

Hobsbawm, Eric, and Terrence Ranger, eds. 1983. *The Invention of Tradition.* Cambridge: Cambridge University Press.

Hogan, Steve, and Lee Hudson. 1998. *Completely Queer: The Gay and Lesbian Encyclopedia.* New York: Henry Holt.

Holtzman, Avner. 1994. "Karov Ve-asur Lanu Sham: Yerushalayim Ha-'hatsuya Bi-r'i Ha-sifrut Ha-'ivrit." In *Yerushalayim Ha-ḥatsuyah, 1948–1967: Mekorot, Sikumim, Parshiyot Nivḥarot ve Homer 'Ezer,* edited by Avi Bar'eli, 202–23. Jerusalem: Yad Yitzhak Ben-Zvi.

———. 2003. "Yerushalayim Ha-mandatorit Ba-sifrut Ha-'ivrit." In *Yerushalayim Bi-tkufat Ha-mandat: Ha-'asiya Veha-moreshet,* edited by Yehoshua Ben-Arieh, 98–115. Mishkenot Sha'ananim, Jerusalem, Israel: Yad Yitzhak Ben-Zvi.

Holzhacker, Ronald. 2013. "State-Sponsored Homophobia and the Denial of the Right of Assembly in Central and Eastern Europe: The 'Boomerang' and the 'Ricochet' between European Organizations and Civil Society to Uphold Human Rights." *Law & Policy* 35 (1/2): 1–28.

Hulme, David. 2006. *Identity, Ideology, and the Future of Jerusalem.* New York: Palgrave.

Huppert, Shmuel. 1989. "Veha-makhbesh Haya Muval—Ke-merkevet Ha-mashi'a'h . . . : 'Iyun Be-ya'haso Shel Uri Tsvi Grinberg el Tnu'at Ha-'avoda Kefi She-hu Mishtakef Be-shirato." In *Ha-sifrut Ha-ivrit U-tnu'at Ha-avoda,* edited by Pinhas Ginossar, 98–115. Beer Sheva, Israel: Ben-Gurion University of the Negev.

———. 2006. *"Kodkod-esh": Be-me'hitsato Shel Ha-meshorer Uri Tsvi Grinberg.* Jerusalem: Karmel.

Hurd, Elizabeth Shakman. 2004. "The Political Authority of Secularism in International Relations." *European Journal of International Relations* 10 (2): 235–62.

Hurgronje, C. Snouck. 1970. *Mekka in the Later Part of the 19th Century: Daily Life, Customs and Learning of the Moslims of the East-Indian Archipelago.* Leiden, Netherlands: E. J. Brill.

Ilan, Shahar. 2006. "Pride of Place." *Haaretz,* July 24.

Inbar, Efraim. 2009. "The Rise and Demise of the Two-State Paradigm." *Orbis* (Spring): 265–83.

Inbari, Motti. 2007. "Religious Zionism and the Temple Mount Dilemma—Key Trends." *Israel Studies* 12 (2): 29–47.

———. 2009. *Who Will Build the Third Temple? Jewish Fundamentalism and the Temple Mount.* Albany: State University of New York Press.

Ingram, Edward. 1997. "The Wonderland of Political Science." *International Security* 22 (1) (Summer): 53–63.

———. 2001. "Hegemony, Global Reach, and World Power: Great Britain's Long Cycle." In *Bridges and Boundaries: Historians, Political Scientists, and the Study of International Relations*, edited by Colin Elman and Miriam Fendius Elman, 223–51. Cambridge, MA: MIT Press.

International Crisis Group. 2012a. "Extreme Makeover? (I): Israel's Politics of Land and Faith in East Jerusalem." *Middle East Report* 134 (December 20).

———. 2012b. "Extreme Makeover? (II): The Withering of Arab Jerusalem." *Middle East Report* 135, December 20.

International Lesbian and Gay Association (ILGA). 2005. "10,000 Participants at Jerusalem's 4th Gay Pride Parade." *IGLA News Online*, July 1. http://ilga.org /ilga/en/article/665.

Ioannides, Dimitri, and Mara W. Cohen Ioannides. 2002. "Pilgrimages of Nostalgia: Patterns of Jewish travel in the United States." *Tourism Recreation Research* 27 (2): 17–25.

Ioannides, Mara W. Cohen, and Dimitri Ioannides. 2006. "Global Jewish Tourism: Pilgrimages and Remembrance." In *Tourism, Religion and Spiritual Journeys*, edited by D. J. Timothy and D. H. Olsen, 156–71. London: Routledge.

Ir Amim. 2008. *State of Affairs—Jerusalem Political Development and Changes on the Ground.* Jerusalem: Ir Amim. http://www.ir-amim.org.il.

Isaac, Jad, and Suhail Khalilieh. 2011. "The Jerusalem Saga: Current Realities in Jerusalem." *Palestine-Israel Journal of Politics, Economics and Culture* 17 (1/2): 109–34. http://www.pij.org/current.php?id=74.

Israel Democracy Institute. 2008–. The Peace Index. http://www.peaceindex.org.

Israeli, Raphael. 2002. *Jerusalem Divided: The Armistice Regime 1947–1967.* London: Frank Cass.

Issacharoff, Avi, and Amos Harel. 2010. "Palestinian Villagers Trapped by Permanent Red Light." *Haaretz*, May 24.

Jacobson, Abigail. 2001. "The Sephardi Jewish Community in Pre-World War I Jerusalem." *Jerusalem Quarterly* 14 (Autumn): 23–33.

———. 2011. *From Empire to Empire—Jerusalem between Ottoman and British Rule.* Syracuse, NY: Syracuse University Press.

Jarman, Neil. 1997. *Material Conflicts: Parades and Visual Displays in Northern Ireland.* Oxford, UK: Berg.

Jarman, Neil, and Dominic Bryan. 1996. *Parade and Protest: A Discussion of Parading Disputes in Northern Ireland.* Ulster, Northern Ireland: Centre for the Study of Conflict, University of Ulster. http://cain.ulst.ac.uk/csc/reports/parade3.htm.

Jerusalem Is Proud to Present. 2007. Directed by Nitzan Gilady. Documentary film. Tel Aviv: Cinephil.

Jerusalem Post. 2009. "Anti-Gay Pride Protest Set for Sakhnin." June 22.

———. 2011. "PM Advisor's Letter to the NY Times." December 16. http://www .jpost.com/Diplomacy-and-Politics/PM-advisers-letter-to-New-York-Times.

Jervis, Robert. 2002. "An Interim Assessment of September 11: What Has Changed and What Has Not?" *Political Science Quarterly* 117 (1): 37–54.

Johnston, Lynda. 2005. *Queering Tourism: Paradoxical Performances at Gay Pride Parades.* New York: Routledge.

Ju'beh, Nazmi. 2001. "Jewish Settlement in the Old City of Jerusalem." *Palestine-Israel Journal of Politics, Economics and Culture* 8 (1): 48–54.

Jurik, Nancy, and Gray Cavender. 2004. "Feminism, Multiculturalism and the Justice Studies Movement." In *The Criminal Justice System and Women*, edited by Barbara Raffel Price and Natalie J. Sokoloff, 577–80. Boston: McGraw Hill.

Justice and Social Inquiry. 2012. "Homepage: About Us." Tempe, AZ: School of Social Transformation, Arizona State University. http://justice.clas.asu.edu /about.

Kalus, Ludvik, and Claude Guilot. 2004. "Réinterprétation des plus anciennes stèles funéraires islamiques nousantariennes: II. La stèle de Leran (Java) datée de 475/1082 et les stèles associées" [Reinterpretation of the earliest Islamic funerary steles in the Nousantarian Area: II. The stele from Leran (Java) dated of 475/1082 and the associated steles]. *Archipel* 67:17–36.

Kaminker, Sarah. 1997. "For Arabs Only: Building Restrictions in East Jerusalem." *Journal of Palestine Studies* 26 (4): 5–16.

Kaniel, Yehoshua. 1981. "Ha-Yishuv ha-Yashan ve-ha-Hityashvut ha-Hadasha." In *Sefer ha-Aliya ha-Rishona*, edited by Mordechai Eliav, 269–88. Jerusalem: Yad Yitzhak Ben-Zvi.

———. 1982. *Hemshech u-Temura: Ha-Yishuv ha-Yashan ve-ha-Yishuv he-Hadash bi-Tekufat ha-Aliya ha-Rishona ve-ha-Sheniya.* Jerusalem: Yad Yitzhak Ben-Zvi.

Kaoma, Kapya. 2012. "Exporting the Anti-Gay Movement." *American Prospect*, April 24. http://prospect.org/article/exporting-anti-gay-movement.

Kark, Ruth, and Michal Oren-Nordheim. 2001. *Jerusalem and Its Environs: Quarters, Neighborhoods, Villages 1800–1948*. Jerusalem: Magnes Press, The Hebrew University of Jerusalem; and Detroit: Wayne State University Press.

Karmi, Ghada. 2001. "Jerusalem: Excursion Up a Blind Alley?" *Palestine-Israel Journal of Politics, Economics and Culture* 8 (1): 26–31.

Kates, Steven, and Russell Belk. 2001. "The Meanings of Lesbian and Gay Pride Day: Resistance through Consumption and Resistance to Consumption." *Journal of Contemporary Ethnography* 30 (4): 392–429.

Katz, Kimberly. 2005. *Jordanian Jerusalem: Holy Places and National Spaces*. Gainesville: University of Florida Press.

Katz, Sue. 2002. "Israeli Queers Revolt." *Z Magazine* December. http://www.zcommunications.org/zmag/dec2002.

Katzenstein, Peter J., Robert O. Keohane, and Stephen D. Krasner. 1999. "International Organization and the Study of World Politics." In *Exploration and Contestation in the Study of World Politics*, edited by Peter J. Katzenstein, Robert Keohane, and Stephen Krasner, 5–45. Cambridge, MA: MIT Press.

Keissar, Adi. 2013. "Look Out Tel Aviv: Israel's Gay Scene Thrives in Unexpected Places." *Haaretz*, November 19.

Kershner, Isabel. 2013a. "Compromise Is Proposed on Western Wall Praying." *New York Times*, April 9.

———. 2013b. "Court Rules for Women in Western Wall Dispute." *New York Times*, April 11.

Khalidi, Rashid. 1992. "The Future of Arab Jerusalem." *British Journal of Middle Eastern Studies* 19 (2): 133–43.

———. 1998. *Palestinian Identity*. New York: Columbia University Press.

———. 2001. "The Centrality of Jerusalem to an End of Conflict Agreement." *Journal of Palestine Studies* 30 (3): 82–87.

———. 2005. "A Research Agenda for Writing the History of Jerusalem." In *Pilgrims, Lepers and Stuffed Cabbage*, edited by Issam Nassar and Salim Tamari, 12–27. Ramallah and Jerusalem: Institute of Jerusalem Studies and the Center for Jerusalem Studies at al-Quds University.

———. 2006. *The Iron Cage: The Story of the Palestinian Struggle for Statehood*. Boston: Beacon.

Khalidi, Walid. 1978. "Thinking the Unthinkable: A Sovereign Palestinian State." *Foreign Affairs* 56 (4): 695–713.

Khamaisi, Rassem, and Rami Nasrallah. 2006. "Jerusalem: From Siege to a City's Collapse." In *City of Collision: Jerusalem and the Principles of Conflict Urbanism*, edited by Philip Misselwitz and Tim Rieniets, 162–69. Basel: Birkhäuser.

Kim, Samuel S., Dallen J. Timothy, and Hag-Chin Han. 2007. "Tourism and Political Ideologies: A Case of Tourism in North Korea." *Tourism Management* 28:1031–43.

Kimmerling, Baruch. 2001. *The Invention and Decline of Israeliness*. Berkeley: University of California Press.

Kittrie, Orde. 2003. "Intellectual Relations: More Process than Peace." *Michigan Law Review* 101 (May): 1661–1712.

Klein, Aaron. 2005. "Petition: No 'Gay Pride' in Holy City: Christian group, Rabbis Demand Mayor Cancel Global Homosexual Event." *WorldNetDaily.com*, March 11.

Klein, Julie Thompson. 1990. *Interdisciplinarity: History, Theory and Practice*. Detroit: Wayne State University Press.

———. 1996. *Crossing Boundaries: Knowledge, Disciplinarities, and Interdisciplinarities*. Charlottesville: University Press of Virginia.

Klein, Menachem. 2001. *Jerusalem: The Contested City*. London and New York: C. Hurst and New York University Press.

———. 2002. "Rule and Role in Jerusalem: Israel, Jordan, and the PLO in the Peace-Building Process." In *Jerusalem: A City and Its Future*, edited by Marshall J. Breger and Ora Ahimeir, 137–74. Syracuse, NY: Syracuse University Press.

———. 2003. *The Jerusalem Problem: The Struggle for Permanent Status*. Gainesville: University Press of Florida.

———. 2004. "Jerusalem without East-Jerusalemites? The Palestinians as the 'Other' in Jerusalem." *Journal of Israeli History* 23 (2): 174–99.

———. 2005. "Old and New Walls in Jerusalem." *Political Geography* 24 (1): 53–76.

———. 2007. *A Possible Peace between Israel and Palestine: An Insider's Account of the Geneva Initiative*. New York: Columbia University Press.

———. 2008. "Jerusalem as an Israeli Problem: A Review of Forty Years of Israeli Rule Over Arab Jerusalem." *Israel Studies* 13 (2): 54–72.

———. 2010. *The Shift: Israel Palestine from Border Struggle to Ethnic Conflict*. London and New York: C. Hurst and Columbia University Press.

———. 2011. "The Shift—Israel's New Goals in Jerusalem." *Palestine-Israel Journal of Politics, Economics and Culture* 17 (1/2): 135–40.

Kliot, Nurit, and Yoel Mansfield. 1997. "The Political Landscape of Partition—The Case of Cyprus." *Political Geography* 16:495–521.

———. 1999. "Divided Cities: Case Studies of Conflict and Territorial Organization." *Progress in Planning* 52:167–226.

Kollek, Teddy. 1977. "Jerusalem." *Foreign Affairs* 55 (4): 701–16.

———. 1990. Letter from Mayor of Jerusalem to John Cardinal O'Connor, Archbishop of New York. May 13.

Kotek, Joël. 1999. "Divided Cities in the European Cultural Context." *Progress in Planning* 52:227–37.

Kraft, Dina. 2009. "Can Gay Friendliness Boost Israel's Image?" *JTA: The News Service of the Jewish People*, June 16.

Krakover, Shaul. 2002. "The Holocaust Remembrance Site of Yad Vashem Welcomes Visitors." *International Research in Geographical and Environmental Education* 11 (4): 359–62.

———. 2005. "Attitudes of Israeli Visitors towards the Holocaust Remembrance Site of Yad Vashem." In *Horror and Human Tragedy Revisited: The Management of Sites of Atrocities for Tourism*, edited by Gregory Ashworth and Rudi Hartmann, 108–17. New York: Cognizant.

Kuhl, Jorgen. 2003. *The National Minorities in the Danish-German Border Region.* Aabenraa, Denmark: Danish Institute of Border Region Studies.

Kurzweil, Baruch. 1966. *Beyn 'Hazon Le-veyn Ha-absurdi: Prakim Le-derekh Sifrutenu Ba-me'a Ha-'esrim.* Jerusalem: Shoken.

Kusno, Abidin. 2003. "The Reality of One-Which is Two: Mosque Battles and Other Stories—Notes on Architecture, Religion and Politics in the Javanese World." *Journal of Architectural Education* 57 (1): 57–67.

LaCapra, Dominick. 2001. *Writing History, Writing Trauma.* Baltimore: Johns Hopkins University Press.

Laclau, Ernesto, and Chantal Mouffe. 1985. *Hegemony and Socialist Strategy: Towards a Radical Democratic Politics.* Translated by Winston Moore and Paul Cammack. London: Verso.

Lamont, Michele, and Virag Molnar. 2002. "The Study of Boundaries in the Social Sciences." *Annual Review of Sociology* 28:167–95.

Lapidoth, Ruth. 1994. "Jerusalem and the Peace Process." *Israel Law Review* 28 (2–3): 402–34.

———. 1994. "Jerusalem: The Legal and Political Background." *Justice* 3 (August): 7–14.

Laplanche, Jean, and J. B. Pontalis. 1973. *The Language of Psycho-analysis*. New York: Norton.

Laqueur, Walter. 2009. *A History of Zionism: From the French Revolution to the Establishment of the State of Israel*. New York: Random House.

Laqueur, Walter, and Barry Rubin, eds. 2001. *The Israel-Arab Reader: A Documentary History of the Middle East Conflict*. 6th ed. New York: Penguin.

Lauderdale, Pat, and Gray Cavender. 1986. "The Study of Justice." *Legal Studies Forum* 10 (1): 87–96.

Laufer, Shlomi. 2008. "Proudly Introducing Gay Tel Aviv." *Ynet*, March 16.

Lebow, Richard Ned. 2000–2001. "Contingency, Catalysts, and International System Change." *Political Science Quarterly* 115 (4): 591–616.

———. 2003. "A Data Set Named Desire: A Reply to William R. Thompson." *International Studies Quarterly* 47 (3): 475–78.

———. 2007. "Counterfactual Thought Experiments." *History Teacher* 40 (2). http://www.historycooperative.org/journals/ht/40.2/lebow/htm.

Lefkovits, Etgar. 2006. "Gay Parade Tensions Rise in Tel Aviv." *Jerusalem Post*, November 2.

Levin, Gabriel. 1982. "Contemporary Hebrew Poetry on Jerusalem: 'A Tunnel Calls to Its Hollow.'" *Ariel* 52:107–20.

Levine, Lee I., ed. 1999. *Jerusalem: Its Sanctity and Centrality to Judaism, Christianity, and Islam*. New York: Continuum.

———. 2008. "Jerusalem in Jewish History, Tradition, and Memory." In *Jerusalem: Idea and Reality*, edited by Tamar Mayer and Suleiman A. Mourad, 27–46. New York: Routledge.

Levinson, Chaim. 2011. "US Jewish Group Appeals against Placing 'Jerusalem, Israel' on Passports." *Haaretz*, November 1.

Lévi-Strauss, Claude. 1963. *Structural Anthropology*. New York: Basic Books.

———. 1966. *The Savage Mind*. London: Weidenfeld & Nicolson.

Levontin, Zalman David. 1924. *Le-Eretz Avoteinu*. Tel Aviv: Eitan and Shoshani.

Levontin, Zalman David, and Menahem Sheinkin. 1906. Letter to David Wolffsohn [in Hebrew]. (October 25). Collection A24, File 60/8, Central Zionist Archives.

Levy, Jack S. 2001. "Explaining Events and Developing Theories: History, Political Science, and the Analysis of International Relations." In *Bridges and Boundaries: Historians, Political Scientists, and the Study of International Relations*, edited by Colin Elman and Miriam Fendius Elman, 39–83. Cambridge, MA: MIT Press.

Lidman, Melanie. 2011. "40,000 March for Jerusalem Day; 24 Arrested." *Jerusalem Post*, June 2.

Lindholm, Charles. 1995. "The New Middle Eastern Ethnography." *Journal of the Royal Anthropological Institute* (N.S.) 1:805–20.

Lior, Ilan, and Jonathan Lis. 2013. "Haaretz Poll Finds 70% of Israelis Support Equality for Gay Community." *Haaretz*, December 15.

Liphshiz, Cnaan. 2009. "Israel Advocates Play Gay Card." *Haaretz*, June 12.

Liptak, Adam. 2011. "Dispute Over Jerusalem Engages Court." *New York Times*, November 8.

Lis, Jonathan. 2008. "Jerusalem Official to High Court: Gay Parade Desecrates Holy City." *Haaretz*, June 20.

———. 2013a. "Habayit Hayehudi: Yes to Civil Union, But Not for Gay Couples." *Haaretz*, November 5.

———. 2013b. "Opposition Urges Netanyahu: Recognize Gay Rights in Israel." *Haaretz*, December 18.

Liverani, Mario. 2005. *Israel's History and the History of Israel*. Translated by Chiara Peri and Philip R. Davies. London: Equinox.

Lugg, Catherine, and Madelaine Adelman. Forthcoming. "Legal, Political, Social & Policy Contexts." In *American Educational Research Association Research on LGBTQ in Education: Using and Investing in Building Knowledge*, edited by Felice J. Levine, George L. Wimberly, and Karen Graves. Washington, DC: American Education Research Association (AERA).

Lukens-Bull, Ronald, and Mark Fafard. 2007. "Next Year in Orlando: (Re)Creating Israel in Christian Zionism." *Journal of Religion and Society* 9:1–20.

Luongo, Michael. 2006. "The Lebanon War Comes to a Gay Pride Rally." *WorldPride*, August 14. Originally published by Slate.com. http://www.worldpride.net/indiex.php?id=1215.

Lustick, Ian S. 1993–94. "Reinventing Jerusalem." *Foreign Policy* 93 (Winter): 41–59.

———. 2008. "Yerushalayim, al-Quds, and the Wizard of Oz: The Problem of 'Jerusalem' after Camp David II and the Aqsa *Intifada*." In *Jerusalem: Idea and Reality*, edited by Tamar Mayer and Suleiman A. Mourad, 283–302. New York: Routledge.

Lyman, Stanford, and Marvin B. Scott. 1968. "Territoriality: A Neglected Social Dimension." *Social Problems* 15:236–49.

MacGregor, Susanne. 1994. "Reconstructing the Divided City: Problems of Pluralism and Governance." In *Managing Divided Cities*, edited by Dunn Seamus, 228–43. Ryburn, UK: Keele University Press.

MacLeish, Kenneth. December 1968. "Reunited Jerusalem Faces Its Problems." *National Geographic* 134 (6): 835–71.

Magal, Tamir, Neta Oren, Daniel Bar-Tal, and Eran Halperin. 2012. "Psychological Legitimization: Views of the Israeli Occupation by Jews in Israel, Data and Implications." In *The Impacts of Lasting Occupation: Lessons from Israeli Society*, edited by Daniel Bar-Tal and Izhak Schnell. New York: Oxford University Press.

Maikey, Haneen, and Jason Ritchie. 2009. "James Kirchick's 'Queers for Palestine?'" *Advocate*, April 26. Reprinted as "Israel, Palestine and Queers." *MRZine*, a project of the Monthly Review Foundation, April 28, 2009. http://mrzine.monthlyreview.org/2009/mr280409.html.

Majalah Islam Sabili. 2006. June 29, 60–61.

Makovsky, David. 2006. *Olmert's Unilateral Option: An Early Assessment*. Washington, DC: Washington Institute for Near East Policy.

Man, K. L. (Kadish Yehuda Silman). 1910. "Al 'Bezalel' ve-al Yotzro." *Ha-Po'el Ha-Tza'ir* 3 (18) (July 6): 7–9.

Manor, Dalia. 2005. *Art in Zion: The Genesis of Modern National Art in Jewish Palestine*. London: Routledge.

Mansfeld, Yoel, Amos Ron, and Dorit Gev. 2000. *Moslem Tourism to Israel*. Haifa: Center for Tourism, Pilgrimage and Recreation Research, University of Haifa.

Maoz, Moshe, and Sari Nusseibeh, eds. 2000. *Jerusalem: Points of Friction—and Beyond*. Cambridge, UK: Kluwer Law.

Marciano, Ilan. 2006. "Arab MK: 'No Gays in Muslim Society.'" *Ynet*, July 4.

Marcuse, Peter. 1995. "Not Chaos, but Walls: Postmodernism and the Partitioned City." In *Post-Modern Cities and Spaces*, edited by Sophie Watson and Katherine Gibson, 243–53. Oxford, UK: Blackwell.

Margalit, Dan. 2000. "As Long As Terrorism Is Kept at Bay." *Haaretz*, September 4.

Mark, Cylde R. 2005. *CRS Issue Brief for Congress: Libya*. Washington, DC: Congressional Research Service, Library of Congress.

Markwell, Kevin, and Gordon Waitt. 2009. "Festivals, Space and Sexuality: Gay Pride in Australia." *Tourism Geographies: An International Journal of Tourism Space, Place and Environment* 11 (2): 143–68.

Matthews, Laura. 2012. "Gay Pride Banned in St. Petersburg, Russia, after Complaints; LGBT Activists to Defy Orders." *International Business Times*, July 6. http://www.ibtimes.com/articles/360432/20120706/gay-pride-banned-st-petersburg-russia-defy.htm.

Matthews, Victor H. 1995. "The Anthropology of Clothing in the Joseph Narrative." *Journal for the Study of the Old Testament* 20 (65): 25–36.

Mayer, Tamar. 2008. "Jerusalem In and Out of Focus: The City in Zionist Ideology." In *Jerusalem: Idea and Reality*, edited by Tamar Mayer and Suleiman A. Mourad, 224–44. New York: Routledge.

Mayer, Tamar, and Suleiman Ali Mourad. 2008. "Introduction." In *Jerusalem: Idea and Reality*, edited by Tamar Mayer and Suleiman A. Mourad, 1–13. London and New York: Routledge.

McGirk, Tim. 2006. "Hatred (of Gays) Unites Jerusalem's Feuding Faiths." *Time Magazine*, November 3.

McKnight, Stephen. 1989. *Sacralizing the Secular: The Renaissance Origins of Modernity*. Baton Rouge: Louisiana State University Press.

Meir Amit Intelligence and Terrorism Information Center (ITIC). 2008. "Jerusalem as a Focus for Terrorism." July 23. Ramat HaSharon, Israel: Israeli Intelligence and Heritage Commemoration Center. http://www.terrorism-info.org.il/.

Messing, Jill, Madelaine Adelman, and Alesha Durfee. 2012. "Gender Violence and Transdisciplinarity." *Violence Against Women*, 18 (6): 641–52.

Metreveli, Marina, and Dallen J. Timothy. 2010. "Religious Heritage and Emerging Tourism in the Republic of Georgia." *Journal of Heritage Tourism* 5 (3): 237–44.

Migdal, Joel S. 2004. "Mental Maps and Virtual Checkpoints: Struggles to Construct and Maintain State and Social Boundaries." In *Boundaries and Belonging: State and Societies in the Struggle to Shape Identities and Local Practices*, edited by Joel S. Migdal, 3–23. Cambridge: Cambridge University Press.

Miller, J. Maxwell, and John H. Hayes. 2006. *A History of Ancient Israel and Judah*. 2nd ed. Louisville, KY and London: Westminster John Knox Press.

Miron, Dan. 1987. *Im Lo Tihiye Yerushalayim: Ha-sifrut Ha-'ivrit Be-heksher Tarbuti-Politi*. Tel Aviv: Ha-kibuts Ha-me'u'had.

———. 1996. "Depictions in Modern Hebrew Literature." In *City of the Great King*, edited by Nitza Rosovsky, 241–87. Cambridge, MA: Harvard University Press.

———. 1999. *Ha-adam Eyno Ela—:'Hulshat-Ha-koa'h, 'Otsmat-Ha-'hulsha: 'Iyunim Be-shira*. Tel Aviv: Zmora-Bitan.

———. 2002. *Akdamot Le-atsag*. Jerusalem: Mosad Biyalik.

Mishal, Shaul, and Reuven Aharoni. 1994. *Speaking Stones: Communiques from the Intifada Underground*. Syracuse, NY: Syracuse University Press.

Misselwitz, Philip, and Tim Rieniets. 2006. *City of Collision: Jerusalem and the Principles of Conflict Urbanism*. New York: Springer and Birkhäuser Basel.

Montefiore, Simon Sebag. 2011. *Jerusalem: The Biography*. New York: Knopf.

Moore, Henrietta, ed. 1999. *Anthropological Theory Today*. Oxford, UK: Polity Press.

Morgan, Phoebe, Madelaine Adelman, and Stephen Soli. 2008. "Dueling Trage-dies: A Critical Read of the Lautenberg Story." *Law, Culture and the Humanities* 4 (3): 424–51.

Morris, Benny. 1999. *Righteous Victims: A History of the Zionist-Arab Conflict, 1881–1999*. New York: Knopf.

———. 2002. "Camp David and After: An Exchange (An Interview with Ehud Barak)." *New York Review of Books* 49 (June 13): 10.

———. 2008. *1948: A History of the First Arab-Israeli War*. New Haven, CT: Yale University Press.

———. 2009. *One State, Two States*. New Haven, CT: Yale University Press.

Mourad, Suleiman Ali. 2008. "The Symbolism of Jerusalem in Early Islam." In *Jerusalem: Idea and Reality*, edited by Tamar Mayer and Suleiman A. Mourad, 86–102. New York: Routledge.

Mukerji, Chandra. 1997. *Territorial Ambitions and the Gardens of Versailles*. Cambridge: Cambridge University Press.

Murphy, Kim. 1990. "Most Israelis Leave Hospice in Old City: Jerusalem: But 20 Stay to Care for Building. That Sets Off a Shouting Match with Greek Priests." *Los Angeles Times*, May 2, A4.

Muwassi, Faroug. 1996. *Jerusalem in Modern Palestinian Poetry* [in Arabic]. Nazareth, Israel: Mawaqif.

Naor, Arye. 2005. "Behold, Rachel, Behold: The Six Day War as a Biblical Experience and Its Impact on Israel's Political Mentality." *Journal of Israeli History* 24 (2): 229–50.

Nassar, Issam. 2005. "Laqatat mughayireh: Al-tasweer Al-mahali Al-mubaker fir Falastin, 1850–1948." *Different Snapshots: Palestine in Early Photography* [in Arabic]. London and Beirut: al-Qattan Foundation and Kutub.

———. 2006. "'Biblification' in the Service of Colonialism: Jerusalem in Nineteenth-Century Photography." *Third Text* 20 (3/4): 317–26.

Nessman, Ravi. 2006. "Faiths in Jerusalem United over Gay March." *Boston Herald*, July 12.

Neumann, Boaz. 2011. *Land and Desire in Early Zionism*. Waltham, MA: Brandeis University Press.

Newby, Gordon. 1989. *The Making of the Last Prophet: A Reconstruction of the Earliest Biography of Muhammad*. Columbia: University of South Carolina Press.

Newman, David, ed. 1985. *The Impact of Gush Emunim: Politics and Settlement in the West Bank*. London: Croom Helm.

———. 1999. "Real Space, Symbolic Space: Interrelated Notions of Territory in the Arab-Israeli Conflict." In *A Road Map to War—Territorial Dimensions of International Conflict*, edited by Paul F. Diehl, 3–36. Nashville: Vanderbilt University Press.

Newman, David, and Anssi Paasi. 1998. "Fences and Neighbors in the Postmodern World: Boundary Narratives in Political Geography." *Progress in Human Geography* 22:186–207.

Nicholson, Robert W. 2012. *Managing the Divine Jurisdiction: Sacred Space and the Limits of Law on the Temple Mount (1917–1948).* Unpublished thesis, Master of Arts in history, Syracuse University, Syracuse, NY.

Nielsen, Christian Axboe. 2013. "Stronger than the State? Football Hooliganism, Political Extremism and the Gay Pride Parades in Serbia." *Sports in Society* 16 (8): 1038–53.

Nietzsche, Friedrich. (1887) 1994. *On the Genealogy of Morality.* Translated by Carol Diethe. Edited by Keith Ansell-Pearson. *Cambridge Texts in the History of Political Thought.* Cambridge: Cambridge University Press.

Nissenbauma, Dion. 2006. "Organizers Cancel Controversial Jerusalem Gay Pride March." *Arizona Republic*, November 10.

Nitzan-Shiftan, Alona. 2006. "To Nationalize and to Cover—Jerusalem's Concept of Place" [in Hebrew]. *Alpayim* 30:134–70.

Nowersztern, Abraham. 2000. "Ha-or Veha-efer: Ha-gavrut Ha-'ola: Mivne U-mashma'ut." In *Ha-matkonet Veha-dmut: Me'hkarim Ve-'iyunim Be-shirat Uri Tsvi Grinberg*, edited by H. Weiss, 171–210. Ramat-Gan, Israel: Bar Ilan University.

Nowotny, Helga. 2004. "The Potential of Transdisciplinarity." In *Rethinking Interdisciplinarity*, proceedings of conference sponsored by Centre National de la Recherche Scientifique (CNRS), Society of Information, and Institute Nicod, February 9, 48–52. http://www.interdisciplines.org/medias/confs/archives /archive_3.pdf

Nusseibeh, Sari. 2007. *Once Upon a Country: A Palestinian Life.* New York: Farrar, Straus and Giroux.

———. 2008. "Negotiating the City: a Perspective of a Jerusalemite." In *Jerusalem: Idea and Reality*, edited by Tamar Mayer and Suleiman A. Mourad, 198–204. New York: Routledge.

O'Mahoney, Anthony, ed. 1995. *The Christian Heritage of Jerusalem.* London: Scorpion.

Ofran, Hagit. 2012. "A New Settlement in Beit Hanina." *Eyes on the Ground in East Jerusalem* (blog), August 20. http://settlementwatcheastjerusalem.wordpress .com/.

Okkenhaug, Inger Marie. 2002. *The Quality of Heroic Living, of High Endeavour and Adventure: Anglican Mission, Women and Education in Palestine, 1888–1948.* Leiden, The Netherlands: Brill.

Oleh Regel. 1903. "Be-Vo'I Li-Yerushalayim (b)." *Hashkafa* 4 (27) (26 Nissan 5663/ April 23): 217.

Olsen, Daniel H. 2006. "Tourism and Informal Pilgrimage among the Latter-Day Saints." In *Tourism, Religion and Spiritual Journeys,* edited by Dallen J. Timothy and Daniel H. Olsen, 254–70. London: Routledge.

Olsen, Daniel H., and Jeanne K. Guelke. 2004. "Spatial Transgression and the BYU Jerusalem Center Controversy." *Professional Geographer* 56 (4): 503–15.

Omer, Dan. 1987. "Homa shel otiyot (Yerushalayim Ba-sifrut)." In *Ha-rov'a Ha-yehudi Ba-'it Ha-'atika Yerushalayim,* edited by M. Na'or, 482–535. Jerusalem: Ha-'hevra Le-shikum Ul-fitu'a'h Ha-rova' Ha-yehudi Ba-'ir Ha-'atika Bi-yerushalayim.

Omer-Sherman, Ranen. 2006. "Yehuda Amichai's Exilic Jerusalem." *Prooftexts* 26 (1–2): 212–39.

Openhaimer, Yo'hai. 2003. *Ha-zkhut Ha-gdola Lomar Lo: Shira Politit Be-yisra'el.* Jerusalem: Magnes Press, Hebrew University of Jerusalem.

Oppenheimer, Yehudit. 2011. "An Explosive Situation in Silwan." *Palestine-Israel Journal of Politics, Economics and Culture* 17 (1/2): 31–34.

Orbach, Lily. 1993. "Mipuy Efsharuyot Shel 'Itsuv Yerushalayim Ba-sifrut," *'Alon La-more Le-sifrut* 14:124–40.

Oren, Michael. 2005. "The Revelations of 1967: New Research on the Six Day War and Its Lessons for the Contemporary Middle East." *Israel Studies* 10 (2): 1–14.

Orme, William A. Jr. 1999. "Christian Churches Plan a Joint Protest of Nazareth Mosque." *New York Times,* November 5.

Otto, Rudolf. 1917. *The Idea of the Holy.* London: Oxford University Press.

Oz, Amos. 2006. *How to Cure a Fanatic.* Princeton, NJ: Princeton University Press.

Paasi, Anssi. 1999. "Boundaries as Social Processes: Territoriality in the World of Flows." In *Boundaries, Territory and Post-Modernity,* edited by David Newman, 69–88. London: Frank Cass.

Pape, Robert A. 2003. "The Strategic Logic of Suicide Terrorism." *American Political Science Review* 97 (3): 343–61.

Parmenter, Barbara McKean. 1994. *Giving Voice to Stones: Place and Identity in Palestinian Literature.* Austin: University of Texas Press.

Parush, Iris. 2004. "Another Look at the 'Life of Dead Hebrew'—Intentional Ignorance of Hebrew in Nineteenth-Century Eastern European Jewish Society." *Book History* 7:171–214.

Peace Now (Israel) and Americans for Peace Now (USA). 2013. *Bibi's Settlements Boom: March–November 2013.* November 7. http://peacenow.org.il/eng/8monthsreport.

Pearce, Susan, and Alex Cooper. 2014. "LGBT Movements in Southeast Europe: Violence, Justice and International Intersections." In *Handbook of LGBT Communities, Crime and Justice,* edited by Dana Peterson and Vanessa Panfil, 311–38. New York: Springer.

Pecora, Vincent. 2006. *Secularization and Cultural Criticism: Religion, Nation, and Modernity.* Chicago: University of Chicago Press.

Pedaya, Haviva. 2007. "Na'hal Kidron—Po'etika Shel Makom: 'Re'hovot Ha-nahar' Ba-tavekh She-beyn 'Eyma Gdola Ve-yare'a'h' Le-veyn 'Le-sa'if Sela' 'Eytam'." In *'Re'hovot Ha-nahar' Le-Uri Tsvi Grinberg: Me'hkarim Ve-te'udot,* edited by Aminadav Lipsker and Tamar Wolf-Monzon, 159–86. Ramat Gan, Israel: Bar Ilan University.

Peleg, Ilan, and Dov Waxman. 2007. "Losing Control? A Comparison of Majority-Minority Relations in Israel and Turkey." *Nationalism and Ethnic Politics* 13 (3): 431–63.

Petachia. 1903. "Tzidduk ha-Din." *Hashkafa* 4 (26 Nissan 5663/April 23): 27.

Peters, Francis E. 1985. *Jerusalem: The Holy City in the Eyes of Chroniclers, Visitors, Pilgrims, and Prophets from the Days of Abraham to the Beginnings of Modern Times.* Princeton, NJ: Princeton University Press.

———. 1989. *The Contested Inheritance: A Primer on the Shared Patrimony and Development of Judaism, Christianity and Islam.* Princeton, NJ: Center for Near Eastern Studies, Princeton University.

———. 2008. "Jerusalem: One City, One Faith, One God." In *Jerusalem: Idea and Reality,* edited by Tamar Mayer and Suleiman A. Mourad, 14–26. New York: Routledge.

Petts, Judith, Susan Owens, and Harriet Bulkeley. 2008. "Crossing Boundaries: Interdisciplinarity in the Context of Urban Environments." *Geoforum* 39:593–601.

Philpott, Daniel. 2002. "The Challenge of September 11 to Secularism in International Relations." *World Politics* 55:66–95.

Pinto, Nino. 1999. "Nazareth Compromise Threatens Papal Visit." *Haaretz,* October 15.

Pinto, Nino, and Joseph Algazy. 1999. "Ministers to Present Nazareth Compromise Today: Ben-Ami 'Certain' of Pope's Visit." *Haaretz*, October 13.

Pinto, Nino, Joseph Algazy, and Sharon Gal. 1999. "Muslims Tell Pope to Stay out of Nazareth's Affairs: Government Set to Allow Small Mosque Near Basilica." *Haaretz*, October 7.

Porat, Dan A. 2004. "It's Not Written Here, but This Is What Happened: Students' Cultural Comprehension of Textbook Narratives on the Israeli-Arab Conflict." *American Educational Research Journal* 41 (4): 963–96.

Poria, Yaniv, and Yaniv Gvili. 2006. "Heritage Site Websites Content: The Need for Versatility." *Journal of Hospitality and Leisure Marketing* 15 (2): 73–93.

Poria, Yaniv, Avital Biran, and Arie Reichel. 2007. "Different Jerusalems for Different Tourists." *Journal of Travel and Tourism Marketing* 22 (3/4): 121–38.

Pressman, Jeremy. 2003. "The Second Intifada: Background and Causes of the Israeli-Palestinian Conflict." *The Journal of Conflict Studies* 23 (2): 114–41.

Prior, Michael. 1994. "Pilgrimage to the Holy Land, Yesterday and Today." In *Christians in the Holy Land*, edited by Michael Prior and William Taylor, 169–99. London: World of Islam Festival Trust.

Protocol [in Hebrew]. 1902. Archives of Mordechai Krishevsky-Ezrahi, Central Zionist Archives A39, file 5–4, 15 Elul 5662/September 17.

Pundak, Ron. 2001. "From Oslo to Taba: What Went Wrong?" *Survival* 43 (3): 31–45.

QUIT (Queers Undermining Israeli Terrorism). 2005. "Op-Ed: Boycott World Pride Jerusalem: Apartheid Pride? No Thanks!" *Bay Area Reporter*, May 12.

Rabbani, Mouin. Spring 2001. "Rocks and Rockets: Oslo's Inevitable Conclusion." *Journal of Palestine Studies* 30 (3): 68–81.

Rabinovich, Itamar. 1999. *Waging Peace: Israel and the Arabs at the End of the Century*. New York: Farrar, Straus and Giroux.

Rabinowitz, Dan. 2002. "Oriental Othering and National Identity: A Review of Early Israeli Anthropological Studies of Palestinians." *Identities: Global Studies in Culture and Power* 4:305–24.

Raivo, Petri. 2000. "Landscaping the Patriotic Past: Finnish War Landscapes as a National Heritage." *Fennia* 178 (1): 139–50.

Ram, Uri. 2005. "Jerusalem, Tel Aviv and the Bifurcation of Israel." *International Journal of Politics, Culture and Society* 19:21–33.

Ramon, Amnon. 2002. "Delicate Balances at the Temple Mount, 1967–1999." In *Jerusalem: A City and its Future*, edited by Marshall J. Berger and Ora Ahimeir, 269–332. Jerusalem and New York: Jerusalem Institute for Israel Studies and Syracuse University Press.

Rapoport, David C. 1996. "The Importance of Space in Violent Ethno-Religious Strife." *Nationalism and Ethic Politics* 2 (2): 258–85.

Ravid, Barak, Natasha Mozgovaya, and Jack Khoury. 2010. "Netanyahu and Obama to Meet Tuesday in Washington." *Haaretz*, March 21.

Ray, James Lee. 1995. *Democracy and International Conflict: An Evaluation of the Democratic Peace Proposition.* Columbia, SC: University of South Carolina Press.

Reiter, Yitzhak. 2002. "Jewish-Muslim Modus Vivendi at the Temple Mount/al-Haram al-Sharif Since 1967." In *Jerusalem: Essays Toward Peacemaking*, edited by Marshall J. Berger and Ora Ahimeir, 269–95. Jerusalem and Syracuse, NY: Jerusalem Institute for Israel Studies and Syracuse University Press.

———. 2007. "'All of Palestine is Holy Muslim *Waqf* Land: A Myth and Its Roots." In *Law, Custom, and Statute in the Muslim World*, edited by Ron Shaham, 172–97. Boston: Brill.

———. 2008. *Jerusalem and Its Role in Islamic Solidarity.* New York: Palgrave.

———. 2009. "Contest or Cohabitation in Shared Holy Places? The Cave of the Patriarchs and Samuel's Tomb." In *Holy Places in the Israeli-Palestinian Conflict: Confrontation and Co-existence*, edited by Marshall J. Berger, Yitzhak Reiter, and Leonard Hammer, 158–77. New York: Routledge.

———. 2013. "Narratives of Jerusalem and Its Sacred Compound." *Israel Studies* 18 (2): 115–32.

Reiter, Yitzhak, and Lior Lehrs. 2010. *The Sheikh Jarrah Affair: The Strategic Implications of Jewish Settlement in an Arab Neighborhood in East Jerusalem: JIIS Studies Series, 404.* Jerusalem: Jerusalem Institute for Israel Studies. http://jiis.org/.upload/sheikhjarrah-eng.pdf.

Reiter, Yitzhak, Marlen Eordegian, and Marwan Abu Khalaf. 2001. "Jerusalem's Religious Significance." *Palestine-Israel Journal of Politics, Economics and Culture* 8 (1): 12–19.

Rekhess, Elie. 2008. "The Palestinian Political Leadership in East Jerusalem after 1967." In *Jerusalem: Idea and Reality*, edited by Tamar Mayer and Suleiman A. Mourad, 266–82. New York: Routledge.

Rhoten, Diana. 2003. *Final Report: A Multi-Method Analysis of the Social and Technical Conditions for Interdisciplinary Collaboration.* September. San Francisco, CA: Hybrid Vigor Institute.

Ricca, Simone. 2005. "Heritage, Nationalism and the Shifting Symbolism of the Wailing Wall." *Jerusalem Quarterly* 24:39–56.

Ricklefs, Merle Calvin. 2001. *A History of Modern Indonesia Since 1200.* Palo Alto, CA: Stanford University Press.

Ringkes, Douwe. 1996. *Nine Saints of Java*. Kuala Lumpur, Malaysia: Malaysia Sociological Research Institute.

Rogers, Sarah. 1999. "Painting Territorial Claims on Canvas: Images of Jerusalem by Contemporary Palestinian and Israeli Artists." Unpublished dissertation, Tufts University, Medford, MA.

Romann, Michael, and Alex Weingrod. 1991. *Living Together Separately: Arabs and Jews in Contemporary Jerusalem*. Princeton, NJ: Princeton University Press.

Ron, Amos S. 2009. "Towards a Typological Model of Contemporary Christian Travel." *Journal of Heritage Tourism* 4 (4): 287–97.

Ron, Moshe, and Michal Peled-Ginsburg. 2003. "Yerushalayim Shel Sha'har." *Me'hkarey Yerushalayim Be-sifrut 'Ivrit* 19:273–304.

Rosenblum, Mark. 1998. "Netanyahu and Peace: From Sound Bites to Sound Policies?" In *The Middle East and the Peace Process: The Impact of the Oslo Accords*, edited by Robert O. Freedman, 35–80. Gainesville: University Press of Florida.

Ross, Dennis. 2004. *The Missing Peace: The Inside Story of the Fight for Middle East Peace*. New York: Farrar, Straus and Giroux.

———. 2007. "Don't Play with Maps." *New York Times*, January 9.

Royal Embassy of Saudi Arabia. 1994. Monthly newsletters, April and June. Washington, DC.

Rudoren, Jodi. 2012. "A Divide over Prayer at a Sacred Site." *New York Times*, December 23.

———. 2013a. "New Apartments Will Complicate Jerusalem Issue." *New York Times*, March 17.

———. 2013b. "1,500 Units to Be Added in Settlement, Israel Says." *New York Times*, October 30.

———. 2013c. "Israeli Move over Housing Poses a Threat to Peace Talks." *New York Times*, November 12.

Rumjanceva, Nadja. 2013. "At Jerusalem Gay Parade, No Pomp But Plenty of Pride." *Haaretz*, August 4.

Sa, Creso M. 2008. "'Interdisciplinary Strategies' in U.S. Research Universities." *Higher Education* 55:537–52.

Sadeh, Danny. 2005. "The Pink City." *Ynet*, November 15.

Safier, Michael. 2001. "The 'Jerusalemite' Question." *Palestine-Israel Journal of Politics, Economics and Culture* 8 (3): 47–63.

Said, Edward. 1978. *Orientalism*. New York: Pantheon.

Sales, Ben. 2013. "Laying the Groundwork for Third Temple." *Jewish News of Greater Phoenix*, July 19.

Samman, Khaldoun. 2007. *Cities of God and Nationalism: Mecca, Jerusalem, and Rome as Contested World Cities*. Boulder, CO: Paradigm.

Saposnik, Arieh Bruce. 2005. "Exorcising the 'Angel of National Death'—National and Individual Death (and Rebirth) in Zionist National Liturgy in Palestine, 1903–1914." *Jewish Quarterly Review* 95 (3): 557–78.

———. 2008. *Becoming Hebrew: The Creation of a Hebrew National Culture in Ottoman Palestine*. Oxford: Oxford University Press.

———. 2009. "A New Zionist Sacred in the Making of the 'New Jew'" [in Hebrew]. *Yisra'el: A Journal for the Study of Zionism and the State of Israel—History, Culture, Society* 16:165–94.

Sattath, Noa. 2013. "Women, the Wall, and the Struggle for Jewish Pluralism in Israel." *Fathom*, September 13. http://www.fathomjournal.org.

Scham, Sandra A. 2001. "A Fight over Sacred Turf: Who Controls Jerusalem's Holiest Shrine?" *Archaeology* 54 (6): 62–67, 72–74.

Scham, Sandra A., and Adel Yahya. 2003. "Heritage and Reconciliation." *Journal of Social Archaeology* 3 (3): 399–416.

Schatz, Boris. 1906a. "Bet ha-nechot Bezalel." *Hashkafa* 8 (October 19; 30 Tishrei 5667): 61.

———. 1906b. Letter to Bezalel Jaffe, November 1 (13 Heshvan 5667). Collection L42, file 10, Central Zionist Archives.

———. 1906c. Letter to Bezalel Jaffe, December 27 (10 Tevet 5667). Collection L42, file 10, Central Zionist Archives.

———. 1906d. Letter to Menahem Ussishkin, November 9 (21 Heshvan 5667). Collection A24, file 60/8, Central Zionist Archives.

———. 1911. "The Bezalel Institute." In *Zionist Work in Palestine*, edited by Israel Cohen, 58–64. London and Leipzig: T. Fischer Unwin.

Schroeder, Paul W. 1997. "History and International Relations Theory: Not Use or Abuse, but Fit or Misfit." *International Security* 22 (1): 64–74.

———. 2001. "International History: Why Historians Do it Differently than Political Scientists." In *Bridges and Boundaries: Historians, Political Scientists, and the Study of International Relations*, edited by Colin Elman and Miriam Fendius Elman, 403–16. Cambridge, MA: MIT Press.

Schwartz, Yigal. 2003. "Yerushalayim Ve-eretz Yisra'el Bi-tkufat Ha-mandat." In *Yerushalayim Bi-tkufat Ha-mandat: Ha-'asiya Veha-moreshet*, edited by Yehoshua Ben-Arieh, 401–4. Mishkenot Sha'ananim, Jerusalem: Yad Yitzhak Ben-Zvi.

Segal, Jerome M., Shlomit Levy, Nadar Izzat Sa'id, and Elihu Katz. 2000. *Negotiating Jerusalem*. Albany: State University of New York Press.

Segal, Rafi, David Tartakover, and Eyal Weizman, eds. 2003. *A Civilian Occupation: The Politics of Israeli Architecture*. New York: Norton.

Segev, Tom. 2007. *1967: Israel, the War, and the Year That Transformed the Middle East*. New York: Metropolitan.

Seidemann, Daniel. 2005. "Why 'Separationism' Won't Work." *Haaretz*, February 18.

Sela, Neta. 2006a. "Gay Pride Leaves Jerusalem?" *Ynet*, July 7.

———. 2006b. "J'lem mayor: Gay Parade a Provocation." *Ynet*, May 4.

———. 2006c. "Pride Parade No; Hasidic Protest: Why Not?" *Ynet*, August 6.

———. 2006d. "Prize Offered to Whoever Kills Gay Person." *Ynet*, July 11.

———. 2006e. "Rabbi Amar to Pope: Thwart J'lem Gay Parade." *Ynet*, July 5.

Seligman, Adam B., Robert P. Weller, Michael J Puett, and Bennett Simon. 2008. *Ritual and Its Consequences: An Essay on the Limits of Sincerity*. New York and Oxford: Oxford University Press.

Shabbaneh, Luay. 2006. "Jerusalem's Shifting Demographic Profile." *Jerusalem Quarterly* 27:6–14.

Shachar, Arie, and Noam Shoval. 1999. "Tourism in Jerusalem: A Place to Pray." In *The Tourist City*, edited by Dennis R. Judd and Susan S. Fainstein, 198–211. New Haven, CT: Yale University Press.

Shaked, Gershon. 1998. "Yerushalayim Ba-sifrut Ha-'ivrit." *Mad'ey Ha-yahadut* 38:15–32.

Shalakany, Amr A. 2002. "Privatizing Jerusalem or an Investigation into the City's Future Legal Stakes." *Leiden Journal of International Law* 15:431–44.

Shamseyeh, Haleem Abu. 1999. "Settling the Old City: The Policies of Labor and Likud." *Jerusalem Quarterly* 6:30–42.

Shankman, Paul. 1996. "The History of Samoan Sexual Conduct and the Mead-Freeman Controversy." *American Anthropologist* 103 (3): 555–67.

Shanks, Hershel, ed. 2004. *The City of David: Revisiting Early Excavations*. Washington, DC: Biblical Archaeology Society.

Shapin, Steven. 1998. "Placing the View from Nowhere: Historical and Sociological Problems in the Location of Science." *Transactions of the Institute of British Geographers* 23:5–112.

Sharansky, Natan. 2008. "The Diaspora Debate." *World Jewish Digest* March: 15.

Shavit, Ari. 2002. "Letter from Jerusalem: No Man's Land—The Idea of a City Disappears." *New Yorker*, December 9, 56–60.

Sheleg, Yair. 2006. "Frightening but Liberating." *Haaretz*, November 11.

Sher, Gilead. 2006. *The Israeli-Palestinian Peace Negotiations, 1999–2001*. New York: Routledge.

———. 2008. "Negotiating Jerusalem: Reflections of an Israeli Negotiator." In *Jerusalem: Idea and Reality*, edited by Tamar Mayer and Suleiman A. Mourad, 303–20. New York: Routledge.

Shiddiq, Abdul. 2000. *Sunan Kudus*. Jakarta: Gunara Kata.

Shilo-Cohen, Nurit, ed. 1983. *Bezalel Shel Schatz: 1906–1929*. Jerusalem: Israel Museum.

Shindler, Colin. 2000. "Likud and the Christian Dispensationalists: A Symbiotic Relationship." *Israel Studies* 5 (1): 153–82.

Shlaim, Avi. 2001. "Israel and the Arab Coalition in 1948." In *War for Palestine: Rewriting the History of 1948*, edited by Eugene Rogan and Avi Shlaim, 79–103. Cambridge: Cambridge University Press.

Shokeid, Moshe. 1992. "Commitment and Contextual Study in Anthropology." *Cultural Anthropology* 7:464–77.

Shorter Oxford English Dictionary on Historical Principles. 2003. 5th ed. Oxford and New York: Oxford University Press.

Shragai, Nadav. 1995. *Har Ha-Merivah: Ha-Ma'avak al-Har Ha-Bayit: Yehudim u-Muslemim, Dat u-Politikah Meaz 1967* [Contentious Mountain: The Struggle over the Temple Mount: Jews and Muslims, Religion and Politics since 1967]. Jerusalem: Keter.

———. 2005. "Opinion Poll: 91% of Jews Unwilling to Relinquish the Western Wall For Peace." *Haaretz*, March 10.

———. 2008. "Jerusalem: The Dangers of Division, An Alternative to Separation from the Arab Neighborhoods." *Strategic Perspectives* (Jerusalem Center for Public Affairs) 3:3–27.

Silberman, Neil A. 2001. "If I Forget Thee, O Jerusalem: Archaeology, Religious Commemoration and Nationalism in a Disputed City, 1801–2001." *Nations and Nationalism* 7 (4): 487–504.

Silverstein, Paul A., and Ussama Makdisi. 2006. "Introduction: Memory and Violence in the Middle East and North Africa." In *Memory and Violence in the Middle East and North Africa*, edited by Paul A. Silverstein and Ussama Makdisi. Bloomington: Indiana University Press.

Slater, Jerome. 2001. "What Went Wrong? The Collapse of the Israeli-Palestinian Peace Process." *Political Science Quarterly* 116 (2): 171–99.

Sloterdijk, Peter. 2010. *God's Zeal: The Battle of the Three Monotheisms*. Translated by Wieland Hoban. Cambridge, UK and Malden, MA: Polity.

Smith, Anthony D. 2003. *Chosen Peoples—Sacred Sources of National Identity*. Oxford: Oxford University Press.

Smooha, Sammy. 2002. "The Model of Ethnic Democracy: Israel as a Jewish and Democratic State." *Nations and Nationalism* 8 (4): 475–503.

———. 2004. "Arab-Jewish Relations in Israel: A Deeply Divided Society." In *Israeli Identity in Transition*, edited by Anita Shapira, 31–67. Westport, CT: Praeger.

Snyder, Jack. 2000. *From Voting to Violence: Democratization and Nationalist Conflict.* New York: Norton.

Soebardi, Soebakin, ed. and trans. 1975. *The Book of Cabolek: A Critical Edition with Introduction, Translation, and Notes: A Contribution to the Study of Javanese Mystical Tradition.* The Hague: Martinus Nijhof.

Sorkin, Michael, ed. 2002. *The Next Jerusalem.* New York: Monacelli.

———, ed. 2005. *Against the Wall: Israel's Barrier to Peace.* New York: New Press.

Spivak, Gayatin Chakravorty. 2003. *Death of a Discipline.* New York: Columbia University Press.

Spolsky, Bernard, and Robert Cooper, eds. 1991. *The Languages of Jerusalem.* Oxford: Oxford University Press.

Sprinzak, Ehud. 1991. *The Ascendance of Israel's Radical Right.* New York: Oxford University Press.

Spruyt, Hendrik. 2005. *Ending Empire: Contested Sovereignty and Territorial Partition.* Ithaca, NY: Cornell University Press.

Stahl, Julie. 2005. "Jerusalem Court Rules in Favor of Homosexual Parade." *Cybercast News Service (CNS) News.com*, June 27.

StandWithUs. N.d. "Why Does Israel Look Like Paradise to Gay Palestinians?" (flyer). Los Angeles: StandWithUs. https://www.swuconnect.com/insys/npoflow.v.2/_assets/pdfs/flyers/whydoesIsrael.pdf.

Sterman, Adiv. 2013. "Aiming to Calm Critics, Netanyahu Cancels Massive Settlement Plan." *Times of Israel*, November 13.

Stoil, Rebecca Anna, and Dan Izenberg. 2006. "High Court to Discuss Parade Petitions." *Jerusalem Post*, November 7.

Stotkin, Richard. 1996. *Gunfighter Nation: The Myth of the Frontier in 20th Century America.* New York: Atheneum.

Strauss, Leo. 1997. *Philosophie und Gesetz-Frühe Schriften (Gesammelte Schriften).* Vol. 2. Edited by Heinrich Meier, with Wiebke Meier. Stuttgart and Weimar: J. B. Metzler.

Sulzberger, C. L. 1978. "Tilting towards Israel." *Journal of Palestine Studies* 7 (2): 156–59.

Swedenburg, Ted. 1989. "Occupational Hazards: Palestine Ethnography." *Cultural Anthropology* 4:265–72.

———. 1992. "Occupational Hazards Revisited: Reply to Moshe Shokeid." *Cultural Anthropology* 7:478–95.

Talhami, Ghada Hashem. 2000. "The Modern History of Islamic Jerusalem: Academic Myths and Propaganda." *Middle East Journal* 7 (2): 113–29.

Tamari, Salim. 1983. "In League with Zion: Israel's Search for a Native Pillar." *Journal of Palestine Studies* 12 (4): 42–56.

———. 1991. "The Palestinian Movement in Transition: Historical Reversals and the Uprising." *Journal of Palestine Studies* 20 (2): 57–70.

———. 1992a. "Left in Limbo: Leninist Heritage and Islamist Challenge." *Middle East Report* 22 (6): 16–22.

———. 1992b. "Soul of the Nation: The *Fallah* in the Eyes of the Urban Intelligentsia." In *Review of Middle East Studies: Israel—Fields for Identity*, vol. 5, edited by Glenn Bowman, 74–83. London: Scorpion Cavendish.

———, ed. 1999. *Jerusalem 1948: The Arab Neighbourhoods and Their Fate in the War.* Jerusalem: Institute of Jerusalem Studies and Badil Resource Center.

———. 2002. *Jerusalem 1948: The Arab Neighborhoods and Their Fate in the War.* Jerusalem and Ramallah: Institute for Jerusalem Studies.

———. 2004a. "Lepers, Lunatics and Saints: The Nativist Ethnography of Tawfiq Canaan and his Circle." *Jerusalem Quarterly* 20:24–43.

———. 2004b. "Years of Delicious Anarchy: Crowds, Public Space, and the New Urban Sensibilities in War-Time Jerusalem, 1917–1921." Occasional Papers, South-South Exchange Program for Research on the History of Development (SEPHIS). Kolkata, India: Centre for Studies of Social Sciences–Calcutta (CSSSC).

———, ed. 2005. *Pilgrims, Lepers and Stuffed Cabbage: Essays on Jerusalem's Cultural History.* Jerusalem and Ramallah: Institute of Jerusalem Studies and The Centre for Jerusalem Studies at al Quds University.

———. 2009. *Mountain against the Sea: Essays on Palestinian Society and Culture.* Berkeley: University of California Press.

Telhami, Shibley, and Steven Kull. 2013. *Israeli and Palestinian Public Opinion on Negotiating a Final Status Agreement.* Washington, DC: Saban Center for Middle East Policy, Brookings Institution.

Terrestrial Jerusalem. 2012. "East Jerusalem Settlements and the Imminent Demise of the Two-State Solution." January.

Thompson, William R. 2003. "A Streetcar Names Sarajevo: Catalysts, Multiple Causation Chains, and Rivalry Structures." *International Studies Quarterly* 47 (3): 453–74.

Timothy, Dallen J. 2001. *Tourism and Political Boundaries*. London: Routledge.

———. 2007. "Introduction: The Political Nature of Cultural Heritage and Tourism." In *The Political Nature of Cultural Heritage and Tourism*, edited by Dallen J. Timothy, 9–18. Aldershot, UK: Ashgate.

———. 2011. *Cultural Heritage and Tourism: An Introduction*. Bristol, UK: Channel View.

Timothy, Dallen J., and Stephen W. Boyd. 2003. *Heritage Tourism*. London: Prentice Hall.

Timothy, Dallen J., and Thomas Iverson. 2006. "Tourism and Islam: Considerations of Culture and Duty." In *Tourism, Religion and Spiritual Journeys*, edited by Dallen J. Timothy and Daniel H. Olsen, 186–205. London: Routledge.

Toren, Haim. 1968. *Yerushalayim Bi-yetsirat Ha-dorot: Mi-ram'hal 'ad Yameynu: Pirkey Sifrut Muv'harim*. 2nd ed. Tel Aviv: Yavne.

Traiman, Alex. 2006. "Violence in Israel Caused by 'Gay' Event?" WorldNetDaily .com, July 19.

Trémouille, Marie-Claude. 1997. *Hebat: Une Divinité Syro-Anatolienne*. Firenze: LoGisma editore.

Tsimhoni, Daphne. 2005. "Christians in Jerusalem: A Minority at Risk." *Journal of Human Rights* 4:391–417.

Tunbridge, J. E., and Gregory J. Ashworth. 1996. *Dissonant Heritage: The Management of the Past as a Resource in Conflict*. Chichester, UK: Wiley.

Udasin, Sharon. 2009. "Pride of Place." *Jewish Week*, May 20.

Uriely, Natan, Aviad Israeli, and Arie Reichel. 2003. "Religious Identity and Residents' Attitudes toward Heritage Tourism Development: The Case of Nazareth." *Journal of Hospitality and Tourism Research* 27 (1): 69–84.

Van der Haven, Alexander. 2008. "The Holy Fool Still Speaks: The Jerusalem Syndrome as a Religious Subculture." In *Jerusalem: Idea and Reality*, edited by Tamar Mayer and Suleiman A. Mourad, 103–22. New York: Routledge.

Van Evera, Stephen. 1994. "Hypotheses on Nationalism and War." *International Security* 18 (4): 5–39.

———. 1997. *Guide to Methods for Students of Political Science*. Ithaca, NY: Cornell University Press.

Van Gennep, Arnold. 1909. *The Rites of Passage* [in French]. Paris: Emile Nourry.

Vaughn, Andrew G., and Ann E. Killebrew, eds. 2003. *Jerusalem in Bible and Archaeology: The First Temple Period*. Atlanta, GA: Society for Biblical Literature.

Vinitzky-Seroussi, Vered. 1998. "'Jerusalem Assassinated Rabin and Tel Aviv Commemorated Him': Rabin Memorials and the Discourse of National Identity in Israel." *City and Society* 10 (1): 183–203.

Vitullo, Anita. 2005. "The Long Economic Shadow of the Wall." In *Against the Wall: Israel's Barrier to Peace*, edited by Michael Sorkin, 100–121. New York: New Press.

Vukonić, Boris. 2006. "Sacred Places and Tourism in the Roman Catholic Tradition." In *Tourism, Religion and Spiritual Journeys*, edited by Dallen J. Timothy and Daniel H. Olsen, 237–53. London: Routledge.

Walt, Stephen M. Spring 1999. "Rigor or Rigor Mortis? Rational Choice and Security Studies." *International Security* 23 (4): 5–48.

Walzer, Lee. 2000. *Between Sodom and Eden: A Gay Journey Through Today's Changing Israel*. New York: Columbia University Press.

Warner, Carolyn M., and Stephen G. Walker. 2011. "Thinking about the Role of Religion in Foreign Policy: A Framework for Analysis." *Foreign Policy Analysis* 7:113–35.

Wasserstein, Bernard. 2001. *Divided Jerusalem: The Struggle for the Holy City*. London: Profile.

———. 2002. *Divided Jerusalem: The Struggle for the Holy City*. New Haven, CT: Yale University Press.

———. 2003. *Israelis and Palestinians: Why Do They Fight? Can They Stop?* New Haven, CT: Yale University Press.

Waxman, Dov. 2008. "From Controversy to Consensus: Cultural Conflict and the Israeli Debate Over Territorial Withdrawal." *Israel Studies* 13 (2): 73–96.

Webber, Jonathan. 1985. "Religions in the Holy Land: Conflicts of Interpretation." *Anthropology Today* 5:3–10.

Weizman, Eyal. 2007. *Hollow Land: Israel's Architecture of Occupation*. New York: Verso.

Wharton, Annabel J. 2006. *Selling Jerusalem: Relics, Replicas, Theme Parks*. Chicago: University of Chicago Press.

———. 2007. "Death in Jerusalem: Palestine Archeological Museum." Paper presented at the Jerusalem Across the Disciplines conference, Arizona State University, February 19–21.

Wheatley, Paul. 1969. *City as Symbol: An Inaugural Lecture Delivered at University College*. London: H. K. Lewis.

Winer, Stuart. 2013. "Jerusalem Mayor Faces a Council as Fragmented as His City." *Times of Israel*, October 23.

Woodward, Mark. 1988. "The Slametan: Textual Knowledge and Ritual Performance in Central Javanese Islam." *History of Religions* 28 (1): 54–89.

———. 1989. *Islam in Java: Normative Piety and Mysticism in the Sultanate of Yogyakarta*. Tucson: University of Arizona Press.

———. 1991. "The Garebeg Malud in Yogyakarta: Veneration of the Prophet as Imperial Ritual." *Journal of Ritual Studies* 5 (1): 109–32.

———. 1998. "Order and Meaning in the Yogyakarta *Kraton*." In *Structuralism's Transformations: Order and Revision in Indonesian and Malaysian Societies*, edited by Susan D. Russell and Lorraine V. Aragon, 235–80. Tempe: Arizona State University, Program for Southeast Asian Studies Monograph Series (PSEAS).

Yair, Gad, and Samira Alayan. 2009. "Paralysis at the Top of a Roaring Volcano: Israel and the Schooling of Palestinians in East Jerusalem." *Comparative Education Review* 53 (2): 235–57.

Yehoshua, A. B. 1992. *Mr. Mani*. Translated by Hillel Halkin. New York: Doubleday.

Yehoshua, Yam. 2002. "TA Grants Gay Couples Eligibility for Benefits." *Haaretz*, October 5.

Yeivin, Yehoshua Heschel. 1949. *Be-'ikvey Ha-shir*. Jerusalem: Ha-Milo.

———. 1974. "Ha-zikaron Veha-kosef Be-shirat Uri Tsvi Grinberg." In *Uri Tsvi Grinberg: Miv'har Ma'amarey Bikoret 'al Yetsirato*, edited by Y. Friedlander, 11–29. Tel Aviv: 'Am 'Oved. First published 1949 in *Be'ikvey Hashir*, vol. 1.

Yellin, David, Isaiah Press, and Leib Levi. 1903. "Michtav La-Rabanim." *Hashkafa* 4 (27) (26 Nissan 5663/April 23): 212–13.

Yisraeli, Y. 1913. "Hashkafa Mekomit," *Ha-Ahdut* 5 (1–2) (14 Tishrei 5674/October 15): 34.

Yitzhaki, Yedidya. 2002. "Al "Hurban Yerushalayim' Ve-'al 'Binyan Yerushalayim." *'Iton* 77 (274): 18–21.

Ynet. 2012. "Tel Aviv Named World's Best Gay City." January 11. http://www.ynet news.com/articles/0,7340,L-4174274,00.html.

Yoaz, Yuval. 2006. "In Precedent-Setting Ruling Court Says State Must Recognize Gay Marriage." *Haaretz*, November 21.

Zank, Michael. "Holy City: Jerusalem in Time, Space, and the Imagination." *Transformations: The Journal of Inclusive Scholarship and Pedagogy* 19 (1): 40–67.

Zertal, Edith, and Akiva Eldar. 2007. *Lords of the Land: The War Over Israel's Settlements in the Occupied Territories, 1967–2007*. New York: Nation Books.

Zias, Joe. 1983. "Anthropological Evidence of Interpersonal Violence in First-Century A.D. Jerusalem." *Current Anthropology* 24 (2): 233–34.

Zunes, Stephen. 2011. "Obama's Mideast Speech: Two Steps Back, One Step Forward." *Huffington Post*, May 22.

Zwiep, Irene E. 1998. "To Remember and to Forget—Jerusalem in Jewish Poetical Memory." *European Judaism* 31 (2): 54–66.

About the Authors

Madelaine Adelman is associate professor of justice and social inquiry, Arizona State University (ASU). She received her Ph.D. in cultural anthropology and a Women's Studies Graduate Certificate from Duke University. Her scholarship centers on violence, law, and culture, in which she connects everyday family life with the development of state-level policy and global movements for social change. She also conducts research on the struggle over identity, violence and democracy in schools, inspired by her advocacy work with the Gay, Lesbian & Straight Education Network (GLSEN). Adelman's research has been supported in part by the ASU Center for the Study of Religion and Conflict. Her solo- and co-authored research has been published in *Companion to Gender Studies* (Blackwell, 2005); *Women, Violence and Media* (Northeastern University, 2009); *International Handbook of Criminology* (Taylor & Francis, 2010); and *Research on LGBTQ in Education: Using and Investing in Building Knowledge* (AERA, forthcoming); as well as in journals such as *Affilia: Journal of Women and Social Work*, *American Anthropologist*, *American Ethnologist*, *Feminist Criminology*, *Human Organization*, *Journal of LGBT Youth*, *Journal of Poverty*, *Innovations on Social, Political & Economic Inequalities*, *Law, Culture and Humanities*, *Law Journal for Social Justice*, *Law & Society Review*, *Police & Society*, *Political and Legal Anthropology Review (PoLAR)*, and *Violence Against Women*. She is currently writing a book on the politics of domestic violence in Israel, and co-editing with Donna Coker (University of Miami School of Law) a special issue on "Teaching about Domestic Violence" for *Violence Against Women*. Adelman is president of the Association for Political and Legal Anthropology (APLA).

Glenn Bowman is reader in social anthropology at the University of Kent where he convenes the MA programs in the Anthropology of Ethnicity, Nationalism and Identity and Visual Anthropology Program, as well as directs the new interdisciplinary Liberal Arts Program. Bowman studied literature and critical theory in the United States before coming to Oxford in the late seventies to work under

Edwin Ardener and Michael Gilsenan at the Institute of Social Anthropology. His doctoral field research (1983–85) was carried out on the topic of Christian pilgrimage in Jerusalem and gave rise to further regionally based interests in shrines, monumentalization, tourism and—with reference to the Palestinian people—nationalism and conflict, diasporic and local identities, and secularist versus sectarian strategies of mobilization. He has worked on nationalist mobilization in the former Yugoslavia, as well as Muslim-Christian shrine sharing in Macedonia (F.Y.R.O.M.). Since 1989 he has been engaged in a longitudinal study of the mixed Christian-Muslim town of Beit Sahour, near Bethlehem, which had played a substantial role in the Palestinian intifada (uprising). Bowman has been honorary editor of the *Journal of the Royal Anthropological Institute* and is on the editorial boards of *Critique of Anthropology, Focaal,* and *Anthropological Theory.* He has published extensively on anthropological theory, Jerusalem, the occupied territories, the former Yugoslavia, the tourist market in the Holy Land, and the Muslim-Christian community in Palestine. His work appears in *Man* (now *Journal of the Royal Anthropological Institute*), *Identities, Social Anthropology, Critique of Anthropology, History and Anthropology, Religion Compass,* and *Anthropological Theory,* among other journals, and he has collaborated on numerous book projects related to the city of Jerusalem, political identity, shrines and pilgrimage.

Miriam Fendius Elman is associate professor of political science at the Maxwell School of Syracuse University, and faculty research director in the Program for the Advancement of Research on Conflict and Collaboration (PARCC). Prior to joining the Maxwell School, she was an assistant and associate professor of political science and faculty affiliate of the Jewish Studies Program at Arizona State University, where she taught from 1995 through 2008. Elman received her Ph.D. in political science from Columbia University and completed her B.A. in International Relations at the Hebrew University of Jerusalem. Elman is the editor of *Paths to Peace: Is Democracy the Answer?* (MIT Press, 1997), and the co-editor of *Bridges and Boundaries: Historians, Political Scientists, and the Study of International Relations* (MIT Press, 2001) and *Progress in International Relations Theory: Appraising the Field* (MIT Press, 2003). Her latest book is *Democracy and Conflict Resolution: The Dilemmas of Israel's Peacemaking* (Syracuse University Press, 2014), co-edited with Oded Haklai and Hendrik Spruyt. Elman's research has been supported by the US Department of Education, Arizona State University's Center for the Study of Religion and Conflict (CSRC), and Harvard University's Belfer Center for Science and International Affairs (BCSIA), where she was a Security Fellow from 1995 to 1996 and from 1998 to 2000. Her publications have appeared in the *British Journal* *of Political Science, American Political Science Review, Asian Security, International Security, International Studies Quarterly, Millennium: Journal of International Studies, Security Studies, International History Review, Palestine-Israel Journal of Politics, Economics and Culture,* and other journals. Elman serves on the editorial boards of the journals *International Security* and *Foreign Policy Analysis,* and on the advisory boards of the Center on American and Global Security (CAGS) at Indiana University and the Israeli Institute for Regional Foreign Policies (MITVIM), and was past president of the American Political Science Association's Foreign Policy Division. In Syracuse, she is a member of the Syracuse Area Middle East Dialogue (SAMED), a thirty-year-old public advocacy organization devoted to realizing a just and lasting resolution to the Israeli-Palestinian conflict.

Chad F. Emmett is associate professor in the Department of Geography at Brigham Young University. He received a Ph.D. in geography from the University of Chicago. His graduate degrees are in international relations and geography with emphases on the Middle East, political geography, and religion. Much of his work has centered on Israel/Palestine including a book: *Beyond the Basilica: Christians and Muslims in Nazareth;* several articles: "The Status Quo Solution for Jerusalem," in *Journal of Palestine Studies;* "The Capital Cities of Jerusalem," in *The Geographical Review;* "Conflicting Loyalties and Local Politics in Nazareth," in *The Middle East Journal;* "Nationalism Among Christian Palestinians," in *The Arab World Geographer;* "Political Manifestations in the Religious Landscape of Jerusalem," in *Architecture and Behavior;* and a book chapter: "Sharing Sacred Space in the Holy Land," in *Cultural Encounters with the Environment.* Current projects include a study of how the siting of mosques and churches can be used as an indicator of Christian-Muslim relations, a study of the status of Christians in the Islamic world, and a study of Christian-Muslim relations in Indonesia.

Roger Friedland is a cultural and religious sociologist (Ph.D., University of Wisconsin) and professor in the departments of religious studies and sociology at the University of California, Santa Barbara. Previously, he has been a visiting professor of social research and public policy at New York University, Abu Dhabi; a Fulbright Research Professor at the University of Rome, La Sapienza; and a visiting faculty member at The Hebrew University of Jerusalem. He has authored or coauthored several books, including *The Fellowship: The Untold Story of Frank Lloyd Wright and the Taliesin Fellowship,* with Harold Zellman (Harper Perennial, 2007); *Matters of Culture: Cultural Sociology in Practice,* with John Mohr (Cambridge University Press, 2004); *To Rule Jerusalem,* with Richard Hecht (University of California

Press, 2000); and numerous articles on religion, nationalism, and violence; political sociology; and the relationship between cities and the welfare state. He is currently engaged in comparative explorations of politicized religions, particularly their gender and sexual preoccupations. He is collaborating with Colleen Windham on a book on the implications of politicized religious movements, and with Janet Afary on the relationship of religion, gender, and intimate life in Egypt, Tunisia, Iran, and Turkey. Friedman teaches courses on the emergence of Christianity out of Judaism, cultural theory, and the history and theory of religion; he is also teaching a series of seminars with philosopher Tom Carlson on the ways in which the sacred is immanent in the organization of the profane world, ranging from science and technology to political authority, money, property, and love.

Shai Ginsburg is assistant professor of Hebrew and Israeli cultural studies in the Department of Asian and Middle Eastern Studies at Duke University. His research focuses on the formation of a Hebrew discourse of a nation. He is the author of *Rhetoric and Nation: The Formation of Hebrew National Culture, 1880–1990* (Syracuse University Press, 2014).

Richard D. Hecht is professor of religious studies at the University of California, Santa Barbara. His publications include *The Sacred Texts of the World: A Universal Anthology* (with Ninian Smart, 1983, and reprinted several times, most recently in 2007) and *To Rule Jerusalem* (with Roger Friedland, 1996 and 2000). Hecht and Friedland have written a series of essays, chapters, and articles on the politics of sacred space in Jerusalem and in other places. Their most recent work is "The Powers of Place" in *Religion, Violence, Memory, and Place*, edited by Oren Baruch Stier and J. Shawn Landres (2006), which explores the relationship of memory and place at Bet Ha-Am in Jerusalem, parish churches in Boston, and Dodger Stadium in Los Angeles. He is completing a book on religious pluralism in Southern California with his colleagues Wade Clark Roof and David Machacek (forthcoming, University of California Press), and another book with Linda Ekstrom, his UCSB colleague in studio art in the College of Creative Studies, titled *Saved From Matter: The Religious Cultures of Contemporary Art*.

Menachem Klein is professor in the Department of Political Science at Bar-Ilan University, Israel. Klein studied Middle East and Islamic studies at the Hebrew University of Jerusalem, and in 1992–93 and 2001–2002 was a fellow at St. Antony's College, Oxford University. In 2006 he was a visiting professor at the Massachusetts Institute of Technology (MIT), and in 2010 he was a Fernand Braudel Senior

Fellow at the European University Institute, Florence. In 2011 Klein was a visiting scholar in Leiden University, Netherlands. Klein has served as an adviser for Jerusalem affairs and Israel-PLO final status talks for Israel's minister of foreign affairs, Professor Shlomo Ben-Ami, and was a member of the advisory team convened by Prime Minister Ehud Barak. Since 1996 he has been active in many unofficial negotiations with Palestinian counterparts. In October 2003, Klein signed, together with prominent Israeli and Palestinian negotiators, the Geneva Agreement—a detailed proposal for a comprehensive Israeli-Palestinian peace accord. He is a board member of Ir Amim and the *Palestine-Israel Journal of Politics, Economics and Culture.* Between 2004 and 2010, Klein was a board member of B'Tselem, The Israeli Information Center for Human Rights in the Occupied Territories. His latest book is *Lives in Common: Arabs and Jews in Jerusalem, Jaffa, and Hebron* (C. Hurst, 2014). Previous books include *The Shift: Israel-Palestine from Border Conflict to Ethnic Struggle* (C. Hurst and Columbia University Press, 2010), *A Possible Peace between Israel and Palestine—An Insiders' Account of the Geneva Initiative* (Columbia University Press, 2007), *The Jerusalem Problem: The Struggle for Permanent Status* (University Press of Florida, 2003), and *Jerusalem: The Contested City* (C. Hurst and New York University Press, 2001). Klein's research on diverse topics related to the Israeli-Palestinian conflict, including the evolution of Hamas, the city of Jerusalem, and the 1948 Palestinian refugees, has appeared in numerous journals and edited volumes, including the *Middle East Journal; Political Geography; Journal of Israeli History;* Michael Dumper (editor), *Palestinian Refugee Repatriation in Global Perspective;* and E. Benvenisti, C. Gans, and S. Hanafi (editors), *Israel and the Palestinian Refugees.*

Arieh Saposnik is associate professor at the Ben-Gurion Institute for the Study of Israel and Zionism at the Ben-Gurion University in the Negev. He is currently on leave from the University of California, Los Angeles, where he is an associate professor in the Department of Near Eastern Languages and Cultures and holder of the Rosalinde and Arthur Gilbert Foundation Chair in Israel Studies and is the founding director of the Younes & Soraya Nazarian Center for Israel Studies. He is the author of *Becoming Hebrew: The Creation of a Jewish National Culture in Ottoman Palestine,* published in 2008 by Oxford University Press. His research focuses on the history of Zionism and Israel and on the varieties of Jewish nationalism, imagery and symbolism of the sacred in the making of Jewish nationalism generally, and Zionism and Israeli culture in particular.

Dallen J. Timothy is professor of community resources and development at Arizona State University (ASU), senior sustainability scientist at ASU's Global

Institute of Sustainability, and visiting professor at Indiana University and UiTM University, Malaysia. He received a Ph.D. in geography from the University of Waterloo, Canada. His graduate degrees are in political and cultural geography, with emphases on tourism, security, and political boundaries. His primary research interests include contested heritage, religious tourism, socio-economic development in peripheral and developing regions, consumption, ethnicity in tourism, and conflict in tourism. He has published over 150 scholarly journal articles and book chapters on these subjects in the past two decades, as well as twenty books, with three more in progress. He is the editor in chief of the *Journal of Heritage Tourism* and serves on the editorial boards of thirteen international scholarly journals.

Mark Woodward is associate professor of religious studies at Arizona State University and visiting professor of comparative religion at Sunan Kalijaga State Islamic University in Yogyakarta, Indonesia. He received his Ph.D. in anthropology from the University of Illinois in 1985, and also studied at the History of Religions Program at the University of Chicago's Divinity School. His research interests center on Islam and politics in Southeast Asia and on religious and ethnic conflict. He is the author or editor of six books and more than sixty scholarly articles. He is currently engaged in long-term research on counter-radical Muslim discourse in Europe, West Africa, and Southeast Asia, and on the history of Salafi Islam in Indonesia, Malaysia, and Singapore.

Michael Zank is professor of religion at Boston University and director of the Elie Wiesel Center for Judaic Studies. Trained in protestant theology and Near Eastern and Judaic studies, Zank teaches undergraduate courses on topics ranging from the Bible to the modern critique of religion, and graduate courses in continental philosophy of religion and Jewish thought. He has written on the philosophy of Hermann Cohen, the early writings of Leo Strauss, the work of Martin Buber, and the thought of Franz Rosenzweig. Currently, he is working on a volume of essays on modern Jewish philosophy and completing a brief history of Jerusalem. Zank blogs on Jerusalem-related issues at http://unholycity.blogspot.com.

Index

Photos, illustrations, and figures are indicated by an italicized page number.